Insurgent Supremacists: The U.S. Far Right's Challenge to State and Empire

Matthew N. Lyons

PMPRESS

KER
SPL
EBE
DEB

2018

Insurgent Supremacists:
The U.S. Far Right's Challenge to State and Empire
Matthew N. Lyons

copyright Matthew N. Lyons, 2018
this edition copyright Kersplebedeb

ISBN: 9781629635118
Library of Congress Control Number: 2017964730

Kersplebedeb Publishing and Distribution
CP 63560
CCCP Van Horne
Montreal, Quebec
Canada H3W 3H8
www.kersplebedeb.com
www.leftwingbooks.net

PM Press
P.O. Box 23912
Oakland, CA 94623
www.pmpress.org

Layout by Kersplebedeb
Cover Design by John Yates

Printed in the USA by the Employee Owners of
Thomson-Shore in Dexter, Michigan
www.thomsonshore.com

Contents

Introduction

For people who thought the U.S. far right was an irrelevant lunatic fringe, the 2016 presidential race seemed like madness. It was bad enough that the victor was a right-wing populist who called for excluding people from the country based on ethnicity or religion, advocated torture, boasted about sexually assaulting women, and encouraged his supporters to beat up dissenters at campaign rallies. But on top of that, his campaign received important help from a network of activists known as the alternative right or alt-right, who want to break up the United States into racially segregated "ethno-states." Styling themselves "fashy goys" (fascistic non-Jews), alt-rightists bombarded social media with gas chamber jokes, rape and death threats against women, and internet memes that vilified both liberal multiculturalists and mainstream conservatives. The alt-right helped Donald Trump score upset victories over his Republican rivals and Democrat Hillary Clinton, gaining unprecedented visibility and attention in return. But alt-rightists were never committed Trump fans, and just a few months after he took office they were bitterly criticizing Trump for abandoning the "America First" nationalism of his campaign for a more conventional conservatism. Around the same time, many began to shift their focus from online activism to street protests and fighting.

Before 2015 or 2016, most mainstream reporters and political pundits had never heard of the alt-right, and they scrambled to figure out what the movement was and what it stood for. Because alt-rightists didn't look or act like stereotypical neonazis, people accused them of trying to hide their white supremacist politics behind a "benign" label, even though in fact many of them went out of their way to sound as offensive and bigoted as possible. Because alt-rightists were explicitly white nationalist, many observers didn't notice that they also promoted a misogyny so extreme that even many neonazis criticized it.[1] And because some "anti-globalist" conservatives started using the alt-right label, many critics missed the distinction between fellow travelers and committed adherents—between those Trump supporters who wanted to reclaim control of the American republic for white Christian men and those who hoped for the republic's collapse. Although media coverage of the alt-right gradually improved, this initial confusion underscored the need to rethink superficial, overgeneralized, and outmoded conceptions, and to recognize the far right as a dynamic, changing collection of movements.

This book is about far right politics in the United States. It is an effort to understand movements such as the alt-right: what they want, what they do, who they appeal to, and how they interact with other political forces. It is also an effort to place these movements in historical context, to analyze how and why they have developed over the past half-century, and how current circumstances affect their strengths and limitations.

The term "far right" needs clarification, since it has been used in many different ways. Depending on the user and the context, far right may refer to white supremacist ideology or hard-line conservatism, authoritarianism or laissez-faire economics, a fascist vision of a new order, or a reactionary drive to turn back the clock. Each of these concepts is relevant to the subject of this book to some degree, but none of them really describes what it is about.

Instead of focusing on a specific doctrine, my approach begins with a specific historical turning point: in the 1970s and 1980s, for the first time since World War II, rightists in significant numbers began to withdraw their loyalty from the U.S. government. This marked a sharp break with the right's traditional role as defender of the established order, as one of the forces helping economic and political elites to maintain social control. In my view, the resulting division between oppositional and system-loyal rightists is more significant than ideological differences about race, religion, economics, or other factors.

As an imprecise working definition (not for all times and places but for the United States today), "far right" is used here to mean political forces that (a) regard human inequality as natural, inevitable, or desirable and (b) reject the legitimacy of the established political system. This definition cuts across standard ideological divisions. It includes insurgent factions among both white supremacists (whose supremacist vision centers on race) and Christian rightists (who advocate social and political hierarchy based on gender and religion, among other factors). It also includes many Patriot movement activists, who may or may not advocate racial or religious oppression but who champion unregulated capitalism and the economic inequality it produces. The definition excludes system-loyal white supremacists, Christian rightists, and Patriot activists, as well as other rightists who want to roll back liberal reforms but leave the basic state apparatus in place. The definition also draws a line between the far right and radical leftists, who reject the existing political system but, at least in theory, seek to transform society based on egalitarian principles.

My analysis of the far right is based on a number of core premises:

The far right is made up of regular human beings. The people who join the far right are not especially crazy or irrational or stupid or fanatical or opportunistic, although these are all common stereotypes. Far right organizations attract and keep supporters because they speak to human hopes and fears, grievances and aspirations, and because they offer appealing explanations for big problems and confusing changes in society. Understanding the far right's human appeal is important because it helps us to combat it more effectively and relate that struggle to the larger struggles for human liberation.

The far right grows out of an oppressive social order. The far right is often described as an extremist threat to democracy, yet the United States is not and never has been a democracy. It is a deeply unequal society where a tiny capitalist elite holds most economic and political power and multiple systems of dominance/subordination shape most human relations. These systems foster scapegoating and demonization of oppressed groups—and violence against them—by far right and mainstream forces alike, a dynamic that will not be eradicated as long as these systems remain in place.

This doesn't mean that the United States is a dictatorship. It has always been a shifting mix of pluralistic openness and repression, where real political space has been won for some people and some ideas that would not be permitted in a wholly authoritarian system, including opportunities to organize, debate, participate in electoral politics, and criticize those in power. Pluralistic space has provided an important tool for managing conflict and a safety valve for popular discontent. Yet those who seriously challenge the underlying structures of power risk jail or worse, and many people (especially low-income people of color) routinely face police harassment and the threat or reality of violence— up to and including death. Such political repression has increased during various crisis periods in U.S. history and has been trending upward for the past several decades.

The far right is politically autonomous. While some liberals have glossed over the deep connections between far right politics and mainstream institutions, some leftists have made the opposite mistake by treating far rightists simply as tools of the ruling class. It is certainly true that economic or political elites have sometimes found white supremacist and fascist forces useful—for attacking the left or the labor movement, for example—but the relationship between them is at best ambivalent. In calling for the U.S. political system to be abolished or broken up, far rightists do not speak for any significant faction of the capitalist elite, although that could change.

The U.S. far right has a contradictory relationship with the established order, reinforcing it in some ways and attacking it in others. This tension is often expressed in a kind of double-edged ideology. On the one side, far right groups offer people a way to defend the relative social privileges and power that they enjoy over oppressed groups such as people of color, women, LGBT people, and immigrants, and speak to fears that traditional privileges have been lost or are under threat. But the far right also speaks to people's sense of being disempowered and downtrodden by groups above them, by denouncing groups that they identify with elite power, such as the federal government, liberal intellectuals, global corporations, or Jewish bankers.

Far right ideology is not just about race. When people say "far right" they often mean white supremacist or white nationalist. There are several problems with this. For one thing, people who want a society dominated and defined by people of European descent don't all necessarily want to overthrow or secede from the United States. And equating the far right with white nationalism leaves out important rightist forces that reject the legitimacy of the U.S. political system but don't put race at the center of their ideology. A prime example is the Christian right's hardline faction—embodied most clearly in Christian Reconstructionism— which wants to replace the U.S. government with a full-scale theocracy based on biblical law. In addition, while all major far right currents in the United States are predominantly white, some have made real efforts to recruit people of color, and these efforts could grow.

Far right politics don't stand still. The Marxist historian Isaac Deutscher commented once that after World War I, many German leftists thought the main danger from the right was going to be efforts to restore the monarchy. They were blindsided when the main rightist danger turned out to be a movement that had no interest in restoring the monarchy, but instead carried a red flag and put both "Socialist" and "Workers" in the name of its organization—the National Socialist German Workers Party, also known as the Nazis.

One of the most striking features of the U.S. far right over the past half-century has been its repeated efforts to develop new doctrines, arguments, strategies, and forms of organization. As an example, many opponents assume that far rightists remain oriented toward classical fascism's vision of a strong state and a disciplined, top-down political organization. In reality huge swaths of the far right have abandoned this approach and have embraced some form of political decentralism, ranging from the neonazi-based "leaderless resistance" strategy to Christian Reconstructionism's vision of a locally based theocracy enforced through the small-scale institutions of church and family.

The far right presents multiple kinds of threats. In the short term, it's extremely unlikely that far rightists could seize power and bring about the kind of society they envision. While this cannot be ruled out in the longer term, there are several more immediate reasons to take the far right seriously. First, far rightists carry out harassment and violence against targeted groups, and they encourage other people to do the same. Second, far rightists create more space for system-loyal forces to intensify their own bigotry, scapegoating, and violence, both by offering an example for system-loyal groups to learn from, and also by providing an "extreme" example that helps more "moderate" versions look legitimate by comparison. Third, far rightists can exploit popular grievances to draw support away from left-wing liberatory alternatives. Fourth, far rightists can infect the left itself with their poisonous ideas or recruit leftists to work with them.

This book builds on earlier projects. In the 1990s I worked with Chip Berlet on the book *Right-Wing Populism in America: Too Close for Comfort*, which was published by Guilford Press in 2000. As Chip and I use the term, populism means an ideology or movement that aims to rally "the people" against sinister elites. Although some forms of populism have advocated moves toward social justice and equality, many have not. *Right-Wing Populism in America* traces a long series of U.S. political movements reaching back to the colonial period that have combined twisted forms of anti-elitism with efforts to intensify oppression of specific groups. An important early example was Jacksonianism, one of the first mass political movements in the United States. Jacksonians, who first came together in the 1820s around the campaign to elect General Andrew Jackson as president of the United States, created the Democratic Party that remains in existence today. Jacksonians glorified the common man and denounced "the money power," but also championed increased white violence and oppression against black and Indigenous people.

As we argued in *Right-Wing Populism in America*:

> Historically, right-wing populist movements have reflected the interests of two different kinds of social groups, often in combination:
>
> 1. Middle-level groups in the social hierarchy, notably middle- and working-class Whites, who have a stake in traditional social privilege but resent the power of upper-class elites over them, and,
>
> 2. "Outsider" factions of the elite itself, who sometimes use distorted forms of antielitism as part of their own bid for greater power.
>
> The original Ku Klux Klan of the late 1860s, for example, represented an alliance between some lower- and middle-class southern Whites (outraged that Black emancipation and Reconstruction had eroded their social privilege), and southern planters (who sought to win back some of the power they had lost to northern capitalists in the Civil War). The Klan combined racist terrorism against Black people and their allies with demagogic antielite rhetoric about northern "military despotism."[2]

Two other concepts central to *Right-Wing Populism in America* merit special mention because of their role in the contemporary far right. One is producerism, an ideology that draws a phony distinction between good producers and evil parasites. The Jacksonians, for example, envisioned an alliance of "productive" white farmers, artisans, planters, and entrepreneurs against "parasitic" bankers, speculators, monopolists — and people of color. The effect was to bolster white supremacist violence, blur actual class divisions, and attack some elite groups while glorifying others. Many later right-wing populist movements have echoed producerist themes, from the anti-Chinese crusade of the late nineteenth century to the Patriot movement of recent decades. By the 1920s, thanks largely to Henry Ford, the auto manufacturer who later became an important American supporter of Hitler's Nazi regime, producerism had converged with antisemitic attacks against "parasitic" Jews.

Another key concept in the right-wing populist tradition is conspiracism, an ideology that treats conspiracy theories as the main explanation for social conflict. While some conspiracy theories focus on supposed subversives such as communists or labor radicals, anti-elite conspiracism focuses on supposed plots by sinister elites. Anti-elite conspiracism blames oppression on a subjective, alien force that distorts the normal workings of society. This may be either a subgroup within the actual elite or a group that does not really dominate society at all. Either way, opposition is diverted away from the broader systems of power that are actually integral to the social order. In times past, conspiracy theorists have targeted sinister plots by Freemasons, Roman Catholics, Northern industrialists, the British government, and Ivy League–educated New Deal bureaucrats. Today's far right conspiracists tend to focus on globalists, secular humanists, Jews, and — most recently — Muslims. Conspiracist thinking can also be found among many Americans who don't identify with the far right, including some leftists, providing an opening for far right ideas to spread.

Following *Right-Wing Populism in America*, in the 2000s my work centered largely on the concept of fascism. Against many liberals and leftists, I argued that George W. Bush's presidential administration was not fascist, and that it was strategically important to delineate fascism from authoritarian conservatism.[3] My thinking was strongly influenced by two distinct approaches: (1) In the 2002 book *Confronting Fascism: Discussion Documents for a Militant Movement*, independent Marxists Don Hamerquist and J. Sakai argued that fascism feeds on popular hostility to big business and aims to bring down the capitalist state and create a new order based on plunder and genocide. (2) In *The Nature of Fascism* (1991) and later writings, liberal historian Roger Griffin offered a nuanced ideological analysis of fascism as a totalitarian populist ideology driven by a myth of "palingenesis," or national or racial rebirth after a period of profound crisis or decline.[4] From different standpoints, Griffin, Sakai, and Hamerquist all argued that fascism should be understood as an autonomous right-wing revolutionary force that has to mobilize masses of people to gain power and transform society. I attempted to synthesize these approaches in the 2008 essay "Two Ways of Looking at Fascism," which is included in this book as an appendix, and offered a new compound definition: *fascism is a revolutionary form of right-wing populism, inspired by a totalitarian vision of collective rebirth, that challenges capitalist political and cultural power while promoting economic and social hierarchy.*

During this period I also began writing for the website *Three Way Fight*, a follow-up project to *Confronting Fascism* that was initiated by a group of radical antifascist activists in 2004. As *Three Way Fight*'s editors explained the project:

> The contributors to this site consider the fracturing of the global capitalist system to be a real possibility. However, there is no guarantee that political opposition to global capital will coalesce around a radical liberatory alternative. There is another opposition emerging—a reactionary neofascism that aims to overthrow the current capitalist hegemony and institute a radically different oppressive social order. This leads us to conclude that we are in a three way contest where the faultlines don't conform to a simple "Us" and "Them."[5]

Three Way Fight brought together both anarchist and Marxist perspectives and sought to inspire open discussion and debate among leftists and greater understanding of the interconnections between antifascism and other kinds of radical activism. Over the years, the website has advanced a number of propositions that have come to characterize its approach:

■ Dualistic "oppressor versus oppressed" models of struggle are inadequate.

- The left isn't the only insurgent force that tries to speak to people's grievances and needs.

- Antifascism is a necessary component of radical politics, not a diversion from it.

- Fascistic tendencies can appear on the left and in the guise of liberation, for instance, by replacing systemic analysis of oppression with antisemitic conspiracy theories.

- Repression isn't necessarily fascist and can even come in the name of antifascism, as when the Roosevelt administration used the war against the Axis powers to justify strikebreaking and the mass imprisonment of Japanese Americans, for instance.

Several of the chapters in this book are derived from or incorporate writings that originally appeared in *Three Way Fight*.

In recent years I have scaled back my emphasis on the concept of fascism, out of concern that it may be more trouble than it's worth. The word fascism is now used in so many different ways and has accumulated so much emotional baggage that it is hard to agree on what we are talking about. Many people seem to think that (a) fascism is some objective thing and it's just a matter of finding the right words to describe it, and (b) if we accurately categorize a movement or regime as fascist, we can predict how it will behave and develop. I disagree with both of these claims. As Roger Griffin has argued, fascism is an analytic category—not a fixed, objective thing. Definitions of fascism help us clarify what we mean, but they aren't objectively true—just more or less useful for helping us understand the differences and relationships between various political movements and regimes. In addition, I see no reason to assume that fascist movements or regimes today will behave the way they have in the past under very different circumstances. I still think my compound definition (above) is useful, but it takes a lot of work to unpack and hasn't won any converts as far as I know. Rather than argue about definitions, I am more concerned to communicate the substance of my analysis.

I started reframing my approach in 2013, when I was invited to write an overview of the U.S. far right for the German leftist publishing house Unrast Verlag. This resulted in the 2015 book *Arier, Patriarchen, Übermenschen: die extreme Rechte in den USA* (Aryans, Patriarchs,

Supermen: The Far Right in the USA), which contained earlier versions of chapters 1, 2, 3, and 5 in German translation.[6] In *Arier* I first laid out the concept of "far right" as used in this book. This framework allows me to avoid some of the problems associated with the concept of fascism. Although there is no more definitional consensus about far right than about fascism, the term is significantly less emotionally loaded. Even if people don't agree with my definition of far right, they are much less likely to get upset about it. This is particularly important, because it would be controversial to label as fascist some of the political movements and initiatives that I define as far right. Christian Reconstructionism, for example, fits my definition of fascism but would be excluded from many others, since its ideology centers on religion, not nationality or race. Several political currents that I define as far right also repudiate classical fascism's goal of a strong state, which means some scholars of fascism would consider them borderline examples at best. And there are some forces that I consider far right but not fascist, including many Patriot movement groups and Keith Preston's *Attack the System*/American Revolutionary Vanguard, because they promote politics that are both insurgent and antiegalitarian but do not aim to impose one single ideological vision on society.

Historically, far right movements as I've defined them here have not been endemic to U.S. politics. While racism, nativism, and xenophobia were hallmarks of the right, to hold these views in no way put one in opposition to the United States itself. Indeed, the rightist belief in social inequality found much to celebrate in a system founded on slavery, genocide, patriarchy, and capitalism. Tensions between the white masses and elites have repeatedly spawned right-wing populist movements, but most of these have embraced or been readily co-opted into established political channels. Generally rightists did not challenge the political system's legitimacy in significant numbers. (There were two important exceptions. First, in the years after the Civil War, the original Ku Klux Klan and other vigilante organizations spearheaded a successful drive to overthrow the Radical Reconstruction governments across the former

Confederacy and reestablish overt white supremacy. Later, in the 1930s and early '40s, an array of pro-Axis groups denounced Franklin Roosevelt's New Deal as part of a Jewish-Communist conspiracy and advocated some form of fascist or quasi-fascist state, a movement that collapsed when the U.S. entered World War II.)[7]

As recently as fifty years ago, the insurgent U.S. far right as we know it today did not exist. The hard-line right-wing movements of that time were focused on protecting old hierarchies and fighting communism. Ku Klux Klan factions used vigilante terrorism to defend Jim Crow segregation and keep black people from voting. The John Birch Society, Christian Anti-Communism Crusade, and other Cold Warriors warned of a Red plot to take over America. These groups hated the civil rights movement, labor unions, and welfare state institutions such as Social Security, and they distrusted the political elites who dominated both major parties. But their politics were about defending or restoring the past. None of them targeted the U.S. political system itself, and none of them envisioned setting up a new social or political order.[8]

Some of the seeds of today's far right were there. For example, the handful of people in the National Renaissance Party (founded 1949) were beginning to reinterpret National Socialist ideology for post–World War II circumstances, while R.J. Rushdoony had just founded the Chalcedon Foundation (in 1965) and had laid the philosophical groundwork for the theocratic doctrine of Christian Reconstructionism.[9] But the political movements that would elaborate these ideas and turn them against the state were still in the future.

The modern U.S. far right took shape in stages and in response to a complex series of developments involving popular struggles for social justice, shifts in the federal government's role and direction, and structural changes in both the U.S. and global economy and social hierarchy. In very broad terms, we can say that the U.S. far right emerged and developed both in conjunction with and in reaction against the rise of the neoliberal political system.

By "political system" I am referring here to the constellation of doctrines and policies that dominates U.S. party politics and determines the federal government's overall stance in a given period. Neoliberalism followed the New Deal system, which held sway from the mid-1930s until the late 1970s. Developed originally to mitigate the effects of the Great Depression and to both safeguard and stabilize capitalist rule, the New Deal system included welfare state programs, Keynesian economics, accommodation of organized labor, and limited efforts to reduce economic inequality. After World War II, it also included a network of international economic agreements, foreign aid, large-scale overseas troop deployments, and military interventions to maintain U.S. hegemony, contain the Communist bloc, and suppress nationalist and leftist movements in Asia, Africa, and Latin America. Although the Democratic Party created the New Deal system and remained its chief standard-bearer throughout, the Republican Party's dominant wing came to embrace it as well.[10]

With its origins in a period of militant labor activism, the New Deal system was modified in the 1960s and '70s to accommodate new pressures from below. During this period, the black liberation movement and its allies overthrew Jim Crow segregation, re-enfranchised black people, and helped to make explicit racism unacceptable in many areas of public life. Black activism also helped to inspire anti-racist and anti-colonial struggles among Latinos, Asians, and Indigenous peoples; the anti–Vietnam War movement and the New Left; a resurgent feminist movement; a new movement against homophobia; environmental activism; and rank-and-file labor militancy. These movements promoted new concepts of grassroots activism, defiance of authority, and political critiques of "personal" issues such as family relations, sexuality, and health.

Both preemptively and in response to these social change movements, the federal government actively intervened to protect African Americans' right to vote in the South and banned many forms of discrimination based on race, sex, religion, or nationality. The 1965 immigration law abolished the old racist quota system and made it possible for large numbers of immigrants of color to enter the United States. Supreme Court decisions banned racial discrimination in schools, strengthened the rights of prisoners and criminal defendants, temporarily abolished capital punishment, and legalized some forms of abortion. The federal government—under both Democrat Lyndon Johnson and Republican Richard Nixon—also instituted a range of new social welfare programs, expanded regulation of business, and strengthened protection of the environment and workplace health and safety.[11]

Two major factors brought about the end of the New Deal system and the rise of neoliberalism. One was a shift within the business community away from Keynesianism and welfare state policies. The New Deal system had worked well for big business during the long post–World War II economic boom, but became increasingly untenable starting in the mid-1970s, as the boom ended and the U.S. faced growing economic challenges from other countries. To maintain profits, capitalists and their political representatives looked for ways to shift costs and societal burdens onto those below them in the social order. They stepped up attacks on labor unions, moved factories from the old industrial heartland in the Northeast and Midwest into lower-wage areas in the Sunbelt and overseas, and brought in immigrant workers to fill badly paid industrial, farming, and service jobs. They also increasingly pressed for cuts in social programs and corporate taxes, deregulation of business, reductions in trade barriers to allow the most profitable shifting of capital and goods across international borders, and expansion of the U.S. military to protect investments abroad.[12]

This rightward shift within the business community intersected with a grassroots backlash among many middle- and working-class whites to defend traditional social hierarchies and rules against challenges from below. Although explicit white supremacy was marginalized, coded racist appeals (which have since become known as "dog-whistle politics") attracted strong support, as did campaigns invoking explicit sexism and homophobia. Evoking the producerist tradition, right-wing populist initiatives accused liberal elites of giving special favors to communities of color, women, and poor people over "hardworking" white men. Social welfare programs, taxes, and the federal government as a whole became scapegoats for these white people's economic woes and general sense of disempowerment.[13]

The late 1970s and 1980s saw a general resurgence of right-wing political forces, including a new activist coalition of religious and secular conservatives backed by a growing faction of the business community, which helped elect Ronald Reagan as president in 1980 and 1984. The Reagan "Revolution" decisively moved the federal government away from the New Deal system to what has come to be known as neoliberalism, but the shift was actually initiated by President Jimmy Carter in the late 1970s, and it paralleled similar changes in Western Europe, notably Thatcherism in Britain.[14] The leaderships of both the Republican and Democratic parties, and all presidents from Reagan through Obama, have worked to implement this neoliberal system.

Neoliberalism involves a set of economic policies, including minimal regulation of business, reduction or privatization of social services, low taxes for businesses and the wealthy, free trade, and relatively unrestricted immigration. These policies are based on a philosophy that sees competition as the defining characteristic of human relations. It redefines citizens as consumers, whose democratic choices are best exercised by buying and selling, a process that rewards merit and punishes inefficiency.... The organization of labour and collective bargaining by trade unions are portrayed as market distortions that impede the formation of a natural hierarchy of winners and losers. Inequality is recast as virtuous: a reward for utility and a generator of wealth, which trickles down to enrich everyone.[15]

Unlike the New Deal system, which co-opted movements for social justice and promoted the federal government as an instrument to reduce inequality, neoliberalism denies—and thus protects—structural inequality behind an ideology of individual freedom. This ideology plays a social control function by blaming people for their own disempowerment and weakening solidarity between members of oppressed groups. As part of its strategy of social control, the neoliberal system has also dramatically expanded the state's repressive apparatus—including mass incarceration, mass surveillance, and the militarization of policing—under both Republican and Democratic leadership.[16]

Some versions of neoliberal ideology have used coded racist appeals to white resentment or claims that people of color are benefiting from "reverse discrimination." Others have promoted color-blindness, the false claim that racial disparities do not exist and any attempt to address them is itself racist. Still other neoliberal versions have promoted a kind of multiculturalism, celebrating the opportunity for members of all groups to compete and rise as individuals, while rejecting any structural redistribution of wealth and power. Similarly, some expressions of neoliberal ideology have rejected feminism and LGBT pride as inherently damaging to the social fabric, while others have offered back individualistic caricatures that redefine liberation as seeing a few members of your group included in the elite or in positions of cultural prominence.[17]

The shift from the New Deal system to neoliberalism has framed the U.S. far right's development, but the dynamic has been complex. The contemporary far right's initial formation in the 1970s and '80s was largely an offshoot of the grassroots backlash against social change movements and the welfare state. Unlike system-loyal activists, far rightists regarded the federal government as not just politically misguided but irredeemably evil, and they felt no hesitation about proclaiming their racial doctrines openly. Still, far rightists both benefited from and contributed to conservative attacks on civil rights—neonazi and Klan leader David Duke, for example, was one of the first to smear affirmative action with the label "reverse racism" in the 1970s—helping to clear the ground for a more right-wing ruling ideology.

Different far right currents have also to varying degrees supported some elements of neoliberalism. For example, Christian Reconstructionists have generally applauded the privatization of public services, while Patriot activists have called for rolling back environmental regulations and have embraced the ethos of individual property rights as a cornerstone of freedom, just as neonazis and other racists have endorsed the rollback of social programs identified with people of color.

Yet despite such support, since the 1990s far right politics has largely developed in reaction against neoliberalism itself. Non-European immigration and multinational free trade agreements are cornerstones of the neoliberal system and prime targets of far right rage. Far rightists have also denounced the U.S. economy's trend toward runaway financial speculation (an organic consequence of the deregulatory policies of the past three decades), persistent military interventionism overseas, and even—when it targets white people—militarization of the police. This ambivalence about neoliberalism, as much as anything else, expresses the far right's contradictory relationship with established systems of power.[18]

To a large extent, the far right's rise is rooted in capitalism's ongoing process of revolutionizing economic, social, and political relations. Historically, capitalism reinforced or created many boundaries, divisions, and social hierarchies to help enforce order and extract labor from subordinate groups. But now many of these old social structures are being reconfigured or replaced through large-scale economic changes—such as industry moving to the Global South and millions of immigrant workers moving from the Global South into the United States. Far right politics expresses, in concentrated form, the fear and anger of groups whose historical privileges have eroded or seem to be under threat. Far rightists offer not just a backlash against "economic progress" but alternative visions for who should be in charge of class society and how it should be organized.[19]

This book is divided into three parts. Part I includes a chapter on each of the U.S. far right's four major currents—neonazism, the theocratic wing of the Christian right, the Patriot movement, and the alt-right—examining each current's origins and development, core beliefs, and activities. The order of chapters reflects a loose chronology of far right upsurges: the neonazi campaigns of the 1980s, the 1990s explosion of the Patriot movement (strongly influenced by both neonazis and Christian Reconstructionists), and the alt-right's rise since 2010. A brief fifth chapter discusses the LaRouche network, a small but persistent formation that does not fit into any of the other categories but which illustrates the potential for far right politics to take unexpected forms.

Part II consists of three chapters on the "neglected themes" of gender and sexuality, anti-imperialism, and decentralism. These topics reflect political developments and concerns that span across the different currents and highlight the far right's complex responses to leftist politics—repudiating some elements while appropriating others in distorted form. These themes help us delineate the contemporary far right from its predecessors. They are often underemphasized or ignored altogether in discussions of these political movements, precisely because they do not fit standard preconceptions.

Part III looks at several examples of how other political actors have conceptualized and interacted with the far right. Chapter 9 examines federal security forces' complicated and shifting relationships with rightist vigilantes and paramilitaries—from collaboration and sponsorship to crackdown to neglect—and the role of both aiding and repressing rightist violence in the state's larger project of maintaining social control. Chapter 10 traces the specter of fascism in leftist and liberal discourse over seventy-five years, from Communists denouncing the early New Deal to liberals condemning George W. Bush. These misplaced claims of impending fascism have pressured leftists alternately to abandon militancy in order to defend "democracy" or to dismiss the distinction between liberal-pluralism and dictatorship as a sham. Chapter 11 addresses Donald Trump's presidential campaign and the first half-year of his presidency, analyzing their political character and how organized far rightists responded to them.

Because the question of fascism underpins this book's analysis but is not central to it, I have included the essay "Two Ways of Looking at Fascism" as an appendix. As noted above, this work argues for a synthesis of Roger Griffin's ideology-based theory of fascism together with an independent Marxist tradition, spanning from August Thalheimer to Hamerquist and Sakai, that treats fascism as an autonomous force that challenges capitalist political control. Most—although not all—of the far right forces discussed in this book meet my definition of fascism. This point is worth exploring and may be of interest to some readers but is secondary to my main argument here.

Insurgent Supremacists is not a comprehensive study of the U.S. far right. I have tried to provide both an overall framework for analysis as well as a sense of the subject's nuances and complexities, but there are many issues that I have omitted or that deserve fuller treatment. This book also does not address the vital question of antifascist or anti–far right strategy. Fortunately, many thoughtful people are writing critically about the far right and the struggle against it, and the pool of useful literature on these topics continues to grow. I hope that this book will contribute to the discussion.

Acknowledgements

This book is dedicated to my parents. To David, who taught me to write clearly. And to Sandy, who taught me to organize by talking to people, one at a time.

Writing this book proved to be a much bigger and more difficult project than I initially envisioned, and I could not have completed it without many kinds of help from many people.

First and foremost, I am grateful to my partner, Claire, and our son, Leo, who supported and affirmed the project in countless ways. Claire also acted as scribe and sounding board when I needed help getting unstuck. Leo's deepening political awareness has both grounded and inspired me.

My thanks to the staff of PM Press, particularly Ramsey Kanaan and Sasha Lilley, and to Karl Kersplebedeb of Kersplebedeb Publishing for agreeing to this project and for asking me to rework a scattered assortment of writings into something resembling a cohesive whole. As book editor, Karl has been an invaluable colleague and comrade throughout the process, and I am grateful for his guidance, encouragement, and thoughtful comments on matters large and small.

Thanks to John Yates for the cover design, and to laurie prendergast for preparing the index.

Many parts of this book grow out of previously published writings. Thanks to Xtn and the other founders of *Three Way Fight*, a forum where I hashed out much of my analysis of far right politics. For their support and editorial help, I owe thanks to Marvin Mandell and the late Betty Reid Mandell of *New Politics*; Kathryn Joyce, Tarso Ramos, Gabriel Joffe, and Greeley O'Connor of Political Research Associates; Geoff of *Red Skies at Night*; and Victor Wallis and Jonathan Scott of

Socialism and Democracy. Special thanks to Gabriel Kuhn, who acted as translator—and much more than translator—for my 2015 book *Arier, Patriarchen, Übermenschen* (Aryans, Patriarchs, Supermen).

A number of organizations and individuals hosted or helped to organize speaking events that helped me develop ideas that went into the book. Thanks particularly to the A-Space Anarchist Community Center, Big Blue Marble Bookstore, *Insurgent Notes*, Kingston OPIRG, Brady McGarry, Sayrah Namaste, Philly Antifa, Resistance in Brooklyn, Southside Anti-Racist Action, and Wooden Shoe Books.

I am grateful to the many people who offered critical comments, shared ideas, raised questions, alerted me to sources, transcribed recordings, wrote dust jacket quotes, or provided other forms of practical or emotional support that made this book possible. Thanks particularly to Sulaiman Abdul-Hakeem, Virgil Addison, Alice in New Zealand, Dana Barnett, Dan Berger, Chip Berlet, Shane Burley, Jamie Buss, Karen Carr, Philip Cohen, Emily Deming, Alex DiBranco, Nava EtShalom, Preston Enright, John Garvey, Sharon Gershoni, John Goetz, Loren Goldner, Joi Gresham, Roger Griffin, Don Hamerquist, Rebecca Hill, Karl Kersplebedeb, Kieran Frazier Knutson, Bob Lederer, Sarra Lev, Sasha Lilley, David Lyons, Emily Lyons, Jeremy Lyons, Sandy Lyons, Clifford McGuire, Matt Meyer, Donna Minkowitz, Phillip Neel, Michelle O'Brien, Dair Obenshain, Nick Paretsky, Jason Perna, Kate Porterfield, laurie prendergast, Michael Pugliese, Mary Ramos, John Riley, Clarissa Rogers, Mark Rupert, J. Sakai, Terry Schleder, Jarrod Shanahan, Davey Silon, Virginia St. Claire, Meg Starr, Michael Staudenmaier, Ruby Steigerwald, Suzy Subways, Elisabeth Sullins, Spencer Sunshine, Tom Thomson, Donovan Waite, JM Wong, Xtn, and Allison Zibelli.

Earlier versions of chapters 1, 2, 3, and 5, as well as parts of the Introduction, were published in German translation in the book *Arier, Patriarchen, Übermenschen: die extreme Rechte in den USA* [Aryans, Patriarchs, Supermen: The Far Right in the USA] (Mainz, Germany: Unrast Verlag, 2015).

An earlier version of chapter 4 and part of chapter 6 were first published as the title essay of the book *Ctrl-Alt-Delete: An Antifascist Report on the Alternative Right* (Montreal: Kersplebedeb Publishing, 2017) and as "Ctrl-Alt-Delete: The Origins and Ideology of the Alternative Right," *Political Research Associates* (website), January 20, 2017.

An earlier version of chapter 7 was first published as "Anti-Imperialism and the U.S. Far Right," *Red Skies at Night*, no. 3 (February 2016).

Part of chapter 14 is based on the essay "Is the Bush administration fascist?" *New Politics* 11, no. 2 (Winter 2007).

Various sections of this book, including portions of chapters 6, 10, 12, and 13 among others, originated as blog posts on *Three Way Fight* between 2005 and 2016.

The Appendix, "Two Ways of Looking at Fascism," was first published in the journal *Socialism and Democracy* issue 47 (vol. 22, no. 2; July 2008) and is reprinted here courtesy of Taylor & Francis.

Part I

Ideological Currents

1. Neonazis

Neonazis are just one branch of the U.S. far right, but they have played a key role in bringing the modern U.S. far right into being. In the 1980s, neonazis spearheaded a pathbreaking merger of white supremacist ideology, militant and often illegal activities targeting the state, and a vision of right-wing revolution. In the decades since then, neonazis' anti-state activities have been more limited, but their ideology and political strategies have strongly influenced a variety of groups and tendencies, for instance, the Patriot movement and the alt-right, as well as system-loyal currents such as paleoconservatism.

Today, the terms neonazi, white nationalist, and white supremacist are sometimes used interchangeably, but their differences are important to my analysis of the far right. Since word usage varies and can change over time, I want to clarify how I am using these terms here:

White supremacy can refer either to the system of white racial oppression or to white supremacist ideology. *White racial oppression* is the web of social, economic, political, and cultural institutions and practices whereby people identified as "white" hold privilege and varying degrees of power over other people. This system has been central to the U.S. social order since the colonial period, and for most of that time has involved the explicit and legal subordination and exclusion of people of color. Today, formal racial discrimination is mostly gone, but less explicit forms of racial oppression and violence are still the norm in policing, employment, education, housing, health care, and many other areas, often with equally deadly consequences. Open racism is widely discredited, but subtler ideologies such as "color-blindness" help to mask and thereby protect racist oppression as a persistent system.

White supremacist ideology says that racial categories are natural and fundamental to human experience; that white people are better and more important than other races; and that whites should hold social, economic, and political power over others. White supremacist ideology promotes traditional racist stereotypes but is fundamentally an ideology of violence, in that it justifies and promotes both direct physical attacks and systemic harm against people of non-European descent.

White nationalism is a form of white supremacist ideology that focuses on racial identity as the basis for nationhood. Although the term is sometimes applied broadly to any ideology that privileges white people in a national framework, I am following Leonard Zeskind's usage, in which white nationalism specifically refers to the belief that "white people should have a homeland of their own and run a white nationalist state."[1] This would be achieved, depending on the version, through voluntary migration by whites, forced displacement of nonwhites, and/or genocide. In this usage, white nationalism is fundamentally at odds with the continued existence of the United States in its current form.

Neonazism is a form of white nationalism that borrows or shares key elements of German National Socialist (Nazi) ideology, above all the emphasis on racial antisemitism, Jews being viewed as an evil nonwhite super-race. Neonazis don't simply copy German Nazi doctrine but reinterpret it in various ways, for example, by disavowing the classical fascist ideal of a large, centralized dictatorship or by embracing the German Nazi movement's "leftist" dissidents like the brothers Otto and Gregor Strasser. Some neonazis celebrate their political heritage openly, while others mask it in various ways.

As examples to illustrate how I use these terms, advocates of Jim Crow segregation (in which whites violently subordinated and isolated blacks and other people of color while relying on their labor for everything from farming to childcare) were white supremacist, the League of the South (which glorifies the Confederacy and advocates secession of a white-dominated southern nation) is white nationalist, and the National Socialist Movement (which models its ideology and much of its symbolism after Hitler's movement) is neonazi.

This chapter will focus on neonazism's role in leading many white supremacists to abandon and repudiate their longstanding loyalty to the United States. This shift took various forms and invoked a number of political reference points—including memories of the Confederacy, which waged war against the U.S. government to uphold slavery—but it was neonazism, above all, that gave it definition, purpose, and plans of action. The term white nationalism came into common usage following this shift and replaced earlier terms such as "white power" and "white separatism."

Neonazis such as David Duke were among the first white supremacists to popularize the myth that civil rights legislation and affirmative action have made whites an oppressed group within the United States. Going further, neonazis pioneered the myth of "white genocide," which claims there is a deliberate elite program to make white people extinct through a combination of non-European immigration, legal abortion, promoting interracial marriage, and other measures.

Neonazis have also led the way in placing antisemitism at the center of white nationalist theories of power. Old-style white supremacists often promoted classic antisemitic myths: that Jews are greedy, dirty, bloodthirsty, cowardly, and deceitful, and manipulate institutions and events from behind the scenes. But neonazis regard Jews as the main enemy, the superpowerful masterminds who manipulate people of color and white "race traitors" as part of a grand scheme to destroy the white race. As in classical antisemitism, Jews and Jewish power are identified with banks and other financial institutions, so that hatred of Jews serves as a way to harness and channel people's anger at finance capital and capitalists more generally. In this way, antisemitism functions as a distorted anti-elitism, what nineteenth-century German socialist August Bebel called "the socialism of fools." Adapting European racial theories that were embraced by Hitler and his followers, neonazis sometimes refer to non-Jewish whites as Aryans.[2]

Neonazis sometimes mask their antisemitism as "anti-Zionism." There are good reasons to criticize the Israeli state's system of apartheid rule, racist violence, and mass displacement of Palestinians. But for neonazis and many other white nationalists, anti-Zionism is based on hatred of Jews, not solidarity with Palestinians. For them, "Zionism" is a code word for Jewish conspiracy, a malevolent international power whose reach goes far beyond Israel and Palestine. Since the 1980s, neonazis have promoted the antisemitic fiction that America is under the control of a Zionist Occupation Government, or "ZOG" for short.[3]

Neonazis argue that men and women are fundamentally different by nature and should have different social roles. Most of them advocate male dominance over women and suppression of homosexuality or any kind of gender nonconformity. As in classical fascism, there is sometimes tension between a family-centered patriarchal view that women should obey their fathers and husbands and a more race-centered view that white women's main duty is to have lots of babies—a view that led German Nazism to encourage out-of-wedlock births among "racially pure" Germans. Neonazis have debated whether abortion should be used eugenically to weed out "inferior" offspring and improve the racial stock. As discussed in chapter 6, since the 1980s some neonazis have criticized certain forms of sexism within the movement, arguing that "racially conscious" white women should be encouraged to use their full talents and even take on leadership roles, but in recent years neonazis involved in the alt-right have promoted much harsher and more exclusionary forms of misogyny.[4]

Historical forerunners

U.S. neonazis combine European fascist influences with homegrown white supremacist traditions. Since the seventeenth century, European Americans have periodically mobilized to enforce or intensify the subjugation of Indigenous, black, Mexican, and Asian people, and even European immigrant groups considered ethnically inferior. Some of these initiatives, such as the slave patrols of the pre–Civil War South, have been more or less official arms of the state. But others have been grassroots movements at odds with the established power structure, reflecting conflicts between lower- and upper-class whites or between different factions of the elite. The most famous of these was the original Ku Klux Klan, which formed in the states of the former Confederacy shortly after the Civil War and the abolition of slavery. The Klan was an underground armed insurgency against the new Radical Reconstruction state governments, under which black men could vote and hold office on a large scale for the first time. In defiance of the federal government and northern elites, the Klan and other paramilitary groups terrorized newly freed African Americans and their white allies, and reversed most of the political gains blacks had made.[5]

A related movement during the same period was the anti-Chinese crusade, which was based among white workers in the Pacific Coast and Mountain regions. At a time when railroad owners and other capitalists promoted Chinese immigrants as a source of cheap labor, most white labor and socialist organizations demanded their total exclusion. In the 1880s, many Chinese were lynched and whole communities were driven out, culminating in Congress banning all Chinese immigration in 1884.[6]

After lying dormant for several decades, the Klan was refounded in 1915 by Atlanta resident William J. Simmons as the Knights of the Ku Klux Klan. For a few years in the early 1920s, it was a mass movement with millions of supporters and influence in every region. The 1920s Klan targeted not only African Americans but also Catholics, Jews, and immigrants. Unlike the original KKK, this Second Klan wasn't an armed insurgency against the state, but in many places it used populist appeals to challenge local elites for political power. Although hostile to "foreign labor radicals," the Klan sometimes supported strikes by white workers and even backed Socialist Party candidates on occasion. The semi-autonomous Women of the Ku Klux Klan, which had hundreds of thousands of members, blended racial and religious bigotry with calls to expand white Protestant women's social, economic, and political rights. Yet the Second Klan lacked a coherent program, and internal conflicts, leadership scandals, and counterattacks by its opponents caused it to decline rapidly after 1925.[7]

The 1920s Klan was influenced by an upsurge of antisemitism. For most of U.S. history, Jews of European descent have been considered white, which has mostly insulated them from systemic discrimination. But during the period roughly from the 1880s to the 1930s, Eastern European Jews (and other immigrants from Southern and Eastern Europe) were widely considered nonwhite. This temporarily intensified antisemitism against all Jews, who found themselves the periodic targets of mob violence; excluded from jobs, housing, and educational institutions; and subjected to antisemitic scapegoating far beyond anything the United States had previously experienced. The twin stereotypes of the Jew as "banker" and "Bolshevik" embodied a dual image of Jews as both oppressors and subversives.[8]

The German Nazi movement, which arose during the same period as the refounded Klan, drew on many aspects of the U.S. racial order, such as the doctrine of Manifest Destiny, the system of Jim Crow segregation, and the eugenics-based compulsory sterilization laws that many states passed in the early twentieth century. Adolf Hitler especially admired the auto manufacturer Henry Ford, who in the early 1920s launched an antisemitic propaganda campaign that reinterpreted the *Protocols of the Elders of Zion* (a Czarist forgery supposedly describing a Jewish plot to conquer the world) for the modern industrial age.[9]

During the Great Depression in the 1930s, a new crop of rightist groups blended white supremacist and anti-Jewish politics with sympathy for European fascist governments. The most important leader in this movement was Father Charles Coughlin, a Catholic priest whose political radio broadcasts had millions of listeners. Coughlin played a leadership role for two organizations: the National Union of Social Justice (active 1934–1937) and the more hard-line Christian Front (1938–1940). Coughlin began as a liberal supporter of President Franklin Roosevelt's New Deal policies but moved steadily to the right and by the late 1930s openly supported Hitler. Like many fascists, Coughlin vilified bankers (commonly associated with Jews) as "bloodsuckers" who victimized both workers and industrialists, and proposed that the U.S. government be replaced with an authoritarian "Corporate State" modeled after Mussolini's government in Italy. Coughlin's movement and other pro-fascist groups quickly fell into disrepute following the Japanese attack on Pearl Harbor and the U.S. entry into World War II in 1941.[10]

In the 1950s and 1960s, the white supremacist movement focused mainly on defending racial segregation and keeping black people from voting, efforts that were eventually defeated. Fascist politics was largely subordinated to the Cold War, as many former Nazi collaborators sided with the U.S. government against the Soviet Union. George Lincoln Rockwell's original American Nazi Party, founded in 1959, celebrated Hitler but remained loyal to the American political system. As white nationalist Gregory Hood has commented, Rockwell's "National Socialism was not an ideology so much as a tactic, an attempt to build a fighting conservatism capable of defeating the militant left." Rockwell targeted blacks, Jews, and communists but reported regularly to the FBI about his party's activities.[11] The National Renaissance Party (NRP) was more radical. Founded in 1949, the NRP came to support Third World revolutions and, along with early neonazi writer and activist Francis Parker Yockey, considered the USSR a lesser threat than the United States. While the NRP probably never had many more than fifty members, it forged relations with a number of different organizations and individuals, and developed themes that would be taken up more broadly in later years.[12]

Another hard-line rightist organization active in this period was the Minutemen, an anticommunist paramilitary organization founded by Robert DePugh in or around 1961. The Minutemen stockpiled weapons and compiled dossiers on political opponents to prepare against the supposed threat of a Communist invasion or government takeover. The group promoted a kind of right-wing conspiracism similar to the John Birch Society (of which DePugh was also a member) and did not officially support white supremacist or antisemitic ideology, but its membership overlapped heavily with white supremacist organizations. De Pugh himself took part in the 1962 convention of the National States Rights Party, a white supremacist group. The Minutemen prefigured the 1980s neonazi movement by operating partly underground, training for guerrilla warfare, and threatening (and in one case attempting) to assassinate members of Congress. DePugh was convicted in 1969 of conspiracy to rob a bank and spent four years in prison; before his death in 2009 he would become associated with the Christian Identity movement.[13]

A movement comes together

The social upheavals of the 1960s, above all the black liberation movement's defeat of formal, explicit white rule, led growing numbers of white supremacists to question the legitimacy of the U.S. political order. Antisemitism offered them a way to make sense of what had happened and chart a way forward. As Eric K. Ward explains:

> The successes of the civil rights movement created a terrible problem for White supremacist ideology. White supremacism—inscribed de jure by the Jim Crow regime and upheld de facto outside the South—had been the law of the land, and a Black-led social movement had toppled the political regime that supported it. How could a race of inferiors have unseated this power structure through organizing alone? ... Some secret cabal, some mythological power, must be manipulating the social order behind the scenes. This diabolical

evil must control television, banking, entertainment, education, and even Washington, D.C. It must be brainwashing White people, rendering them racially unconscious.[14]

In the late 1960s and the 1970s, while some white supremacists continued to advocate a return to old forms of white dominance, many began to regard the U.S. political framework as incompatible with their racial goals and moved toward oppositional strategies that blended white supremacism with a new emphasis on antisemitism.[15] In this period, several distinct white nationalist currents took shape, including the following:

American Nazi Party offshoots. After Rockwell's death in 1967, various successor groups took the party's politics in more radical directions. The most important of these was the National Alliance, which William Pierce founded in 1974 and led until his death in 2002. In 1978, Pierce published *The Turner Diaries*, a fictional account of a Nazi revolution against the U.S. government, which later served as an inspiration and blueprint for a series of underground armed initiatives. Also worth mentioning is the short-lived National Socialist Liberation Front, headed by Joseph Tommasi until his violent death in 1975, one of the first neonazi groups to stake out an unambiguously revolutionary position. Another former Rockwell recruit, James Mason, inspired by Tommasi, further elaborated an anti-systemic philosophy in his *Siege* newsletter, which is still an important source for neonazis today.[16]

Ku Klux Klan. In the 1970s, former Nazi student activist David Duke formed a new Knights of the Ku Klux Klan in a bid to revitalize the most famous branch of U.S. white supremacy. Duke used media skillfully, welcomed Catholics and women as members, and claimed that the group was simply defending whites against unfair discrimination. Duke also initiated a Klan "border watch" to oppose illegal immigration from Mexico. At the same time, he increased the Klan's emphasis on the "Jewish problem" and criticized segregationism as a "system of weakness and degeneration." "We of the Ku Klux Klan are not reactionaries longing to return to a previous era of White racial history," his group declared—instead, they advocated the creation of an all-white nation-state.[17]

Crypto-fascists. Willis Carto's Liberty Lobby (founded 1957) was for many years a leading antisemitic publisher. Carto was an admirer of neonazi Francis Parker Yockey, yet consistently presented himself as a conservative or populist, not a fascist. Initially Carto sought to build a broad coalition of anti-Jewish conspiracy theorists and mainstream conservatives, though in the late 1960s he tried briefly to create a street-fighting force to attack the student and black left. From the 1970s until his death in 2015, Carto promoted fascist ideology through a variety of ostensibly non-fascist organs, including the Populist Party and the Institute for Historical Review, a leading Holocaust denial publisher, which Carto founded but later lost control of. In 1980, the Liberty Lobby's newspaper, *The Spotlight*, reached a peak circulation of over three hundred thousand, and the Liberty Lobby's radio program was broadcast on 410 radio stations.[18]

Posse Comitatus. Founded in 1971, Posse Comitatus was a loose political network that promoted a militant mix of white supremacy, antisemitic conspiracy theories, and arcane pseudo-legal doctrines, while rejecting the legitimacy of all government above the county level. (The group's name means "power of the county.") One of Posse's first leaders, Henry Lamont Beach, was a veteran of the 1930s fascist group the Silver Shirts. Posse Comitatus was rooted in the right-wing tax protest and survivalist subcultures and strongest in the Midwest and Mountain West. The network gained some popular support in the 1980s with its claims that the Midwest farm crisis was caused by a conspiracy of Jewish bankers. One of the first martyrs of the emerging revolutionary movement was Gordon Kahl, a former Posse organizer and income tax resister, who died in a shootout with police in 1983.[19]

Christian Identity. Many Posse Comitatus members promoted this racist version of Christianity, which teaches that Anglo-Saxons or northern Europeans more generally are the real descendants of the ancient children of Israel and that the Jews of today are evil impostors—in some versions, literally descended from the Devil. Christian Identity adherents also believe that people of color are subhumans who result from a separate creation from whites. In the 1970s, the neonazi group Aryan Nations was established as the political arm of a leading Christian Identity church, Richard Butler's Church of Jesus Christ-Christian. Aryan Nations went on to become a major influence and force within the broader revolutionary white nationalist movement.[20]

These five currents remained disunited through the 1970s, but in the early 1980s they began to coalesce into one movement. A major turning point came in 1979, when a coalition of Klansmen and neonazis calling itself the United Racist Front opened fire and killed four members and one supporter of the Communist Workers Party, a small Marxist-Leninist organization, at a "Death to the Klan" rally organized by the CWP in Greensboro, North Carolina. Although this operation had federal government support (an FBI informant and an agent of the Bureau of Alcohol, Tobacco, and Firearms were active participants in planning the massacre) it softened the traditional distrust between Klan and Nazi groups and encouraged many white supremacists to embrace revolutionary politics.[21]

One of the first leftists to grasp the meaning of this change was Ken Lawrence of the National Anti-Klan Network and the Sojourner Truth Organization. Speaking in 1982, Lawrence highlighted the new convergence of two distinct traditions: KKK racist terror and fascism. "It is the genius of the Klan leaders today that they have managed to merge those two movements into a single whole, and to create a coherent ideology out of those two divergent strains." In the 1960s, the Klan had been "essentially a backward-looking movement attempting to preserve what was most reactionary and most peculiar of the institutions of the segregated white South. It was under that banner … that it went out and did its beatings, bombings, lynchings, mutilations, and castrations." But by the early 1980s, the resurgent Klan had embraced a fascist political vision and strategy:

> [T]he role of racism and the role of anti-Semitism and the role of scapegoating in general is quite different ideologically for a fascist movement from that of a right-wing conservative movement or a traditional Klan-type movement. That is, it is *not* to put people in their place. It is *not* to make a sub-class out of them and to exploit, or super-exploit, their labor. It is *genocidal*. It is *exterminationist*.[22]

The key text embodying this new vision was *The Turner Diaries* by William Pierce. In its account of an armed revolution whose targets include the FBI and the U.S. military, Pierce's novel marked a dramatic shift for many white supremacists. *The Turner Diaries* draws a sharp line between revolutionaries and conservatives, who are dismissed as "the world's greatest cowards."[23] The revolutionaries are organized in a centralized underground network known simply as the Organization, which in turn is run by a secretive inner circle called the Order. The Organization uses bombings, assassinations, and the resulting repression to disrupt business as usual and cause the social and political order to disintegrate. In the words of Pierce's narrator, Earl Turner:

> [O]ne of the major purposes of political terror, always and everywhere, is to force the authorities to take reprisals and to become more repressive, thus alienating a portion of the population and generating sympathy for the terrorists. And the other purpose is to create unrest by destroying the population's sense of security and their belief in the invincibility of the government.[24]

Yet the Organization wins white people's support less by gaining their sympathy than by terrorizing them. As Turner puts it, "we will make them fear us more than they fear the System."[25] Turner thinks this approach is based on anticolonialist guerrilla warfare, but as Ken Lawrence pointed out, Pierce is really copying the "strategy of tension," which was developed by European neonazis in the 1970s.

As an example of the kind of revolution *The Turner Diaries* envisions, here is a passage from late in the novel, when civil war and nuclear strikes have destroyed much of the economic infrastructure, starvation is rampant, and both the Organization and the System control a patchwork of enclaves:

> Those who were admitted—and that meant only children, women of childbearing age, and able-bodied men willing to fight in the Organization's ranks—were subjected to much more severe racial screening than had been used to separate Whites from non-Whites in California. It was no longer sufficient to be merely White; in order to eat one had to be judged the bearer of especially valuable genes.

> In Detroit the practice was first established (and it was later adopted elsewhere) of providing any able-bodied White male who sought admittance to the Organization's enclave with a hot meal and a bayonet or other edged weapon. His forehead was then marked with an indelible dye, and he was turned out and could be readmitted permanently only by bringing back the head of a freshly killed Black or other non-White. This practice assured that

precious food would not be wasted on those who would not or
could not add to the Organization's fighting strength, but it took
a terrible toll of the weaker and more decadent White elements.[26]

Eventually the System collapses, and the Organization gains control
of North America and finishes killing all people of color and Jews on
the continent. This is followed by bloody white uprisings against the
Jewish overlords in Europe and the Soviet Union, and the systematic
depopulation of Asia through the massive use of chemical, biological,
and nuclear weapons. The specific fates of Africa and Latin America are
not described, but by the end of the novel the only human beings left
alive are non-Jewish whites.

Predictably, Pierce's novel relies on racist caricature of the most vi-
cious kind: the black characters are brutes who live in filth, rape white
women at every opportunity, and resort to cannibalism when food gets
scarce. The Jews are evil, deceitful wirepullers who use the rhetoric of
anti-racism to manipulate other people, but, when pressed, "shriek and
gibber" in Hebrew and work themselves into a frenzy of hatred against
whites. Perhaps more surprisingly, the vast majority of whites, too, are
presented as bestial creatures who deserve contempt—and death—for
allowing Jews to rule over them. The revolutionaries massacre thousands upon thousands of whites for participating in the Jewish-run state
or for sexually "defiling their race." This is the book that, Lawrence
reported in 1982, all of the resurgent Klan groups were selling at a bulk
discount, and which became one of the most influential writings within
the U.S. far right.

Following their success in Greensboro, Klansmen and Nazis joined
forces again in 1981, this time along with members of the Canadian
far right, in a failed plot to seize control of the Caribbean nation of
Dominica.[27] Over the following few years, several prominent Klan leaders moved from KKK groups to Nazi-oriented ones: Robert Miles and
Louis Beam became ambassadors-at-large for the Aryan Nations; Tom
Metzger founded White Aryan Resistance (WAR); Don Black founded the *Stormfront* online discussion forum; and Frazier Glenn Miller
(a participant in the Greensboro massacre) remade his Confederate
Knights of the Ku Klux Klan as the White Patriot Party. In the years
ahead, some Klan groups remained wary of the shift, but the most successful ones tended to be those that embraced neonazism or worked
together with overt neonazis.[28]

During the 1980s and '90s, neonazism developed along several lines that still shape the movement today. Like Hitler and Mussolini, some movement activists used electoral campaigns to spread their message. In 1984, Willis Carto helped found the Populist Party, which brought together activists from older white supremacist groups such as the National States Rights Party, the Christian Patriots Defense League, and the KKK. The Populist Party denounced the Federal Reserve, monopoly finance capitalism, and world government, as well as immigration, gun control, and homosexuality. The party lasted into the mid-1990s. Its 1988 presidential candidate was David Duke, who had resigned as head of the Knights of the Ku Klux Klan in 1980 to form the National Association for the Advancement of White People. In 1989, Duke won a seat in the Louisiana state legislature as a Republican. He then ran strong campaigns for U.S. senator in 1990 and Louisiana governor in 1991, both times losing but securing a majority of white votes.[29]

In contrast to Duke and Carto, Tom Metzger's White Aryan Resistance, founded in 1983, developed a militant, street-fighting presence. Through its affiliate, Aryan Youth Movement, WAR was one of the first neonazi groups to welcome and promote skinheads, who with their shaved heads, tattoos, suspenders, and combat boots have since become a prominent fixture of the far right. Skinhead youth culture started in Britain in the late 1960s and later spread to other countries, including the United States. Skinheads project a working-class ethos, strong group loyalty, and a readiness to fight. Some skinheads are antiracist and antifascist, but others have embraced neonazi ideology and symbols. Initially, the most important neonazi skinhead groups often consisted of crews in particular cities—Chicago Area Skinheads (CASH), Detroit Area Skinheads (DASH), etc.—though as the movement grew so too did groups not confined to one locale, for instance, the American Front and Hammerskin Nation. Neonazi skinheads have repeatedly been implicated in violent, sometimes lethal, attacks against people of color, Jews, queers, and antifascist activists. They have also helped to build a significant music scene with various bands and recording companies that have served as vehicles for spreading white nationalist propaganda and as an important source of revenue.[30]

The third major current of neonazism, distinct from both WAR's street-fighting orientation and Carto's electoralism, was what Leonard Zeskind has called the movement's "vanguardist" wing—those who believed that the white race's future depended on a committed minority acting in secret to destroy Jewish power. For instance, William Pierce aimed to build his National Alliance into a revolutionary cadre by recruiting from "an elite minority carefully sifted out of the overall White population."[31]

Meanwhile, in the early 1980s Robert Miles and Louis Beam promoted the concept of the Fifth Era Klan, which like the original Reconstruction-era Klan would take up arms in a guerrilla war against the U.S. government. Both men were former KKK grand dragons (state leaders). Miles was a former Michigan insurance executive who spent six years in prison for a 1971 bombing of school buses used for racial integration. Beam was a Vietnam veteran and former leader in David Duke's Knights of the KKK. A pioneer in the Klan's paramilitary turn, he had organized training camps for white supremacists, as well as a terror campaign against Vietnamese fishermen in Galveston Bay in 1981. In his writings during this period, Beam argued for a break with system-supportive conservatism and prioritizing attacks on the government and leaders of the "International Satanic Anti-Christ Conspiracy." Through their *Inter-Klan Newsletter & Survival Alert*, Beam and Miles promoted a decentralized strategy to protect the underground movement from being infiltrated and crushed. Miles wrote of organizing "a WEB, instead of a chain" of command, and Beam wrote an influential article advocating a program of "Leaderless Resistance," in which cells or even individuals would operate independently, making them less vulnerable to repression.[32]

In 1983, National Alliance member Robert Mathews founded an underground cell known as The Order (after the fictitious revolutionary leadership group in *The Turner Diaries*), also known as the Aryan Resistance Movement or Silent Brotherhood. The group issued a "declaration of war" against the U.S. government and conducted a series of robberies, killings, bombings, and other illegal actions before its members were arrested or killed in shootouts with police.[33] The Order was influenced by both Pierce's elitism and Beam and Miles's call for immediate action. The group's members were recruited from the National Alliance, Aryan Nations, Posse Comitatus, and two Klan organizations, among others, embodying the convergence of a revolutionary movement.[34]

The Order brought an organized section of the U.S. right into armed conflict with the state for the first time in over one hundred years. In doing so, it helped to define a new era of far right militant opposition to the state. The federal government sentenced the surviving members of The Order to long prison terms, rounded up members of several other far right paramilitary groups, and tried fourteen movement activists—including Miles, Beam, and Aryan Nations head Richard Butler—for seditious conspiracy. Although the latter trial resulted in acquittals, the overall crackdown significantly weakened the neonazi movement and turned many activists away from an underground guerrilla warfare strategy. At the same time, the imprisoned Order members were celebrated as political prisoners or prisoners of war, similar to the way imprisoned members of left-wing guerrilla groups have been celebrated on the left. Order prisoner David Lane's famed "14 words"—"We must secure the existence of our people and a future for white children"—quickly became a watchword for fascists around the world, just as December 8, the day Order founder Robert J. Mathews perished in a standoff with the FBI, would be commemorated in later years by neonazis as Martyr's Day.

The Order also helped to inspire a series of other paramilitary groups and initiatives over the following decades, such as the Aryan Republican Army and Aryan People's Republic in the 1990s and the 1995 bombing of the Oklahoma City federal building, carried out by neonazi Timothy McVeigh and others, which killed 168 people. There have also been various "lone wolf" attacks by individual white nationalists in different places against federal institutions, people of color, Jewish institutions, women's health clinics, and other targets.[35]

Debates within the movement

The 1980s not only crystallized strategic debates between electoralists, street fighters, and vanguardists but disagreements on several other issues as well, such as religion. While key groups such as Aryan Nations and Posse Comitatus helped spread Christian Identity to others in the movement, some neonazis rejected any form of Christianity as an offshoot of Judaism. Many Nazi skinheads and others have advocated Odinism, a form of neopaganism derived from Norse mythology, as supposedly more appropriate for Aryan or Nordic people. A third contender is the Creativity Movement, a religion founded in 1973 by former

Florida state legislator Ben Klassen as the Church of the Creator, whose theology centers on the concept of Racial Holy War, or RAHOWA, against Jews and the other "mud races" of the world. Other religious doctrines, including Satanism, occultism, and "Hitlerism" (the worship of Adolf Hitler), as well as mainstream Christianity and atheism, have also found supporters, while some groups have downplayed religion or avoided taking any particular position on the issue.[36]

A more practical debate concerned centralization versus decentralization, an issue that split the vanguardist current among neonazis. Some groups, such as William Pierce's National Alliance, have followed classical fascism in promoting a highly centralized political organization and a powerful state apparatus. But other neonazis have advocated various kinds of decentralism, as discussed more fully in chapter 8. Posse Comitatus's suspicion of all government above the county level influenced not only neonazi activism but also the Patriot and sovereign citizens movements. Posse's localism may have influenced Louis Beam's 1983 call for "Leaderless Resistance," which in turn was taken up by many other neonazis, as well as Patriot activists and the Christian rightist Army of God. But Pierce and some others within the movement strongly disagreed with leaderless resistance as a strategy and argued that a centralized command structure is needed. This debate has continued.[37]

A related issue was whether neonazis should aim to take power in the entire United States or just a part of it. *The Turner Diaries* had envisioned white revolutionaries conquering the globe, and The Order claimed "a territorial imperative which will consist of the entire North American Continent north of Mexico."[38] But many neonazis advocated regional secession instead. The Christian Patriots Defense League wanted a "Mid-America Survival Zone" bordered by the Appalachians and the Rockies. The White Patriot Party envisioned a Southern White Republic.[39] Most influential of all was Robert Miles's call for a white nation-state in the Northwest, specifically Idaho, Montana, Oregon, Washington, and Wyoming. In Leonard Zeskind's words, Miles "proposed an out-trek by white nationalists, from inside a multinational empire they once controlled, but no longer did, to a territory where they could reinvent themselves."[40] Aryan Nations, based in rural Idaho, promoted the plan and drew many movement activists to settle in the region. Today the idea lives on in Harold Covington's Northwest Front and other initiatives and as a more diffuse utopian dream drawing far right individuals to move to the area.[41]

To some extent, neonazis have also disagreed about capitalism. Many groups, echoing Hitler's party, draw a phony distinction between "productive" industrial capital and "parasitic" finance capital (supposedly controlled by "usurious" Jews), and many criticize multinational corporations for hurting white workers, for example, by moving industrial jobs overseas. They advocate at most limited economic reforms that echo welfare state or social democratic politics. The National Alliance in 1993 praised capitalism for giving people strong incentives, so that "the strong, aggressive, and clever rise and prosper, and the weak, indecisive, and stupid remain at the bottom." But they also cautioned that unrestricted capitalism could lead to "endemic class hostility and even to class warfare" and could also promote "racially harmful activity, such as stifling competition or importing non-White labor." The National Socialist Movement, founded in 2004, modeled its program on the German Nazi Party's 25-Point Program and declared that it stood "explicitly for private property" but called for a number of economic reforms, such as abolishing "unearned income" and "interest slavery," confiscating "war profits," nationalizing trusts, establishing profit-sharing in "large industrial enterprises," and ensuring that people have affordable housing and adequate health insurance.[42]

"Third Position" fascism, which stands for a rejection of both communism and capitalism, goes further. Italian and British fascists initiated Third Position politics in the 1970s, and Tom Metzger's White Aryan Resistance first brought it to prominence in the U.S. far right. WAR proclaimed itself an anti-capitalist, white working-class movement, denounced U.S. military intervention in Central America and the Middle East, embraced environmentalism, celebrated Third World anti-imperialist struggles, and sponsored an Aryan Women's League that advocated white power and women's power. WAR celebrated the German Nazi movement's "left" wing, associated with the brothers Gregor and Otto Strasser, which emphasized class struggle against conservative elites and capitalists. Third Position has also been promoted by other groups, such as the skinhead-based American Front. The ideology also influenced National-Anarchism, an offshoot of British neonazism that envisions a decentralized system of racially segregated communities. National-Anarchism established a small presence in the United States starting in 2007.[43]

In the 2010s, a small offshoot of American Front called New Resistance declared that "we do not extend any tribal loyalty to white capitalists or their lackeys. In any conflict between the system and non-white/mixed-race workers, we will always side with the latter." New Resistance called for the dissolution of multinational corporations and collective control of major industries, the abolition of "wage slavery and landlordism," equitable land redistribution, free universal health care, and a guaranteed annual income—measures that many other far right groups would denounce as communistic.[44] New Resistance calls its political philosophy Fourth Position, after *The Fourth Political Theory* by Russian far right theorist Aleksandr Dugin. A former leader of the National Bolshevik Party, which blended Stalinism and fascism, Dugin advocates an authoritarian Eurasian empire in opposition to U.S. and Western European global power. In keeping with Dugin's politics, New Resistance voiced wide-ranging support for ostensible opponents of U.S. imperialism, including Syria, Iran, Muammar Gaddafi's Libya, Hugo Chávez's Venezuela, and even North Korea. They also disavowed anti-Jewish bigotry and affirmed "the right of Jews...to live in peace and according to their own traditions."[45]

Post–Cold War developments

Since its initial upsurge in the 1980s, the neonazi movement has failed to achieve the breakthrough that its leaders hoped for. It has neither attracted a mass following nor sustained an organized armed conflict with the state. As a movement, it has been isolated and fragmented, plagued by infighting, prosecutions and lawsuits, and bad leadership, as well as vocal opposition from leftists, liberals, and many conservatives. At the same time, neonazis have remained a significant political force as a pole of right-wing anti-systemic opposition. They have continued to spread their message and have contributed to two important broader movements, the Patriot movement and the alt-right.

The collapse of the Soviet bloc and end of the Cold War in 1989–1991 indirectly aided the shift toward oppositional politics on the right. For decades, shared hatred of the "Red Menace" had united diverse right-wingers behind U.S. foreign policy, even repeatedly bringing fascists and conservatives together within the same structures with an anticommunist focus, such as the World Anti-Communist League, the

Neonazis   21

Anti-Bolshevik Bloc of Nations, and others.⁴⁶ Support for the South
African apartheid regime and for various anticommunist guerrilla forces
throughout the Third World were shared concerns.

With that unity gone—due the fall of the Soviet Union and subse-
quent cooling of U.S. ruling-class support for the now less useful anti-
communist guerrilla groups and political networks—old debates began
to reemerge, and more rightists began to voice opposition to sections of
the U.S. political and economic elite. Some conservative intellectuals,
declaring themselves "paleoconservatives," invoked the legacy of the
America First movement of the early 1940s, which had opposed U.S.
entry into World War II and harbored many sympathizers with Nazi
Germany. The paleocons defined themselves in opposition to the "neoconservatives," a network of former Cold War liberals who had moved
rightward and who advocated an aggressive foreign policy, staunch
support for Zionism, and relatively open immigration policies. The paleocons spoke out against U.S. interventionism and Washington's close
alliance with Israel, often in terms with anti-Jewish undertones, and
many of them contributed to the growth of the anti-immigrant movement in the 1990s. Such developments provided a wider field in which
neonazis could operate and from which they could draw recruits. And
while paleocons remained loyal to the U.S. political order, they interacted dynamically with neonazism and helped to extend its impact. For
example, David Duke's electoral activism directly inspired paleocon
Patrick Buchanan to run for president in the 1992 and 1996 Republican
presidential primaries. Each time, Buchanan received about three million votes. Paleocons such as Sam Francis helped to build a new crop
of white nationalist organizations, such as the Council of Conservative
Citizens, that presented a more respectable face than neonazism.⁴⁷ In
the 2000s, paleoconservatives such as Paul Gottfried helped launch the
alt-right, as discussed in chapter 4.

During this same period, as I discuss in chapter 3, neonazis contributed to the explosive growth of the Patriot movement, which highlighted the potential for white nationalist paramilitarism to develop into
something much larger. The majority of Patriot groups have seen themselves as fending off tyranny rather than seeking to overthrow the state,
yet they began to form dual power institutions that challenged federal
authority in ways directly influenced by Posse Comitatus and other
neonazis. Many Patriot activists have disavowed white nationalism
and racial bigotry, yet some of them have had direct ties with neonazi

groups, and political ideas rooted in neonazi supremacist ideology have become commonplace in Patriot movement circles.

Despite this influence, the neonazi movement has struggled to build and maintain a significant organizational network. Most of the leading groups of the 1980s have fragmented or disappeared. Willis Carto lost control of the Holocaust-denying Institute for Historical Review in 1993. By 2001, an ongoing legal battle with the IHR's new leadership bankrupted the Liberty Lobby and forced it to fold, although Carto replaced *The Spotlight* with another newspaper, *The American Free Press*.[48] White Aryan Resistance and Tom Metzger were bankrupted by a 1990 wrongful death judgment for their role in the 1988 racist murder of Ethiopian student Mulugeta Seraw in Portland, Oregon, and never regained their former influence.[49] Aryan Nations maintained a national network and hosted an annual World Congress for movement activists through the 1990s, but in 2000 it too was hit with a multimillion-dollar judgment because of a shooting incident. After Richard Butler's death in 2004, Aryan Nations splintered into competing factions. The National Alliance built a relatively strong organization in the 1990s, with 1,400 dues-paying members and one million dollars in annual revenues by 2002. But that year William Pierce died suddenly, and over the following years the National Alliance collapsed under mismanagement and scandals. In 2000, David Duke replaced the National Association for the Advancement of White People with the National Organization For European American Rights, renamed European-American Unity and Rights Organization (EURO) the following year, but it has been little more than a platform to promote Duke's writings.[50]

Yet as some organizations have declined, others have risen. The World Church of the Creator grew rapidly in the late 1990s, collapsed in 2004 when Matt Hale, its leader at the time, was sentenced to forty years for solicitation of murder, then regrouped as the Creativity Movement and rebounded to a degree. The National Socialist Movement, founded in 1974, has had more staying power to date, partly through its policy of welcoming members who also belong to other white supremacist groups. As of 2009, the NSM had sixty-one chapters in thirty-five states, and the Southern Poverty Law Center called it the largest neonazi group in the United States. Among neonazi skinhead groups, the Vinlanders Social Club, founded in 2003, has gained prominence alongside the more fragmented and older Hammerskins.[51]

Reaching out

Despite these upheavals, neonazis have continually sought to forge ties with others outside their own ranks. U.S. neonazis have a long history of collaborating with far rightists in other countries. As early as 1962, American Nazi Party head George Lincoln Rockwell helped to found the World Union of National Socialists, which today claims affiliate organizations in some twenty-five countries. William Pierce made a number of visits to Europe and formed ties with neo-fascist groups in Britain, Germany, Greece, and elsewhere, and David Duke has attended many political meetings in Russia and Eastern Europe.[52] Because the United States does not have the legal prohibitions against "hate speech" that exist in many countries, U.S. groups have been an important illicit source of far right newspapers and other literature internationally. Gary Lauck's National Socialist German Workers Party/Overseas Organization (NSDAP/AO), based in Lincoln, Nebraska, has been supplying propaganda to groups in Germany and other European countries since the 1970s. More recently, American neonazis have helped to host foreign-language websites on U.S. servers. In the early 1990s, the NSDAP/AO helped recruit foreign mercenaries to fight for Croatia in its war for independence from Yugoslavia.[53]

Neonazis have also cultivated ties with the Aryan Brotherhood (AB), a white supremacist prison gang with an estimated fifteen to twenty thousand members nationwide. AB has a history of extreme violence against people of color, but it is primarily a criminal syndicate rather than a political organization and sometimes sets aside its racist ideology for the sake of profit. At the same time, many AB members joined Aryan Nations during the latter's peak in the 1980s, and in 2000, AB leaders allegedly explored the possibility of making bombs to use against federal officials and buildings.[54]

Some neonazis have made overtures to right-wing black nationalist groups, such as Louis Farrakhan's Nation of Islam, or to Islamic rightist groups. Some even applauded the September 11, 2001, attacks that destroyed the World Trade Center and killed three thousand people as courageous blows against Jewish power. Bill Roper, deputy membership coordinator of the National Alliance, wrote on 9-11:

> The enemy of our enemy is, for now at least, our friends. We may
> not want them marrying our daughters, just as they would not

want us marrying theirs. We may not want them in our societies, just as they would not want us in theirs. But anyone who is willing to drive a plane into a building to kill jews [sic] is alright [sic] with me. I wish our members had half as much testicular fortitude.[55]

In 2005, Aryan Nations head August Kreis called for an alliance between neonazis and al-Qaeda against ZOG. "You say they're terrorists, I say they're freedom fighters. And I want to instill the same jihadic feeling in our peoples' heart, in the Aryan race, that they have for their father, who they call Allah."[56]

But other white supremacists rejected any collaboration with non-white Muslims and applauded the upsurge of anti-Muslim hostility and violence that followed the 9-11 attacks. In 2010, some contributors to the neonazi website *Stormfront* even praised Islamophobic articles by Pamela Geller of the group Stop Islamization of America, despite the fact that Geller is Jewish.[57] Neonazis have taken part in anti-immigrant initiatives such as the Minuteman Project and Minuteman Civil Defense Corps, vigilante groups formed in the early 2000s to keep Mexicans from crossing the U.S. border. As nativist activism has intensified in recent years, a number of white supremacist groups have made it a major focus.[58]

Neonazis have also tried to build alliances with leftists around shared opposition to the U.S. power structure or global capitalism—sometimes from opportunism, but sometimes as a serious strategy to join with other political dissidents. Willis Carto sought to ally with leftist anti–Vietnam War protesters in the late 1960s and offered advice in the 1970s to Lyndon LaRouche, who at that time was moving from Marxism to the far right. In the 1990s, supporters of Carto's Liberty Lobby distributed propaganda at anti–Gulf War rallies. Both Louis Beam and Matt Hale of World Church of the Creator praised the 1999 anti-globalization protests in Seattle, and the New Alliance created a bogus Anti-Globalism Action Network in 2002 in an effort to lure leftist support. Some neonazis endorsed or tried to join the left-oriented Occupy movement of 2011–2012.[59]

Music has become an important arena for extending neonazi influence. Neonazi music in the 1980s was centered on Oi!, a punk subgenre that became associated with white power skinheads, but it now includes bands working in many other genres, including black metal, neo-folk, martial industrial, and others. Some of these bands are explicitly white nationalist, while others claim to be non-political but consistently use fascist imagery, themes, and historical references in positive ways. Many concerts and music-related forums have become meeting grounds between far rightists and people who are apolitical or even anti-racist in their leanings. These changes allow neonazi ideology to reach a wider range of U.S. music audiences than previously.[60]

One of the most significant, but also most difficult to gauge, opportunities for outreach used by neonazis is the internet. Neonazis were quick to recognize the potential of online activism in breaking through the isolation that comes with having highly unpopular views. In the early 1980s, neonazis began building computer boards, and in the 1990s the *Stormfront* website (established by former Klansman Don Black in 1995) became the main far right hub for internet discussion. *Stormfront* and similar websites made the writings of William Pierce and David Duke accessible to millions of people who might have never heard of them otherwise. As the internet has increased its importance in the general culture, it has also become a main site of organization for neonazis. For instance, the Atomwaffen Division was founded in 2015, largely as a result of discussions on the *Ironmarch.org* website.

Lately, neonazis' most dramatic opportunity for dialogue with a broader public has been the alt-right, or alternative right, a far right movement that mostly exists online, and that gained sudden prominence and influence through its relationship with Donald Trump's 2016 presidential campaign. As I discuss in chapter 4, the alt-right is predominantly white nationalist but also overlaps with various other anti-egalitarian ideological currents. The movement includes some neonazis, such as the Traditionalist Youth Network/Traditionalist Worker Party and Andrew Anglin's *The Daily Stormer*, but most alt-rightists have other political roots and many disagree with neonazism to varying degrees, for example, on the possibility of an alliance with Zionist Jews. Like the Patriot movement of the 1990s, the alt-right is dangerous in part because it is a political coalition between neonazis and other right-wing opposition forces.

Conclusion

Far right politics is often defined in terms of white supremacist and anti-semitic ideology, placing neonazis at the center of the discussion. While I disagree with that approach, there is no question that neonazism has been pivotal for articulating a modern right-wing opposition to the existing U.S. political order. This opposition has taken different forms, from street combat and guerrilla warfare to electoral campaigns, and has also brought neonazis into broader oppositional initiatives, from the Patriot movement's dual power-building to the alt-right's online activism. Whether or not neonazis ever again take up arms against the U.S. government on a significant scale, they are likely to remain an important source of supremacist insurgency.

2. Theocrats

The Christian right, which has been a major force in American politics since the late 1970s, aims to impose a conservative or reactionary interpretation of Christian morality on society as a whole. Although a majority of Christian rightists seek change within the existing political system, this chapter focuses on the movement's hard-line minority, which wants to replace that system with a full-blown theocracy.

While white nationalists emphasize race, Christian rightists emphasize gender and sexuality. Sexism and heterosexism are nothing new in American politics, but in the past they were largely taken for granted. The Christian right—responding to the rising feminist and LGBT movements of the 1960s and after—is the first U.S. mass movement to put the reassertion of heterosexual male dominance at the center of its program. Christian rightists are also pro-capitalist and hostile to all non-Christian belief systems. Since the 9-11 attacks, the movement has embraced the wave of Islamophobia that portrays Muslims as a threat to Western civilization. Rejecting secularism, the Christian right has promoted an attack on science and the very concept of evidence-based knowledge. This attack resonates with the estimated 35–40 percent of Americans who believe that human beings did not evolve from other animals but were created by God in their present form.[1]

Unlike white nationalists, most Christian right groups disavow racial ideology, and many have emphasized "racial reconciliation" or reached out to conservative Christians of color in an effort to build a larger and ethnically more diverse movement. For decades, most movement groups took moderate positions on immigration so as not to alienate conservative Latino evangelicals. But in the 2000s, pressure from the Christian right grassroots led many movement leaders to embrace

hard-line anti-immigrant politics. The Christian right remains predominantly white and promotes many policies that implicitly bolster
racial oppression, such as opposition to government assistance for low-
income people. And as we will see, hard-line Christian rightists have
made common ground with neonazis and other white nationalists on a
number of occasions.[2]

The Christian right is strongest among middle-class suburbanites
of the Sunbelt region (South, Southwest, and Pacific Coast). In religious terms, the Christian right is based primarily among evangelical
Protestants and Catholics. Roughly speaking, evangelicals emphasize
being spiritually "born again," seeking personal salvation through
belief in Jesus Christ, and actively proselytizing their religion. Many
evangelicals in the Christian right are fundamentalists, who believe that
the Bible is the error-free word of God, and that after a cataclysmic
struggle against evil known as the End Times, Jesus will return to earth.
Charismatics are Protestant evangelicals or Catholics who believe that
through faith they can gain supernatural powers such as miracle healing,
prophesying, and "speaking in tongues" (unknown languages). The ear-
liest Charismatic churches, formed in the early twentieth century, were
Protestant and are called Pentecostal; the Catholic Charismatic movement dates from the 1960s.[3]

Catholics and evangelical Protestants each account for about a quarter of the U.S. population. Those Christians who identify as born again,
or as Charismatics, have each been estimated at more than a third of
Americans in recent polls. However, only a fraction of these people support the Christian right as a political movement (by one estimate, 12.9
percent of the electorate in 2008), and fewer still support the movement's hard-line wing.[4]

This chapter primarily addresses the Protestant Christian right.
Catholic and Protestant rightists have cooperated, most famously in
the anti-abortion movement, but also in several anticommunist campaigns, yet right-wing Catholics often have their own separate organizations and different philosophical and political reference points. The
most hard-line far right Catholics, often known as Traditionalists or
integralists, are grouped in organizations like the Society of St Pius X
and the Society of St Pius V and around magazines like *The Remnant*.
They are more concerned with control of the church hierarchy and the
Vatican (which they believe have been taken over by a coalition of Jews,
Freemasons, and globalists) than with control of the United States.[5]

Thus Catholic Traditionalism falls outside of the scope of this book, although it is a significant influence in some sectors of the far right, both in the United States but more especially in historically Catholic countries around the world.

Hard and soft dominionists

A core tenet of the Christian right is dominionism, the belief that the United States was founded as a Christian nation and that Christians need to "take dominion" over society to return the country to its original principles. Yet from the beginning, the movement has encompassed two poles of thought on this question. Soft dominionists want to make changes within the existing political system, such as outlawing abortion and homosexuality and allowing creationism to be taught in public schools. They have pursued a reformist strategy, building a power base oriented toward the Republican Party and cultivating influence with members of the economic and political elites. Hard dominionists advocate systematic, revolutionary change—they want to get rid of all secular and pluralistic institutions and replace the existing political system with a totalitarian theocracy. Their ties with economic and political elites have been much more limited, and they have worked largely outside mainstream political channels. There are other differences between the movement's two wings, based in both politics and theology. Generally speaking, soft dominionists have been closely aligned with the Republican Party establishment on foreign policy, promoting an interventionist role in the world and strongly supporting the state of Israel (and especially its right-wing Zionist parties). In contrast, hard dominionists (like other U.S. far rightists) tend toward anti-interventionism and anti-Zionism.[6]

In the terms we are using in this book, hard dominionists are on the far right, while soft dominionists represent a kind of militant conservatism. But within the Christian right, the line between the two wings is not clearly emphasized or sharply defined. It has brought tension and conflict but also productive exchange of ideas and strategies. In this context, far rightists have been able to extend their influence far beyond their own numbers. The pool of people who share many of their values and beliefs, who they can pull rightward and potentially recruit, is massive.

The rise of a mass movement

Several factors contributed to the rise of the Christian right in the late twentieth century. One has been the steady and dramatic increase in the numbers of Protestant evangelicals. Another factor was conservative Christians' growing outrage at what they saw as erosions of public morality, such as the rise of feminism, the increased visibility and militance of lesbians and gay men, and the U.S. Supreme Court's decisions banning prayer in public schools (1962 and 1963) and legalizing abortion (1973). A third factor was activists' growing ability to forge a multidenominational movement, by mobilizing many fundamentalists who had traditionally avoided politics and by setting aside sectarian theological disputes (especially Protestant anti-Catholicism), which had traditionally made it difficult for Christians from different denominations to work together.[7]

The Christian right in its current form first emerged as a visible political force in 1979, with the founding of Jerry Falwell's Moral Majority organization. Christian right groups were a major part of the "New Right" coalition that elected Ronald Reagan as president in 1980 and 1984. With lavish funding from right-wing businesspeople and their own media networks, Christian rightists built an extensive web of organizations ranging from think tanks and lobbying organizations to local prayer groups, with supporters in the tens of millions. The movement established itself as a major power base within the Republican Party, although sections of the movement have supported political initiatives well to the right of the Republicans.[8]

Christian right leaders made a strategic decision to mobilize support by emphasizing issues related to family, gender, sex, and reproduction. These efforts have included statewide ballot initiatives to protect discrimination against LGBT people and ban same-sex marriage, local school board campaigns to have public schools teach creationism or "abstinence only" sex education, and legislation to limit women's access to abortion. The movement has mobilized not only men but also millions of women behind its attack on feminism, arguing that "natural" gender roles and "traditional" marriage offer women respect, safety, and love, and constrain men to support and protect women and children. At the same time, the Christian right has used feminist ideas and social gains, encouraging women to learn professional skills, speak publicly, and take leadership roles—in the service of women's subordination.[9]

Christian right leaders have also focused on foreign policy, for example, supporting anticommunist military operations in Central America, southern Africa, and the Philippines in the 1980s, or backing the U.S. government's War on Terror in the 2000s. Most Christian right groups have rallied behind policies of aggressive intervention to promote U.S.-oriented regimes, and staunch support for the state of Israel, especially the Israeli right. Although the movement's drive to Christianize American society is anti-Jewish by definition, the fact that most Christian right groups are pro-Zionist has enabled the movement to present itself as a friend to Jews. This "Christian Zionism" is rooted in the belief of many Protestant fundamentalists that the gathering of Jews in the Holy Land is a crucial step leading toward Jesus's return, after which all Jews will either die or convert to Christianity.[10]

Christian Reconstructionism

Within the mass movement that is the Christian right, a major node of far right politics is the doctrine of Christian Reconstructionism. Reconstructionist ideology is an offshoot of Presbyterianism (itself a branch of Calvinism) that was founded by Rev. R.J. Rushdoony in the 1960s. Leading Reconstructionist organizations include the Chalcedon Foundation (headed by Rushdoony from 1965 until his death in 2001), the Institute for Christian Economics (founded by Gary North), and American Vision (founded by Gary DeMar and now headed by Joel McDurmon). One of Reconstructionism's core principles is that Christianity is the basis for all knowledge and anything that departs from it is sinful, evil, satanic. As a result, Christians have a duty to take control of all human institutions to bring them in line with God's commands. Pluralism must be rejected because the very idea of human reason separate from God's authority is anti-Christian and wrong.[11]

For these reasons, Reconstructionists advocate a totalitarian theocracy based on their interpretation of Old Testament law. In their ideal society, only men from approved Christian churches could vote or hold office, slavery would once again be legal, and death (preferably by stoning) would be applicable punishment for homosexuality, adultery (by women), striking a parent, heresy, blasphemy, and many other offenses.

Women would be permanently "in submission" to men and expected to bear as many children as possible. Workers would have a duty to obey their employers, and labor unions would be forbidden.[12]

Unlike most theocracies, the Reconstructionist model does not involve a highly centralized state, but rather puts most of the coercive authority either with local government or with nongovernmental institutions, especially the family and the church. Reconstructionists have been called "libertarian theocrats" because they want to dismantle most of the central state apparatus—deregulate businesses, abolish public schools and social services, and get rid of most taxes—and because interchange between Reconstructionists and the libertarian political movement goes back more than half a century. For example, Rushdoony worked for a libertarian publishing house before founding the Chalcedon Foundation, and Gary North has written regularly for the libertarian website *LewRockwell.com*. North also worked briefly for prominent libertarian and former U.S. Congressmember Ron Paul, and coauthored a Ron Paul homeschool curriculum, which was launched in 2013.[13]

There have never been very many Reconstructionists, but their reach has extended far beyond their numbers. One reason for this is that Reconstructionist theology is unusually well suited to political activism. Most Protestant evangelicals are premillennialists, who believe that Christ will return to earth and reign for a thousand years before Judgment Day. But Reconstructionists are postmillennialists—they say that Christ will return only *after* his kingdom has been in place for a thousand years. This belief places the responsibility squarely on Christians to take control of society now. Largely thanks to Reconstructionism's example, the idea that Christians should "take dominion" has become a unifying principle across the Christian right, although with many different interpretations. The interdenominational Coalition on Revival served largely as a megaphone for Reconstructionist ideas in the 1980s, and Reconstructionism influenced key figures such as Pat Robertson, whose Christian Coalition was one of the most important Christian right organizations in the 1990s.[14]

Anti-abortion activism

One of the most dramatic arenas where Reconstructionism has had an impact is anti-abortion activism, which has been central to the Christian right's crusade against feminism and women's autonomy. From the late 1970s onward, a growing number of Christian rightists took part in protests and civil disobedience at women's health clinics, in an effort to disrupt or temporarily shut down facilities where abortions were or might be performed. But a few activists went much further, invading clinics, engaging in vandalism, planting firebombs, or shooting clinic personnel. To some extent, the escalation of tactics reflected activists' growing frustration with the federal government's "failure" to outlaw abortion under Republicans and Democrats alike. Bomb attacks against abortion clinics surged in the mid-1980s and again in the early 1990s. Between 1993 and 2009, a series of murders and attempted murders were carried out against physicians and other employees at abortion clinics.[15]

A shadowy entity called the Army of God (AOG) claimed responsibility for many of the most violent attacks. First appearing in 1982, AOG is ostensibly an underground network of people who practice and promote violence as a means to stop abortion. It is unclear whether this is or was a functioning organization or simply a dramatic-sounding moniker that like-minded people have periodically invoked. There is an AOG website that features writings by imprisoned anti-abortion activists, and AOG has been supported by aboveground groups that defend the killing of abortion providers as "justifiable homicide," such as Missionaries to the Preborn and the former American Coalition of Life Activists. Many of these groups also promote hard-line positions on other issues, such as virulent homophobia. In 2002, for example, the AOG website applauded the beheading of three gay men in Saudi Arabia. The AOG website also links to the article "Leaderless Resistance" by neonazi Louis Beam.[16]

Christian Reconstructionism helped to shift the anti-abortion movement toward insurgent politics. In the late 1980s, Gary North personally tutored Randall Terry, who as head of Operation Rescue led a series of aggressive civil disobedience actions at women's health clinics, but who also began to echo Reconstructionist ideas. At this time, North urged anti-abortion activists to build a theocratic movement and declared that Operation Rescue's clinic actions were the first step in a larger war against pluralism and secular humanism. Other Reconstructionists involved in anti-abortion activism have included Paul Hill (a former Presbyterian minister who murdered a physician and his bodyguard outside a clinic in Pensacola, Florida, in 1994), Michael Bray (a Lutheran pastor who spent four years in prison for firebombing a series of clinics in the 1980s, and who has called himself chaplain of the Army of God), and Matthew Trewhella (a Pentecostal minister and founder of Missionaries to the Preborn, who in 1994 called for forming church-based militias).[17]

Interconnections with white nationalism

In the 1990s, Christian Reconstructionists joined forces with neonazis and other white nationalists to help launch the Patriot militia movement and related groups such as the U.S. Taxpayers' Party, as discussed in the next chapter. Reconstructionists have also aided or joined the neo-Confederate movement, a branch of white nationalism that glorifies the Confederate States of America and, in some versions, advocates a new secession by southern states. Reconstructionism founder R.J. Rushdoony argued that the American Civil War was not about slavery, but rather was a contest between an orthodox Christian nation (the Confederacy) and a heretical one (the Union), a position that has been labeled the "theological war thesis." He also claimed that black people had been better off under American slavery than in any other time or place. Since the 1990s, Christian Reconstructionists have promoted these and similar claims. They have also increased collaboration with neo-Confederate groups and have helped make the theological war thesis predominant across the neo-Confederate movement.[18]

Reconstructionists have also joined the chorus of white nationalists, Christian rightists, and others attacking Islam. Following the 9-11 attacks, for example, *Chalcedon Report* repeated the claim that Islam was an evil civilization threatening the West. R.J. Rushdoony's son Mark wrote that Islam was a "false" religion that promoted forced conversion, slavery, prostitution, sexual debauchery, treachery, despotism, oppression, and murder.[19]

Antisemitism is another point of connection between Reconstructionists and white nationalists. Going beyond the veiled anti-Jewishness that is standard in the Christian right, a 2007 entry on the Chalcedon

Foundation blog complained that Jews in the U.S. society controlled the banking industry, the media, the courts, military policy, political lobbying, and other areas. Rushdoony claimed that fewer than one million Jews died in Nazi custody during World War II, and most of them from the cold. Gary North, too, has engaged in Holocaust denial.[20]

Meanwhile, neonazis and other white nationalists have emulated Christian rightists in targeting LGBT people with homophobic actions ranging from street protests to murder. Ku Klux Klansmen and members of the Third Positionist group American Front have taken part in anti-abortion protests at women's health clinics. Several white nationalists have conducted Army of God–type actions, such as Scott Roeder, who murdered Dr. George Tiller in 2009, and Eric Rudolph, who bombed the 1996 Atlanta Olympics to protest the U.S. government's support for abortion (and the Games' promotion of "global socialism"). Rudolph also bombed two women's health clinics and a lesbian bar between 1996 and 1998.[21]

Building a "biblical" culture

While taking part in overtly political activism, Reconstructionists have worked quietly to reshape grassroots social institutions as a way to begin implementing their ideas and also build a long-term base of support. These efforts parallel the "metapolitical" initiatives advocated by the European New Right and its supporters, as discussed in chapter 4. As early as the 1960s, Rushdoony called on Christian parents to take their children out of public schools and educate them at home, so as to shield them from secular humanism and mold them according to biblical principles. His ideas helped to inspire the Christian homeschooling movement, which in recent decades has grown to include hundreds of thousands of students and their families. Many of the teaching materials and activities these families use are based on Reconstructionist ideology.[22]

Reconstructionists have been a driving force in the biblical patriarchy movement, which guides many Christian homeschoolers. Biblical patriarchy declares that rigid gender roles are divinely ordained, that women must obey their fathers and husbands in all matters, and that for women to speak for themselves or make decisions for themselves is selfish, sinful, and a revolt against God. Biblical patriarchy advocates urge men to keep close control over everything that their wives and children do, from the books they read to the time they go to bed. Doug Phillips headed Vision Forum, a Reconstructionist organization that was a leading proponent of biblical patriarchy. "Can you call your husband 'Lord'? If the answer is no, you shouldn't get married," Phillips told young women at one homeschoolers' convention. (Vision Forum closed its doors in 2013 after Phillips admitted having an extramarital affair.)[23]

One specific branch of biblical patriarchy is the Quiverfull movement, which tells women that their greatest religious duty is to have as many children as possible. The movement's name comes from Psalm 127: "Like arrows in the hands of a warrior are sons born in one's youth. Blessed is the man whose quiver is full of them." Quiverfull supporters reject not only abortion but any form of birth control (even the rhythm method) as contrary to God's authority. The image of children as arrows in a quiver embodies the movement's belief that raising a big, male-run family is an act of spiritual warfare, a counterattack against feminism and related evils. Author Kathryn Joyce estimates that the Quiverfull movement numbers in the tens of thousands and argues that its beliefs are influencing more mainstream evangelical churches.[24]

In 1982, Reconstructionist leader Gary North outlined how such initiatives fit into a long-term political strategy:

> So let us be blunt about it: we must use the doctrine of religious liberty to gain independence for Christian schools until we train up a generation of people who know that there is no religious neutrality, no neutral law, no neutral education, and no neutral civil government. Then they will get busy in constructing a Bible-based social, political, and religious order which finally denies the religious liberty of the enemies of God. Murder, abortion, and pornography will be illegal. God's law will be enforced. It will take time. A minority religion cannot do this. Theocracy must flow from the hearts of a majority of citizens, just as compulsory education came only after most people had their children in schools of some sort.[25]

There have been signs in recent years that Reconstructionists' belief that the U.S. political system is beyond repair has been spreading within the Christian right. Writing in 2014, journalist Frederick Clarkson found "powerful indications" that sections of the Christian right, spurred by "the accelerating advance of LGBTQ rights," among other trends, "have lost confidence in the bright political vision of the United States as the once and future Christian nation—and that they are desperately seeking alternatives." He cited a growing popularity of southern secessionism among evangelicals, as well as a 2013 essay by David Lane, a high-level Republican political strategist (no relation to the neonazi of the same name). Lane declared that "Christian America is in ruins" and approvingly quoted Reconstructionist Peter J. Leithart on the need for martyrs to help separate "heretical Americanism" from "Christian orthodoxy."[26]

Clarkson also cited Father C. John McCloskey, a member of the right-wing Catholic organization Opus Dei, who since 2001 has argued that conservative Christian strongholds may need to secede from the United States. While right-wing Catholics have been involved in anti-abortion violence, and organizations such as Human Life International have interpreted Catholic doctrine in reactionary terms, they have rarely called the U.S. political system into question. Yet McCloskey envisions a civil war that would result in a fragmented country. He is a former Wall Street stockbroker who has helped convert leading politicians to Catholicism, including Sam Brownback (governor of Kansas) and Newt Gingrich (former speaker of the House of Representatives). Given McCloskey's elite connections, his secessionist views indicate the potential reach of far right politics.[27]

New Apostolic Reformation

One of the most important and fastest growing Christian right branches that reflects Reconstructionist theocratic influence is New Apostolic Reformation (NAR). It is also known by other names, such as the Apostolic and Prophetic movement or Kingdom Now theology. NAR was formally launched in 1996, and today over three million Americans belong to churches that embrace its teachings, along with millions more in other countries. A few of the many NAR organizations include International Coalition of Apostles, Harvest International Ministries, and God TV. The movement has a significant presence in such far-flung countries as Nigeria, South Korea, Australia, and Guatemala. In Uganda, New Apostolics helped foment a wave of anti-gay activism and violence that included a 2014 law (later ruled invalid on a technicality) making homosexual sex punishable by life in prison.[28]

NAR grows out of the Pentecostal/Charismatic movement, or more precisely the Christian right–fostered coalition and dialogue between Reconstructionists and politically conservative Charismatics such as Pat Robertson in the 1980s. Pentecostals and Charismatics are not only much more numerous, they are also more ethnically diverse than Reconstructionists, most of whom are white.[29]

C. Peter Wagner, who gave New Apostolic Reformation its name and was its prime mover until his death in 2016, described NAR's theology as dominionism and cited Rushdoony as an intellectual forebear. Like Reconstructionism, NAR theology declares that Christians are called to "take dominion" over all areas of society in preparation for Christ's return. NAR leaders phrase this in terms of taking control of "Seven Mountains," i.e., seven key societal institutions: government, media, family, business/finance, education, church/religion, and arts/entertainment.[30]

At the same time, NAR differs from Reconstructionism in important ways. To begin with, Reconstructionists are decentralizers, who want to take dominion mainly through local and private institutions, but NAR is a centralizing ideology, whose leaders want to gain control of big government and make it bigger. Connected with this, NAR promotes a new and highly centralized organizational structure. Traditionally, most evangelical Protestant churches in the U.S. have been governed in a participatory manner, with congregants electing their own leaders. But NAR claims that God has now restored the church offices of apostle (to govern the church) and prophet (to receive divine revelation). In practice, this means that thousands of churches have stopped governing themselves and now submit themselves to the authority of a single leader within one of various "apostolic networks," which are in turn joined together by coordinating bodies such as the Apostolic Council of Prophetic Elders. In other words, NAR combines a theocratic vision with an organizational structure that is far more centralized and authoritarian than most on the Christian right.[31]

Far more than Reconstructionism, NAR uses prayer and worship as aggressive weapons of spiritual warfare. In the past, Christians have sometimes tried to exorcise demons from individuals, but NAR leaders use "strategic-level" spiritual warfare to cast out evil spirits that are supposedly ruling over whole cities, regions, or countries—or over whole groups of people, such as homosexuals or Muslims. One tactic they use is "prayerwalking," in which a team of people walks through the area controlled by a particular demon and battles it with prayer. Another tactic is public confession of the collective sins that are believed to have given the evil spirit entry. In 2007, for example, NAR leaders had Senator Sam Brownback of Kansas apologize to American Indian leaders on behalf of the United States, for atrocities against Indigenous people that had enabled evil spirits to rule over the U.S.[32]

Totally unlike Reconstructionism, but in keeping with its Charismatic roots, NAR puts a big emphasis on miracles. NAR leaders teach that their adherents will develop vast supernatural powers, such as defying gravity or healing every person inside a hospital just by laying hands on the building. Eventually, these people will become "manifest sons of God," who essentially have God-like powers over life and death. In the End Times, too, some one or two billion people will convert to Christianity, and God will transfer control of all wealth to the NAR apostles. It's not difficult to imagine how these beliefs, held by millions of people who see themselves as engaged in a cataclysmic struggle against absolute Evil, could serve as an invitation to coercion and violence on a large scale.[33]

New Apostolics, like the majority of Christian rightists, are pro-Zionist, because they believe Jews gathering in Israel plays a key role in bringing Jesus back to earth. This, too, sets them apart from Reconstructionists, who don't assign any special role to Jews in the End Times. But in NAR's new version of the End Times narrative, only Jews who accept Jesus as their savior can help bring about his return, which has led New Apostolics to proselytize Jews aggressively in Israel and elsewhere.[34]

Conclusion: between loyalty and opposition

While each can be described as "dominionist," in practical political terms, Reconstructionists and New Apostolic Reformers have staked out very different positions. Although some Reconstructionists have worked with mainstream institutions such as the Republican Party, for the most part they have aligned themselves with political initiatives that reject conventional politics and established political elites: the Army of God, the U.S. Taxpayers/Constitution Party, the Patriot movement. In recent years they have focused mainly on low-key base-building activities, which bring them relatively little public visibility but could produce dramatic results in the long run.

By contrast, NAR leaders have forged ties with conventional conservative politicians such as Sarah Palin (former governor of Alaska and 2008 Republican vice presidential candidate) and Rick Perry (former governor of Texas and now secretary of energy).[35] So far, NAR leaders seem to be pursuing the same basic strategy that Jerry Falwell and Pat Robertson did before them: mobilize right-wing Christians as a base with which to cut a deal with the conservative wing of the ruling class. Yet there is an inherent tension between this approach and the absolutist implications of NAR's ideology and organizational structure. The movement might continue on its current course, or it might be pulled in a more radical direction, into a full-scale break with the established political system. Either way, given its debt to Reconstructionism, NAR is testimony to the far right's power to shape the political landscape.

3. The Patriot Movement

The Patriot movement brings together people who believe that there is a conspiracy by globalist elites to disarm the American people, overthrow the Constitution, and impose a dictatorship. The movement suddenly appeared as a national force in 1994, as activists began forming hundreds of armed "militias" to defend against an expected crackdown, or organized so-called common law courts that claimed legal authority in place of the existing court system. The movement's size and strength has waxed and waned, reaching a peak in the mid-1990s, dropping almost to nothing in the early 2000s, and surging to even higher levels in the middle of Barack Obama's presidency. The Patriot movement is a political hybrid, a meeting place for several different rightist currents. Although all Patriot movement activists are hostile to the federal government to a degree, some have taken an essentially defensive posture while others reject the federal government in principle, and a few have planned or carried out physical attacks against federal institutions or personnel.

Patriot groups have tended to be most active in western and midwestern regions of the United States. The movement has particular strength in rural areas and among military veterans, although by some accounts it has also attracted more women and families in recent years than during its first boom in the 1990s. The movement's loose organization makes size difficult to estimate. One study estimated that closed online groups oriented toward the Three Percenters, a leading Patriot network, grew from twelve thousand at the end of 2014 to eighty-five thousand in early 2016. The Anti-Defamation League has estimated that the Oath Keepers, another mainstay of the movement, has at least two thousand members, but the group itself has claimed forty thousand.[1]

The Patriot movement puts a big emphasis on unrestricted gun rights as a cornerstone of liberty, and an armed citizenry as protection against tyranny. Patriot groups draw heavily on the ideas, language, and symbols of the American Revolution and early Republic, from phrases borrowed out of the Declaration of Independence or U.S. Constitution to the Gadsden flag, which features a coiled rattlesnake and the words, "Don't tread on me."

From the beginning, the Patriot movement has been strongly influenced by both white nationalism and the Christian right. The movement's common denominator and strongest ideological current is a kind of militant, conspiracist libertarianism, which emphasizes individual freedom from government intrusion. Patriot groups also promote dramatic and sometimes wildly implausible conspiracy theories, for example, that the U.S. government has secretly built hundreds of concentration camps and stockpiled thousands of guillotines as preparation for rounding up dissenters, that the United Nations is part of a plot to impose world government, or that security services orchestrated the 1995 Oklahoma City bombing and 9-11 attacks to whip up popular fear of terrorism and push repressive laws through Congress. Some, but not all, of these conspiracy theories are rooted in antisemitism or racism.[2]

Many Patriot groups disavow racism and promote an ideology of "color-blindness." Yet ideas rooted in white supremacist or antisemitic ideology circulate freely, such as the belief that black people have far fewer legal rights than whites, because most of them did not become U.S. citizens until passage of the Fourteenth Amendment to the Constitution after the Civil War. Anti-immigrant politics and the implicitly racist claim that Barack Obama wasn't born in the United States (and therefore was ineligible to be president) also became major movement themes in recent years. At the same time, the movement has long included a small number of people of color, and Patriot activists have occasionally spoken out directly against racial oppression.[3]

Factors behind the movement's growth

The Patriot movement is often seen as outgrowth of the white supremacist movement, especially Posse Comitatus, which rejected the federal government's legitimacy and pioneered the forming of militias and
common law courts in the 1980s. Some Patriot groups later borrowed
Posse's antisemitic conspiracy theories about the banking system and its
bogus legal theory that the Fourteenth Amendment to the Constitution
established a different class of citizenship (for black people) from that
held by whites.[4]

However, several other political currents besides Posse Comitatus
also helped to lay the groundwork for Patriot movement ideology.
Starting in the 1970s, the gun rights movement (spearheaded by the
National Rifle Association and the even more hard-line Gun Owners
of America) promoted an insurrectionary interpretation of the Second
Amendment — the idea that the Founding Fathers saw an armed populace
as a vital counterweight to deter government from amassing too much
power.[5] Mormon ultraconservatives such as Cleon Skousen blended
hostility to most federal government activities, John Birch Society–type
conspiracy theories, and a belief that the U.S. Constitution was divinely
inspired. Christian Reconstructionists offered a whole framework for
broad-based far right activism in the 1983 book *Theology of Christian
Resistance*, edited by Gary North. This "theology," as summarized by
sociologist James Scaminaci III, included "the idea that the county was
the ideal level of government; that lower magistrates should interpose
themselves between individuals in local communities and the federal
government to thwart tyranny; that arming individuals for self-defense
and resistance to tyranny was biblically and constitutionally mandated;
and, that a well-armed local militia was needed to resist violently federal tyranny as a last resort."[6] In 1990, the Coalition on Revival, which
brought Reconstructionists together with other Christian rightists,
echoed these ideas when it called for establishment of "county militias"
and a "Christian court system."[7]

Another big influence on Patriot groups was the so-called Wise Use
movement, which coalesced in the late 1980s to oppose environmental
laws and regulations, mainly in the western United States. Wise Use
groups were funded by big business interests such as timber and energy companies but enjoyed some grassroots support among farmers,
ranchers, and workers in industries subject to environmental controls.

The Wise Use movement defined its struggle largely as a defense of individual property rights against federal government intrusion, and in many locales Wise Use merged with the movement for county supremacy, which was based directly on ideas from Posse Comitatus and Christian Reconstructionism. Today, anti-environmentalism remains a major Patriot movement theme.[8]

By the late 1980s, a "Christian Patriot" movement representing several of these ideological threads was active, at least in the rural Northwest. As analyzed by sociologist James Aho based on field research he conducted in Idaho, this movement included "Identity Christians" (who believed there was a powerful Jewish conspiracy to destroy America), "Christian Constitutionalists" (who believed the conspiracy was not ethnically specific), and "Issue-oriented Patriots" (who focused on a specific issue such as abortion or education and did not necessarily see themselves pitted against a grand conspiracy).[9]

An important point of connection between the gun rights movement and Christian Reconstructionism was Larry Pratt, longtime executive director of Gun Owners of America and, if not an adherent, certainly a close supporter of Reconstructionism.[10] Pratt wrote the essay in *Theology of Christian Resistance* that advocated "a well armed local militia" as a tool for resisting tyranny, and he was credited with drafting the Coalition on Revival's 1990 call to form county militias. Also in 1990, Pratt published the book *Armed People Victorious*, which celebrated the use of "citizen defense patrols" (paramilitary death squads) to fight communism in Central America and the Philippines.[11] The book was based largely on Pratt's experience as secretary of the Council for Inter-American Security, a right-wing think tank, lobbying organization, and spy network close to the World Anti-Communist League that played a leading role in promoting Central American counterrevolution in the 1980s. Just as Louis Beam had adapted the concept of leaderless resistance from Cold War anticommunism to far right insurgency, Pratt did the same with the concept of militias.

In broader terms, the Patriot movement's rise reflected the end of the Cold War between 1989 and 1991, as some of the hatred long directed against communism was now redirected against the "totalitarian" federal government. The movement's anti-globalism is in large part a reaction to the growing power of multinational corporations and financial institutions, expansion of international free trade agreements, and movement of industry from the U.S. to the Global South and of workers from the Global South to the United States. Many Patriot activists see these trends, typical of neoliberalism, as threats to the sovereignty, economic health, and cultural integrity of the United States. And while leftists have interpreted these trends as results of the capitalist system, Patriot activists believe they are caused by elite conspiracies that distort the "normal" workings of free enterprise.[12]

Several events in the early 1990s contributed to the Patriot movement's sudden upsurge in 1994:

In 1991, Pat Robertson, one of the Christian right's most prominent leaders, published *The New World Order*, which showcased John Birch Society–style conspiracy theories about globalist plots by the Illuminati and Freemasons (as well as a few claims drawn directly from antisemitic sources).[13]

Also in 1991, Christian Reconstructionist Howard Phillips founded the U.S. Taxpayers' Party (USTP), which emphasized biblical law, gun rights, hostility to the federal government, and conspiracy theories about global elites. The USTP brought together Christian rightists and white nationalists and in the mid-1990s served as a connecting link between militias and the anti-abortion rights movement. Renamed the Constitution Party in 1999, it was for several years in the 2000s the third largest political party in the United States.[14]

In the 1992 Republican presidential primaries, Pat Buchanan ran against incumbent George Bush, declaring, "He is a globalist and we are nationalists. ... He would put America's wealth and power at the service of some vague New World Order; we will put America first."[15] In this statement, Buchanan identified Bush with collectivist world government and himself with the America First Committee, which had opposed U.S. entry into World War II.

In 1993, President Bill Clinton signed the Brady Act, which set up a national background check system for gun purchasers. This was followed a year later by the Federal Assault Weapons Ban, which outlawed certain semiautomatic weapons such as the AR-15 rifle, as well as large-capacity magazines. Both laws sparked bitter opposition from gun rights advocates.

Above all, two brutal raids by federal agents precipitated the mobilization that became the Patriot movement: the 1992 siege and arrest of white supremacists Randy Weaver and Kevin Harris at Ruby Ridge, Idaho, (in which Weaver's wife and teenage son were killed, as was a U.S. marshal) and the 1993 federal assaults on the Waco, Texas, compound of the Branch Davidian religious cult, in which eighty-two cult members (including twenty-two children) and four federal agents died. Both the Weaver home and Branch Davidian compound were targeted because of illegal firearms charges, and both raids involved massive displays of deadly force by heavily armed federal agents. Right-wing activists across the country were justifiably outraged. To many of them, the events at Ruby Ridge and Waco signaled the rise of a police state intent on disarming the populace, and required an immediate response.[16]

Right-wing fears of growing state violence had a basis in reality. Throughout the 1980s and early 1990s, policing in the United States became increasingly militarized. More and more police departments formed paramilitary units, including police forces in smaller cities, and paramilitary cops were used more and more in relatively routine operations, such as drug raids. Cooperation and integration grew between local, state, and federal police. The U.S. military became increasingly involved in domestic police work, providing equipment, training, and intelligence to law enforcement agencies, and military units began to hold training exercises in cities across the United States.[17]

These trends brought an increase in police repression, which—as has been true throughout U.S. history—came down most heavily and most frequently against people of color. For example, in a 1985 confrontation with the black liberation organization MOVE, Philadelphia police dropped an incendiary bomb on the group's home in a mostly black section of the city, killing eleven people, destroying sixty-five houses, and leaving 250 people homeless. The MOVE bombing evoked no protests from right-wing gun rights activists, even though it resulted partly from illegal weapons charges against MOVE members.[18] But when this same kind of police violence was directed against white people, rightists reacted.

Patriot movement organizing reflected its ideologically varied roots. Many accounts have emphasized the importance of a 1992 meeting at Estes Park, where 160 far right leaders gathered to formulate a response to the Ruby Ridge raid. The attendees included many white nationalists, such as Louis Beam, who reiterated his 1983 call for "leaderless resistance," but also Larry Pratt, who presented his own ideas about militias to the gathering, and whose Gun Owners of America was much larger than any of the Christian Identity or neonazi groups represented.[19] The Estes Park meeting was convened by Pete Peters, a Christian Identity minister who repeatedly invited Reconstructionists to his church and helped to spread Reconstructionist ideas in Identity circles, forging important links between the most militant branches of the Christian right and white nationalism.[20]

One of the Estes Park attendees was John Trochmann, who in 1994 cofounded the Militia of Montana. But other early militia organizers were not particularly connected to either white nationalism or Christian Reconstructionism. These included Samuel Sherwood, who founded the Idaho-based U.S. Militia Association and publicized it via a Mormon homeschooling network, Jon Roland, who cofounded the Texas Constitutional Militia, and Norm Olson, who cofounded the Michigan Militia. As Robert Churchill has argued, Trochmann (as well as video and shortwave radio propagandist Mark Koernke) represented a white nationalist current within the Patriot movement, while Sherwood, Roland, and Olsen "offered a more constitutionalist, civic, and racially inclusive vision of the militia."[21]

Writing about the militia movement's early years, Churchill argues that the movement's predominant racial ideology was "color-blind racism," not white nationalism. Color-blind racists in the movement advocated formal equality and opposed explicit racial bigotry, while denying that racial oppression remained a significant force. They claimed to treat everyone as individuals and made tokenistic efforts to welcome people of color; they replaced old-style racial stereotypes with less blatant forms of "ethnic racial disdain."[22] They acted, in other words, the way millions of mainstream white liberals and conservatives act all the time.

Within these parameters, racial politics was a point of conflict within the Patriot movement. On one hand, figures such as Koernke promoted blatant racism, claiming for example that the federal government was recruiting black gang members to go house to house and confiscate people's guns, with the implicit understanding that they would be allowed to loot and rape in the process.[23] On the other hand, some Patriot groups denounced racial and religious discrimination, barred white supremacists from joining, and some of them directly confronted or harassed white nationalist groups such as the Ku Klux Klan.[24]

These debates were interwoven with other disagreements: advocates of secrecy versus advocates of organizing openly, apocalyptic conspiracists versus those who regarded federal tyranny as a straightforward result of power's tendency to corrupt, and those who called for a defensive response to growing police repression versus those who advocated aggressive, preemptive action.

Decline and resurgence

The Patriot movement grew fast from 1994 to 1996, then declined sharply, for a number of reasons. The April 19, 1995, Oklahoma City bombing—often described at the time as the "deadliest terrorist attack on American soil," with 168 people killed and more than 680 others in-jured—was widely blamed on the militias, although the men convicted of the crime were not actively involved in any militia groups. In the aftermath of the bombing, conflict over ideology and strategy intensi-fied within the movement and caused a number of Patriot groups to split or collapse. Government investigation of the movement increased and some activists were convicted of planning armed attacks or for il-legal weapons possession. Other Patriot activists dropped out or shifted back into mainstream politics, especially after Republican George W. Bush was elected president in 2000. The movement was mostly dormant during Bush's eight years in office, but surged back after Barack Obama was elected the first black president of the United States in 2008 (and shortly after the country entered the worst economic recession since the 1930s). Within a few years, the movement had grown beyond its 1990s peak.[25]

Key meetings held in 2009 helped to relaunch the Patriot movement. The second of these, dubbed a continental congress, took place outside Chicago and drew more than one hundred delegates from forty-eight states. The meeting produced a document called "Articles of Freedom," which warned that the federal government "now threatens our Life, Liberty and Property through usurpations of the Constitution" and de-clared that it was time to "cast off tyranny." The Articles declared the U.S. to be independent of all supra-national bodies and called on the federal government to repeal all gun control and domestic surveillance laws, stop fighting undeclared wars or meddling in other countries, abolish the income tax and social welfare programs, slash environmental laws and foreign aid, and start enforcing immigration law. Underscoring the movement's libertarian roots, the Articles claimed that "The United States is the only nation on earth specifically based on the premise of the right of individuals to own and control private property" and that own-ing private property is "the root of our individual Freedom."[26]

The Patriot movement resurgence has included the growth of sev-eral new groups. Oath Keepers, founded in 2009, is an organization for police and military service people who pledge to defy orders that conflict with the Constitution, such as imposing martial law or helping foreign troops to occupy the U.S. The Three Percenters, founded in 2008, is a much looser organization than Oath Keepers and tends to be more militant and confrontational, although the two groups share many views and overlap to some extent. The Three Percenters' name refers to the supposed proportion of the colonial population that took up arms against the British in the Revolutionary War. A third key group, the Constitutional Sheriffs and Peace Officers Association, was founded in 2010 by Richard Mack, who is a former lobbyist with Larry Pratt's Gun Owners of America and also sits on the Oath Keepers' board.[27]

Conflicted racial politics

More than in the 1990s, Patriot groups have attempted to delineate themselves from the white nationalist movement, yet they have also increased ties with other rightist currents that promote thinly veiled forms of racist politics. For example, the resurgence of Patriot groups during Barack Obama's presidency paralleled the rise of the Tea Party, a conservative movement characterized by a kind of militant populist libertarianism. As the two movements grew, Patriot ideology spread to sections of the Tea Party, and many Patriot groups adopted the belief (common among Tea Partiers) that Barack Obama was born in Africa and thus was ineligible to be U.S. president. (This falsehood was also promoted for years by Donald Trump.) Interconnections have also grown between the Patriot and anti-immigrant movements. While Patriot activists have taken part in vigilante border patrols and have echoed claims that Mexico is using undocumented immigrants to help reconquer the southwestern United States, many anti-immigrant vigilantes such as the Minuteman groups have embraced the sovereign citizens doctrine or conspiracy theories about an impending globalist takeover. The Patriot Coalition, formed in 2009, brought together a number of anti-immigrant and Patriot groups in a formal alliance.[28]

The book *Up in Arms: A Guide to Oregon's Patriot Movement*, which is jointly published by the Rural Organizing Project and Political Research Associates, argues that the Patriot movement today is "implicitly racist," in that it opposes "the redistribution of social and economic power in society across racial lines" and assumes white cultural norms (as well as patriarchal, heterosexual, and Protestant ones) when discussing the United States.[29] Spencer Sunshine and the other authors of *Up in Arms* argue that, in contrast to the movement in the 1990s, open racism is now rare among the movement's leadership but still common at the grassroots. "Most Patriot groups," they write, "have a colorblind approach," which means they oppose explicit racial bigotry but also frequently deny (and thus protect) the continuing reality of both structural and interpersonal racism.[30]

In the 1990s, the Patriot movement, although predominantly white, included a small number of people of color. J.J. Johnson, an African American man, cofounded the Ohio Unorganized Militia and described militias as "the civil rights movement of the 1990s." Johnson urged black people to join the Patriot movement and argued, "If our ancestors would have been armed, they would not have been slaves!" Again today, the Patriot movement includes a few people of color, whose involvement helps the movement project an image of inclusiveness.[31]

Oath Keepers vividly illustrates the movement's conflicted racial politics.[32] Oath Keepers declares that its opposition to government tyranny is "not about race" but is meant to protect all Americans regardless of color. The group's website features videos in which people of color are prominently featured as Oath Keepers members. Yet Oath Keepers has also called for a crackdown against "illegal aliens," who it warns are being brought in as part of a large-scale "invasion" of the United States, and some individual Oath Keepers have made racist statements, such as one who referred to President Obama as a "mulatto" and suggested he was a Muslim born in Kenya—right-wing code-speak for "a black man has no business being in the White House."[33] Oath Keepers has cosponsored two "Racial Reconciliation of the Races" events with African American pastor James David Manning, whose vision of white-black unity centers on intense homophobia.[34]

In 2014 and 2015, during Black Lives Matter protests in Ferguson, Missouri, over the police killing of Michael Brown, Oath Keepers sent heavily armed men (apparently all white) into Ferguson. The group said the men were there to guard businesses and homes against arsonists and looters, and to protect reporters with *Infowars.com*, Alex Jones's right-wing conspiracist website. Many people interpreted the move as a white supremacist show of force to intimidate Black Lives Matter protesters. Support for this interpretation could be found in a statement by the

New York state chapter of Oath Keepers, which dismissed Black Lives Matter as a pawn of Communist, anti-American "race-baiters."[35]

Yet before sending the armed men to Ferguson, Oath Keepers had harshly condemned the Ferguson police force for violating people's right to protest and offered detailed criticisms of its "spectacularly unsafe weapons discipline and methodology," such as pointing automatic weapons at unarmed protesters. The group also wrote an open letter to the people of Ferguson, which declared that "you have an absolute, God given, and constitutionally protected right to protest and speak your mind" and that "the police have no right, no authority, and no power to violate those rights.... " The letter specifically urged black military veterans to form armed patrols and neighborhood watches to keep Ferguson safe, and cited the Deacons for Defense and Justice (whose armed members protected 1960s civil rights marchers in the Deep South and helped to inspire the Black Panther Party) as a "proud and noble" example to follow.[36] By urging African Americans to arm themselves, Oath Keepers repudiated one of the traditional core principles of U.S. white supremacy, that black people must never practice—or be able to practice—self-defense.

But Oath Keepers would only take this so far. When St. Louis County Oath Keepers leader Sam Andrews announced plans to hold a march through downtown Ferguson in which Oath Keepers members would accompany fifty African Americans armed with long barrel rifles, the group's national leadership withdrew support. Andrews and his "tactical team," as well as a group of Oath Keepers in Florida, resigned from Oath Keepers in protest, and Andrews commented, "I can't have my name associated with an organization that doesn't believe black people can exercise their First and Second Amendment rights at the same time."[37]

The emphasis on gun rights helps us understand the Patriot movement's conflicted racial politics. In the United States there is an organic connection between racism and guns, because an armed white male populace was historically one of the cornerstones of the whole system of racial oppression. Frontier settlers needed guns for conquering Indigenous and Mexican lands, and white men in the South needed to be armed to keep control over enslaved black people, who were not allowed to have guns. The Ku Klux Klan, lynch mobs, and a host of vigilante groups continued this tradition of armed, decentralized white rule. Yet people of color and their allies, too, have invoked the right to

bear arms—from anti-slavery activists to Chicano land rights defenders
and the Black Panther Party. As a result, gun control has sometimes
been used to enforce white rule, as in the late 1960s, when conservatives advocated stricter gun laws because they were afraid of the Black
Panthers and other black radicals.[38]

Ideological contradictions around race show up dramatically in a bi-
zarre Patriot movement offshoot known as the sovereign citizens movement. Sovereign citizens claim that at some point in the past the U.S.
government was secretly replaced by a hidden government, and that
anyone can declare themselves beyond its jurisdiction if they use the
right terminology. This belief leads them to write fake checks, refuse
to pay taxes, drive without a license, and file elaborate pseudo-legal
claims.[39] The Southern Poverty Law Center estimates that some three
hundred thousand people participate to some degree in the sovereign
citizen subculture, which extends well beyond the Patriot movement
itself. Even though the sovereign citizen theory derives from Posse
Comitatus's racist and antisemitic ideology—including the belief that
whites enjoy a higher form of citizenship than blacks, who are mere
"14th Amendment Citizens"—many of its adherents are unaware of its
racist origins, and in fact a large number of sovereign citizens are black,
including members of the Moorish Science Temple of America, a black
nationalist religious group.[40]

An "inside/outside" strategy

Patriot movement activism challenges the legitimacy of the U.S. political
system in a variety of ways. The movement promotes the belief that local governments can veto or ignore federal laws.[41] Creating new bodies,
such as common law courts, that claim legal authority reflects what leftist revolutionaries have long termed a "dual power" strategy: simultaneously withholding loyalty from established state institutions and prefiguring the system that activists hope to create. Looking more broadly,
Up in Arms describes the Patriot movement approach as an "inside/out-
side" strategy: "some parts of the movement work inside of established
government structures to change them, while at the same time other
parts work outside of the system to undermine it."[42] As an example,

Patriot activists have been elected to local office and have spread many of their ideas widely within the Republican Party, yet some, such as Three Percenters founder Mike Vanderboegh, have openly called for a revolutionary uprising to overthrow the government.[43]

The Patriot movement also embodies what *Up in Arms* calls "a political culture of violence." Patriot activists have extensively and repeatedly threatened and harassed political opponents and elected officials.[44] Between 2009 and 2014, there were seventeen documented shooting incidents between movement activists and law enforcement, including several in which Patriot activists wounded or killed police officers. One of the most dramatic confrontations occurred in April 2014 on the Nevada ranch of Cliven Bundy. Bundy, a sovereign citizen, refused to recognize the U.S. government and for twenty years had been grazing his cattle on federal lands without paying the grazing fees. Bundy declared that the area was "public land for the people of Clark County," that he had "preemptive rights" to raise cattle there, and that the federal government, not he, was the trespasser.[45]

When the Bureau of Land Management seized Bundy's cows to cover part of the one million dollars he owed in back fees and fines, hundreds of Patriot movement activists descended on his ranch to defend his supposed private property rights. The heavily armed, professionally coordinated militiamen took up sniper positions, forcing federal agents to leave and let Bundy retrieve his cattle. The Southern Poverty Law Center commented, "Almost never has a group of heavily armed right-wing radicals, facing large numbers of equally heavily armed law enforcement, forced the government to back down." Patriot activists hailed this as a movement victory. Even many mainstream conservatives praised Bundy as a hero, but many of them backed away when he was videotaped making racist comments about black people.[46]

In January 2016, Cliven Bundy's son Ammon Bundy led an armed occupation of the Malheur National Wildlife Refuge in southeastern Oregon under the auspices of a Patriot group, Citizens for Constitutional Freedom.[47] The occupation was ostensibly in support of two Oregon ranchers who were convicted of arson after setting controlled-burn fires that damaged federal lands, and who received mandatory five-year sentences under the 1996 Antiterrorism and Effective Death Penalty Act.[48] But the occupiers' motivations went much further, as Ammon Bundy explained:

[W]e're planning on staying here for several years. And while we're here, what we're going to be doing is freeing these lands up, and getting the ranchers back to ranching, getting the miners back to mining, getting the loggers back to logging, where they can do it under the protection of the people, and not be afraid of the tyranny that's upon them.... Harney County will begin to thrive again.... [O]ne time they were the wealthiest county in the state, and now they're the poorest county, and we will reverse that in just a few years by freeing up their land and resources, and we're doing this for the people, we're doing this so the people can have the land and their resources back.... [49]

As Zach Schwartz-Weinstein commented, in Ammon Bundy's usage the term "the people" "appears synonymous with extractive industries like timber and mining as well as cattle ranching." These industries relied on the federal government's seizure of land from the Indigenous inhabitants (specifically the Northern Paiutes in southeastern Oregon)—the "enclosure" of land that had previously been held in common. "The Bundys and other ranchers have benefitted from these enclosures for well over a century, but now they want to further enclose what is already enclosed, to privatize what the Northern Paiutes had to be dispossessed of before the land could be made public."[50]

After leaving the occupiers virtually unimpeded for weeks, the FBI and Oregon State Police eventually arrested Bundy and several other occupiers; after fleeing by car, Citizens for Constitutional Freedom spokesperson LaVoy Finicum was fatally shot three times in the back during this operation. The last of the occupiers surrendered two weeks later.

Conclusion

The Bundy ranch confrontation and the Malheur occupation highlighted some key features of the Patriot movement in the last years of Obama's presidency. First, while it not clear how many Patriot activists rejected the U.S. government in principle, a significant current within the movement not only embraced insurgent politics but had enough organization, training, and weapons to confront the federal government directly and in the open. Second, while old-style supremacist views played a significant role within the movement, its driving force was a vision of unregulated property rights, an ideology of capitalist individualism. This is a doctrine of social inequality based not on biology or God, but on market competition. Ironically, this ideology is closely related to the free trade neoliberalism of the global corporate elites who the Patriot movement sees as its main enemy.[51]

4. The Alt-Right

The alt-right, short for "alternative right," is the most recent incarnation of far right politics in the United States. The alt-right coalesced as an intellectual current around 2010 and first gained prominence in 2015 as a loosely organized movement sharing a contempt for both liberal multiculturalism and mainstream conservatism; a belief that some people are inherently superior to others; a strong internet presence and embrace of specific elements of online culture; and a self-presentation as being new, hip, and irreverent. Alt-right ideology combines white nationalism, misogyny, antisemitism, and authoritarianism in various forms and in political styles ranging from intellectual argument to violent invective. White nationalism constitutes the movement's center of gravity, but some alt-rightists have been more focused on reasserting male dominance or other forms of elitism rather than race. The alt-right has relatively little formal organization but has used internet memes effectively to gain visibility, rally supporters, and target opponents. Most alt-rightists rallied behind Trump's presidential bid, yet as a rule alt-rightists regard the existing political system as hopeless and call for replacing the United States with one or more racially defined homelands.

Ideological roots

Two intellectual currents played key roles in shaping the early alternative right: paleoconservatism and the European New Right. As discussed in chapter 1, paleoconservatives trace their lineage back to the

"Old Right" of the 1930s, which opposed New Deal liberalism, and to the America First movement of the early 1940s, which opposed U.S. entry into World War II. In the 1980s, devotees of the Old Right began calling themselves paleoconservatives as a reaction against neoconservatives, formerly liberal and leftist intellectuals who were predominantly Jewish and Catholic and who were gaining influential positions in right-wing think-tanks and the Reagan administration. After the Cold War ended in 1989–1991, paleocons criticized U.S. military interventionism, the U.S.-Israel alliance, free trade, open immigration, and the welfare state. Paleoconservatives tended to be unapologetic champions of European Christian culture, and some of them gravitated toward white nationalism. To some extent paleocons also began to converge with more hard-line white supremacists in this period.[1]

Paleocons attracted little elite support and were mostly frozen out of political power. But they drew significant popular support, as reflected in Pat Buchanan's campaigns in the 1992 and 1996 Republican presidential primaries. Paleocons played key roles in building the anti-immigrant and neo-Confederate movements in the 1990s and influenced the Patriot movement in this period. Some self-described libertarians, such as former Congressmember Ron Paul, embraced paleocon positions on culture and foreign policy.[2] After the September 11, 2001, attacks, the resurgence of military interventionism and neoconservatives' prominent roles in the George W. Bush administration solidified the paleocons' position as political outsiders.[3]

The alt-right's other significant forerunner, the European New Right (ENR), developed along different lines. The ENR began in France in the late 1960s and then spread to other European countries as an initiative among far right intellectuals to rework fascist ideology, largely by appropriating elements from other political traditions—including the left—to mask their fundamental rejection of the principle of human equality.[4] The ENR has long been a far-flung constellation of groups, publications, and writers—"a school of thought, not an organization"—but its chief intellectual has been Alain de Benoist, its flagship publication *Nouvelle Ecole*, and its center of gravity the Groupement de Recherche et d'Études sur la Civilization Européenne (GRECE; trans.: Research and Study Group on European Civilization). Eclecticism and a "big tent" approach were firmly encouraged, as were overtures to non-fascist political traditions; nonetheless, most ENR members came to embrace a core set of positions, including sociobiology (pseudo-scientific racism), anti-Americanism, anti-capitalism, and anti-Christianity, all firmly grounded in an anti-egalitarian framework and resting on various theories about a distinct ancient "Indo-European" civilization. European New Rightists championed "biocultural diversity" against the homogenization supposedly brought by liberalism and globalization. They argued that true anti-racism requires separating racial and ethnic groups to protect their unique cultures, and that true feminism defends natural gender differences, instead of supposedly forcing women to "divest themselves of their femininity." ENR writers also rejected the principle of universal human rights as "a strategic weapon of Western ethnocentrism" that stifles cultural diversity.[5]

European New Rightists dissociated themselves from traditional fascism in various other ways as well. In the wake of France's defeat by anticolonial forces in Algeria, they advocated anti-imperialism rather than expansionism and a federated "empire" of regionally based, ethnically homogeneous communities, rather than a big, centralized state. Instead of organizing a mass movement to seize state power, they advocated a "metapolitical" strategy that would gradually transform the political and intellectual culture as a precursor to transforming institutions and systems. In place of classical fascism's familiar leaders and ideologues, European New Rightists championed more obscure far right intellectuals of the 1920s, '30s, and beyond, such as Julius Evola of Italy, Ernst Jünger and Carl Schmitt of Germany, and Corneliu Codreanu of Romania.

ENR ideology began to get attention in the United States in the 1990s, resonating with paleoconservatism on various themes, notably opposition to multicultural societies, nonwhite immigration, and globalization.[6] On other issues, the two movements tended to be at odds: reflecting their roots in classical fascism, but in sharp contrast to paleocons, European New Rightists were hostile to liberal individualism and laissez-faire capitalism, and many of them rejected Christianity for its universalism (and, implicitly, for its origins in Judaism) in favor of paganism. Nonetheless, some kind of dialogue between paleocon and ENR ideas held promise for Americans seeking to develop a white nationalist movement outside of traditional neonazi/Ku Klux Klan circles.

Early years and growth

The term "alternative right" was introduced by Richard Spencer in 2008, when he was managing editor at the paleocon and libertarian *Taki's Magazine*. At *Taki's Magazine* the phrase was used as a catch-all for a variety of right-wing voices at odds with the conservative establishment, including paleocons, libertarians, and white nationalists.[7] Two years later, Spencer left to found a new publication, *AlternativeRight. com*, "an online magazine of radical traditionalism." Joining Spencer were two senior contributing editors, Peter Brimelow (whose anti-immigrant VDARE Foundation sponsored the project) and Paul Gottfried (one of paleoconservatism's founders and one of its few Jews). *AlternativeRight.com* quickly became a popular forum among dissident rightist intellectuals, especially younger ones. The magazine published works of old-school "scientific" racism along with articles from or about the European New Right, Italian far right philosopher Julius Evola, and figures from Germany's interwar Conservative Revolutionary movement. There were essays by National-Anarchist Andrew Yeoman, libertarian and Pat Buchanan supporter Justin Raimondo of *Antiwar.com*, male tribalist Jack Donovan, and black conservative Elizabeth Wright.[8]

AlternativeRight.com developed ties with a number of other white nationalist intellectual publications, which eventually became associated with the term alternative right. Some of its main partners included *VDARE.com*; Jared Taylor's *American Renaissance*, whose conferences attracted both antisemites and right-wing Jews; *The Occidental Quarterly* and its online magazine, *The Occidental Observer*, currently edited by prominent antisemitic intellectual Kevin MacDonald; and *Counter-Currents Publishing*, which was founded in 2010 to "create an intellectual movement in North America that is analogous to the European New Right" and "lay the intellectual groundwork for a white ethnostate in North America."[9]

In 2011, Richard Spencer became head of the white nationalist think-tank National Policy Institute (NPI) and its affiliated Washington Summit Publishers. He turned *AlternativeRight.com* over to other editors the following year, then shut it down completely, establishing a new online magazine, *Radix Journal*, in its place. (The other editors then reestablished *Alternative Right* as a blog.) Compared with *AlternativeRight.com*'s broad ideological approach, Spencer's later entities were more sharply focused on promoting white nationalism. Starting in 2011, NPI held a series of high-profile conferences that brought together intellectuals and activists from various branches of the movement. In 2014, the think-tank, together with supporters of Russian ENR theorist Aleksandr Dugin, cosponsored a "pan-European" conference in Budapest, although the Hungarian government deported Spencer and denied Dugin a visa.[10]

Starting in 2015, a much larger array of writers and online activists embraced the alt-right moniker. As *Anti-Fascist News* put it, "the 'alt right' now often means an internet focused string of commentators, blogs, Twitter accounts, podcasters, and Reddit trolls, all of which combine scientific racism, romantic nationalism, and deconstructionist neo-fascist ideas to create a white nationalist movement that has almost no backwards connection with neo-Nazis and the KKK."[11] Some online centers of this larger, more amorphous alt-right included the imageboard websites *4chan* and *8chan*, various *Reddit* sub-communities, and *The Right Stuff* blog and podcasts. Some alt-right outfits offered neonazi-based politics (such as *The Daily Stormer*, the Traditionalist Youth Network, and its electoral offshoot, Traditionalist Worker Party), while others did not (such as *Occidental Dissent*, *The Unz Review*, *Vox Popoli*, and *Chateau Heartiste*).

On many sites, alt-right politics were presented in terms intended to be as inflammatory as possible, bucking a decades-old trend among U.S. far rightists to tone down their beliefs for mass consumption. Previously, antisemitic propagandist Willis Carto and neonazi-turned-Klan leader David Duke had made careers of dressing up fascism as "populism" or "conservatism"; now alt-rightists confidently derided antifascism in the way 1960s radicals had derided anticommunism: "We might not all be proper fascists," *The Right Stuff* columnist Lawrence Murray wrote in 2015, "but we're all a little fash whether we want to be or not. We're fashy goys—we think a lot of nasty thoughts that keep leftists up at night during their struggle sessions. Might as well embrace it...."[12]

The alt-right's rapid growth partly reflected trends in internet culture, where anonymity and the lack of face-to-face contact have fostered widespread use of insults, bullying, and supremacist speech. More immediately, it reflected recent political developments, such as a backlash against the Black Lives Matter movement and, above all, Donald Trump's presidential candidacy, which the alt-right in turn helped promote. A majority of alt-rightists supported Trump's campaign because of his anti-immigrant proposals; defamatory rhetoric against Mexicans, Muslims, women, and others; and especially his clashes with mainstream conservatives and the Republican Party establishment.

The alt-right's growth also reflected a demographic shift within the far right, as younger activists and leaders joined or replaced an earlier generation of white nationalists. The antifascist website *It's Going Down* commented that these activists were "more interested in reaching out to college educated, urban based, and financially secure men than rural, poor, or working-class people"—in contrast to earlier organizers who focused on racist skinheads or rural survivalists. There were exceptions to this pattern, and *IGD's* comment specifically excluded the Traditionalist Worker Party/Traditionalist Youth Network, which made special efforts to ally with more established neonazi groups, but the description has seemed to hold true across most of the alt-right.[13]

White nationalists, high- and low-brow

The original *AlternativeRight.com* magazine helped set the parameters of alt-right white nationalism. In "Why an Alternative Right is Necessary," published in 2010, soon after the magazine was launched, columnist Richard Hoste offered a paleocon-style criticism of the War on Terror and mainstream conservatives, coupled with a blunt new emphasis on race:

> One would think that the odds of a major terrorist attack happening would depend on how many Muslims are allowed to live in the United States. Reducing Islamic immigration in the name of fighting terror would receive widespread public support, be completely practical in a way installing a puppet regime in Afghanistan wouldn't, and not lead us to kill or torture anybody.... The idea that nothing must be done to stop the March Of Diversity is so entrenched in the minds of those considered of the Right that they will defend America policing the entire planet, torture, indefinite detentions, and a nation on permanent war footing but won't mention immigration restriction or racial profiling.

We've known for a while through neuroscience and cross-adoption studies—if common sense wasn't enough—that individuals differ in their inherent capabilities. The races do, too, with whites and Asians on the top and blacks at the bottom. The Alternative Right takes it for granted that equality of opportunity means inequality of results for various classes, races, and the two sexes. Without ignoring the importance of culture, we see Western civilization as a unique product of the European gene pool.[14]

A few months later, Greg Johnson at *Counter-Currents Publishing* declared that:

The survival of whites in North America and around the world is threatened by a host of bad ideas and policies: egalitarianism, the denial of biological race and sex differences, feminism, emasculation, racial altruism, ethnomasochism and xenophilia, multiculturalism, liberalism, capitalism, non-white immigration, individualism, consumerism, materialism, hedonism, anti-natalism, etc.

He also warned that white people would not survive unless they "work to reduce Jewish power and influence" and "regain political control over a viable national homeland or homelands."[15]

In 2016, following the alternative right's rapid growth, Lawrence Murray in *The Right Stuff* proposed a summary of the movement's "big tent" philosophy: inequality of both individuals and populations is "a fact of life"; "races and their national subdivisions exist and compete for resources, land and influence"; white people are being suppressed and "must be allowed to take their own side"; men and women have separate roles and heterosexual monogamy is crucial for racial survival; "the franchise should be limited" because universal democracy "gives power to the worst and shackles the fittest"; and "Jewish elites are opposed to our entire program."[16] Alfred W. Clark in *Radix Journal* offered a slightly different summary. In his view, alt-rightists recognize human biodiversity; reject universalism; want to reverse Third World immigration into the West; are skeptical of free trade and free market ideology; oppose mainstream Christianity from a variety of religious viewpoints (traditionalist Christian, neopagan, atheist, and agnostic); and often (but not always) support Donald Trump. Unlike Murray, Clark noted that alt-rightists disagree about the "Jewish question," but generally agree "that Jews have disproportionately been involved in starting left-wing movements of the last 150 years."[17]

Like other far rightists, members of the alt-right have endorsed some views usually considered liberal or leftist. Defying laissez-faire conservatives, many alt-rightists have supported single-payer health insurance as a way to help working-class whites, a position which echoes the "welfare chauvinism" of France's Front National and some other rightist parties in Europe. Some alt-rightists, like Hitler's National Socialists, have also advocated a kind of racist environmentalism.[18]

Alt-rightists have promoted their ideas in a variety of ways. Some have used moderate-sounding intellectual tones, often borrowed from the European New Right's euphemistic language about respecting "difference" and protecting "biocultural diversity." For example, the National Policy Institute has promoted "identitarianism," a concept that was developed by the French New Right and popularized by the French group Bloc Identitaire. In 2015, Richard Spencer introduced an NPI essay contest for young writers on the theme, "Why I'm An Identitarian":

> Identitarianism … eschews nationalist chauvinism, as well as the meaningless, petty nationalism that is tolerated, even encouraged, by the current world system. That said, Identitarianism is itself not a universal value system, like Leftism, monotheism, and most contemporary versions of "conservatism." To the contrary, Identitarianism is fundamentally about difference, about culture as an expression of a certain people at a certain time. … Identitarianism acknowledges the incommensurable nature of different peoples and cultures—and thus looks forward to a world of true diversity and multiculturalism.[19]

Other movement activists have offered very different versions of alt-right politics. *The Right Stuff* website used a mocking, ironic tone, with rotating tag lines such as "Your rational world is a circle jerk"; "Non-aggression is the triumph of weakness"; "Democracy is an interracial porno"; "Obedience to lawful authority is the foundation of manly character"; and "Life isn't fair. Sucks for you, but I don't care." An article by "Darth Stirner," titled "Fascist Libertarianism: For a Better World," further illustrated this style:

Dear libertarian, take the rose colored glasses of racial egalitarianism off. Look around and see that other races don't even disguise
their hatred of you. Even though you don't think in terms of race,
rest assured that they do. Humanity is composed of a series of racial corporations. They stick together, and if we don't...Western
civilization is doomed....

Progressives, communists, and degenerates of various stripes will
need to be interned—at least during the transition period. Terrorism
and guerrilla warfare can be prevented with this measure. In the instance of a coup d'état it would be reasonable to detain every person who might conceivably be an enemy of the right-wing revolution. Rather than starving or torturing them they should be treated
well with the highest standard of living reasonably possible. Most
of them will simply be held until the war is over and the winner
is clear. This is actually much more humane than allowing a hotly
contested civil war to occur.[20]

The Right Stuff didn't just offer quasi-irony, however, but also naked
bigotry, as summarized by *Anti-Fascist News*:

[On The Right Stuff] they choose to openly use racial slurs, de-
grade women and rape survivors, mock the holocaust and call for
violence against Jews. Their podcast, The Daily Shoah, which is a
play on The Daily Show and the Yiddish term for The Holocaust,
is a roundtable discussion of different racists broadcasting under pseudonyms. Here they do voice "impressions" of Jews, and
consistently use terms like "Nig Nog," "Muds["] (referring to
"mud races," meaning non-white), and calling people of African
descent "Dingos." The N-word, homophobic slurs, and calls for
enforced cultural patriarchy and heteronormativity are commonplace....The use of rhetoric like this is almost entirely missing
from groups like American Renaissance, Counter-Currents, Radix
Journal, Alternative Right, and even Stormfront, the main hub for
racist groups who recently banned swastikas and racial slurs.[21]

Anti-Fascist News argued that different branches of the alternative right
use different language to appeal to different target audiences. "The
Right Stuff tries to mimic the aggression and reactionary insults of

right-wing talk radio like Rush Limbaugh, while Radix would love to look a lot more like that trendy Critical Theory journal young grad students are clamoring to be published in."[22] This is more division of labor than factional conflict, as a number of alt-right intellectual figures have appeared on *The Right Stuff* podcasts, for example.

Stylistic differences aside, alt-rightists have sometimes voiced different positions on core issues. When discussing how a white homeland would be achieved, alt-rightists have usually tried to sound moderate and reasonable, as when Greg Johnson called for "moving populations around and redrawing maps ... in a completely humane way" or Richard Spencer advocated "peaceful ethnic cleansing." But as the movement gained public visibility, some alt-rightists argued for mass violence. In March 2017, "Padishah Emperor Julius Ebola" wrote that "Aryan Revolution ... requires an expansive foreign policy, and that foreign policy must be supremacy in our hemisphere." Other activists, echoing *The Turner Diaries*, bluntly advocated genocide against Jews and people of color, claiming that this is simply a normal part of biological competition between nations and races.[23]

Alt-rightists have also taken different positions on whether white nationalists should work with Jews, or at least some Jews. The movement's most influential theorist on "the Jewish Question" has been Kevin MacDonald, a retired evolutionary psychology professor who now edits the *Occidental Observer*. Since the 1990s, MacDonald has argued, in Ben Lorber's words, "that Judaism represents a 'group evolutionary strategy', developed and perfected over two millennia of Jewish adaptation in the diaspora, whereby a tight-knit Jewish 'ingroup' embeds itself, like a virus, within the pores of its host nation, siphoning off resources, rising to the elite and disarming all defenses against their invasion." MacDonald argues further that Jews have been the prime agents directing all attacks against white society, such as the civil rights movement, changes in immigration laws, and enforced "political correctness."[24]

Anti-Jewish views such as MacDonald's have been prevalent across most of the movement, but with important variations and qualifications. For those alt-rightists who identify with neonazism, such as Andrew Anglin of the *Daily Stormer*, uncompromising antisemitism is the overriding core principle.[25] To *The Right Stuff* blogger "Auschwitz Soccer Ref," Jews as a group have engaged in "2,000 years of non-stop treachery and backstabbing" and are "remorseless enemies who seek the destruction of the people they hate, which is us." As a result, "anyone who self-identifies as a Jew or anyone who makes excuses for a continued Jewish presence in White homelands should be unapologetically excluded from this movement, and none of these people should ever be allowed to speak at alt-right conferences no matter how pro-White they may seem."[26]

Not all alt-rightists agree. *American Renaissance*, one of the movement's central institutions, pioneered a version of white nationalism that avoided antisemitism. Besides publishing Jewish authors, both Jews and antisemites have been welcome at AmRen events as long as they set aside their disagreements.[27] Richard Spencer, too, initially welcomed Jewish writers and cited them as useful contributors to the movement, although he later shifted toward antisemitism.[28] Even alt-rightists who view Jews as dangerous outsiders don't necessarily regard them as the embodiment of pure evil. Serbian-American author Srdja Trifkovic wrote that "the Jews" had disproportionately contributed to the erosion of European civilization. Nevertheless, he hoped for an alliance with Jews against their common enemy, "the brown, black, and yellow multitudes" whose eventual attacks on the Jewish community might "easily exceed in ferocity and magnitude the events of 1942–45."[29] Similarly, *Counter-Currents* writer M.K. Lane described Jews as "a self-segregating and culturally arrogant people," yet hoped that a significant number of Jews could be won over to ally with white nationalism since, "if we go down, they go down." Of course, in such an alliance white nationalists "must not allow ourselves to become stooges." Jews "living in our midst … could either be allowed to live in their own communities, assimilate in small numbers, or move to Israel. Anything as long as they refrain from subverting our societies. … "[30]

Manosphere

As it grew, the alt-right became closely intertwined with the so-called manosphere, an online antifeminist male subculture that has grown rapidly in recent years, largely outside traditional right-wing networks. The manosphere includes various overlapping circles, such as Men's Rights Activists (MRAs), who argue that the legal system and media unfairly discriminate against men; Pickup Artists (PUAs), who help men learn how to manipulate women into having sex with them; Men Going Their Own Way (MGTOWs), who protest women's supposed dominance by avoiding relationships with them; and others.[31]

Manospherians have emphasized male victimhood—the false belief that men in U.S. society are oppressed or disempowered by feminism or by women in general. This echoes the concept of "reverse racism," the idea that white Americans face unfair discrimination, which white nationalists have promoted since the 1970s.

Like the alt-right, manosphere discourse ranges from intellectual arguments to raw invective, although the line between them is often blurred. Paul Elam's *A Voice for Men*, founded in 2009, became one of the manosphere's most influential websites with intentionally provocative articles arguing, for example, that the legal system was so heavily stacked against men that rape trial jurors should vote to acquit "even in the face of overwhelming evidence that the charges are true."[32] Elam also "satirically" declared October "Bash a Violent Bitch Month," urging men to fight back against physically abusive female partners. He offered "satire" such as:

> I don't mean subdue them, or deliver an open handed pop on the face to get them to settle down. I mean literally to grab them by the hair and smack their face against the wall till the smugness of beating on someone because you know they won't fight back drains from their nose with a few million red corpuscles.[33]

At the PUA site *Return of Kings*, Daryush Valizadeh, who writes under the name Roosh V, has argued that women should not be allowed to make life decisions for themselves because they are "significantly less rational than men."[34]

Two events in 2014 helped bring the manosphere's misogyny to public attention. In May, Elliot Rodger murdered six people and injured fourteen in Isla Vista, California, after posting a 140-page "manifesto" that rationalized his killing spree as retribution for women's refusal to have sex with him. Rodger had been a participant in manosphere forums such as PUAhate.com, and manosphere ideology infused his manifesto. He complained that "the most beautiful of women choose to mate with the most brutal of men, instead of magnificent gentlemen like myself," and declared that "women should not have the right to choose who to mate and breed with." In fact, women were so "evil and depraved" that they "don't deserve to have any rights" but should be locked up in concentration camps, where most of them should be starved to death.[35]

Manospherians denied that misogyny played any role in Rodger's mass murder. Valizadeh declared that the killings could have been prevented if Rodger had learned "game" (techniques for seducing women). The problem, according to Valizadeh, was not misogyny or men's sense of entitlement, but rather society's unreasonable limitations on men's access to sex with women:

> Until you give men like Rodger a way to have sex, either by encouraging them to learn game, seek out a Thai wife, or engage in legalized prostitution—three things that the American media and cultural elite venomously attack, it's inevitable for another massacre to occur.[36]

The other 2014 event that brought the manosphere to public attention was the Gamergate controversy. Starting that year, a number of women who worked in—or were critical of sexism in—the video game industry were subjected to large-scale campaigns of harassment, coordinated partly with the #Gamergate Twitter hashtag. Supporters of Gamergate claimed that the campaign was a defense of free speech and journalistic ethics and against political correctness, but it included streams of misogynistic abuse, rape and death threats, as well as doxxing (public releases of personal information), which caused several women to leave their homes out of fear for their physical safety.[37] The Gamergate campaign took the pervasive, systematic pattern of threats and abuse that has been long used to silence women on the internet and sharpened it into a focused weapon of attack.[38] Gamergate, in turn, strongly influenced the alt-right's own online activism, as I discuss below.

Beyond its broad aims to weaken or destroy feminism and reintensify men's dominance over women, the manosphere does not have an agreed upon political program and is too diffuse to characterize as far right. However, there has been significant overlap and interchange between the manosphere and the alt-right. Both are heavily active on discussion websites such as *4chan*, *8chan*, and *Reddit*, and a number of prominent alt-rightists—such as Matt Forney, Theodore Beale (pseudonym: "Vox Day"), James Weidmann ("Roissy"), and Andrew Auernheimer ("weev")—have also been active in the manosphere. Many other alt-rightists have absorbed and promoted manosphere versions of gender ideology.

But there have also been tensions between the two rightist movements. In 2015, Valizadeh ("Roosh V") began to build a connection with the alternative right, attending an NPI conference and quoting extensively from antisemite Kevin MacDonald in a lengthy post about "The Damaging Effects Of Jewish Intellectualism And Activism On Western Culture."[39] Some alt-rightists responded favorably. One blogger commented that the manosphere was "not as stigmatized" as white nationalism and the alt-right, and suggested hopefully that, "since the Manosphere has a very broad appeal it is possible that bloggers such as Roosh and Dalrock [a Christian manospherian] might serve as a stepping stone to guide formerly apathetic men towards the Alternative Right."[40] Matt Parrott of the Traditionalist Youth Network praised Valizadeh's "What is Neomasculinity?" as "a masterful synthesis of human biodiversity knowledge, radical traditionalist principle, and pragmatic modern dating experience."[41]

But the relationship soured quickly, largely because Valizadeh is Persian American. Although Andrew Anglin of *The Daily Stormer* tweeted that Valizadeh was "a civilized and honorable man,"[42] many white nationalists denounced him as nonwhite and an enemy. One tweeted that he was "a greasy Iranian" who "goes to Europe to defile white women and write books about it."[43] After studying Valizadeh's accounts of his own sex tourism, *Counter-Currents Publishing* editor-in-chief Greg Johnson concluded that Roosh "is either a rapist or a fraud" and "it is not just feminist hysteria to describe Roosh as a rape advocate." More broadly, Johnson wrote, "for all its benefits … the manosphere morally corrupts men. It does not promote the resurgence of traditional and biologically based sexual norms."[44] Valizadeh responded by blogging "The Alt Right Is Worse Than Feminism in Attempting to Control Male Sexual Behavior."[45]

Male tribalism

Jack Donovan, an early contributor to *AlternativeRight.com* who remained active in the alt-right until 2017, has offered a related but distinct version of male supremacist ideology. In a series of books and articles over the past decade, Donovan has advocated a system of patriarchy based on "tribal" comradeship among male warriors. Drawing on evolutionary psychology, he argues that in the past men have mostly organized themselves into small, close-knit "gangs," which fostered true masculinity and men's natural dominance over women. Yet modern "globalist civilization" "requires the abandonment of human scale identity groups for 'one world tribe.'" A combination of "feminists, elite bureaucrats, and wealthy men," he writes, has promoted male passivity and put women in a dominant role.[46]

Donovan's social and political ideal is a latter-day tribal order that he calls "The Brotherhood," in which all men would affirm their sacred loyalty to each other against the outside world. A man's position would be based on "hierarchy through meritocracy," not inherited wealth or status. All men would be expected to train and serve as warriors, and only warriors—meaning no women—would have a political voice. In this version of patriarchal ideology, unlike the Christian right version, male comradeship is central and the family is entirely peripheral. An example of the kind of community Donovan envisions is the Odinist group Wolves of Vinland, which Donovan joined after visiting their off-the-grid community in rural Virginia in 2014. The Wolves use group rituals (including animal sacrifice) and hold fights between members to test their masculinity.[47] The Wolves of Vinland have also been praised by white nationalist groups such as *Counter-Currents Publishing*, and one of their members has been imprisoned for attempting to burn down a black church in Virginia.[48]

Donovan has written that he is sympathetic to white nationalist aims such as encouraging racial separatism and defending European Americans against "the deeply entrenched anti-white bias of multiculturalist orthodoxies." White nationalism dovetails with his beliefs that all humans are tribal creatures and human equality is an illusion. But in contrast to most alt-rightists, race has not been Donovan's main focus or concern. "My work is about men. It's about understanding masculinity and the plight of men in the modern world. It's about what all men have in common." His "Brotherhood" ideal is not culturally specific, and he's happy to see men of other cultures pursue similar aims. "For instance, I am not a Native American, but I have been in contact with a Native American activist who read *The Way of Men* and contacted me to tell me about his brotherhood. I could never belong to that tribe, but I wish him great success in his efforts to promote virility among his tribesmen."[49] In August 2017, after the Unite the Right rally and the killing of antifascist protester Heather Heyer in Charlottesville, Virginia, Donovan disavowed the alt-right and declared he would no longer allow white nationalists to publish his writings.[50]

Donovan has also embraced the term "anarcho-fascism," which he explained in terms of the original fascist symbol, the *fasces*, a bundle of wooden rods that stands for strength and unity. Rejecting the common belief that fascism equals a totalitarian state or top-down bureaucratic rule, he identified the fasces with the "bottom-up idea" of "a unified male collective.... True tribal unity can't be imposed from above. It's an organic phenomenon. Profound unity comes from men bound together by a red ribbon of blood." "[T]he modern, effeminate, bourgeois 'First World' states can no longer produce new honor cultures. New, pure warrior-gangs can only rise in anarchic opposition to the corrupt, feminist, anti-tribal, degraded institutions of the established order.... Ur-fascism is the source of honor culture and authentic patriarchal tradition."[51]

Elsewhere, Donovan cautioned that he isn't "an anarchist or a fascist proper," but simply wanted to make the point that "revitalizing tribal manliness will require a chaotic break from modernity."[52] Still, there are strong resonances between Donovan's ideas and early fascism's violent male camaraderie, which took the intense, trauma-laced bonds that World War I veterans had formed in the trenches and transferred them into street-fighting formations such as the Italian *squadristi* and German storm troopers. Donovan also echoes the 1909 *Futurist Manifesto*, a document that prefigured Italian Fascism with statements such as, "We want to glorify war—the only cure for the world—militarism, patriotism, the destructive gesture of the anarchists, the beautiful ideas which kill, and contempt for woman."[53] Thus it's not surprising he favors the term anarcho-fascism, which he identifies with referring to "a unified male collective...bound together by a red ribbon of blood."[54]

In the alternative right and among rightists in general, the most controversial part of Donovan's ideology is that he advocates and practices "androphilia," by which he means love or sex between masculine men.

Many alternative rightists consider homosexuality in any form to be immoral and a threat to racial survival, and Donovan has been vilified on many alt-right sites for his sexuality, yet his work has also won widespread support within the movement. *Anti-Fascist News* has noted a broader trend among many white nationalists to include openly homosexual writers (such as James O'Meara) and musicians (such as Death in June leader Douglas Pearce), while continuing to derogate gay culture.[55]

Right-wing anarchists

As part of its project to bring together a range of dissident right-wing voices, the original *AlternativeRight.com* published articles by self-identified anarchists Andrew Yeoman of Bay Area National Anarchists (BANA) and Keith Preston of the website *Attack the System* (ATS). National-Anarchism, which advocates a decentralized system of "tribal" enclaves, was initiated in the 1990s by Troy Southgate, a veteran of British neonazism.[56] Over the following years, National-Anarchist groups formed in a number of countries across Europe, the Americas, and Australia/New Zealand. The first U.S. affiliate, BANA, began in 2007, and Southgate formally launched the National-Anarchist Movement (N-AM) in 2010.[57]

National-Anarchism is a white nationalist ideology. Like identitarianism, it draws heavily on the ENR doctrine that ethnic and racial separatism is needed to defend so-called biocultural diversity. The *N-AM Manifesto* declares that race categories are basic biological facts and some people are innately superior to others. National-Anarchists also repeat classic antisemitic conspiracy theories and, like many neonazis, promote neopaganism and closeness to nature.[58] But National-Anarchists reject classical fascism for its emphasis on strong nation-states, centralized dictatorship, and collaboration with big business. Instead, they call for breaking up society into self-governing tribal communities, so that different cultures, beliefs, and practices can coexist side by side.[59]

National-Anarchists have not had a significant presence in the alternative right since BANA disbanded in 2011, but self-described anarcho-pluralist Keith Preston has continued to participate in alt-right forums, for example, speaking at National Policy Institute conferences and on

The Right Stuff podcasts. Preston is a former left-wing anarchist who moved to the right in the 1990s and then founded the group American Revolutionary Vanguard, better known today by the name of its website, *Attack the System*.[60] ATS brings together a number of right-wing currents, including National-Anarchist, libertarian, white nationalist, Duginist, and others among its editors and contributors, but Preston's own ideology is distinct from all of these.[61]

Preston has called himself a "fellow-traveler" of National-Anarchism, and like the National-Anarchists he advocates a decentralized, diverse network of self-governing communities, while rejecting left-wing anarchism's commitment to dismantle social hierarchy and oppression. Authoritarian and supremacist systems would be fully compatible with the anarcho-pluralist model, as long as they operated on a small scale. But unlike National-Anarchists, Preston frames his decentralist ideal in terms of individual free choice rather than tribalism, and he is not a white nationalist.[62] Although Preston has echoed some racist ideas such as the claim that non-European immigrants threaten to destroy Western civilization, his underlying philosophy is based not on race but rather a generic, Nietzschean elitism that is not ethnically specific.[63] While Preston himself is white, several of his closest associates in the *Attack the System* inner circle are people of color.

By his own description, Preston "has remained peripherally associated with the Alt-Right milieu" since its early years; for example, he spoke at the National Policy Institute conferences in 2011 and 2015.[64] He has offered several reasons for his involvement in the alternative right. He saw the movement as an important counterweight to what he calls "totalitarian humanism" (supposedly state-enforced progressive values, i.e., political correctness), he regarded the alt-right's foreign policy non-interventionism and economic nationalism as superior to what the Republican or Democratic parties advocate, and he shares many alt-rightists' interest in earlier European "critics of liberal capitalism and mass democracy,"[65] meaning people like Julius Evola, Carl Schmitt, and Ernst Jünger. In addition, the alt-right allowed Preston to avoid political isolation, as his efforts to reach out to left-wing anarchists have been almost completely rejected.

Preston gained respect within the alternative right, and his antistatist vision has appealed to some white nationalists in the movement. For example, *Counter-Currents* author Francisco Albanese has argued that it provides "the best and most viable option for the ethnic and racial survival" of whites in regions where they form a minority of the population. In addition, "it is only outside the state that whites can come to understand the true essence of community and construction of a common destiny."[66] At the same time, anarcho-pluralism offers potential common ground between white nationalists and other critics of the existing order, such as anarcho-capitalists and other "market anarchists," whose ideas are regularly featured on *Attack the System*, as well as the "libertarian theocrats" of the Christian Reconstructionist movement.[67]

Preston's approach to political strategy takes this bridge building further. Echoing Third Position fascists, who denounce both communism and capitalism, Preston and ATS call for a broad revolutionary alliance of all those who want to destroy U.S. imperialism and the federal government. Within U.S. borders, this would involve a "pan-secessionist" strategy uniting groups across the political spectrum that want to carve out self-governing enclaves free of federal government control.[68] As a step in this direction, ATS supported a series of North American secessionist conventions, which brought together representatives of the neo-Confederate group League of the South, the Reconstructionist-influenced Christian Exodus, the libertarian Free State Project, advocates of Hawaiian independence, the left-leaning Second Vermont Republic, and others.[69]

Neoreaction

Neoreaction is another dissident right-wing current that has emerged online in the past decade, which overlaps with and has influenced the alternative right. Like the alt-right and much of the manosphere, neoreaction (often abbreviated as NRx and also known as Dark Enlightenment) is a loosely unified school of thought that rejects egalitarianism in principle, argues that differences in human intelligence and ability are mainly genetic, and believes that cultural and political elites wrongfully limit the range of acceptable discourse. Blogger Curtis Yarvin (writing under the pseudonym Mencius Moldbug) first articulated neoreactionary ideology in 2007, but many other writers have contributed to it. Neoreaction emphasizes order and restoring the social stability that supposedly prevailed before the French Revolution, along with technocratic and futurist concerns such as transhumanism, a movement that hopes to radically "improve" human beings through technology. NRx theorist Nick Land is a leading advocate of accelerationism, which in his version sees global capitalism driving ever-faster technological change, to the point that artificial intelligence essentially replaces human beings. One critic wrote that neoreaction "combines all of the awful things you always suspected about libertarianism with odds and ends from PUA culture, Victorian Social Darwinism, and an only semi-ironic attachment to absolutism. Insofar as neoreactionaries have a political project, it's to dissolve the United States into competing authoritarian seasteads on the model of Singapore.... "[70]

Neoreactionaries, who are known for their arcane, verbose theoretical monologues, appear to be mostly young, computer-oriented men, and their ideas have spread partly through the tech startup scene. PayPal cofounder and Trump supporter Peter Thiel has voiced some neoreactionary-sounding ideas. In 2009, for example, he declared, "I no longer believe that freedom and democracy are compatible" and "the vast increase in welfare beneficiaries and the extension of the franchise to women...have rendered the notion of 'capitalist democracy' into an oxymoron."[71] Both Yarvin and fellow NRxer Michael Anissimov have worked for companies backed by Thiel.[72] This doesn't necessarily mean that Thiel is intentionally bankrolling the neoreactionary movement per se, but it points to resonances between that movement and Silicon Valley's larger techno-libertarian discourse.

"At its heart, neoreaction is a critique of the entire liberal, politically-correct orthodoxy," commented "WhiteDeerGrotto" on the NRx blog *Habitable Worlds*. "The Cathedral, a term coined by Moldbug, is a description of the institutions and enforcement mechanisms used to propagate and maintain this orthodoxy"—a power center that consists of Ivy League and other elite universities, the *New York Times*, and some civil servants. "The politically-correct propagandists assert that humans are essentially interchangeable, regardless of culture or genetics, and that some form of multicultural social-welfare democracy is the ideal, final political state for all of humanity. Neoreaction says no. The sexes are biologically distinct, genetics matter, and democracy is deeply flawed and fundamentally unstable."[73]

While alt-rightists largely agree with these neoreactionary ideas, and some outsiders have equated the two movements, alt-right and neoreaction differ significantly. Alt-rightists might or might not invoke popular sovereignty as an achievement of European civilization, and try to strike a populist or anti-elitist pose, but neoreactionaries all regard regular people as utterly unsuited to hold political power—"a howling irrational mob" as NRx theorist Nick Land has put it.[74] Some NRxers advocate monarchy; others want to turn the state into a corporation with members of an intellectual elite as shareholders.[75] Conversely, neoreactionaries might or might not translate their genetic determinism into calls for racial solidarity, but for most alt-rightists race is the basis for everything else.[76] Unlike most alt-rightists, leading neoreactionaries have not supported Donald Trump.[77] In addition, while many alt-rightists emphasize antisemitism, neoreactionaries generally do not, and some neoreactionaries are Jewish or, in Yarvin's case, of mixed Jewish and non-Jewish ancestry.[78] Indeed, in *The Right Stuff*'s lexicon of alt-right terminology, "Neoreaction" translates as "Jews."

At the same time, many alt-rightists regard neoreaction as a related movement that offers many positive contributions. Some writers, such as Steve Sailer, have had a foot in both camps. Alt-rightist Gregory Hood has argued that white nationalism and neoreaction are complementary: "I've argued in the past that race is sufficient in and of itself to serve as a foundation for state policy. However, just saying that tells you very little about how precisely you execute that program. NRx and its theoretical predecessors are absolutely core to understanding how society works and how power functions."[79] Anarcho-pluralist Keith Preston applauded a proposal by NRxer Michael Anissimov to create breakaway enclaves in "low-population, defensible regions of the United States like Idaho."[80] On its own, neoreaction seems too esoteric to have much of a political impact, but its contribution to alt-right ideology might be significant.

Political strategy debates

Alt-rightists' embrace of Trump followed several years in which they argued about whether to work within existing political channels or reject them entirely. During this period, *American Renaissance* columnist Hubert Collins called on white nationalists to use the electoral process and ally with more mainstream anti-immigrant groups to keep whites at as high a percentage of the U.S. population as possible.[81] In contrast, Gregory Hood of *Counter-Currents Publishing* declared that the United States was "beyond reform" and political secession was "the only way out." Sidestepping this issue, many alt-rightists have followed the European New Right lead and focused on a "metapolitical" strategy of seeking to transform the broader culture. In Lawrence Murray's words, "When the idea of White nationalism has taken root among enough of our people, the potential to demand, demonstrate, and act will be superior to what it currently is."[82] Jack Donovan has argued that the U.S. is on the road to becoming a failed state and urged alt-rightists to "build the kinds of resilient communities and networks of skilled people that can survive the collapse and preserve your identities after the Fall."[83] To Donovan, this is an optimistic scenario: "In a failed state, we go back to Wild West rules, and America becomes a place for men again—a land full of promise and possibility that rewards daring and ingenuity, a place where men can restart the world."[84]

Whether or not to work within established political channels has been debated at movement events, with some alt-rightists moving from one position to another. Richard Spencer, for example, argued in 2011 that "the GOP could unite a substantial majority of white voters by focusing its platform on immigration restriction." This strategy "would...ensure that future Americans inherit a country that resembles that of their ancestors."[85] But two years later, Spencer seemingly turned his back on the Republican Party and called for creating a separate white ethnostate in North America. He declared, "the majority of children born in the United States are non-White. Thus, from our perspective, any future immigration-restriction efforts are meaningless." Spencer also argued that "restoring the Constitution," (going back to an aristocratic republic run by property-owning white men) as some white nationalists advocated, would only lead to a similar or worse situation.[86]

One approach has been to propose working within the system in order to weaken it, advocating changes that sound reasonable but require radical change—a right-wing version of the Trotskyist transitional demand strategy. Ted Sallis, for example, urged white nationalists to "demand a seat at the multicultural table, represented by *real* advocates of White interests, not groveling patsies." This would involve using the language of multiculturalism to complain about "legitimate" cases of discrimination against whites or members of other dominant groups.

The aim here would not be "reforming the System. It is instead using the contradictions and weaknesses of the System against itself...."[87]

To a large extent, alternative rightist support for Trump's presidential candidacy followed a related approach of using the system against itself. Alt-rightists began praising Trump in 2015, and by mid-2016 most of the movement was applauding him. But this support was qualified by the recognition that Trump was not one of them and was not going to bring about the change they wanted. Brad Griffin, who blogs at *Occidental Dissent* under the name Hunter Wallace, hoped in late 2015 that Trump "provokes a fatal split that topples the GOP." The Traditionalist Youth Network declared:

> While Donald Trump is neither a Traditionalist nor a White nationalist, he is a threat to the economic and social powers of the international Jew. For this reason alone as long as Trump stands strong on deportation and immigration enforcement we should support his candidacy insofar as we can use it to push more hardcore positions on immigration and Identity. Donald Trump is not the savior of Whites in America, he is however a booming salvo across the bow of the Left and Jewish power to tell them that White America is awakening, and we are tired of business as usual.[88]

At *The Right Stuff*, "Professor Evola-Hitler" argued that Trump had broken important taboos on issues such as curtailing immigration and ending birthright citizenship, damaged the Republican Party's pro-Israel coalition, shifted the party closer to ethnic nationalism, and "offers the opportunity for the Alt-Right to expand quickly," but cautioned, "We need to be taking advantage of Trump, not allow Trump to take advantage of us."[89]

Not all alt-rightists supported Trump. *The Right Stuff* contributor "Auschwitz Soccer Ref" argued that alt-rightists shouldn't support Trump since two of his children had married Jews, making him "naturally loyal" to Israel.[90] Jack Donovan suggested that a Hillary Clinton presidency would be preferable, because she would "drive home the reality that white men are no longer in charge...and that [the United States] is no longer their country and never will be again,"[91] while Keith Preston commented, "The alt-right's attachment to Trump seems to be a mirror image repeat of the religious right's attachment to Reagan, i.e. the case of an insurgent, somewhat reactionary, populist movement

being taken for a ride by a thoroughly pro–ruling class centrist politician motivated primarily by personal ambition."[92] However, these anti-
Trump voices were squarely in the minority.

Internet memes and harassment campaigns

The main way that alt-rightists helped Trump's campaign was through
online activism. A pivotal example came in the summer of 2015, when
alt-rightists promoted the #cuckservative meme to attack Trump's GOP
rivals as traitors and sellouts to liberalism. "Cuckservative" combines
the words "conservative" and "cuckold," meaning a man whose wife has
sex with other men. As journalist Joseph Bernstein pointed out, "The
term's connotations are racist. By alluding to a genre of porn in which
passive white husbands watch their wives have sex with black men, it
casts its targets as impotent defenders of white people in America."[93]
During the weeks leading up to the first Republican presidential debate,
alt-rightists spread the meme across social media to boost Trump and
vilify his GOP rivals, as in a Tweet that showed a picture of Jeb Bush
with the words, "Please fuck my country, Mexico. #Cuckservative."[94]
As *Anti-Fascist News* pointed out, this initiative "allowed racialist discourse to shift into the public, making #cuckservative an accusation that
mainstream Republicans feel like they have to answer to."[95]

Alt-rightists also turned online harassment and abuse into a potent
tactic for frightening and silencing opponents, borrowing directly from
the manosphere's Gamergate campaign discussed above. In the spring of
2016, for example, anti-Trump protesters at Portland State University
were flooded with racist, transphobic, and antisemitic messages, doxxing, and rape and death threats sent from anonymous social media accounts. Reflecting the manosphere's influence, alt-right harassment often emphasized sexual violence and the humiliation of women and girls,
even when men were the supposed targets.[96] David French, staff writer
at the conservative *National Review*, described the yearlong stream
of relentless online abuse his family has endured because he criticized
Trump and the alt-right:

I saw images of my daughter's face in gas chambers, with a smiling Trump in a Nazi uniform preparing to press a button and kill her. I saw her face photoshopped into images of slaves. She was called a "niglet" and a "dindu." The alt-right unleashed on my wife, Nancy, claiming that she had slept with black men while I was deployed to Iraq, and that I loved to watch while she had sex with "black bucks." People sent her pornographic images of black men having sex with white women, with someone photoshopped to look like me, watching.[97]

One of the alt-right's most skillful uses of social media in 2016 was the #DraftOurDaughters meme, which was trending on Twitter the week before the election. As the website *Know Your Meme* explained, "#DraftOurDaughters is a satirical social media hashtag launched by supporters of Donald Trump which encourages American women to register for Selective Service in preparation for hypothetical scenarios of United States military operations that would supposedly be launched by Hillary Clinton if she were elected as President of the United States." The campaign included a series of fake Clinton campaign ads, many of which feature images of women in military uniform and slogans such as "Hillary will stand up to Russian Aggression. Will you stand with her?," "I'd rather die in a war than live under bigotry," and "In the White House or on Russian soil. The fight for equality never stops."[98]

#DraftOurDaughters portrayed the Clinton campaign as fusing feminism/multiculturalism and aggressive militarism. Since that was a reasonably accurate description of Clinton's politics, the meme was equally effective as either disinformation or satire. A number of alt-right sites, such as *Vox Popoli* and *The Daily Stormer*, promoted the campaign.[99] Along with spreading the "ads" themselves, alt-rightists also spread the phony claim that mainstream media had been taken in by them.[100]

The alt-lite

As the alt-right grew and attracted increased attention, it also developed complicated relationships with more moderate rightists. The movement has largely defined itself and drawn energy by denouncing conservatives, and some conservatives have returned the favor, including the prestigious *National Review*.[101] At the same time, other conservatives have taken on the role of apologists or supporters for the alt-right, helping to spread a lot of its message without embracing its full ideology or its ethnostate goals. Richard Spencer and his comrades began to call this phenomenon the "Alt Right-lite" or simply the "Alt Lite." Alt-rightists have relied on the alt-lite to help bring its ideas to a mass mainstream audience, but to varying degrees they have also regarded alt-lite figures with resentment, as ideologically untrustworthy opportunists.

Breitbart News Network is the preeminent example of alt-lite politics. Founded in 2007, *Breitbart* featured sensationalist attacks on liberals and liberal groups, praise for the Tea Party's anti–big government populism, and aggressive denials that conservatives were racist, sexist, or homophobic. Under Steve Bannon, who took over leadership in 2012, the organ began to scapegoat Muslims and immigrants more directly.[102] In March 2016, *Breitbart* published "An Establishment Conservative's Guide to the Alt-Right," by Allum Bokhari and Milo Yiannopoulos, which asserted—without evidence—that most alt-rightists did not believe their own racist propaganda, but were actually just libertarians trying to shock people.[103] The article helped boost the alt-right's profile and acceptability in mainstream circles, yet many alt-rightists criticized it for glossing over their white nationalist ideology.[104]

Over the following months, Yiannopoulos—a flamboyantly gay man of Jewish descent and a political performer who vilifies Muslims and women and refers to Donald Trump as "Daddy"—became publicly identified with the alt-right himself, to mixed reviews from alt-rightists.[105] Meanwhile, Steve Bannon declared *Breitbart* "the platform of the Alt Right" and began publishing semi-veiled antisemitic attacks on Trump's opponents, all while insisting that white nationalists, antisemites, and homophobes were marginal to the alt-right.[106] Richard Spencer was pleased when Donald Trump hired Bannon to run his campaign, commenting that "Breitbart has acted as a 'gateway' to Alt Right ideas and writers" and that the media outlet "has people on board who take us seriously, even if they are not Alt Right themselves."[107] But other alt-rightists were more critical of the alt-lite phenomenon. At *Occidental Dissent*, Brad Griffin described the alt-lite as "basically conservative websites pushing Alt-Right material in order to generate clicks and revenue," and asked, "What the hell does Milo Yiannopoulos—a Jewish homosexual who boasts about carrying on interracial relationships with black men—have to do with us?" Many alt-rightists were pleased when Yiannopoulos's political career collapsed following circulation of a video interview in which he said that sexual relationships between young teenage boys and adult men could be "hugely positive."[108]

Within the U.S. far right's larger history, the alt-right stands out in several ways. Other far right movements have embraced up-to-date technology (neonazis were using computer bulletin boards in the early 1980s), but the alt-right is the first such movement to organize and conduct its activism mostly online. Other movements have brought together different ideological currents (witness the neonazi-Klan convergence in the 1980s or the Patriot movement's roots in neonazism, Christian Reconstructionism, Birchite conspiracism, and gun rights) but the alt-right has been unusually successful in combining a big tent ideological framework with hard-line rejection of the established order. And other far rightists have engaged with electoral politics and some of them have offered limited support to mainstream politicians, but the alt-right is the first such movement to enjoy a strong symbiotic connection with a major party presidential candidate—let alone put him in the White House. As I have noted, the alt-right's relationship with Donald Trump is complex. How that relationship has unfolded since Trump's inauguration is part of the subject of chapter 11.

5. The LaRouche Network

Not all far rightists focus on race, religion, guns, or gender. In this short chapter I will look at the Lyndon LaRouche network, a small formation that does not fit into standard ideological categories and rarely figures in discussions of the U.S far right. Yet LaRouchites, too, argue that humans are fundamentally unequal and that the U.S. political system has to be radically transformed. They deserve attention here because they illustrate the far right's ideological diversity and capacity to rework elitism in different ways.

For years, Lyndon LaRouche has been widely dismissed as a political crackpot, but he has had an impact well out of proportion to his following's small size. Since the mid-1970s, the LaRouche network has maintained a cohesiveness, propaganda output, and international reach that most far right groups can only dream of. In the 1980s, the LaRouchites raised funds, fielded candidates, gathered intelligence, and peddled political dirty tricks on an unprecedented scale. Although their influence today is more limited, they have continued to find new audiences and remake themselves in the face of new circumstances.[1]

Building a network

Virtually alone on the U.S. far right, the LaRouche network started out as a leftist organization. Lyndon LaRouche spent seventeen years in the Socialist Workers Party, a Trotskyist organization, then formed the National Caucus of Labor Committees (NCLC) in 1968 as a Marxist offshoot of Students for a Democratic Society. But in 1973, LaRouche used cult psychology techniques to establish dictatorial control over the NCLC. He then launched his followers in a series of physical attacks against members of the Communist Party and other Marxist groups, cutting them off from the rest of the left.[2]

Over the following years, the LaRouchites developed a unique populist ideology centered on anti-elite conspiracy theories and built a network of organizations, businesses, and publications in several countries. LaRouche became a perennial candidate for U.S. president, first on the U.S. Labor Party ticket, and after 1980 in the Democratic Party primaries. His network fielded thousands of candidates for federal, state, and local office in every region of the country. Most LaRouchite electoral efforts were marginal, but there were exceptions. A LaRouche-sponsored California ballot initiative to "quarantine" people with AIDS won 2 million votes in 1986 and 1.7 million votes in 1987. Although the measure lost both times, the mass support it garnered helped the LaRouchites look legitimate and bolstered other efforts to exploit the AIDS crisis to attack gay rights.[3]

In the 1970s and '80s, LaRouchites established political organizations in a number of European countries, especially Germany, as well as Canada, Mexico, Australia, the Philippines, and elsewhere. The LaRouchites built an international network for intelligence gathering, propaganda, and dirty tricks, an endeavor assisted through their close relationship with Mitch WerBell, an anticommunist mercenary who was close to the World Anti-Communist League, and who provided paramilitary training to NCLC members at his Georgia compound. LaRouchites helped conservative Republican candidates and corrupt labor union bureaucrats by conducting smear campaigns against their opponents. They ingratiated themselves with nuclear power executives and scientists by attacking the environmental movement. They developed contacts at the CIA and other spy agencies and sold intelligence reports to right-wing dictatorships, while also meeting privately with KGB agents and other Soviet officials for almost a decade. The LaRouchites also developed an impressive fundraising machine, which in the 1980s alone brought in an estimated $200 million.[4]

For much of the 1980s, the LaRouchites were on friendly terms with President Ronald Reagan's conservative Republican administration. But in 1986–1988, after it came to light that they had defrauded thousands of elderly Republicans out of millions of dollars, the federal government cracked down on the LaRouchites' illegal fundraising activities, and LaRouche himself spent five years in prison for fraud and conspiracy.[5] Many people thought this would end his political career, but it didn't. In the 1990s and 2000s, the LaRouchites took on new vitality by shifting to more "leftist" positions. They were active in campaigns against the U.S.-led wars against Iraq, the NATO bombing of Yugoslavia, and in the mostly progressive Occupy Wall Street movement.[6] The LaRouchites also expanded their ties with political elites in other countries, especially Russia, where their attacks on free trade and conspiracy theories about international bankers won favor among policymakers close to President Vladimir Putin.[7]

Today the LaRouchites present themselves as defenders of President Franklin Roosevelt's legacy of welfare state liberalism, although they applaud Donald Trump and denounced Barack Obama as a fascist madman.[8] Their efforts have enabled them to recruit a new crop of young activists. Lyndon LaRouche is now in his mid-nineties, yet the network he established is likely to continue.

LaRouchite ideology

Despite many changing details, the LaRouche network's underlying ideology has remained basically the same since the 1970s. Unlike most U.S. far rightists today, the LaRouchites advocate a program of centralized economic development, driven by high-tech industry and massive infrastructure projects to expand transportation, power generation, and water management. They argue (rightly) that this approach is a continuation of the old "American system" of high tariffs to protect young industries, government-sponsored "internal improvements" such as canal building, and public credit to support productive investment. Formulated in opposition to the "British system" of free trade, the American system guided federal policy for much of U.S. history, for example, under Alexander Hamilton (George Washington's secretary of the treasury) and Presidents John Quincy Adams and Abraham Lincoln. The LaRouchites also celebrate Franklin Roosevelt's New Deal policies of the 1930s, which sought to lift the U.S. out of the Great Depression with federal jobs programs, public works development, banking reform, Social Security and federal unemployment insurance, some protection of workers' right to organize, and other interventionist measures.[9]

The LaRouchites regard all human history as defined by a massive Manichean struggle between good "humanists" and evil "oligarchs," both of whom manipulate events through elaborate conspiracies. The center of oligarchic power has supposedly shifted at various points in history but is today based in Britain, specifically among British financiers, who secretly exercise enormous global power through many seemingly unconnected and even conflicting institutions, doctrines, and cultural practices. These oligarchic-directed forces include most financial institutions, free market economics, Marxism, Zionism, the Christian right, neoconservatism, the illegal drug trade, the environmental movement, homosexuality, and rock music. This eclectic mix of targets allows the LaRouchites to present themselves as "progressive" in one situation and "conservative" in another.[10]

The LaRouche network's conspiracist ideology is rooted in antisemitism, but the relationship is complex. In the early 1970s, LaRouchite conspiracy theories centered on the Rockefellers, a non-Jewish family of super-wealthy industrialists and bankers. In the late 1970s, at the suggestion of the far rightist Liberty Lobby, they began to target Jewish bankers and prominent Jews such as former Secretary of State Henry Kissinger.[11] In the 1990s, they were the first group to promote conspiracy theories centered on liberal financier George Soros, who is Jewish, and who has since become one of the most popular targets of right-wing scapegoating and implicit Jew-hatred.[12] Yet the LaRouchites have consistently denied being antisemitic, a claim bolstered by the fact that many of LaRouche's followers were and are Jews, including some of his top lieutenants.

Over time, the LaRouchites have become more careful and sophisticated at deflecting the charge of antisemitism, while continuing to exploit the emotional power of historically antisemitic themes. Generalized vilification of Jews is difficult if not impossible to find in current-day LaRouchite propaganda, and non-Jews typically outnumber Jews in their lists of evildoers. When they attack Jewish leaders or organizations, they are more likely to portray them as tools or dupes of the oligarchs, rather than as the top wire-pullers. When they do target Jews, they often describe them as Nazis, implying that they are in fact defenders, not scapegoaters, of Jews.[13]

Yet many of the LaRouchites' conspiracist motifs are borrowed directly from anti-Jewish literature. The false dichotomy between "evil" finance capital and "good" industrial capital has long been a central theme in antisemitic propaganda, as has the claim that (Jewish) bankers secretly orchestrated the rise of Marxism and international communism. The idea that oligarchs spread drugs and non-classical music to undermine civilization echoes Henry Ford's *The International Jew* (published 1920–1922), which charged that Jews were promoting bootlegging and jazz to weaken America. Anglophobia has been tied to antisemitism since the late nineteenth century, based on the idea that the Rothschild banking family controlled Britain. In the United States in the 1930s and early 1940s, Nazi sympathizers such as Charles Lindbergh, the famous aviator, often lumped Jews and British together as interconnected powerful groups pressuring the U.S. to join World War II on the side of the Allies.[14]

LaRouchites have also changed the way they talk about people of color. In the 1970s, the LaRouchites repeatedly referred to nonwhites in overtly racist terms. In 1977, for example, LaRouche wrote that it was "correct for the American branch of European humanist culture to absorb the territories occupied by a miserable, relatively bestial culture of indigenous Americans," since "we do not regard all cultures and nations as equally deserving of sovereignty or survival."[15] In this period, the LaRouchites also formed an alliance with Pennsylvania Ku Klux Klan leader Roy Frankhauser and helped to fund Posse Comitatus.[16] Yet today LaRouchite organizations welcome people of color as members. LaRouchite publications celebrate the legacy of antislavery and anti-racist struggles and hold up African American supporters of LaRouche, such as the late activists James Bevel and Amelia Boynton Robinson, as heroes of the civil rights movement. In the 1990s, the LaRouchites also cultivated a friendly relationship with the Nation of Islam, a right-wing black nationalist organization headed by Louis Farrakhan. They declared African American spiritual music to be "the basis for an American Classical culture"—in stark contrast to "the completely synthetic organized-crime phenomenon known as 'rock and roll.'"[17] At the same time, the LaRouchites have sometimes reverted to open racism, as in LaRouche's periodic references to Barack Obama as a "monkey" or "chimpanzee."[18]

Along the same lines, in the 1970s, LaRouche blamed women (especially "sadistic" mothers) for causing both sexual and political impotence in men, and engaged in shrill diatribes against feminists and lesbians. In recent decades he has stopped doing this and has written and said little about feminism or women as a group.[19]

The LaRouchites present themselves as saviors of humanity locked in a desperate struggle with the forces of darkness. For decades they have warned that the United States or the world itself is on the brink of imminent economic collapse, full-scale fascist dictatorship, or nuclear war. LaRouche and his followers routinely describe him as one the greatest thinkers in the world and one of the few people able to lead us out of the crisis. They don't just criticize people they disagree with, such as Barack Obama or British Queen Elizabeth II, but demonize them as both subhuman and utterly evil.[20]

LaRouche has argued repeatedly that people can be divided into three levels of "moral development." At the bottom are people who live a "bestial" existence, giving in to their personal impulses and passions or corrupted by irrational ideas—essentially everyone who embraces oligarch-directed evils such as environmentalism, homosexuality, or laissez-faire economics. At the middle level are people who restrain their impulses when these conflict with "natural law." At the top level are those few people who have embraced a higher, universal moral purpose—in plain language, the LaRouchites themselves and their close allies.[21]

LaRouchites believe that people at the lowest moral level are dangerous to society and should not have the same rights as their moral superiors. LaRouche detailed his vision for how to organize a state in a 1981 "draft constitution" for Canada. Those who espouse "irrationalist hedonism" would have no right to express their views, while those who are "insane" or have a "criminal mind" (both defined as expressions of "irrational hedonism") would be barred from voting or running for office. This means that people who don't subscribe to LaRouchite ideology—or who belong to cultures the LaRouchites consider "bestial"—would have no political voice.[22]

Although widely ridiculed as a "wingnut," LaRouche has been more successful than most far rightists in gaining a wider hearing. He has appeared several times on *The Alex Jones Show*, a syndicated radio program that promotes right-wing conspiracy theories and has millions of listeners. LaRouchite conspiracy theories have also repeatedly reached left-leaning audiences, largely with the help of intermediaries such as the Christic Institute (a public interest law firm active in the

1980s), Ramsey Clark (a former U.S. attorney general who has served as LaRouche's lawyer), and the Centre for Research on Globalisation, also known by its web address, GlobalResearch.ca. Former LaRouche network members such as William Engdahl and Webster Tarpley help to extend the network's influence by peddling similar theories, often with a pseudo-leftist gloss. In recent years both Tarpley and Dennis Speed of *Executive Intelligence Review* have spoken at the Left Forum, a major annual conference in New York City that is attended by radicals of many different political backgrounds.[23]

The LaRouche network goes further than most far rightists in combining elements of left and right and in trying to build connections with leftists. They present themselves not only as anti-globalist and anti–Wall Street but also anti-racist, antiwar, and antifascist. They offer an elaborate, seemingly endless set of conspiracy theories that seem calculated to appeal to sections of both the right and the left. LaRouchite ideology is profoundly anti-egalitarian, but—in sharp contrast to white nationalists—the network has largely moved away from explicitly demonizing specific ethnic groups. They have moved toward a generic elitism similar to that of *Attack the System*'s Keith Preston, another former leftist-turned-far rightist who describes the mass of humanity as beast-like and inferior.

In other respects—their cultural conservatism, glorification of centralized nation-states, and cult of personality around their supreme leader—the LaRouchites seem stuck in a different era. Despite their ideological eclecticism, both leftists and fellow rightists alike tend to view them with hostility or derision. Yet every time we hear someone make an absurd claim about George Soros, we should remember that even a small group of crackpots can have a big impact.

Part II

Neglected Themes

6. Gender and Sexual Identity

Issues of gender and sexuality often get short shrift in discussions of the U.S. far right. The far right is often defined as synonymous with the white nationalist movement, for whom race is the overriding issue, while the Christian right and other currents that emphasize gender and sexuality are treated as separate. Discussions of neonazis and other white nationalists don't necessarily address the ways that gender and sexuality permeate and help define racial politics. In addition, when gender and sexuality are discussed, the treatment does not usually explore complexities, contradictions, or debates within the movement or the ways that far right positions on these issues have evolved over time.

These issues are especially important today. In the modern global economy, women's labor—both paid and unpaid—is a valuable prize that different groups of men are battling over. As Bromma, an independent Marxist, has argued:

> A unifying theme of the new capitalist order is that the labor of working-class women is too valuable to leave in the hands of the "man of the house." Women's labor is now to be controlled more directly by capitalists and their professional agents, without all the clumsy and inflexible local mediation formerly assigned to husbands, fathers and brothers. Working-class women must be "free" to move from country to country, from industry to industry, from household to household. They are needed in the industrial zones, needed in giant factory farms, needed as nurses and "entertainers." Their domestic work is increasingly moved out of their own families and merged into great global service industries.

As women have been drawn into the capitalist labor market, growing numbers of men "have been forced into the margins of the labor market, if not out of it altogether." These changes, Bromma argues, have fueled a powerful male backlash, expressed through both widespread physical violence against women and right-wing political activism.[1] Yet the far right itself offers a variety of models for reasserting male control.

For the past hundred years, far right movements in both Europe and North America have promoted politics of gender and sexuality based on some synthesis—or contradictory mixture—of four ideological themes:

Patriarchal traditionalism: Often formulated in religious terms, this theme promotes rigid gender roles based on a romanticized image of the past. Women are confined to domestic roles as wife, mother, caregiver, plus at most a few (under)paid jobs that extend these roles into the wage economy. Women are to obey men, especially fathers and husbands, who are supposed to provide them security and protection (especially, in racist versions, protection against sexually aggressive men of other ethnicities). Traditionalism emphasizes the family as the main framework for male control over women. Homosexuality and gender nonconformity are strictly taboo and treated as immoral, sick, or part of a deliberate effort to undermine the family and the social order. This is the most conservative current of far right gender politics, although the "traditions" being defended are arbitrary, selective, and often made up.

Demographic nationalism: This theme embodies fears that the nation or race is not reproducing fast enough. A variant says that the quality of the national "stock" is declining because of cultural degeneration or racial mixing, and therefore eugenics programs are needed to control human breeding. Demographic nationalism says women's main duty to the nation or race is to have lots of babies (and, in the eugenics variant, the right kind of babies). This doctrine rejects homosexuality as a betrayal of the duty to reproduce, but also sometimes clashes with patriarchal traditionalism—for example, in the Nazis' program to encourage out-of-wedlock births among "racially pure" Germans. Demographic nationalism (especially eugenicist versions) also tends to centralize male control over women through the state, which weakens patriarchal authority within the family.

Male bonding through warfare: This theme emphasizes warfare (hardship, risk of death, shared acts of violence and killing) as the basis for deep emotional and spiritual ties between men. It is often implicitly homoerotic and sometimes celebrates male homosexuality (especially masculine gay men), and is frequently at odds with "bourgeois" family life. In the resulting cult of male comradeship, women may be targets of violent contempt or simply sidelined as irrelevant and unimportant. In Europe during and after World War I, this current flourished as an ideology that spoke to the camaraderie of the trenches and later street-fighting organizations.

Quasi-feminism: This theme advocates specific rights for women (or at least women of the privileged nation or race), such as educational opportunities, equal pay for equal work, and the right to vote, and encourages such women to engage in political activism, develop self-confidence and professional skills, and take on leadership roles. Quasi-feminism may criticize sexist dynamics within the movement or in society more broadly. At the same time, quasi-feminism accepts men's overall dominance, embraces gender roles as natural and immutable, advocates only specific rights for women rather than comprehensive equality, and often promotes intensified oppression for poor or working-class women or women who are targeted on ethnoreligious grounds.

Far right movements have related to these four themes in different ways. Some far right currents have mainly stuck to one theme, while others have combined two or more, depending on their ideology and constituency, and on the pressures and opportunities of a given historical moment. In the United States of the past several decades, far right politics have responded to the feminist and LGBT movements as well as societal changes in family structures, employment, the legal system, and popular culture. While all of these responses have bolstered male dominance, some have been harshly and explicitly patriarchal while others have borrowed feminist ideas and language in distorted form; some have tried to mobilize women by offering them specific benefits, while others have ignored or excluded them. Similarly, while all far right currents have promoted heterosexism and gender conformity, some have offered limited space for certain forms of male homosexuality while others have not.

To varying degrees, far rightists have also fueled and exploited popular fears and resentments against feminists and LGBT activists. For example, male supremacist and former alt-rightist Jack Donovan has portrayed feminists as a powerful group working with elite bureaucrats and wealthy men to disempower middle- and working-class men.[2] Fear of homosexuality has offered a particularly useful mobilizing tool. As Mab Segrest and Leonard Zeskind have pointed out, "Because homosexuality appears randomly across the population, anybody—or anybody's children—could possibly 'be one,' so the fear of homosexuality affects a much wider audience than the actual presence of gay men and lesbians and provides a convenient lever for the politics of fear."[3]

The Lyndon LaRouche network, for example, has both fueled and exploited homophobia for over forty years. In the 1970s, Lyndon LaRouche gained psychological control over his own followers through cult psychology tactics—including playing on their fears of being homosexual. In the following years, homophobic slurs became a routine part of LaRouche conspiracist propaganda. As mentioned in the previous chapter, in 1986 and 1987, the LaRouchites sponsored two ballot initiatives in California to "quarantine" people with AIDS, exploiting the widely held belief that AIDS was a "gay disease." The measures were defeated but received 2 million and 1.7 million votes, respectively, and, in Dennis King's words, "desensitized millions to the idea of rounding up unpopular minorities."[4]

Historical forerunners

Historically, rightist movements in the United States have addressed gender politics in different ways, attacking but also to varying degrees accommodating women's expanded roles and assertions of social and political autonomy. In the late nineteenth and early twentieth centuries, early Protestant fundamentalists glorified a Victorian ideal of the "true woman" who guarded virtue and spirituality within the family. They denounced "sinful" modern women who challenged sexual constraints, worked outside the home, and demanded the right to vote. In the 1920s, the mass movement "Second Era" Knights of the Ku Klux Klan echoed these sentiments and rationalized their own secrecy and violence as chivalrous defense of morality and Protestant white womanhood. But in this same period, the semi-autonomous Women of the

Ku Klux Klan (WKKK), with half a million members, criticized gender inequality among white Protestants and described the home as a place of "monstrous and grinding toil and sacrifice" for women. The WKKK built directly on earlier women's suffrage and temperance movements, which often blended feminism with racism and nativism.[5]

In the United States, demographic nationalism first came to prominence in the early 1900s, when "race suicide" propagandists—including President Theodore Roosevelt—warned that the birthrate was declining among native-born whites. Roosevelt is widely remembered today as a reformer who attacked (some) corporate monopolies, promoted environmental conservation, and split with conservative Republicans to launch the Progressive (Bull Moose) Party in 1912. But Roosevelt was also militantly antisocialist and an aggressive proponent of global white supremacy (or, as he put it, rule by the "mighty civilized races" over the "barbarian peoples of the world").[6] Roosevelt supported women's suffrage and equalization of property laws and job opportunities for women and men, but also declared that a woman who avoided having children was a "criminal against the race... the object of contemptuous abhorrence by healthy people."[7] Roosevelt promoted gender roles in the framework of national duty: a man's highest obligation was to fight for his country, and a woman's was to raise a family of children. Roosevelt also warned that American men and boys were becoming effeminate and exhorted them to be tough, aggressive, hardworking, and courageous. Roosevelt was influenced by the "muscular Christianity" movement, which emphasized physical fitness and created the Young Men's Christian Association (YMCA), and he helped promote the Boy Scouts as an organization that trained males to be both virile and patriotic.[8]

The eugenics movement took demographic nationalism a step further. Between 1905 and 1922, fifteen states made it legal to involuntarily sterilize institutionalized people who were considered "unfit"—notably those labeled "insane," "feeble-minded," or "sexually degenerate." Eventually, more than thirty states passed such laws, and over sixty thousand people were involuntarily sterilized as a result.[9] These laws later served as a model for Nazi Germany's own eugenics program. In the 1920s, eugenics was a required subject at many U.S. universities, and many public fairs included "fitter family" contests, where blue ribbons went to those with the best pedigrees based on eugenic standards. Like the race suicide theorists, most eugenicists considered women useful mainly as breeders. Eugenics policy later shifted focus from improving the "racial stock" among whites to sterilizing women of color, often without their consent. According to some studies, this led to the eventual sterilization of over one third of Puerto Rican and over one quarter of Indigenous women.[10] Such practices continued into the 1980s and beyond.[11]

During the late 1930s and early '40s, the so-called mothers' movement rallied millions of ultraconservative and pro-fascist women who opposed U.S. support for the Allies in World War II. Organizations such as We the Mothers Mobilize for America and National Legion of Mothers of America represented a significant force within the anti-interventionist movement. These groups offered a curious twist on patriarchal traditionalism: they argued that mothers' nurturing nature made them the strongest champions of peace, yet applauded Nazi Germany.[12] One of the movement's main leaders, Cathryn Curtis, even offered a maternalist version of producerism, claiming that women were the true protectors of productive, industrial capitalism against destructive, male-inspired military capitalism.[13] While the mothers' movement glorified traditional families and rejected feminism, some of its leaders urged women to think for themselves and declared that women could govern better than men.[14]

Homosexuality became more visible in U.S. society during the 1940s. Partly as a result, as historian John D'Emilio has documented, Cold War witch-hunters in the early 1950s targeted gay men and lesbians alongside suspected Communists as a major threat to American society and national security. Thousands of "sexual perverts" were fired from government and private jobs or discharged from the military as undesirable. In right-wing propaganda, gay men and lesbians, like Communists, were dangerously immoral people who had secretly infiltrated all institutions and threatened to corrupt all those with whom they came in contact. "Communists taught children to betray their parents; mannish women mocked the ideals of marriage and motherhood.... Weak-willed, pleasure-seeking homosexuals—'half-men'—feminized everything they touched and sapped the masculine vigor that had tamed a continent."[15]

The modern Christian right, which first emerged on a mass scale in the 1970s, put gender and sexual politics at the center of its program. The movement largely represented a reaction to the 1960s upsurge of movements for women's liberation and gay liberation, and promoted patriarchal traditionalism through initiatives against the Equal Rights

Amendment, abortion rights, and LGBT rights. Christian rightists attacked both feminism and homosexuality as immoral, anti-family, elitist, and part of a secular-humanist conspiracy to weaken and ultimately enslave America.

The Christian right recruited large numbers of women with a contradictory blend of messages. On the one hand, the movement promoted a system of gender roles that offered many women a sense of security and meaning and, in Andrea Dworkin's words, "promise[d] to put enforceable restraints on male aggression."[16] Women were told that if they agreed to be obedient housewives and mothers, their husbands would reward them with protection, economic support, and love. Feminism was denounced as unnatural, man-hating, and a dangerous rejection of the safety that the traditional family supposedly offered women.

Within this overall framework, however, Christian rightists often framed their arguments in terms borrowed from feminism, for example, arguing that abortion "exploits women" or that federal support for childcare is wrong because it supposedly limits women's choices.[17] To varying degrees, some Christian right groups encouraged many women to become more self-confident and assertive, speak publicly, take on leadership roles, and get graduate training—as long as they did so in the service of the movement's patriarchal agenda.[18] In 1976, Christian right leaders Timothy and Beverly LaHaye published a bestselling sex manual, titled *The Act of Marriage*, which declared that (married, heterosexual) women have a right to sexual pleasure, endorsed birth control, and encouraged women to be active in lovemaking.[19]

In 1979, Beverly LaHaye founded Concerned Women for America (CWA), which today claims over half a million members and calls itself "the nation's largest public policy women's organization." CWA vilifies feminism as a threat to the traditional family and healthy moral values, but it also seeks to appeal to a mass audience of women who don't necessarily reject all feminist positions. For example, CWA's president, Penny Nance, has argued that it's a violation of religious liberty to require health insurers to pay for contraception, but the organization doesn't officially oppose contraception itself, claiming its members "hold a variety of views on the subject."[20]

CWA has often used feminist-sounding language about letting women think for themselves and make their own decisions. An article rejecting calls for wage equality between women and men concludes, "Women's career plans come in all different shapes and sizes.

They have different needs....Stop trying to force ill-conceived policies on women that will ultimately hurt them in the workforce! In the rare instances of sex-based wage discrimination, there are already laws on the books which address it. *That* is something which all women should applaud."[21] An article opposing federal funding for birth control accuses feminists of believing that "Women are irresponsible. Women cannot make informed choices. Without the government bailing them out or telling them what to do, women just wander hither and yon like helpless kittens."[22] In such ways, Christian rightists have used the language of women's empowerment to bolster their patriarchal agenda.

But like the rest of the Christian right, CWA has been unambiguous in rejecting LGBT experiences. CWA claims that "homosexual sex is dangerous and destructive to the human body," and has denounced same-sex marriage as "an abomination to God," harmful to children, and "as wrong as giving a man a license to marry his mother or daughter or sister or a group."[23] CWA has also declared that "transgenderism is a form of broken sexuality" at odds with the immutable, physical sex categories that God created.[24]

Driving perversion underground

Within the Christian right, self-avowed dominionists have played a leading role in promoting harsher forms of heterosexist and male supremacist politics. At the same time, there are significant differences in this area between different forms of dominionism. While both Christian Reconstructionism and New Apostolic Reformation have advocated violent repression against homosexuality, Reconstructionists are at the forefront of the biblical patriarchy movement, while some NAR advocates have promoted quasi-feminism to varying degrees.

Like other Christian rightists, Reconstructionists believe that homosexuality is sinful and a serious threat to the social fabric. American Vision has argued, for example, that legalizing same-sex marriage (or, as they put it, "requiring homosexual marriage") would "undermine the created male-female order," stifle religious freedom, sexualize children, legalize incest, and "could bring God's judgment on the Nation."[25] Colorado pastor Kevin Swanson has warned that homosexuality is being promoted through Disney films, women's soccer, day care, country music, and the Girl Scouts.[26]

But unlike many Christian rightists, Reconstructionists also state openly that in their ideal society homosexuality would be punishable by death. Rushdoony declared this in the 1970s, and numerous Reconstructionist leaders have reiterated it in recent years.[27] Reconstructionists explain that the death penalty would only be implemented after most people have embraced their ideology, and it would not be used to wipe out gay people but mainly as a deterrent to suppress their behavior. As Gary DeMar put it, "The law that requires the death penalty for homosexual acts effectually drives the perversion of homosexuality underground, back to the closet, to the dark realm of shameful activity."[28]

By comparison, some adherents of New Apostolic Reformation—a movement that straddles the divide between system-loyal and oppositional politics—have tried to stake out a more moderate public position on homosexuality. NAR prophet Johnny Enlow commented (with an implicit swipe at Reconstructionists' dream of reimposing Old Testament law), "Society does need to know that homosexual behavior is wrong but it would not be defensible to execute homosexuals any more than it would be to execute rebellious children—which is espoused to some measure in Leviticus. . . . [W]e do not need the extreme punishments of the Old Testament." NAR founder C. Peter Wagner went even further: "To legislate against sexual orientation is probably crossing the line. . . . It's much too much of a personal ethical issue."[29] But these disavowals seem insincere, given that many other NAR leaders have aggressively promoted homophobic legislation. For example, Lou Engle, a member of the NAR leadership group, the Apostolic Council of Prophetic Elders, has spearheaded many anti-gay events, such as a 2008 mass rally supporting California's Proposition 8 ballot measure to ban same-sex marriage. Two years later, Engle and other NAR leaders organized a rally in Uganda in support of a bill that would have imposed the death penalty for gay sex.[30]

Calling your husband "Lord"

Christian Reconstructionism and New Apostolic Reformation differ more starkly in their positions regarding women's roles in the family, society, and political life. Over the past three decades, Reconstructionists have spearheaded a shift away from the quasi-feminism exemplified by Concerned Women for America to a much harsher ideology of male dominance. In 2008, when the Republican Party nominated Christian conservative Sarah Palin as its vice presidential candidate, Reconstructionist Doug Phillips commented:

> Today, our friend Janice Crouse of Concerned Women for America offered a press release in which she declared: "Here is a woman of accomplishment who brings a fresh face to traditional values and models the type of woman most girls want to become."... I respectfully disagree with part of that statement. I am confident that Mrs. Palin is a delightful, sincere, thoughtful, and capable woman with many commendable virtues. But in fairness, there is nothing "traditional" about mothers of young children becoming career moms, chief magistrates, and leading nations of three hundred million, nor is this pattern the Biblical ideal to which young women should aspire.[31]

Christian Reconstructionists have led the rise of the biblical patriarchy movement (which emphasizes that a woman's number one religious duty is "submission" to her husband) and its branch known as Quiverfull (which calls for couples to have as many babies as possible). Kathryn Joyce summarizes these doctrines:

> The "biblical" woman wears modest, feminine dress and avoids not only sex but also dating before marriage. She doesn't speak in church or try to have authority over men. She doesn't work outside the home, but within it she is its tireless center: homeschooling her children, keeping house, cooking bulk meals, and helping her husband run a home business or ministry. She checks in with her husband as she moves through her day to see if she is fulfilling his priorities for her. When he comes home, she is a submissive wife who bolsters him in his role as spiritual and earthly leader of the family. She understands it's her job to keep him sexually satisfied

at all times and that it's her calling as a woman to let those relations result in as many children as God wants to bless her with. She
raises families of eight, ten, and twelve children, and she teaches
her daughters to do the same. She's not the throwback to the fif-
ties summoned in media-stoked "mommy wars"; she is a return to
something far older.[32]

This "something far older," in Joyce's view, is Reconstructionism's idealized version of seventeenth-century Puritan society: "a collection of
autonomous patriarchal households under the authority of the local
church. America before democracy." Or to put it in slightly different
terms, "it would be a form of Christian feudalism." In keeping with this
vision, biblical patriarchy advocates oppose women's suffrage, arguing
that it's the husband's role to be the political voice for his family.[33]

The Reconstructionist organization Vision Forum, headed by Doug
Phillips, played a key role in promoting biblical patriarchy from its
founding in 1998 until 2013, when it closed its doors after Phillips admitted having an extramarital affair. Other Reconstructionist proponents
of biblical patriarchy include Scott Brown, director of the National
Center for Family-Integrated Churches, and Kevin Swanson, head of
Christian Home Educators of Colorado.[34] A slightly watered down version of biblical patriarchy known as complementarianism (as in, men's
and women's God-given roles are different but complementary) has a
much wider reach among Protestant evangelicals and is promoted by
groups such as the Council on Biblical Manhood & Womanhood.[35]

Biblical patriarchy's vision of godly husbands and fathers benevo-
lently ruling over their families offers obvious privilege benefits to men.
And as Cheryl Seelhoff, an ex-Quiverfull woman turned feminist, ob-
serves, "many otherwise ordinary men with ordinary jobs who didn't
command high levels of respect, societally, found a way to obtain respect in the Quiverfull community by being the leader of a devout, large
family—the husband of a submissive wife, raising sons who would be
future leaders in the church and daughters who would bear large families and care for them at home, and so on."[36]

What biblical patriarchy offers to women is more complex but also
important. Unlike white nationalism, which aims to remove or extermi-
nate those defined as Other, biblical patriarchy (like most male supremacist doctrines) keeps the subordinate Other within the home on terms
of intimate interdependence. As a result, biblical patriarchy requires

constant indoctrination of women and girls to get them to accept and, if possible, embrace their subordinate position. Many of the authors and bloggers who promote and articulate this ideology are themselves women. Biblical patriarchy praises women who fulfill their appointed roles as wives, homemakers, and mothers of large families, and tells them that "feminism" (which it falsely equates with capitalist mass culture) treats these roles with contempt. It tells them that feminism's vision of independence, freedom, and equality for women is a dangerous illusion. In this view, women can't really choose between freedom and slavery; their choice is slavery to sin or slavery to God. Yet slavery to God is itself the only true freedom: freedom from sin and freedom from burdens that women were never meant to bear, such as having to make decisions for themselves or their families.[37]

Biblical patriarchy tells women and girls that feminism is their original sin—Eve's sin of disobedience to godly authority. It warns them to avoid anything—such as higher education or close friendships with other women—that might come before loyalty to their husband or encourage them to think independently. It teaches them that their body belongs to their husband, not to them. It teaches them to trust men and not themselves. In Seelhoff's words, it teaches them to "believe themselves to be easily deceived, manipulative, likely to deceive, 'unclean,' in need of protection from men, and in great danger if they are out from under men's protection."[38]

In *Building God's Kingdom: Inside the World of Christian Reconstruction* (2015) religious studies scholar Julie Ingersoll describes how the use of "church courts" for resolving marital disputes further helps to disempower women. These courts can punish church members by demanding repentance, denying communion, or ordering excommunication:

> Women are disproportionately vulnerable in these cases in that they often have no financial resources or work experience they can take with them. With the husband as patriarch, it is considered reasonable for the assets to be in his name. Because of the way in which submission teaching is understood, marital problems are frequently blamed on women, and the men in authority close ranks around the husbands. If a husband is unfaithful, questions arise as to the wife's submission to her husband's sexual desires.... The reverse situation is rarely the case: that is, if a woman has an adulterous

relationship she is denounced as a "Jezebel," and it is rare that her failing is attributed to some inadequacy on her husband's part. Furthermore, these judicial processes are administered entirely by men, who have a vested interest in preserving the male privilege afforded by patriarchy. ... The women facing charges, furthermore, are risking additional charges of "gossiping" and insubordination to church authorities if they talk openly to anyone about the case.[39]

In terms of the four gender ideology themes that I outlined above, biblical patriarchy and Quiverfull represent the most extreme version of patriarchal traditionalism, but Quiverfull, specifically, also incorporates a strong secondary element of demographic nationalism. If having big families is primarily about avoiding sin, to Quiverfull advocates, it is also a way to expand the population of faithful Christians and eventually overpower unbelievers through sheer numbers. In addition, Quiverfull advocates (most of whom are in the United States) have made common cause with other Christian rightists in warning Europeans against the threat of "demographic winter." This campaign exploits fears that declining birthrates among white Europeans, coupled with rising numbers of darker-skinned and Muslim immigrants, will destroy Europe's cultural and racial identity. To ward off this fate, Quiverfull advocates urge Europeans to reject the evils of abortion, contraception, and feminism; reaffirm the patriarchal family; and accept their reproductive responsibility. Here, as elsewhere, theocratic ideology incorporates an implicit white nationalism.[40]

All believers called to be priests

The New Apostolic Reformation movement is much more racially diverse and inclusive than Christian Reconstructionism, and it promotes a strikingly different model of women's social and political roles as well. Like Reconstructionism, NAR is a theocratic movement that wants to impose a deeply repressive moral code across all spheres of society, but this vision, unlike biblical patriarchy, allows significant room for women's agency and voice. New Apostolic Reformers declare that God created men and women differently and with different roles, yet in NAR

a number of women not only serve as ministers but hold high international leadership roles in the movement as prophets and apostles—
something that would be inconceivable in Reconstructionism.[41]

A range of positions on this issue can be found within the NAR movement. At the more conservative end, Rick Joyner, head of MorningStar
Ministries and a prominent NAR author, has stated that according to
the Bible the husband is the head of the wife as Christ is the head of the
church, and a godly wife is to obey her husband even if he is ungodly.
But this does not mean "that a godly woman should submit to things
that are ungodly or unlawful." She may resist, "if it is done with respect for her husband, and not in a rebellious spirit," a line that sounds
difficult to walk in practice. Less ambiguously, Joyner has rejected the
"devastating" doctrine that the husband is "the priest" of his home, because "all believers are called to be priests, which includes both men and
women. In fact, women in general, tend to be much better intercessors
and priests in the home than men do." He also disagreed with those who
claim that male headship of the family "puts all women under all men,"
a claim at odds with the authority held by some women in the NAR
movement.[42]

Cindy Jacobs, co-leader of Generals International and one of the top-
ranking women in NAR, has argued more directly for "empowering
women" in an article about her own personal efforts to "break strongholds that strangle destiny." Such "strongholds" included intimidation,
fear of other people's opinions, personal insecurities, and tradition:

> Growing up in the South, in the United States, tradition was an-
> other of my big strongholds. Good Christian Southern women
> simply did not travel around the world and preach the gospel! ... I
> struggled intensely with accepting the call of God upon my life as a
> minister of the gospel. ... I guess I was afraid of people's reactions.
> Now, I am proud (in a righteous way) of sharing what I do in God's
> kingdom.

Jacobs concluded by urging women not to be "bound by the opinion of
man (or woman)" but to follow God's calling, whether to be a homemaker or to be a missionary.[43]

Jacobs's *Generals International* website has also provided a forum for
a number of other female NAR ministers to speak out on gender issues.
In an article reposted on several other NAR websites, Diane Lake of

Christian International Ministries found biblical support for women's leadership, noting that Deborah served as judge in ancient Israel and women worked with Paul in apostolic ministry. She concluded, "The army of God is on the move and about to significantly advance—and *we will not take the kingdom with half an army*."[44] Lonnie Crowe argued that viewing Eve as the conduit through which sin entered Creation was the result of "faulty Biblical exegesis" and declared that "We all, *male and female*, have equality and redemption through our covenant in Christ Jesus."[45]

In a particularly startling article on the *Generals International* website, pastor Tisha Sledd declared that women were "fighting to be freed from" a "system of patriarchal beliefs," starting with the "misguided" belief that men were called to be masters of women. "When Christ died, He wiped out the curse that Eve's sin brought upon women. There is no reason to 'desire to control our husbands,' nor is there a need for our husbands to 'rule over us' (Genesis 3:16). The blood of Jesus obliterated this curse. We are now free." Skillfully reappropriating the concept of wifely submission, Sledd wrote, "I submit to my husband, and he submits to me by giving himself up for me. We submit to one another out of reverence for Christ.... There are no 'masters' in our home.... There can be two powerful people in the home without emasculating the man or defeminizing the woman."[46]

In an article on her own ministry's website entitled "How Patriarchy Is Killing the American Church," Sledd stated that she was a "suffragist" but not a "feminist," because feminism was rooted in "selfishness and anger" and had been "hijacked by women who hate men." In contrast, a suffragist believed that women were "equal to men in every way" and "deserve the right to vote in every facet of society." In the United States, "Women have made great strides in equality in government and in the marketplace [but] when it comes to Christendom, women are not equal in the home or the church."[47] Elsewhere, Sledd recounted her personal "Journey Out of Bondage to Male Headship," in which she experienced spiritual growth faster than her husband and gradually rejected "lies" from others in her original church who wanted her to submit to men.[48]

We should be careful not to overgeneralize from these writings. Given the patriarchal Christendom that Sledd has described, it's unlikely that the average NAR congregation is supportive of women challenging male control. But the fact that articles advocating women's empowerment have been featured in influential NAR forums, coupled with the prominent leadership roles that some women hold in the movement, points to a political culture in which there is far more space for women to speak and act than under Reconstructionist biblical patriarchy. As far as I can tell, this issue has received little or no attention from critics of New Apostolic Reformation, although there has been extensive coverage for years warning about NAR ideology, activism, and political connections. Yet NAR's quasi-feminist tendencies are important both because they force us to rethink standard assumptions about the Christian far right, and because they highlight the far right's capacity to appropriate progressive, egalitarian politics for its own repressive, anti-egalitarian, and anti-humanist goals.

Both warriors and bearers of the race

The neonazi movement, too, has offered a range of positions on women's roles. For neonazis, racial ideology is the overarching framework that shapes their gender politics. In general, neonazis promote subordination for all women, but in different ways depending on racial identity. For example, White Aryan Resistance and other neonazi groups have opposed abortion for white women but supported it for women of color.[49] Drawing on old themes prominent in both U.S. white supremacy and European fascism, many neonazis emphasize a need to control non-Jewish white women's bodies so as to maintain the purity of the race. In propaganda works such as William Pierce's *The Turner Diaries*, combating interracial sex is a major concern, particularly the victimization of innocent white women by black rapists and Jewish pimps, as well as racial treason by white women who willingly have sex with men of color.

In a 1982 article, Pierce offered an overview of sexual rules based on racial ideology:

> [T]he primary purpose of sexual activity is the upbreeding of the race. The strongest taboo, then, must be against any sexual activity which tends to degrade the race.... Next in order of sinfulness is an act of symbolic degradation. The act of a man and woman intended to engender a healthy, white child should be viewed as a

sacramental act. Even when a sex act is not specifically sacramental—i.e., not intended to produce children—it ought not to be of a nature which clashes with sacramental sex or which tends to undermine or distort the basic view of sexual activity. Thus bestiality and homosexuality are beyond the pale, just as interracial sex with a sterile partner (or involving contraception) is.[50]

Although white supremacist rightists have fixated on interracial sex for much of U.S. history, they have focused on homosexuality only since the 1970s, in response to the rise of gay and lesbian activism. Since then, neonazis have been implicated in a number of violent anti-LGBT attacks, such as the 1987 murder of three men at a gay bookstore in Shelby, North Carolina (for which two former members of the White Patriot Party were indicted but not convicted), and Eric Rudolph's 1997 bombing of an Atlanta lesbian bar, which injured five people.[51] Starting in the 1980s, neonazis exploited anti-gay fears associated with the AIDS crisis in an effort to win popular support. Harold Covington argued in his 1987 book *The March Upcountry* that AIDS represented a strategic opportunity for the movement:

> I now feel that any white revolutionary party needs to upgrade the struggle against pervision [sic] significantly.... It is now the area in which the enemy is arguably the most vulnerable, thanks to those four little letters that are God's greatest gift to our cause since the Fuhrer Adolph Hitler himself: A-I-D-S! ... it has galvanized White opinion worldwide in a manner nothing else has done.... At long last, using AIDS as an excuse, White people could really say what they felt about faggots! And from saying and openly admitting what they really feel about queers, it is only a short step to saying what they really feel about those other major AIDS carriers, the blacks.... And who knows? Once Whites get really used to speaking their mind, maybe Yehudi [the Jew] himself might come in for a mention or two.[52]

To some extent neonazis call for implementing sexual rules through patriarchal traditionalism—centered on controlling white women within the family. But many neonazis also emphasize demographic nationalism and—in sharp contrast with Christian rightists—advocate eugenicist policies to improve the white race's fitness and purity. The current

American Nazi Party (not to be confused with the 1960s organization of the same name), for example, has declared that "Aryan men and Aryan women have distinctive but complementary social roles to play, and that just as the man is the natural breadwinner and warrior, so the woman is the natural homemaker." But the party has also called for the state to impose "positive eugenic measures" to promote "propagation of the highest racial elements," as well as steps "to halt the spread of hereditary defects and racially impure blood within the gene pool of the racial community."[53] The National Socialist Movement has called for reestablishing "the nuclear family in which the father works while the mother stays at home and takes care of the children if they so choose." It also advocates "a structured system of pay raises for those that give birth to healthy babies" and prohibiting "abortion and euthanasia, except in cases of rape, incest, race-mixing, or mental retardation."[54]

On the broader questions of women's roles in the movement and in society, neonazis range from hard-line misogyny to quasi-feminism. In the 1980s and '90s, Aryan Nations and National Alliance tended to oppose paid employment and any public political role for women.[55] Aryan Nations declared, "feminism is the means to weaken Aryan masculinity, promoted by the international Jew."[56] More recently, the Vanguard News Network (VNN) has continued this line of thought. VNN founder Alex Linder claimed, for example, that

> Women are repeaters. It is not in them to originate or create anything but a baby except in the most unusual case.... Plenty of women are smart, but only in a mechanical sense.... Smart women are just able to access the answer authority wants to hear quicker than others—but they can't truly think about anything. It really is true, what Schopenhauer (said)—men are what is referred to when we speak of humans. Women are just ways of getting new men.[57]

VNN has also attacked women's supposed political power. One VNN post, entitled "The Female Vote: a Terrible Idea Since 1920," declared:

> And it isn't just female voting that's a problem, it's female power in general: women have much more power today than they did in 1970. They control big businesses. They often hold positions of legislative power, and they often control households as well. That's not a good thing. White men built Western culture and only White

men can manage it properly. One big consequence of more female power is the incredible growth of the federal government. Women, like liberals, are big believers in federal power.[58]

However, quasi-feminism has also been represented in the neonazi movement. For example, in the 1980s and '90s, Molly Gill of St. Petersburg, Florida, edited a neonazi newsletter under a series of titles: *Independent Woman, The Radical Feminist*, and *The Rational Feminist*. Gill wrote that she had been involved in the women's movement since 1977 and served on the Board of Directors of the First Tampa Bay Women's Rape Crisis Center. In the spring 1991 issue, she explained, "We use the term 'radical feminist' to indicate that we agree in general with the principles in the book, *The Sexual Liberals and the Attack on Feminism*" (an anthology of anti-pornography feminist writings published in 1990). "We oppose the exploitation of women in any form, to a greater degree than other feminist factions such as NOW, anarchist feminists, etc."[59] A regular feature of Gill's publication was the "Feminist Counseling Column," which for example argued that "over-controlling, domineering daddies" were often to blame for young women "running with men of other races." "So don't ride herd too hard," Gill cautioned white fathers, "or she's likely to slip in a little miscegenation."[60]

Tom Metzger's White Aryan Resistance (WAR), too, has long promoted a racist quasi-feminism. In the 1980s, WAR sponsored an affiliate called the Aryan Women's League, which declared that white women had important roles to play both as mothers and nurturers on the one hand and as "women warriors fighting to save our noble Aryan race" through direct political activism.[61] Long after its influence in the movement collapsed, WAR's gender politics remained the same. WAR's web page on "Women," posted in or around 2000, conceded that "No intelligent White man or woman would deny the physical, biological and chemical differences between the two sexes," such as average physical strength or "the special bond of a mother and her child." But the page went on to criticize (white) women's oppression and blamed it primarily on Judaism and Christianity, which it rejected as an offshoot of Judaism:

The same religion that wrongly promotes the myth that all men are created equal, also promotes a negative attitude towards our White women. The Right Wing or conservative movement and the racial elements thereof, have perpetuated some very negative attitudes also. These positions have caused, in part, the political flight of many capable women, into the arms of lesbianism and race mixing.... Let's not help our enemies by putting up Middle Eastern and Asiatic based roadblocks to male/female unity.[62]

Along similar lines, the international group Women for Aryan Unity (WAU), founded in 1990, called in its Mission Statement for "reinventing the concept of 'feminism' within the parameters of Race and Revolution." WAU projects included the Frigga Award, for mothers who make special contributions to the Aryan cause, and raising money for imprisoned "Brüder" (brothers) of the paramilitary group The Order. In the 2010s, the Creativity Movement–affiliated group Women's Frontier rejected "the twisted, unnatural Jewish feminist concept of womanhood" and the idea of male-female equality, yet encouraged women to become activists and leaders as well as mothers, wives, and helpers of men. The Women's Frontier website offered a "Women of History" page that features English fascist Diana Mosley and English royals Elizabeth I and Eleanor of Aquitaine, but also Hypatia (a fourth-century Greek-Egyptian philosopher who was murdered by a Christian mob), Emilie du Chatelet (an eighteenth-century French mathematician and physicist), and Edith Flanigen (a twentieth-century chemist who helped improve petroleum refining technology), among others.[63]

Sociologist Kathleen Blee conducted a study of women who were active in "Ku Klux Klan, neo-Nazi, Christian Identity, white-power, skinhead, and other white-supremacist groups" in the mid-1990s.[64] She noted widespread conflict within such groups over women's roles, for example in white supremacist skinhead groups: "Many skin groups are intensely male-dominated and violently misogynist ... " yet "skinhead women are often the racist movements' most physically aggressive women, and at least some prominent skinhead women publicly confront the sexism of male skinhead culture."[65]

Blee also found that female activists' experiences were often much more negative than the propaganda image of Aryan women warriors. While some white supremacist women she spoke with felt empowered by racist activism, many others spoke of "having made great sacrifices to be in a movement that gave them little in return." To some extent this reflected the specific demands that white supremacist groups placed on female members, especially the intense focus on biological reproduction, "ensuring the purity of racial bloodlines ... and increasing white birthrates." But many of the frustrations that these women activists experienced reflected sexist dynamics common to other social movements, including liberal and leftist ones: women were "expected to perform material and wifely roles," relegated to "middle-level and informal leadership positions," and frustrated with their organizations' failure to address their needs."[66]

A matter of privacy and decency

Patriot activists have not addressed gender or sexuality as much as Christian rightists or even neonazis have. The Patriot movement is predominantly male, but women have played a significant if largely overlooked role. One of the movement's early leaders was Linda Thompson, an Indianapolis lawyer who produced a series of influential videos that featured conspiracist claims about federal government repression. In 1994, as self-declared "Acting Adjutant General of the Unorganized Militia of the U.S.A.," Thompson called for an armed march on Washington to try federal officials for treason. (Other Patriot leaders denounced the plan and Thompson canceled the march.) As a Patriot activist, Thompson regularly denounced abortion, but before joining the movement she had been known as "a very feminist, pro-woman civil rights lawyer" and had compared anti-abortion activists to the Ku Klux Klan.[67]

As in some neonazi groups, women's roles in the Patriot movement reflect a mix of patriarchal traditionalism and quasi-feminism. The authors of *Up in Arms: A Guide to Oregon's Patriot Movement* argue that "despite the movement's overwhelmingly macho tone, it is not an entirely male movement, and despite its hostility to feminism, women can take roles as either leaders or 'helpers' in the movement." They cite several examples of Patriot women in movement leadership positions such as lecturer, self-appointed judge, and "intelligence officer."[68] When Patriot activists occupied the Malheur Wildlife Refuge in Oregon in late 2015, men were most of those carrying weapons and giving speeches to the media, while most of the women occupiers cooked, organized supplies, and stayed in the background. "We women, we are helpers," said one. "That's how we are created, and that's what we do here."[69] But other activists disagree. "Women Patriots cannot be stuck in a box—we are free and diverse," proclaimed "Patriot Patricia" on one movement website. "We are daughters, mothers, grandmothers, professionals and business owners. Many of us are smart, educated, independent, and accomplished women, who also love our country's founding princi- ples.... Any man who stands in the way is on the other team."[70]

Journalist Elinor Burkett recounted conversations with many Patriot movement women in her 1998 book, *The Right Women: A Journey Through the Heart of Conservative America.* Carolyn Trochmann (then wife of Militia of Montana leader John Trochmann) told Burkett that women should not have the right to vote because it's a violation of family values, but also declared, "Too many women allow fear to manipulate or control them. They need to work on their self-esteem. I don't need anybody or anything to tell me who I am, what I am capable of doing." Some of those who spoke with Burkett believed that women should not work outside the home, while others opposed restrictions on abortion because—even though they considered it murder—they were more concerned about government controlling citizens' lives.[71]

In many rural western states, Burkett saw Patriot women embody- ing a strong regional tradition that often rejects organized feminism but asserts women's competence and independence. Lee Ann Callear (a campaign organizer for ultraconservative congress member and Patriot movement ally Helen Chenoweth) told her, "I have five sisters and we've all been liberated since birth. The way I figure it, if you want to be liberated, why don't you just be liberated? Why do you have to talk about it all the time? If men are a problem, just go around them like a brick wall. You don't need to bash it down. It's not all that wide."[72]

To the extent that they address issues of sexuality, Patriot groups have offered positions ranging from overt anti-LGBT hostility to a more veiled "I-don't-care-what-homosexuals-do-in-private" stance. Some Patriot activists emphasize the libertarian theme of keeping gov- ernment out of people's personal affairs, while others echo claims that nonconformity in sexuality or gender is either sinful or part of a plot to undermine American society. Both of these positions can be found, for example, in a 2011 discussion thread about "the homosexual agenda" on the *ThreePercenter.org* website. One commenter wrote, "I think it's fairly stupid to attach some type of 'morality' to ones [sic] sexual prefer- ences and fetishes (provided they are non violent and practiced among consenting adults). As far as marriage, removing the government from the institution solves pretty much every problem with the so called 'gay marriage issue'...leave it up to churches/mosques/synaguages [sic]/ temples...." But on the same thread others wrote that "the gay movement" was "just another branch of the socialist tyrannical agenda" and that "It's part of the bigger plan to feminize males so they'll be as intimidated by authority as women and children who have a natural predisposition to want to please over bearing [sic] and threatening authority!"[73]

Oath Keepers has opposed federal efforts to extend civil rights protections to LGBT people as a dangerous and illegal extension of government power. For example, in 2015, Kim Davis, county clerk in Rowan County, Kentucky, refused to issue marriage licenses to same-sex couples; because she was defying a federal court order, she was jailed for several days. In response, Oath Keepers offered to provide Davis with a security team to protect her against possible rearrest by the U.S. Marshals Service. (Davis declined the offer.) Oath Keepers declared, "We would like to stress in the strongest terms possible that we are doing this not because of her views on gay marriage, but because she is an elected public servant who has been illegally arrested and held without due process."[74] But the group has also promoted overt anti-LGBT activism, for example favorably publicizing a Christian right petition to boycott Target stores after Target instituted a policy allowing transgender people to use the bathroom of their choice. Oath Keepers commented, "it is a matter of privacy and decency for men to use men's facilities and women to use women's facilities."[75] More bluntly, Oath Keepers cosponsored two "Racial Reconciliation" rallies with James David Manning, an African American pastor who is virulently homophobic. At the July 2015 event, Manning led the crowd in chanting, "Sodomites, go to Hell!" and offered similar comments throughout his sermon.[76]

Without women getting in the way

In recent years the alt-right has revitalized far right politics in the U.S. with skillful online activism and a dynamic relationship with Donald Trump's political candidacy. Alt-right ideology centers on white nationalism but also draws on other political currents, some of which focus on reasserting male dominance more than on racial issues. Although alt-rightists largely echo neonazi positions on gender and sexuality, there are some notable differences. Alt-rightists have generally repudiated quasi-feminism and thus are, if anything, even more harshly misogynistic than many neonazis of recent decades. At the same time, in sharp contrast to U.S. neonazism, alt-rightists do not necessarily reject homosexuality. A few openly homosexual men have been important participants in alt-right forums, and alt-rightists have actively debated the place of homosexuality in the movement and in the white race's history and future.

As discussed in chapter 4, harassment and vilification of women and girls has been central to the alt-right's political activism. Such tactics reflect an intense misogyny that runs through the movement. Most of the alt-right declares that women are intellectually and morally inferior to men and should be stripped of any political role.

Alt-rightists have claimed that it's natural for men to rule over women and that women want and need this, that "giving women freedom [was] one of mankind's greatest mistakes," that women should "never be allowed to make foreign policy [because] their vindictiveness knows no bounds," and that feminism is defined by mental illness and has turned women into "caricatures of irrationality and hysteria."[77] And while alt-rightists give lip service to the traditionalist idea that women have important, dignified roles to play as mothers and homemakers, the overwhelming message is that women as a group are contemptible, pathetic creatures not worthy of respect.

On some issues, notably abortion, alt-rightists combine race and gender positions in ways that closely parallel the neonazi movement. While some alt-rightists have argued that abortion should simply be banned as immoral, others counter that it plays a useful role as a form of eugenics. They claim that legal abortion is disproportionately used by black and Latina women and potentially could be a way to weed out "defective" white babies as well. Dismissing the idea that women have a right to control their own bodies, *Counter-Currents* editor Greg Johnson commented, "in a White Nationalist society ... some abortions should be forbidden, others should be mandatory, but under no circumstances should they simply be a matter of a woman's choice."[78]

The anti-feminist online subculture known as the manosphere overlaps with the alt-right and has had a significant influence on alt-right ideology and tactics. While some manospherians claim that they simply want equality between the sexes, others advocate patriarchy openly. Some manospherians are family-centered traditionalists, while others celebrate a more predatory sexuality.

Daryush Valizadeh (Roosh V) embodies this tension. His eight thousand–word "What is Neomasculinity?" argues that male and female identities are genetically determined at birth; traditional sex roles are products of human evolution; gender equality is a myth with no scientific basis; patriarchy is the best social system for individual fulfillment and civilization as a whole; the nuclear family with one father and one mother in the same home is the healthiest unit for raising children; and socialism is damaging because it makes women dependent on the government and discourages them from using their "feminine gifts" to "land a husband." Yet the staunch traditionalism of this document contrasts starkly with Valizadeh's role as a pick-up artist. He has written ten how-to books for male sex tourists with titles such as *Bang Ukraine* and *Bang Iceland*. The blurb for *Bang Colombia* says that the book is "for guys who want to go to Colombia mostly to fuck women. It contains tons of moves, lines, and tips learned after six months of full-time research in the city of Medellin, where I dedicated my existence to cracking the code of Colombian women." Valizadeh doesn't dwell on his own glaring inconsistency, but does suggest in "What is Neomasculinity?" that the dismantling of patriarchal rules has forced men to pursue "game" as a defensive strategy "to hopefully land some semblance of a normal relationship."[79]

Manospherians tend to promote homophobia and transphobia, consistent with their efforts to reimpose rigid gender roles and identities. At *Return of Kings*, Valizadeh has denounced the legalization of same-sex marriage as "one phase of a degenerate march to persecute heterosexuals, both legally and socially, while acclimating young children to the homosexual lifestyle."[80] On the same website, Matt Forney warned that trans women who have sex with cis men might be guilty of "rape by fraud."[81] At the same time, some manosphere sites have sought to reach out to gay men. *A Voice for Men* published a series of articles by Matthew Lye that were later collected into the e-book *The New Gay Liberation: Escaping the Fag End of Feminism*, which Paul Elam described as "a scorching indictment of feminist hatred of all things male."[82]

Jack Donovan, who was an active and influential participant in the alt-right from 2010 to 2017, has contributed to some manosphere publications, but offers his own distinctive male tribalist ideology. Donovan's

"Way of the Gang" is a vision of male supremacy based on the shared loyalty of men prepared to fight and die together. This is the ideology of male bonding through warfare in pure form. Donovan rejects any compromises with feminism, ignores demographic nationalism, and clashes head on with patriarchal traditionalism, as can be seen by comparing his ideas with biblical patriarchy doctrine.

Like biblical patriarchy, Donovan's ideology calls for reasserting "traditional" gender roles, confining women to the domestic sphere, and excluding them from any say in running society or the state. But in other ways, the two doctrines are miles apart. A former Satanist, Donovan anchors his ideas in evolutionary psychology, not the Bible—an approach that's probably meaningless, if not satanic, to Adam and Eve creationists. And while even the most hard-core biblical patriarchs aim to recruit women as well as men (claiming their path offers women security and respect, not to mention salvation through Jesus), Donovan does not write for women at all. His audience, his community, his hope for the future, is entirely male.

In Donovan's ideal society, which he calls "The Brotherhood," women's main roles would be to birth and raise children and to help preserve the memory of the ancestors, because "young men should grow up knowing what their great-grandfathers and great-great-grandfathers did, and who they were, and what they believed." To some extent this sounds consistent with biblical patriarchy, but there's a difference. To biblical patriarchy advocates, the family is the basic economic and political unit of society. To Donovan, "The family is a means for the continuation of The Brotherhood, and gives a sacred role to women in The Brotherhood. The ideal woman is Queen Gorgo of Sparta...boasting that only women of her tribe give birth to worthy men."[83] This is a reversal of the idea that men become hunters and warriors to protect and provide for their families. As Jef Costello noted on the white nationalist website *Counter-Currents*, Donovan is saying that women exist in order to bring men into the world, and the family exists because it makes idealized male gang life possible.[84]

Donovan's open homosexuality and advocacy of sexual relationships between masculine men are his most dramatic disagreement with biblical patriarchy.[85] He does not call himself gay, rejects gay culture as effeminate, and justifies homophobia as a defense of masculinity rooted in the male gang's collective survival needs.[86] In Donovan's ideology, "androphilia" is a consummation of the priority that manly men place on each other. As he has commented, "When you get right down to it, when it comes to sex, homos are just men without women getting in the way."[87]

Unlike Christian rightists, who argue that feminism misleads women into betraying their true interests, Donovan sees feminism as an expression of women's basic nature, which is "to calm men down and enlist their help at home, raising children, and fixing up the grass hut." Today, feminists' supposed alliance with globalist elites reflects this: "Women are better suited to and better served by the globalism and consumerism of modern democracies that promote security, no-strings attached sex and shopping." It's not that women are evil, Donovan claims. "Women are humans who are slightly different from men, and given the opportunity they will serve their slightly different interests and follow their own slightly different way." But that slightly different way inevitably clashes with men's interests and therefore needs to be firmly controlled, if not suppressed.[88]

White nationalist alt-rightists place ideas about gender and sexuality within the framework of race, as neonazis have done for decades, but to varying degrees they are also influenced by writers such as Donovan and Valizadeh, for whom race is secondary. In "The Woman Question in White Nationalism," Greg Johnson of *Counter-Currents Publishing* declared, "Preserving our race's biological integrity requires the defeat of feminism and emasculation (male infantilization) and the restoration of sexual roles that are not just traditional but also biological: men as protectors and providers, women as nurturers." In parts of this essay Johnson sounds like a manospherian: "every man knows another man who has been emotionally and financially savaged by the punitive feminist biases now codified in laws governing marriage, divorce, and child custody." Yet he also implicitly rejected the pick-up artist and "men going their own way" lifestyles celebrated by many manospherians: "In a White Nationalist society, men will no longer be allowed to prolong their adolescence into their thirties and forties. They will be expected, encouraged, and enabled to take on adult responsibilities as soon as they are able. They will become husbands and fathers, providers and protectors for their families."[89]

In the alt-right's early years quasi-feminism had a foothold, as when National-Anarchist Andrew Yeoman criticized the "constant litany of abuse and frequent courtship invitations from unwanted suitors" that women faced from men in the movement. Yeoman argued that "We need women's help, now more than ever," yet "nothing says 'you are not important to us' [more] than sexualizing women in the movement."[90] A year later, Greg Johnson also acknowledged that "a sizable and vocal enough minority" of white nationalists were "genuine woman haters," but unlike Yeoman he argued that they should be given free rein and that women activists should simply be "tolerant and understanding" of such misogyny, "as a personal sacrifice to the greater good."[91] More recently, alt-rightists have tended to dismiss or trivialize the issue entirely, as when the Traditionalist Youth Network (TYN) declared that women were underrepresented in the movement because by nature they are "neither designed nor inclined to develop or encourage politically aggressive subcultures."[92] *The Daily Stormer* instituted a policy against publishing anything written by women and called for limiting women's involvement in the movement—in the face of criticism from women on the more old school neonazi discussion site *Stormfront*. Manospherian-turned-alt-rightist Matt Forney declared that "Trying to 'appeal' to women is an exercise in pointlessness.... [I]t's not that women should be unwelcome [in the alt-right], it's that they're unimportant."[93] The few women who have identified themselves with the alt-right have embraced a subordinate role.[94]

TYN has claimed that "women's biological drives are contrary to the best interests of civilization and ... the past century or so of women's enfranchisement and liberation has been detrimental to societal stability." But the group framed this position as relatively moderate because, unlike some manospherians, they didn't believe "that women are central to the destruction of Western Civilization"—they are simply being manipulated by the Jews. "While there's an organic (and not entirely degenerate) thread of indigenous feminist interest in expanding female power and influence in our society, the nature and scope of feminism in the contemporary West is almost entirely Jewish in origin and character." TYN conceded that "western women" "can and should be trusted in a variety of leadership and leading roles in a healthy Western society," although they shouldn't be allowed to vote "in matters relating to foreign policy or immigration policy" because "feminine nurturing impulses" cloud their judgment.[95]

True to its name, the Traditionalist Youth Network/Traditionalist Worker Party takes a patriarchal-traditionalist position with regard to homosexuality, declaring, "In Western pagan and Christian civilization, homosexual behavior has always been looked upon as being a degenerate behavior," and "homosexuality in the 21st century has become the vehicle for a demonically [i.e., Jewish] inspired attack upon our civilization and our culture."[96] According to TYN, homosexuals often molest children and not only spread AIDS recklessly but "in many cases, actively seek the infection as part of a morbid, *homocidal* [sic] sexual fantasy."[97] TYC has also applauded laws in several African countries that banned homosexuality, has denounced a Jewish-orchestrated Western campaign of "promoting homosexuality" in Africa as a new form of "cultural imperialism," and has declared "Nationalists from Europe to Asia to America to Africa are all fighting for the same thing, a healthy future for their descendants and a morally upright world."[98]

Many alt-rightists share TYN's utter rejection of homosexuality—but a significant number of them don't. Writing in 2010, Greg Johnson agreed that "leftist gays really are repulsive" but urged white nationalists to welcome white gays who shared their politics. "Quite a number of homosexual men do not fit the effeminate stereotype. They are masculine, and appreciate masculine things like facts, logic, and forthright action. And even effeminate gay men can make a real contribution." Directly contradicting TYN's positions, Johnson claimed that "homosexual behavior was not only tolerated by ancient Aryan peoples, it was considered normal, in some cases even ideal," and that homophobia—not homosexuality—had been promoted by Jews to divide and weaken the white race. Fear of homosexuality "has chilled same-sex friendships and male bonding, and it is the bonded male group, the *Männerbund*, that is the foundation of all higher forms of civilization, particularly Aryan civilizations."[99]

Johnson's comments here resonate with Jack Donovan's work, and also with the writings of white nationalist and alt-rightist James O'Meara, a homosexual man who, like Donovan, rejects the label "gay." O'Meara has called homosexual men "the natural elite of the Aryan peoples" and argued that "The origin of the handing down (tradition) of culture, at least in the Aryan world, lies not in the family ... but in those who have broken from it and established their own groups for these purposes: the various *Männerbunde* of warriors, priests, scholars, vigilantes, etc."[100] O'Meara has no interest in combating homophobia ("taking pity on some sniveling queen in a closet demanding 'my rights!'") but, unlike Donovan, his vision of male brotherhood has ample room for effeminate as well as masculine members.[101]

Some alt-rightists have also used Islamophobia in a bid to "wedge gays and Muslims," as "Butch Leghorn" put it in a 2016 article on *The*

Right Stuff website. Writing two days after Omar Mateen, an Afghani American, murdered forty-nine people at a gay nightclub in Orlando, Florida, Leghorn declared, "Gays will never be safe from Muslim violence, and the liberals will allow Muslim violence against gays because Muslims are higher ranked on the Progressive stack than gays.... This makes [the Orlando] shooting a very valuable wedge issue. By allowing Muslims into America, the Democrats are in effect choosing Muslims over gays. We simply need to hammer this issue." Leghorn offered several examples of talking points and images to use, such as a rainbow flag with the words "Fuck Islam" superimposed over it.[102] Alt-lite activist and former *Breitbart* journalist Milo Yiannopoulos made similar appeals.[103]

Conclusion

Many far right ideas about gender and sexuality have deep historical roots, but the rise of the feminist and LGBT movements since the 1960s have made these issues more prominent and politically volatile than they were before. Far rightists have responded to these movements in different ways, offering various versions or combinations of patriarchal traditionalism, demographic nationalism, quasi-feminism, and the cult of male comradeship. Some New Apostolic Reformers, part of a movement that has both far rightist and system-supportive aspects, have celebrated women's empowerment and challenged male dominance in ways that belie standard assumptions, and even some neonazis have done the same. But in recent years there has also been a strong trend toward increasingly harsh and explicit male supremacist doctrines, ranging from Christian Reconstructionist–inspired biblical patriarchy to the male warrior culture of Jack Donovan and others. At the same time, some alt-rightists have contested the far right's traditional blanket rejection of homosexuality, either because they want to drive a wedge between LGBT people and liberal/left politics, or as a pure expression of male bonding "without women getting in the way." All of this adds up to a complex, conflicted, and dynamic political landscape that cannot be fought with dismissive stereotypes.

7. Anti-Imperialism

For over thirty years, far rightists have been denouncing U.S. military intervention overseas, from Central America in the 1980s to the former Yugoslavia in the 1990s to Iraq and Syria today. More broadly, far rightists condemn the economic, political, and cultural dominance of globalizing elites, especially U.S.-based ones, both at home and abroad. Many U.S. far rightists also express solidarity with anti-imperialist struggles in the Global South, and some of them have tried to forge alliances with leftists around shared opposition to the U.S. empire.

Far right anti-imperialism doesn't fit old school leftist assumptions that opposition to empire is inherently liberatory or progressive, that far rightists always promote military expansionism, or that fascists are basically tools of the ruling class. These assumptions weren't true in the 1930s or the 1960s, and they're certainly not true now. As the 9-11 attacks in 2001 made clear, some of the most committed and important opponents of U.S. global power are on the far right.

I am using "anti-imperialism" here to refer to groups that oppose the international dominance of economic or political elites or the interventionist policies of the United States and its allies. Unlike leftist anti-imperialism, which at least in theory is predicated on principles of egalitarianism and social justice, far right anti-imperialism assumes that some groups of people are morally and intellectually superior to others and, often, that it is inevitable or desirable for some nations to dominate others. As a result, far rightists offer only partial or distorted critiques of imperialism. This can mean targeting some examples of international dominance or aggression while rationalizing others, or it can mean defining imperialism in ways that reinforce supremacist politics—for example, blaming it on an international Jewish conspiracy.

This chapter explores far right anti-imperialism's major roots and branches, and some of their points of interaction and conflict. Anti-imperialism has not unified the U.S. far right, but it has been a key issue helping to define its rejection of the existing order. To some extent, far right anti-imperialism is a matter of appropriating twisted versions of leftist politics, but it also grows out of rightist traditions that stretch back to the nineteenth century, and it combines homegrown influences with doctrines imported from Europe.

Conservative anti-interventionism

Far rightists aren't the only right-wing anti-imperialists. Although most American conservative groups support policies that promote U.S. military, economic, and political dominance internationally, there have been important exceptions. The roots of conservative anti-imperialism trace back to the 1930s and early 1940s, when a large anti-interventionist or "isolationist" movement opposed U.S. entry into World War II. Groups such as the America First Committee attracted broad support ranging from liberals to pro-Nazi groups, but centered in a kind of anti–Eastern Establishment conservatism. Historian Franz Schurmann writes:

> The isolationists were anti-imperialist, which, in the 1930s and 1940s, meant being against the only world imperialism of the time, the British Empire. They regarded it as a global conspiracy on the part of vast financial interests centered in London abetted by similar interests in New York to dominate the world economy. The ultimate aim of Britain, they believed, was to create a world economic and political monopoly which would stifle the natural expansionist desires of late-comer powers, such as America. The isolationists were indeed expansionists, the true heirs of "manifest destiny." They saw a glorious future for America beyond its borders, but not particularly in Europe or Africa or Western Asia. They looked westward to East Asia and southward to Latin America. They believed in laissez-faire capitalism and were hostile to big government, whose only result could be to suppress freedom, the natural right of every individual to deploy his enterprise in the pursuit of his own interests.[1]

Despite their faith in the "free" market, conservative anti-interventionists also tended to support economic protectionism against foreign (especially British) competition. They denounced the welfare state liberalism of Franklin Roosevelt's New Deal and the moderate wing of the Republican Party.

Conservative anti-interventionism collapsed when the Japanese navy attacked Pearl Harbor in December 1941, bringing the U.S. into World War II, and remained marginal during the Cold War, when former isolationists became aggressive opponents of communism both at home and abroad. But with the breakup of the Soviet bloc starting in the late 1980s, old fault lines reappeared.

Paleoconservatives directly invoked the America First Committee legacy and called for a new anti-interventionist, protectionist foreign policy. In Pat Buchanan's words, "All the institutions of the Cold War, from vast permanent U.S. armies on foreign soil, to old alliances against Communist enemies that no longer exist, to billions in foreign aid, must be re-examined."[2] Many paleocons have also promoted thinly veiled ethnic bigotry, warning that America is threatened by non-European immigrants and a Zionist lobby that supposedly controls Congress. In the 1992 and 1996 Republican primaries, Buchanan captured significant support by denouncing immigration as well as free trade, globalization, multinational corporations, and U.S. military intervention overseas. Buchanan's 1999 book *A Republic, Not an Empire* framed his politics in anti-imperialist terms while defending the United States' own history of westward expansion. Many libertarians have voiced similar anti-interventionist views, such as former congressmember and three-time presidential candidate Ron Paul and *Antiwar.com* founder Justin Raimondo.[3]

Classical fascism

In Europe, anti-imperialism was one of the ideological threads that came together in the early twentieth century to form fascism. Enrico Corradini, a leader of the Italian Nationalist Association, reworked the concept of international class conflict in a way that bolstered capitalist power within nations. Historian David Roberts writes:

The class struggle, said Corradini, was real enough, but it pitted not workers against capitalists within the nation, but poor proletarian nations [such as Italy] against rich plutocratic nations [such as Britain] on the international plane.... "Have" and "have-not" nations competed for economic advantage in perpetual war—sometimes cold war, sometimes hot war. Since some capitalist countries were richer than others, and since the workers of a rich country did share in their nation's wealth, international proletarian solidarity was a sham, a doctrine which served the plutocratic nations by helping to keep proletarian nations like Italy divided along class lines.[4]

While these ideas may bear a superficial likeness to some left-wing observations regarding divisions between oppressor and oppressed nations within the capitalist world-system, Corradini's view differed from these in that it held no place for international solidarity between proletarian nations, nor did it aim to ultimately suppress such unequal relations between peoples. Rather, the goal of Nationalists was to simply fight to make their nation one of the "winners" in this global contest, replicating the Hobbesian war of all against all on a higher level:

Corradini and his colleagues publicized these notions as they worked to drum up support for Italy's imperialist war with Turkey over Libya in 1911 and 1912. Corradini stressed a nation's right to take whatever it could get and its duty to conquer the bases of its own prosperity. Turkey and Libya, of course, were hardly plutocratic nations, but the Nationalist doctrine had no room for international solidarity between proletarian nations.... "No people has an absolute, innate right to a particular territory; rather, all peoples have only a relative right, an historic right, to the territory which they occupy." This right lasts only "as long as a people is a vital and active nation." In the geographical area known as Libya, the Berbers had been overrun by the Arabs centuries ago, and the Arabs had been overrun by the Turks a few centuries later. Italy could now claim title to the same territory by the same never-ending method on conquest from peoples grown too decadent to defend that territory.[5]

After World War I, the Nationalists merged into Benito Mussolini's new Fascist Party, which embraced Corradini's international theories, invading Ethiopia and intensifying colonial rule in Libya.

In Germany during the same period, anger at the punitive Versailles Treaty fueled far rightist claims that Germany had been subjugated by foreign powers, which contributed to the rise of Nazism. Within the Nazi movement, a "left" current associated with the brothers Gregor and Otto Strasser called for Germany to ally with the Soviet Union, as well as India and China, against Britain and France. This current, which focused on recruiting industrial workers and advocated nationalizing big companies and farms, was eventually suppressed by Hitler.[6] Nevertheless, during World War II, both Nazi Germany and Imperial Japan supported anticolonial struggles within the British and French Empires. For example, Hitler's government supported some Arab nationalist opponents of British rule in the Middle East, such as Palestinian leader Haj Amin al-Husseini, who helped recruit Bosnian Muslims into the Waffen SS. Both Germany and Japan backed efforts by Subhas Chandra Bose to end British rule in India. Under Bose's leadership tens of thousands of Indians in the Indian National Army fought alongside Japanese troops.[7]

Yockeyism and Third Position

After World War II, far rightists faced a radically different context, with Fascist and Nazi governments destroyed and discredited, a new Cold War pitting a U.S.-dominated capitalist world against Soviet communism, and a rising tide of anticolonial struggles in Asia and Africa. In the 1950s, Gamal Abdel Nasser's government in Egypt (which clashed with Western powers and eventually allied with the Soviet Union) drew thousands of German ex-Nazis as military advisors, scientists, or propagandists. For example, Johann von Leers, who had been a high-ranking member of Josef Goebbels's Propaganda Ministry in the Nazi government, changed his name to Omar Amin and headed Egypt's Institute for the Study of Zionism. In a 1958 letter to American neonazi H. Keith Thompson, Leers wrote, "One thing is clear—more and more patriot Germans join the great Arab revolution against beastly imperialism.... Our place as an oppressed nation under the execrable Western colonialist Bonn government must be on the side of the Arab nationalist revolt against the West."[8]

In the Cold War atmosphere of the 1950s and 1960s, the vast majority of American rightists aligned themselves with Western imperialism, but not all of them did. Francis Parker Yockey argued that fascists should ally with the USSR against the United States and support Third World anticolonial struggles against the Western powers. Yockey believed that under Stalin the Soviet Union had embraced antisemitism and abandoned proletarian internationalism, whereas the United States was still under Jewish control and thus posed the greater threat. Although staunchly racist and antisemitic, Yockey disagreed with the Nazis' biological racism, arguing instead that race was a reflection of culture and history. This approach was based on the work of German rightist philosopher Oswald Spengler.[9]

Yockey's politics represented a form of National Bolshevism, which promotes a synthesis of right-wing nationalism and communism. His views were rejected by most U.S. rightists of the time, such as American Nazi Party founder George Lincoln Rockwell, who condemned Yockey's anti-Americanism. An exception was the National Renaissance Party (NRP), a tiny neofascist group which cultivated ties with black separatists, Arab nationalists, and representatives of the Soviet Union, and which published a number of Yockey's writings. In a 1960 article, NRP head James Madole praised the Cuban Revolution and compared it to the new nationalist governments of Egypt, Iraq, Pakistan, and Indonesia:

> The peoples of these newly liberated nations wished to throw off the oppressive yoke of foreign colonialism just as our heroic American ancestors rebelled against the unjust taxation and repressive laws of the British Empire in 1776. The Arab, Pakistani, Indonesian, Chinese, Cuban, and Latin American peoples also intend to halt the vicious exploitation of their land, labor, and natural resources by hordes of foreign Jewish parasites operating under the protection of the French, British, American, and Dutch flags. The nefarious activities of these Jews acting as merchants, gambling and narcotics czars, businessmen, and stock speculators, are largely responsible for the intense hatred of America felt by most of the people of Asia, Africa, and Latin America.[10]

A lot of today's far right anti-imperialism is derived from a political tendency known as the Third Position, which originated in Italy in the 1970s. This was a period when Italian underground paramilitary organizations on both the right and the left carried out a series of robberies, bombings, kidnappings, and assassinations, as well as violent street confrontations. There was extensive collusion between neofascist armed groups and members of the state security forces—both of which feared the Italian Communist Party's growing popularity—around a so-called strategy of tension, an effort to create a public atmosphere of chaos and fear so as to justify a repressive crackdown and an end to parliamentary rule. However, some neofascists were unwilling to play this role. As Moyote Project explains:

> Although these groups did essentially agree with the strong anti-communist ideology of the Italian State and intelligence service, they also manifested their own anti-American worldview, embracing anti-imperialism and opposing themselves to the prevailing image of American society as paradigmatically individualistic and composed of a vast array of alienated subjects. This was theorised by Julius Evola, who became known as the neo-fascist "black baron."[11]

The principal organization to uphold this line was Terza Posizione (TP, "Third Position"), founded in 1978, whose name reflected their rejection of both communism and capitalism. Unlike other neofascist groups, they attempted to build working-class support by addressing social issues such as housing, and they periodically called for an alliance of far right and far left against the state.[12] TP also became closely aligned with the Nuclei Armati Rivoluzionari (NAR, "armed revolutionary nuclei"), an underground group that is believed to have carried out the 1980 Bologna train station bombing, which killed eighty-five people. After this attack, several dozen members of TP and NAR fled to England and began to promote Third Position ideology in the British fascist organization National Front. Under their influence, the NF applauded Muammar Gaddafi's Libya, the Islamic Republic of Iran, and Louis Farrakhan's Nation of Islam.[13]

European New Right and Duginism

Another important ideological current contributing to far right anti-imperialism is the European New Right (ENR). This movement was founded in the 1960s by a group of young French far rightists, who began as proponents of colonialism but in the wake of France's defeat in Algeria came to reject it as a threat to ethnic purity. Starting in the 1970s, French New Rightists advocated an alliance of Europe and the Third World against the two Cold War superpowers. In the process they portrayed right-wing authoritarian governments, rather than the revolutionary left, as the Global South's source of inspiration. "Around 1905, the Third World turned towards Japan. Around 1930, it turned towards Germany.... Today it is left with the possibility of turning towards Europe, which, itself seeking a third way, is the potential ally of all the countries of the world which seek to escape the ascendency of the superpowers."[14]

One of the ENR's contributions to far right ideology was to redefine imperialism not as a system of political, economic, or military domination but as a drive to impose cultural values on other peoples. Thus anti-imperialism became above all a project of asserting cultural identity and purity, and could be identified with the ENR's defense of "biocultural diversity" against a dominant "universalism." As French New Rightists Alain de Benoist and Charles Champetier put it:

> The West's conversion to universalism has been the main cause of its subsequent attempts to convert the rest of the world: in the past, to its religion (the Crusades); yesterday, to its political principles (colonialism); and today, to its economic and social model (development) or its moral principles (human rights). Undertaken under the aegis of missionaries, armies and merchants, the Westernization of the planet has represented an imperialist movement fed by the desire to erase all otherness.... [15]

Aleksandr Dugin of Russia is one of the most important figures within the European New Right and one of the most influential fascist theoreticians in the world. He has enjoyed close ties with people in President Vladimir Putin's office, the Duma (national legislature), military, and secret police. Despite these ruling-class connections, Dugin is seen by some Westerners as an innovative radical thinker who offers an important challenge to U.S. imperialism.[16]

In the 1990s, Dugin was co-founder and chief theoretician of the National Bolshevik Party, whose ideology combined fascism and Stalinism. He argued for a "clean, ideal fascism" involving "a new hierarchy, a new aristocracy...based on natural, organic [and] clear principles—dignity, honor, courage, [and] heroism," and claimed that

Mussolini and Hitler had been forced to compromise these ideals by allying with conservatives and capitalists.[17] Like Yockey and his fellow European New Rightists, Dugin disavows biological racism, yet he opposes ethnic mixing and has declared, "wherever there is a single drop of Aryan (Slavic, Turkic, Caucasian, European) blood, there is a chance for racial awakening, for the rebirth of the primordial Aryan conscience." He rejects vulgar antisemitism yet has warned that "the world of 'Judaica' is hostile to us," and that "the Indo-European elite" needs to understand Jews "not 'to forgive,' but 'to defeat'" them.[18]

In recent years, Dugin's political project has centered on Eurasianism—a vision of a renewed Eurasian "empire" in which ethnic Russians will hold a privileged position based on their "messianic" role. Dugin argues that the world faces a basic geopolitical conflict between "sea power" (centered on the Atlanticist alliance between the United States and Britain) and "land power" (centered on Russia). Atlanticism stands for "absolute evil," including the values of individualism, liberalism, consumerism, feminism, and homosexuality, while Eurasianism stands for authoritarianism, hierarchy, traditional religion, patriarchy, and communitarianism. Atlanticism is trying to impose its values on the world—what Dugin calls "a colonization of the spirit and of the mind." Against this, he declares, "Russia is the incarnation of the quest for an historical alternative to Atlanticism. Therein lies her global mission."[19] Dugin has loudly encouraged the Russian government's expansionist moves, such as the 2008 war with Georgia, 2014 annexation of Crimea, and ongoing support for secessionist rebels in eastern Ukraine. At the same time, Dugin insists that "Russia doesn't have an imperialist agenda. Moscow respects sovereignty and wouldn't interfere in the domestic politics of any other country."[20]

Dugin argues further, "To fight this global threat to humanity [Atlanticism], it is important to unite all the various forces that would, in earlier times, have been called anti-imperialist" and "all identitarian forces in any culture that refuse globalism for cultural reasons"— notably including many Islamic rightists. Dugin's "global revolutionary alliance" would cut across the left-right divide:

> Those from either the Right or the Left who refuse American hegemony, ultra-liberalism, strategic Atlanticism, the domination of oligarchic and cosmopolitan financial elites, individualistic anthropology and the ideology of human rights, as well as typically Western

racism in all spheres—economic, cultural, ethical, moral, biological and so on—and who are ready to cooperate with Eurasian forces in defending multipolarity, socio-economic pluralism, and a dialogue among civilizations, we consider to be allies and friends.

Those on the Right who support the United States, White racism against the Third World, who are anti-socialist and pro-liberal, and who are willing to collaborate with the Atlanticists; as well as those on the Left who attack Tradition, the organic values of religion and the family, and who promote other types of social deviations—both of these are in the camp of foe.[21]

Dugin has dismissed the possibility of any independent resistance, rejecting any alternative to siding with either Russia or the West:

There is no "third position," no possibility of that.... The same ugly truth hits the Ukrainian "nationalist" and the Arab salafi fighter: They are Western proxies. It is hard to accept for them because nobody likes the idea to be the useful idiot of Washington....

There is land power and sea power in geopolitics. Land power is represented today by Russia, sea power by Washington. During World War II Germany tried to impose a third position.... The end was the complete destruction of Germany. So when even the strong and powerful Germany of that time wasn't strong enough to impose the third position how [can] the much smaller and weaker groups want to do this today? It is impossible, it is a ridiculous illusion.[22]

Dugin echoes Francis Parker Yockey in his image of Russia/Eurasia as the main bastion against American liberalism and consumer culture, and in his call for an alliance of rightists and leftists against Western imperialism. Dugin's Eurasianism also draws on the ideas of earlier figures such as the Strasser brothers, the German National Bolshevik Ernst Niekisch, and Karl Haushofer (a geopoliticist who was teacher and mentor to Hitler's deputy führer, Rudolf Hess).

Christian Reconstructionism

With this varied ideological heritage, ranging from conservative anti-interventionists to National Bolsheviks, U.S. far rightists offer many different versions of anti-imperialism. Some far right currents emphasize opposition to empire more than others, but to a greater or lesser degree the theme can be found in all sectors of the far right.

Within the Christian right, anti-imperialism is not a major area of focus, but it is an issue that helps delineate the movement's system-loyal majority from its oppositional (far right) minority. Since the 1970s, leading Christian right organizations such as the Moral Majority, Christian Coalition, and Concerned Women for America have generally supported an aggressive U.S. foreign policy on behalf of capitalist interests.[23] The hard-line theocrats of Christian Reconstructionism, however, have rejected this approach. Gary North, one of Reconstructionism's main leaders, has written:

> The United States of America is an empire. ... those who profit from the expansion of the empire are paid by the government to produce the weapon systems which enable the United States government to project power around the world. The foreign aid system ... bribes leaders of countries around the world to keep their mouths shut regarding the extension of American power. This extension of power does not benefit the man in the street. It benefits various special interests, especially the military-industrial complex.[24]

Christian Reconstructionists' anti-imperialism blends America First nationalism, hostility to big government, and Calvinist theology. On American Vision's website, John Crawford has declared that "A Christian bully-state, evidenced in military bases strewn across the globe, is a misuse of God's blessings. ... [O]utside-in, top-down, moral transformation by force is not a biblical strategy for success." And further, "Empires seek to bring about peace or just extend their rule through force. Empires eventually run out of money during the process. This is by the Creator's design."[25]

On the website of the Chalcedon Foundation, Christian Reconstructionism's oldest institution, Tom Rose has argued that "America's military expansion overseas i.e., imperial hegemony" and "the domestic growth of what is known as a security/police state" represent "two aspects of *growing statism*." Rose declared that empire-building is "completely contrary to God's Word," asserting, "To be Biblical, America should abhor foreign possessions and international entanglements like the United Nations, NAFTA, etc." Rose also emphasized the interconnections between foreign expansionism and domestic repression. For example, U.S. military involvement in Southeast Asia contributed to the flow of illegal drugs into United States, which in turn brought on the war on drugs. "This so-called 'war' ... resulted in armed SWAT-team raids all across America and the confiscation of billions of dollars of private property owned by innocent people," as well as the militarization of local police and massive growth of prison populations.[26]

When discussing specific international conflicts, Reconstructionists have often avoided taking sides. For example, in a 2013 article opposing U.S. military intervention in the Syrian civil war, Rob Slane argued that "Syria is a sovereign nation that poses no threat to the US," yet emphasized that this was not a statement of support for Syrian President Bashar al-Assad. "It is possible to oppose Assad without endorsing the rebels. It is possible to oppose the rebels without endorsing Assad. And it is possible to oppose Assad, the rebels and the Western governments rattling their sabres, in the conviction that all three parties are evil and unworthy of support."[27]

Patriot movement and LaRouchites

Like Christian Reconstructionists, Patriot movement groups invoke a homegrown "no foreign entanglements" brand of conservatism and link the dangers of overseas expansion with the threat of big state tyranny. But unlike Reconstructionists, the Patriot groups generally say little about God and much about globalist elite conspiracies. They are hostile to transnational institutions such as the United Nations and the International Monetary Fund, which to their minds represent beachheads in the stealth campaign to impose world government. A distinctive feature of Patriot movement ideology is the persistent fear that the United States is itself a major target of imperialist designs. The movement has promoted a continuous stream of conspiracy theories about supposed plans to strip the United States of its national sovereignty and subjugate its citizens. Many of these theories claim that elites will use foreign soldiers to round up Americans and put down resistance. One Patriot movement blogger in 1997, for example, offered a version of this fear that centered on Chinese troops:

> During the 1950's, the elitists planning for world government made plans to use occupation forces in every country that did not submit to their greedy, arrogant ambitions. Their plan called for using Chinese troops in America.... Now that American soldiers have been used in Kuwait, Somalia, Haiti, Bosnia, and Kosovo, a precedent has been set to bring the red Chinese troops here. The UN could justify such an action if the Black Muslims instigate a race war. I expect this scenario if the Democrats loose [sic] the White House and Congress in the 2000 elections. Comrade Clinton could not be slicker in making himself Commandant of Gulag America.[28]

Unlike Christian Reconstructionists and most Patriot activists, the Lyndon LaRouche network glorifies centralized state power. They denounce imperialism not as an expression of "statism" but as a plot by the evil oligarchs to destroy the nation-state, which they regard as a cornerstone of a healthy and productive society. Although the LaRouchites disavow anti-Jewish bigotry, their analysis echoes modern antisemitism's phony distinction between "productive" industrial capital and "parasitic" finance capital. Evoking age-old stereotypes of the Jewish "usurer," for example, LaRouche has written that "Imperialism was not the result of capitalist development; it was the result of the conquest of power over capitalist nations by a usury-oriented rentier financier interest older than feudalism."[29] LaRouchite anti-imperialism is also bound up with Anglophobia—they argue that the oligarchs' power currently centers on British financiers, and that the British Empire continues to exist in secret. This too evokes antisemitism, because since the late nineteenth century Jew-haters have claimed that the Rothschild banking family controls the British government. At the same time, the LaRouchites' Anglophobia harks back to the America First tradition of the early 1940s, although somewhat incongruously they also celebrate the Anglophile Franklin Roosevelt.

The LaRouchites have often used their positions on international issues—such as opposing U.S. military attacks on Iraq and Yugoslavia or demanding that the International Monetary Fund cancel the debts of countries in the Global South—to help forge ties with liberal and radical activists and infiltrate left-oriented coalitions.[30] In these circles, they have played a disproportionate role beyond their small numbers in promoting a conspiracist analysis of imperialism and elite power.

In recent years, the LaRouche network's international policies have become increasingly oriented toward Russia. Politically marginalized in the United States, the LaRouchites have made concerted efforts since the 1990s to establish a presence in Russian academic and political circles, with some success. Their strong opposition to laissez-faire economics and free trade, coupled with conspiracy theories about international bankers, won sympathy among many members of Russia's political elite. LaRouche denounced former Russian President Boris Yeltsin, a laissez-faire advocate, as a "British puppet" and has praised Putin as a leader who promotes economic development and international cooperation in the face of Western oligarchic attacks. The LaRouche network has formed close ties with some high-ranking Russian political figures, such as Putin advisor Sergei Glazyev, who also has close ties with Duginists. (Although the technophile LaRouchites have little patience for Dugin-style mysticism, they share Dugin's fixation with grand Manichean theories of world history and have long promoted a vision of a "Eurasian land-bridge" as a cornerstone of global economic development, which resonates with Dugin's Eurasianism.)[31]

The LaRouchites have largely aligned themselves with Putin's government regarding recent international flash points, notably Ukraine and Syria. The conflicts in both of these countries involve complex interplays between popular forces, local elites, the United States, Russia, and other external powers, with authoritarian rightists playing major roles on different sides. Yet in both cases, LaRouchites have condemned Western-backed forces while defending those forces backed by Russia. In early 2014, Ukrainian President Viktor Yanukovych was toppled by the Euromaidan movement, a Western-supported uprising that encompassed forces ranging from liberals to neonazis. The LaRouchites— hewing closely to the Russian government line—reduced this to a U.S.-orchestrated fascist coup d'état, ignoring the real popular grievances against Yanukovych and whitewashing the role of pro-Russian fascists on the other side. Similarly, the LaRouchites reduce the Syrian civil war to an "Anglo-Saudi drive to destroy the nation of Syria," in which Iran, Hezbollah, and Russia are helping a democratic government to push back "international terrorists" and "their Syrian collaborators."[32]

Neonazism

While the LaRouche network promotes conspiracy theories rooted in coded antisemitism, most white nationalists explicitly equate empire with international Jewish power. Neonazis' hatred of the "Zionist Occupation Government" led some of them to applaud the 9-11 attacks in 2001 and call for an alliance with al-Qaeda against the U.S. government. Yet some neonazis, like LaRouchites, have also made overtures to leftists around anti-interventionism and anti-imperialism, for example when World Church of the Creator leader Matt Hale praised the 1999 Seattle protests against the World Trade Organization, or when the National Alliance set up a progressive-sounding "Anti-Globalism Action Network" website in 2002.[33] The Third Positionist group White Aryan Resistance (WAR) was pivotal in promoting this approach in the 1980s, as WAR leader Tom Metzger explained:

> We have taken a stand since the late 70s early 80s of opposing imperialist activities by what we would call the transnational corporate leadership in this country that we feel pretty much controls what goes on in Washington, DC. So we came out opposing the Cold War because our logic was simple that if there were any kind of nuclear war it would destroy the ancestral homeland of the entire white race. And from there we began to oppose intervention in the problems of Central America and so forth. ... This would cause massive illegal immigration into the United States. ... [34]

Although WAR has all but disappeared as an organization, Third Positionism remains a significant current within the neonazi movement. A 2011 post on the neonazi discussion forum *Stormfront* argued that Third Position was a more effective framework than white nationalism for promoting fascist ideology to non-fascists. The author, "PolishPatriot82," claimed that while most people associated white nationalism negatively with racism, Third Position represented a combination of leftist and rightist views, so it has the potential to appeal to more people. "For example, Third Positionists are pro-environment and antiwar (the left is happy) yet they are anti-immigration and support traditional values (the right is happy)." PolishPatriot82 also emphasized that Third Positionism was "anticolonial":

Third Positionists believe that every ethnic group and race of people has the human right to independence, freedom and the dignity and RIGHT TO EXIST AS A PEOPLE, A RACE, OR AN ETHNIC GROUP. In this respect, we completely reject what could be called the neo-colonial agenda of the United States in pursuing wars for oil in Iraq and Libya. We are also completely against the military intervention of the United States in Afghanistan or their support of pro-American juntas in Latin America to open up markets for exploitation by American capitalism....

At the same time, the author also argued that globalist elites were trying to destroy European culture first because white Europeans were the most successful race in the world, and the only ones who could and would step in to help others. "[L]eftists know it's true, with no white people around Africa and Asia will fall quickly."[35]

Some neonazis have moved from Third Positionism to Duginism, notably former American Front leader James Porrazzo's group New Resistance and its website, *Open Revolt*. New Resistance has voiced support for a wide range of opponents of U.S. imperialism, including Syria, Iran, North Korea, Gaddafi's Libya, and Hugo Chávez's Venezuela. But while Third Positionists refuse to back any major power, New Resistance has aligned itself with Russia. Porrazzo echoes many of Dugin's geopolitical views as well as his disavowal of old-style racial supremacism and antisemitism.

In 2017, Porrazzo held up Philippines President Rodrigo Duterte as a model of anti-imperialist politics, who "gives hopes to the people of other oppressed nations" and has long campaigned for literacy and women's rights. Dismissing concerns that President Duterte's anti-drug campaign has involved extrajudicial killings of thousands of people, Porrazzo commented that "history has clearly proven that killing as a political tactic for societal rejuvenation is mandatory if the human pox is to be contained." He added that "the great French philosopher Alain De Benoist articulates that 'Human Rights' so to speak, are a bourgeois construct of modernity that conflicts with more organic and traditional collective identities and patterns of self-perception."[36]

Alt-right

Like New Resistance, a number of alt-rightists have criticized imperialism in terms that draw on European New Right arguments and combine leftist and rightist themes. *Counter-Currents* editor Greg Johnson argues that while "Old Right" figures such as Mussolini and Hitler tried to build colonial empires, the "New Right" is "sympathetic to anticolonialism, because what we really believe in is national self-determination for all peoples."

> [T]he New Right basically stands for the idea of ethnonationalism and the idea of a kind of organic society, a society that embraces a lot of critiques of class structure and capitalism and colonialism and imperialism that you find on the Left, a critique of globalization and so forth, but recognizes that the best solution to that problem really is to embrace organic national communities and to seek a world where every nation has its own sovereignty.[37]

In these passages, "national self-determination" and "sovereignty" means racially defined separation and exclusion. Or as Johnson himself puts it, "we have to in the long run recognize that the best interests of all of our peoples is to have our own separate spheres."[38]

In discussing colonialism, Johnson sometimes sounds like a leftist: "I look at the settling of the New World as something that was in many ways driven by an extremely evil model of capitalism."[39] But his bigotry and scapegoating are always close to the surface: "I try to sympathize with the colonized. I sympathize with the Palestinians. Why? Because we're both under Jewish occupation."[40]

Echoing leftist critiques of neocolonialism, Eugene Montsalvat of *Counter-Currents* denounces "America's seemingly anti-colonial foreign policy [after World War II] as merely a fig leaf for financial imperialism. In Africa, the US sought to break down the old colonial empires and impose American lackeys as their new leadership." At the same time, Montsalvat echoes the European New Right's emphasis on defending traditional societies against mass migration and mass culture: "It is in the interest of big business to destroy the traditions of a people and replace them with consumerism, to eliminate the borders that prevent the flow of cheap labor. The capitalist seeks little more than to turn the world into their private plantation."[41]

But while the alt-right is indebted to ENR ideology in broad terms, it has been divided about Aleksandr Dugin's geopolitical ideas, notably his vision of Russia as the hub of a broad global alliance against the Western imperial powers. The Traditionalist Worker Party has criticized Dugin's disavowal of fascism and antisemitism but praised his vision of an international "anti-Atlanticist revolt,"[42] and TWP leader Matthew Heimbach has called Putin "the leader, really, of the anti-globalist forces around the world." National Policy Institute head Richard Spencer has even praised Russia as "the sole white power in the world." *American Renaissance* head Jared Taylor attended the 2015 Russian Imperial Movement conference in St. Petersburg, where he called the United States "the greatest enemy of tradition everywhere." Putin's government has encouraged these developments, which dovetail with its efforts to promote far right organizations internationally.[43]

Other alt-rightists, however, have been much more critical of Russia. Greg Johnson, who regards Dugin as "an apologist for Russian multiculturalism and imperialism," has warned, "Putin is not an ethnonationalist. Indeed, he imprisons Russian nationalists and is committed to maintaining Russia's current borders, which include millions of restive Muslims in the Caucasus." At the *Alternative Right* blog, Colin Liddell has criticized Putin's "suppression of Russian nationalist groups and the thought crime laws he has introduced that are aimed at suppressing historical viewpoints critical of the Red Army and the Holocaust/Holohoax narrative...." Liddell's fellow blogger "Duns Scotus" continued in this same vein in "The Boundless Insanity of Neo-Russian Imperialism": "Along with its geopolitical, temporal, and ideological borderlessness, the Russian imperialist entity... believes firmly in racial, religious, and ethnic borderlessness. Muslims, Jews, atheists, Christians—are all weighed and balanced only in as much as they serve the imperialist entity and its essentially soulless interests."[44]

Alt-rightists' divergent comments about the late President Hugo Chávez of Venezuela illustrate another aspect of this debate. As the leader of Venezuela's "Bolivarian Revolution" for fourteen years before his death in 2013 and a critic of the U.S. government whose friends and allies spanned the political spectrum from Cuba's Fidel Castro to Iran's Mahmoud Ahmadinejad and Russia's Putin, Chávez practiced exactly the kind of global alliance-building that Dugin has advocated. Some alt-rightists applauded Chávez; others did not.[45]

Gregory Hood of *Counter-Currents Publishing* wrote that he

wouldn't want to live in Chávez's Venezuela, citing rampant crime, corruption, and other problems, but praised the "powerful nationalist and even traditionalist overtones" of his policies, his efforts to imbue his people with "a sense of mission and national pride that transcended class," and his break with neoliberal orthodoxy. Hood argued that "White Nationalists and Hugo Chávez share common interests and a common enemy: global capitalism." Also at *Counter-Currents*, Kerry Bolton emphasized Chávez's intellectual debt to Argentinian leader Juan Perón, his image as "an enemy of World Zionism and of World Jewry," and his close relationship with Putin's Russia.[46]

Colin Liddell, however, was sharply critical of the whole premise of an international anti-globalist alliance of rightists and leftists, whites and nonwhites. He dismissed Dugin's Eurasianism as "nothing more than a rehash of Soviet/Russian Imperialism and its Machiavellian tendency to seek strange bedfellows in any tent, mud hut, or igloo on the planet." He derided Chávez as a "burly mulatto populist strongman" and concluded, "A leader who redistributed wealth to the less-White sector of his nation's population and is mourned by the ANC, is hardly a fitting coffin-fellow for White Nationalists."[47]

Alt-rightists have been more unified in their positions regarding the Syrian Civil War, and many of them have looked favorably on Putin's close alliance with the Assad government. Matt Parrott of the Traditionalist Youth Network, for example, referred to the Syrian Civil War as "the first truly winnable 'hot' engagement of the nascent Traditionalist Bloc of nations aligned against the Modernist Bloc in the world order...."[48] In this context Gregory Hood's article "Standing With Syria" staked out a position of qualified support for Russia and Syria against the United States:

> The Russian (and Syrian) alternative is not perfect. It is highly dependent on raw materials, is open to cronyism and corruption, and is at best only a partial exception to the global economic order being pushed by Washington. It is not the kind of system we should seek to emulate. However, it is an exception, and it is tied to hierarchical social systems, a renewal of Tradition, and at least leaves open the possibility of a renewal of patriotism and white racial identity.

Hood's article is also notable for defending Assad's government with progressive sounding arguments:

> Syria, like its protector Russia ... stands for autonomy — a responsi-
> ble governing class that identifies its well-being with that of contin-
> ued survival of the state and the national population, not just some
> economic system or abstract creed. It holds that traditional social
> forms and cultures have a right to survival. It is under the "dicta-
> tor" Assad that marginalized but longstanding groups like Middle
> Eastern Christians or minority Islamic sects can survive in relative
> peace and security. It is under American-backed "democratic" re-
> gimes that such populations are either persecuted or destroyed.[49]

This passage resembles claims by some Marxists, such as the Workers World Party, that the Assad regime is a bulwark of national independence against foreign intervention, and that it protects cultural and religious minorities against persecution or death. The main difference is that Workers World describes the Assad government as leftist and the United States as right-wing, while Hood and other alt-rightists argue the reverse.[50]

Conclusion

As we have seen, U.S. far rightists are carrying forward a long tradition of right-wing opposition to colonialism, multinational capital, and military interventionism. This opposition is rooted in anti-egalitarianism, often conspiracist, and often selective, but it reflects genuine principles and can't be dismissed as mere hypocrisy. This opposition also can't be blamed on Russian manipulation, any more than the anti-interventionist movement of the early 1940s could be blamed on Nazi government propaganda and covert organizing.

At the same time, as the disagreements I've outlined suggest, far right anti-imperialists face important strategic choices. First, in opposing the military-industrial complex or globalist elites or ZOG, should they align themselves with a countervailing force (most immediately Russia, but in the long run maybe China or some other power) or pursue an independent course? Second, should they work internationally with nonwhite and non-Christian forces, such as the Syrian government or the Islamic Republic of Iran, or with left-wing populists such as Hugo Chávez? These issues have been actively debated for years. How they are resolved could significantly affect the kind of organizing work that far rightists do, as well as their capacity to attract supporters.

8. Decentralism

Like fighting globalist elites, breaking up or dismantling political authority is a major focus for many U.S. far rightists. Although a few groups cling to the classical fascist vision of a powerful, centralized state, many more say that they want to shrink the state, secede from it, or get rid of it entirely. Political decentralism can be found across most sectors of the far right—racialist and non-racialist, religious and secular—and serves multiple functions. It taps into many Americans' hostility to "big government," helps far rightists insulate themselves against the charge of fascism, facilitates collaboration between different branches of the far right, and, in a few cases, helps far rightists to present themselves as progressive or to win themselves a hearing amongst leftists.

Just as many leftists have trouble understanding far right anti-imperialism because it doesn't fit our preconceptions, far right political decentralism challenges us to rethink some common beliefs. Both the anarchist and communist traditions identify the dismantling of state power as a key part of creating a free society, whether that dismantling is to happen during the overthrow of capitalism or through the "withering away" of a future workers' state. By contrast, we associate far right politics with the totalitarian state of Nuremberg rallies and secret police, supreme leaders and forced labor camps. In this context, far right political decentralism may seem either nonsensical or phony. But the right has its own antistatist traditions, associated with the mythology of freeing the market from government interference, and in recent decades has developed a variety of new decentralist doctrines. Far rightists often advocate political decentralism as a way to combat tyranny. However, once we scratch the surface, the smaller-scale political entities they envision are highly stratified and often profoundly authoritarian.

Roots of far right decentralism

In many European countries, nation-state formation involved the growth of large centralized bureaucracies and an expectation of deference to the state. But the United States developed a relatively limited and decentralized government apparatus, with locally controlled police, no peacetime military conscription, a profusion of civic associations organized from the bottom up rather than the top down, and a strong tradition of distrust toward central authority. In some ways this decentralist tradition has reflected (and allowed space for) struggles for political freedom and equality, but that is just one side of the story.

Although we often assume that increases in repression involve growth of the centralized state, this is not necessarily true. Throughout U.S. history, local and non-state institutions have often been the main vehicles for enforcing political order and keeping subject populations under control. The organization People Against Racist Terror (PART) addressed an important part of this legacy in a 1995 article commenting on the rise of the Patriot militia movement. "Traditional Marxist analysis has it that the state apparatus is expressed in and relies on 'special bodies of armed men.' But...the U.S., as a settler colonial society, has in fact depended on the armed organization of masses of the settler populace to establish and maintain itself, not merely on the armed state apparatus." PART continues:

> The militias of today are the descendants of the armed settlers who banded together to take land from the indigenous people. They are descendants of the slave posses that enforced the slave codes before there was any law enforcement apparatus. The white supremacist Arizona Rangers who plotted to bomb federal buildings in the '80s are descendants of the 19th century Arizona, Texas, and California Rangers, which developed from lynch mobs terrorizing the conquered Mexican population in the 1840s into the rudimentary apparatus of law enforcement by the Euro-American state in those territories conquered from Mexico.

PART also cited a number of other vigilante organizations, such as the Bald Knobbers of 1880s Missouri, who "took up arms to defend private property and enforce cultural norms," as well as the 1920s Ku Klux Klan, which "was not exclusively white supremacist, but enforced

Protestant 'Americanism,' family values, anti-immigrant hysteria, and Prohibition."[1]

While these vigilante organizations have been accepted or actively supported by the state, others have worked in opposition to the state. As I wrote in 2011:

> For over 300 years, American hostility to "big government" has often been driven by European Americans who wanted freer rein to conquer or dominate people of color without the limitations that central authorities imposed for pragmatic reasons. For example, Bacon's Rebellion in 1676 began with a massacre of Occaneechee Indians by Virginia frontier settlers; the American Revolution was motivated partly by opposition to the Royal Proclamation of 1763, which banned colonial settlement west of the Appalachians. Both the New York City "Draft Riot" of 1863 and the Reconstruction-era Ku Klux Klan combined anti-black terrorism with irregular warfare against the established central government. In the 1880s, the white labor movement in the western U.S. was built largely through anti-Chinese racism, including several pogroms. After World War I, even the refounded Klan often challenged local elites and sometimes aided striking workers. In the 1930s and early forties, a sizeable network of fascist and pro-fascist groups called for overthrowing the government. In the late 1950s, Southern politicians promoted a "Massive Resistance" campaign against federally mandated school desegregation.[2]

Another factor behind right-wing decentralism is that capitalist development in the United States has been unusually decentralized. With the westward movement of people and economic activity during the nineteenth and twentieth centuries, as historian Gabriel Kolko has noted, a series of "new hubs of financial and economic power emerged without the existence of a dominating, centralized financial and capital control."[3] Kolko argued that historians have tended to exaggerate Wall Street's dominance of American finance. For example, "in 1912, New York banks shared only 18 percent of the American banking resources, leaving such critical new industries as automobiles, Southwest oil, and the like for the most part independent of Eastern finance."[4] Historian Mike Davis noted a similar dynamic: "In contrast to the geo-financial centralism of other capitalist countries, the dominance of Wall Street has always been qualified by competition with financial centers in Cleveland, Chicago, San Francisco and, more recently, Los Angeles and Houston." Of particular significance here, these regionally based business groups have repeatedly used political power at the state or city level to challenge older capitalist factions for national dominance.[5]

Also in contrast to other industrialized countries, U.S. businesses have historically taken on many of the core functions we associate with the state. This was especially true between the 1870s and the 1930s, the key period in the development of U.S. industrial capitalism. During this time, capitalists relied on private armies and police forces more than the state to repress workers. In the late nineteenth century, the Pinkerton Detective Agency alone had more men than the U.S. Army.[6] Pinkertons and other private security forces often acted as a law unto themselves without fear of prosecution, even when they killed or wounded workers.

Capitalist takeover of state functions was even more extreme in the thousands of "company towns," where a single business economically dominated or even owned an entire community, and controlled all aspects of public life there. Company towns were "extremely widespread, especially in lumber, textile and coal mining areas in the south, coal and steel areas in the east and midwest, metal and coal mining areas in the mountain west, and lumber, copper and agricultural areas in the far west." According to historian Robert Justin Goldstein, "The Commission on Industrial Relations reported in 1915 that towns either owned or controlled by corporations presented 'every aspect of feudalism except the recognition of special duties on the part of the employer' and that the rights of free speech and assembly were seriously abridged in such areas."[7]

At several points in U.S. history, under pressure from liberal or leftist popular movements, the federal government has redefined its role in ways that limit economic inequality or shift power downward in the social hierarchy. This has repeatedly made the federal government a major target of right-wing opposition. In the 1860s and '70s, during the period of Reconstruction after the Civil War, new amendments to the U.S. Constitution proclaimed a nonracial definition of citizenship, equality before the law, and voting rights for men of color. For a few years, the federal government provided unprecedented social services through the Freedmen's Bureau and used troops to suppress organized racist terror. These measures led the Ku Klux Klan and its allies to denounce northern "military despotism" and a supposed plot by northern elites to stir up black people against southern whites.[8]

In the 1930s, under Franklin Roosevelt's New Deal, the federal government established new social programs such as Social Security, protective measures such as a minimum wage, federal sponsorship for collective bargaining, and a major government-owned public utility (the Tennessee Valley Authority). In the 1960s and '70s, the federal government's redistributive role expanded further, as it established additional programs to combat poverty; banned racial discrimination in voting and many other forms of discrimination; expanded regulation of businesses with regard to the environment, workplace and product safety, and other issues; declared abortion a fundamental right; and expanded civil liberties protections in a number of areas. Rightists opposed these shifts in various terms, for example denouncing Roosevelt as a would-be dictator, accusing an "activist" Supreme Court of usurping legislative authority, charging that the federal government was infringing on states' rights, and warning of sinister conspiracies by Jews, communists, and others.

Free marketeers

One of the main ideological sources of far right decentralism today is the libertarian movement. In many countries, "libertarianism" refers to left-wing philosophies, including anarchism and left communism, that reject both capitalism and authoritarian political organization. But in the United States, the term libertarianism generally refers to right-wing philosophies, rooted in classical liberalism and laissez-faire economics, that center on a call to end state interference with capitalism and property rights. Some libertarians ("minarchists") want to reduce the state to a few specific functions—mainly police, courts, and military—to safeguard persons and property against aggression, while others ("anarcho-capitalists") want to abolish the state altogether.

The libertarian movement in this sense grew out of conservative opposition to the New Deal in the 1930s and after. Right-wing business leaders bankrolled organizations such as the Foundation for Economic Education (FEE), which was founded in 1946 and helped to shape the modern libertarian movement. In its origins, libertarianism was closely intertwined with right-wing conspiracism (FEE board member Robert Welch later founded the John Birch Society) and with right-wing evangelical Protestantism (notably in the 1930s and '40s via the organization Spiritual Mobilization, which advocated a kind of pro-capitalist theology).[9] In the 1960s and '70s, some libertarians opposed the Vietnam War and tried to build ties with the New Left, but most of the movement later shifted back to a more firmly rightist orientation.[10]

Libertarianism offers a vision of individual personal freedom that speaks to the widely held value of "live and let live." Libertarians present their ideology as a deeply American tradition enshrined in the Declaration of Independence and the Bill of Rights but also as uniquely radical—"taking insights about order, justice, and the struggle between liberty and power further and deeper than most standard American liberals, patriots, or old fashioned Jeffersonians."[11] Yet by glorifying the market as a uniquely effective regulator of human relations, libertarianism rationalizes capitalist exploitation and unregulated business practices such as environmental destruction. And by framing liberty only in terms of the individual's freedom from state interference, libertarianism obscures and thus reinforces the many other systems of oppression and power that operate outside of the state. For example, libertarian theorist Murray Rothbard wrote (in an essay dismissing feminism as a "sick" ideology):

> In the free market, every worker tends to earn the value of his product, his "marginal productivity." ... Employers who persist in paying below a person's marginal product will hurt themselves by losing their best workers and hence losing profits for themselves. If women have persistently lower pay and poorer jobs ... then the simple reason must be that their marginal productivity tends to be lower than men's.[12]

In addition to denying non-state-based forms of oppression, libertarians generally reject egalitarianism on principle. Although self-described left-libertarians regard human equality as a worthy goal,[13] the more prevalent view is that equality and liberty are incompatible. Rothbard denounced egalitarianism as "antihuman" and "profoundly evil," asserting that its goals could only be achieved by "totalitarian methods of coercion"; Lew Rockwell has called egalitarianism a "menace."[14] This orientation has helped make libertarian ideas appealing to many far rightists.

Libertarianism has had a strong influence on the Patriot movement. Patriot groups have always emphasized opposition to gun control, which embodies several libertarian themes: defense of individual liberty against government intrusion, celebration of the Bill of Rights, and people directly protecting themselves and their property without relying on the state. In addition, the anti-environmentalist Wise Use movement's emphasis on protecting land use rights against the federal government has also strengthened libertarianism's impact on Patriot movement ideology. The Patriot movement's overarching libertarian framework has made it easier for white nationalists, Christian rightists, John Birch Society–type conspiracists, and others to work together and share their ideas fruitfully.

Libertarianism's relationship with white nationalism, on the other hand, has been complicated. According to *Anti-Fascist News*, many activists in alt-right white nationalist organizations such as the American Freedom Party and the Traditionalist Youth Network were former supporters of libertarian presidential candidate Ron Paul.[15] White nationalist Gregory Hood was written, "For many on the Alt Right, libertarianism is a kind of gateway drug, a safe way of attacking egalitarianism, the establishment conservative movement, and 'the System' more broadly."[16] At the same time, white nationalists have argued that libertarians' individualism conflicts with racial solidarity, and some libertarians have agreed.[17] Justin Raimondo, for example, contributed to *AlternativeRight.com* in 2010 but has repeatedly denounced white nationalists in recent years, arguing that they "are looking for the unearned: they want power, prestige, and money in the bank based on factors over which they had no control, that is, their genetic heritage."[18] Some white nationalists have advocated "national libertarianism" or "libertarianism in one country," meaning that libertarianism is a good idea but can only work in a society limited to members of one ethnicity.[19] The neoreactionary movement, which repudiates democracy in principle and has influenced the alt-right, is an offshoot of libertarianism and has produced various calls for autocracy on a small scale.[20]

Libertarian theocrats

Christian Reconstructionism, which has influenced both the wider Christian right and the Patriot movement, represents a kind of theocratic reinterpretation of libertarianism. R.J. Rushdoony, Reconstructionism's founder and chief theoretician, was actively involved in the fledgling libertarian movement in the 1950s, and in the early 1960s he worked for the William Volker Charities Fund, a wealthy libertarian foundation, before founding the Chalcedon Foundation. Gary North, another important Reconstructionist figure, worked for both the Volker Fund and FEE in the 1960s and for libertarian U.S. Congressmember Ron Paul in the 1970s. In 2013, North co-authored a Ron Paul homeschool curriculum.[21]

Reconstructionists share with mainstream libertarians an emphasis on limited government, laissez-faire economics, and the virtues of the American political tradition, but interpret all of these in terms of hardline Calvinist theology rather than classical liberalism. Rushdoony advocated limited government not to safeguard individual rights but rather to implement biblical law. In his vision, reconstructed Christian men, or "dominion men," would exercise governance across several different spheres, including the family, the church, and the state—with family and church keeping in check the state's "totalitarian" (i.e., non-Calvinist) tendencies. Of the three spheres, Rushdoony—who pioneered the practice of Christian homeschooling—regarded the family as most important and most powerful, while some other Reconstructionists have placed more emphasis on the church.[22]

Limited government under Reconstructionist biblical law would not mean freedom from repression—quite the opposite. As Rushdoony's biographer, Michael McVicar, explains:

> Ultimately, the end of biblical law is God's absolute sovereignty over all aspects of life on earth. This is most clearly illustrated in the various offenses requiring the death penalty. ... God decrees death in cases involving blasphemy, propagating false doctrines, sacrificing to foreign gods, and witchcraft. Another class of capital offenses included refusing to recognize a court ruling or failing to pay restitution for a crime. ... Of all the crimes, however, Rushdoony spent most of the book [*The Institutes of Biblical Law*, his magnum opus] outlining those that amounted to war against the family and therefore necessitated death. Murder, cursing a parent, kidnapping,

adultery, incest, bestiality, homosexuality, rape, and habitual delin-
quency all struck out against the propagative, future-oriented nature of the family. Death was necessary in these cases because each
crime asserted the sovereignty of humanity over God's law.[23]

Rushdoony's description of the American political tradition further illustrates the Reconstructionist concept of political decentralism. Again
quoting from McVicar's biography:

> Rushdoony argued that the American concept of liberty as it de-
> veloped from colonization, through the Revolutionary era, and be-
> yond rested on a Calvinist-derived theocratic "Christian common-
> wealth" that thrived in the northern colonies and parts of the South.
> Rushdoony believed he found evidence that significant portions of
> the civil structure of the early New England and southern colonies
> were, "almost from [their] inception, *a Protestant restoration of
> feudalism*" ... [which] made every man a priest and king of his own
> dominion. As such, Rushdoony argued that this "American feu-
> dal system" undermined the "Babel-like unity" of the centralized
> nation-state emerging contemporaneously in Europe....In this id-
> iosyncratic reading of American history, the Revolution became an
> antistatist "counter-revolution" that denied the concept of *human*
> sovereignty and distrusted the "people."[24]

Power of the county

Related to libertarianism, but more arcane, are the elaborate pseudo-
legal arguments against governmental authority that were developed by
Posse Comitatus in the 1970s. Founded in 1969, Posse blended influences from classical fascism and right-wing tax protesters in developing its own ideological framework.[25] With claims such as that the 16th
Amendment to the U.S. Constitution (which established the modern
federal income tax) was unconstitutional, Posse Comitatus reached peak
activity during the farm crisis of the 1980s, but had little organizational
presence by the end of the decade. Nevertheless, its ideas about the state
influenced other white nationalist currents and were enormously influential in shaping the Patriot movement in the 1990s, as well as related

movements such as the county supremacy movement.[26] Today Posse doctrines are represented most vividly by the Patriot-aligned sovereign citizens movement.

Posse Comitatus ideology is complex and, given the organization's decentralized structure, was never fully unified into a consistent body of ideas. However, most Posse members and supporters agreed on the following claims, all of which are regarded as specious by legal authorities:

- County government is the highest governmental authority in the United States, to which both federal and state governments are subordinate.

- Much of the official governmental and legal system is illegitimate, and the true governmental rules and principles have been hidden for generations by an elaborate conspiracy. These mysteries can be uncovered by searching through old legal documents and decoding secret symbols.

- Common law (which to most of us means case law found in court decisions) is not simply a complement to statutory law, but rather an entirely separate legal system, which can be used as a basis for disregarding statutory law and defying all governmental officials. An example would be establishing a "common law bank" not subject to government regulation.

- The Fourteenth Amendment to the U.S. Constitution created a new form of citizenship in order to take away people's common law rights and impose federal jurisdiction on them. However, Americans can disavow this subordination and declare themselves sovereign citizens who are not subject to federal authority.[27]

Posse members and those who followed them have applied these tenets in a number of ways, ranging from personal efforts to get out of financial obligations to organized protests against specific laws and policies. Especially interesting from a political standpoint have been efforts to establish courts, townships, militias, and other institutions that claim the authority to act as governmental bodies under common law, in defiance of the actual state. To back up their claims, advocates of Posse ideology have harassed government officials with bogus property liens (which are specious but can be difficult and expensive to remove), used death threats, and engaged in physical attacks.[28]

Leaderless resistance

In the 1980s, as Posse Comitatus converged with neonazi and Ku Klux Klan forces to form a new white nationalist insurgency, other activists in this emerging movement also promoted decentralist politics with regard to both goals and strategy. While earlier fascists had envisioned a revolutionary transformation of U.S. society as a whole, several groups now advocated a breakaway white homeland in one region or another. Most influential was the 1985 call by Robert Miles to form an independent white nation in the Northwestern United States, specifically Idaho, Montana, Oregon, Washington, and Wyoming.[29]

Miles was former Michigan grand dragon of the United Klans of America and co-publisher with Louis Beam of the *Inter-Klan Newsletter & Survival Alert*. The two of them advocated a revolutionary "Fifth Era" Klan that would take up armed struggle against the U.S. government. Both Miles and Beam were also ambassadors-at-large of the Aryan Nations organization, which was headquartered in rural Idaho and in the following years helped popularize the goal of a Northwest Republic amongst many white nationalists.

With regard to strategy, in 1983 the *Inter-Klan Newsletter* published Louis Beam's article "Leaderless Resistance." Like Miles, Beam had served in the U.S. military and been a Klan leader (Texas grand dragon in David Duke's Knights of the KKK). He credited the concept of leaderless resistance to Colonel Ulius Amoss, a U.S. intelligence officer, who developed it to combat a possible Communist takeover of the United States. "Col. Amoss feared the Communists. This author fears the federal government. Communism now represents a threat to no one in the United States, while federal tyranny represents a threat to *everyone*."

Beam's rationale for leaderless resistance was pragmatic rather than ideological. He argued that a traditional pyramid system of hierarchical organization was too vulnerable to infiltration and disruption, while a Soviet-style cell system required lots of organization, funding, and outside support, none of which were available to white insurgents. In contrast, the leaderless resistance model was based on independently operating "phantom" cells, which would function much as the Committees of Correspondence had done during the American Revolution:

> [P]articipants in a program of Leaderless Resistance through phantom cell or individual action must know exactly what they are

doing, and how to do it. It becomes the responsibility of the individual to acquire the necessary skills and information as to what is to be done....

[A]ll members of phantom cells or individuals will tend to react to objective events in the same way through usual tactics of resistance. Organs of information distribution such as newspapers, leaflets, computers, etc., which are widely available to all, keep each person informed of events, allowing for a planned response that will take many variations. No one need issue an order to anyone. Those idealist[s] truly committed to the cause of freedom will act when they feel the time is ripe, or will take their cue from others who precede them.

"Such a situation," Beam wrote, "is an intelligence nightmare for a government intent upon knowing everything they possibly can about those who oppose them."[30]

Although some neonazis have rejected the leaderless resistance model, others have embraced it. Its influence can be seen in numerous armed attacks against government targets, most notoriously the 1995 Oklahoma City bombing. Beam's article also influenced the Patriot movement and has been reposted on the website of the anti-abortion Army of God.

Leaderless resistance complements another strategic military framework, fourth generation warfare (4GW), which also was being developed during this period. The term was coined in 1989 by paleoconservative William S. Lind, director of cultural conservatism at Paul Weyrich's Free Congress Foundation, and a number of U.S. Marine Corps officers. It describes a type of asymmetric warfare that is initiated by non-state actors, often motivated by (and exacerbating) religious, ethnic, or cultural conflict.[31] While many observers consider 4GW to be a useful model, which accurately describes trends in conflict in an era of declining nation-state power and increasingly complex and vulnerable economic and technological systems, there was always a clear ideological component to Lind's argument. As sociologist and former United States Army civilian senior intelligence analyst James Scaminaci III has explained:

A sub-component of 4GW is William Lind's conspiracy theory of the internal war for supremacy between what he called "cultural

Marxists" and their ideology of "Political Correctness" or "multiculturalism" and the "traditional American culture" or "Judeo-Christian culture." Lind argued that "cultural Marxists" hate[d] America's "Judeo-Christian culture" and were seeking to destroy it. The losers were to be rich, white, conservative, Christian, heterosexual men....

Mike Vanderboegh, the militia strategist and founder of the Three Percenters, is an avid promoter of Fourth Generation Warfare.

Of note, in 2001, Karen Yurica uncovered a Paul Weyrich–commissioned strategy document on the "New Traditionalist Movement." Weyrich and Lind endorsed the following 4GW operational strategy: "Our strategy will be to bleed this corrupt culture dry. We will pick off the most intelligent and creative individuals in our society, the individuals who help give credibility to the current regime....Our movement will be entirely destructive, and entirely constructive. We will not try to reform the existing institutions. We only intend to weaken them, and eventually destroy them....We will maintain a constant barrage of criticism against the Left. We will attack the very legitimacy of the Left....We will use guerrilla tactics to undermine the legitimacy of the dominant regime....Sympathy from the American people will increase as our opponents try to persecute us, which means our strength will increase at an accelerating rate due to more defections—and the enemy will collapse as a result."[32]

A federation of tribes

At the same time that these new military strategies were being formulated and examined by the far right and that groups like Posse Comitatus and Aryan Nations were replacing traditional fascist strong state ideology with their own decentralist doctrines, a parallel development was taking place in Europe. The European New Right (ENR), which began in 1968 with the founding of GRECE (Research and Study Group for European Civilization) in France, undertook an elaborate intellectual project to develop a new theoretical framework for far right politics.

As in the United States, this effort included a shift away from calls for a large-scale dictatorship toward more decentralized political models. In the United States, ENR ideology has had a defining impact on the alt-right movement.

ENR ideas about political organization start with the concept of "organic democracy," which requires a "sense of ethnic solidarity and a sense of collective meaning grounded in a shared heritage."[33] French New Right co-founder Alain de Benoist has counterposed organic democracy to "liberal democracy" (which treats people as atomized, self-interested individuals) and "egalitarian" or "popular democracy" (represented by Marxist totalitarian regimes), both of which rest on false conceptions and thus are not true democracies. In an organic democracy, "common interest prevails over particular interests," and all citizens hold equal political rights "because they all belong to the same national and folk community."[34] Yet the system is also "perfectly reconcilable with the values of hierarchy, aristocracy, and authority."[35] The emphasis would be on citizens' participation rather than "numbers, suffrage, elections or representation." Organic democracy can accommodate a "pluralism of opinions" but not a "pluralism of values," let alone multiculturalism, which "severely threatens national and folk identity, while stripping the notion of the people of its essential meaning."[36]

De Benoist and other ENRists have advocated a federated political system with most decisions made at the local level:

> Born out of absolute monarchy and revolutionary Jacobinism, the nation-state is now too big to manage little problems and too small to address big ones.... Europe must organize itself into a federal structure, while recognizing the autonomy of all the component elements and facilitating the cooperation of the constituent regions and of individual nations.... Authority at the lower levels should not be delegated to authorities at the upper levels except in those matters which escape the competence of the lower level.[37]

Another French New Rightist, Guillaume Faye, detailed one version of this type of system in his 1999 book *Archeofuturism*. In the book's final chapter Faye envisions a post-catastrophic society, the "Eurosiberian Federation." All non-Europeans have been expelled and the people who remain have organized themselves into ethnically homogeneous regions. The federation's government has absolute authority but is elected by

representatives of all the regions. Each region can choose its own system
of government and exercises a great deal of autonomy. Across the whole
federation, a two-tiered social order has developed. About one-fifth of
the people live in an urban "techno-scientific" economy, while the rest
of the population lives in communities based on farming and crafts at a
medieval technological level.[38] In Faye's words:

> Those who perform subordinate functions in these inegalitarian
> societies will not feel frustrated: their dignity will not be called into
> question, for they will accept their own condition as something
> useful within the organic community—finally freed from the indi-.
> vidualistic hubris of modernity, which implicitly and deceptively
> states that each person can become a scientist or a prince.[39]

National-Anarchism, an offshoot of British neonazism that has spread
to the United States and other countries, has perhaps taken ENR's
decentralist tendencies further than anyone else. While embracing
the European New Right's approach to race and culture, National-
Anarchists reject the central state entirely in favor of a loose network of
self-governing tribalist communities. They have used the anarchist label
in an effort to disavow their neonazi roots and gain acceptance in leftist
spaces. At the same time, they have stated clearly that the purpose of
their anarchism is not to end social oppression or liberate all people to
live full and productive lives, but rather to allow everyone to rise or sink
to their appointed level in a natural human hierarchy. As the *National-
Anarchist Manifesto* puts it:

> To suppose...that humans are somehow "equal" is quite ridicu-
> lous.... Humanity—like the rest of nature—is hierarchical and the
> Left's progressive fantasies about a world in which everyone ac-
> quires the same rank, inevitably manifests itself as a levelling pro-
> cess in which oppressive laws are used to drag the strong down to
> the level of the most weak and resentful.[40]

Closely allied with National-Anarchism, Keith Preston of *Attack the
System* advocates an "anarcho-pluralist" system that blends elements
of ENR ideology with a libertarian emphasis on individual free choice.
Once a left-wing anarchist, Preston now claims he wants to abolish
the centralized state so that a minority of superior people can most

effectively rise above the "herd" of "sheepish" humanity. But compared with National-Anarchism, anarcho-pluralism would accommodate a wider variety of political, economic, and cultural systems at the local level. Preston has advocated this approach, in part, in hopes that it will provide a framework for collaboration between different branches of the far right, as well as those leftists willing to work with them.[41]

Conclusion

One of the most striking features of the U.S. far right's development over the past half-century has been the shift from strong state ideology to political decentralism. Although a few groups, such as the Lyndon LaRouche network, still echo the classical fascist call for a powerful, centralized state, many more far rightists want to reduce, fragment, or abolish centralized political authority. This trend extends across multiple political currents—from neonazi advocates of a regional white home-land to sovereign citizens and county supremacists, from National-Anarchists and alt-right identitarians to the libertarian theocrats of Christian Reconstructionism. It also draws on extraordinarily diverse ideological sources: classical liberalism, Calvinist theology, conspiracist pseudo-legal theories, the European New Right, even U.S. counterin-surgency strategy. The far right's shift to decentralism challenges us to rethink old political categories. Analytical models that equate "right-wing extremism" with a yearning for 1930s-type dictatorships simply don't work any more.

On one level, far right decentralism can be seen as a way to tap into many Americans' aversion to big government and, in some cases, in-sulate far rightists against the charge of fascism. But on a deeper level, it represents a reconceptualization of power, a shift from strong state totalitarianism to a kind of "social totalitarianism," in which repressive control is exercised through non-state networks and local institutions. The far right of the 1930s was a creature of its times. It took shape in an era when Europe's nation-states were still forming and consolidating, an era of large colonial empires and industrial production based on mas-sive factories. The far right of today takes shape in an era when global capitalism puts a premium on mobility, flexibility, and reconfiguring old structures. An era when many public functions—such as education, social services, police, prisons, and even the military—are being privatized, and when policy think tanks put out a "failed states index" so that businesses can profitably navigate the erosion or failure of state structures in different countries. Today's far right is both a reaction to the current era's dislocation and uncertainty, and an effort to meet it and define it in some way.

Part III

Partners, Rivals, Opponents

9. Federal Security Forces and the Paramilitary Right

This chapter explores U.S. security forces' changing relationships with the political far right—especially the paramilitary far right—and its predecessors. There is a long history of right-wing vigilantes helping the government suppress dissent and keep oppressed communities under control, but the federal government has also periodically used fears of right-wing "extremism" to help justify the growth of its own repressive apparatus. Over the past few decades, with the rise of an insurgent far right that rejects the U.S. government's legitimacy and has sometimes taken up arms against it, federal security forces have responded to right-wing paramilitary groups in various ways, from crackdowns to indecision or passivity. In recent years, some liberal policy advocates have promoted a smarter approach to combating the paramilitary right—based on counterinsurgency strategy—that would be both more preemptive and more sensitive to rightist fears of state repression.

Federal security forces in the United States exist, fundamentally, to defend ruling class power. This central purpose is mediated by many other factors—such as legal constraints and directives, agency turf wars, internal ideological biases, and external pressures from politicians, specific business interests, or social movements—and overlain by official rationales such as stopping criminals and terrorists, protecting human rights, and defending democracy. Levels of state repression have waxed and waned at various times, and specific targets and priorities have varied, but in broad terms there has been a long-term trend for many decades toward the growth of an integrated, coordinated national security apparatus that uses increasingly sophisticated techniques and systems to anticipate, monitor, disrupt, and redirect real or imagined threats to elite power and systems of social control. To varying degrees, both conservatives and liberals and both major political parties have actively contributed to this trend and, with marginal exceptions, have shielded federal security forces from scrutiny and critique.[1]

Federal security forces operate largely in secret, and there is a lot we don't know and may never know about what they do. Fortunately, information about their covert activities has periodically been uncovered through the actions of political dissenters (such as the 1971 break-in at an FBI office by antiwar activists that revealed COINTELPRO), independent whistleblowers (such as Edward Snowden's 2013 leak of classified NSA documents to the press), or through Freedom of Information Act requests by journalists or watchdog groups (such as J.M. Berger's discovery of the FBI's PATCON operation, discussed below).

Leftist critiques of federal security forces have highlighted government agencies' illegal activities, violations of civil liberties, targeting of oppressed communities (notably immigrants and people of color), and repression of liberatory movements. To the extent that leftists have addressed security forces' relations with armed right-wing groups, they have mainly focused on the lenient treatment such groups have often received—as well as instances when the government has collaborated with them directly. These are important realities, but they are not the whole story. Federal agencies have sometimes tolerated or even supported rightist vigilantes when doing so has aligned with their goals, but at other times they have regarded them as a threat—or as a useful scapegoat.

Building a security apparatus

Historically, armed right-wing groups actually preceded the federal government as major enforcers of social hierarchy and political obedience. "From the end of the Civil War to the start of World War II," writes Michael Cohen, "America's disciplinary regime...comprised a decentralized and hybrid system of private security firms, vigilantism, and state policing institutions."[2] The federal government's repressive apparatus expanded dramatically during World War I, with passage of the anti–free speech Espionage and Sedition Acts and the growth of several federal intelligence agencies, especially the Justice Department's Bureau of Investigation, which was renamed the Federal Bureau of Investigation (FBI) in 1935. But these agencies relied heavily on rightist vigilante organizations, which offered additional manpower at minimal cost and could use levels of violence that would be more awkward coming from officers of the law. The most important vigilante groups at the national level were the American Protective League (APL), whose members were deputized as federal "agents," and the American Legion, formed by returning veterans shortly after the war. These groups shared federal security services' countersubversion ideology: the belief that workers, immigrants, and people of color were being stirred up to subvert the political and social order by sinister outsiders. The APL, American Legion, and other vigilante groups helped federal agencies and local police break strikes and suppress the Industrial Workers of the World, the Socialist Party, and other radical organizations.

By contrast, during the 1930s and early '40s, the federal security apparatus grew largely by targeting the political right—with dire consequences for the left as well. The fascist and pro-Nazi groups that developed during the Great Depression hated Marxists, people of color, and Jews, but many of them also rejected the legitimacy of the U.S. government—the first significant right-wing forces to do so since the Reconstruction-era Ku Klux Klan. President Roosevelt helped the FBI expand its power by instructing it to investigate foreign-directed fascist and communist activities. In 1934, the House of Representatives created the original Un-American Activities Committee to investigate pro-Nazi propaganda; four years later the committee was reorganized to target Communists and became a major vehicle of the Cold War Red Scare. In 1940, six days after the Nazi conquest of France, President Roosevelt signed the Alien Registration Act (Smith Act), which made it a crime to advocate the violent overthrow of the U.S. government or insubordination in the armed forces and required adult foreigners to register and be fingerprinted. Many liberals and the Communist Party cheered when the Smith Act was used to prosecute both fascist sympathizers and system-loyal anti-interventionists, including a group of thirty-three prominent rightists who were indicted in 1942 and brought to trial in 1944. Although the government eventually dropped the case, it effectively put much of the far right leadership out of commission for the duration of the war. But in practice leftists were the Smith Act's main targets, including eighteen Trotskyists convicted in 1942 as part of a drive to smash labor radicalism, eleven Communist Party leaders convicted in 1949, and about one hundred other Communists convicted over the following seven years.[3]

Many people think of growing state repression as a trend toward fascism. But these events of the 1930s and '40s highlight the fact that *anti*fascism can itself serve as a rationale for increasing repression, as Don Hamerquist has pointed out: "when did this country outlaw strikes, ban seditious organizing and speech, intern substantial populations in concentration camps, and develop a totalitarian mobilization of economic, social, and cultural resources for military goals? Obviously it was during WWII, the period of the official capitalist mobilization against fascism, barbarism and for 'civilization.'"[4]

The FBI and the Ku Klux Klan

Even when rightist vigilantes are loyal to the system and ideologically in sync with federal security forces, significant tensions have sometimes developed between them. The FBI's relationship with the Ku Klux Klan in the 1960s offers a prime example. FBI Director J. Edgar Hoover and his deputies largely shared the Ku Klux Klan's doctrines of white supremacy and anticommunist nationalism, and most Klansmen revered the FBI as an ally defending the American social order against subversion. During the early 1960s, as Klansmen and other white supremacists physically attacked civil rights workers and other African Americans across the South, FBI agents consistently refused to provide protection, claiming that they could only observe and investigate. Below the surface, the bureau's role was much more active. For example, Gary Thomas Rowe, a paid FBI informer inside the Klan in Alabama, helped to plan and lead a mob assault on Freedom Riders in 1961, was part of the team that murdered civil rights worker Viola Liuzzo in 1965, and may have helped to carry out the Birmingham church bombing in 1963.[5] The FBI shielded him from prosecution for any of these activities.

In 1964, under pressure from liberal politicians and Justice Department officials, as well as public outrage at Klan violence, the FBI stepped up its investigations of white supremacist crimes. It also initiated COINTELPRO-White Hate, a covert program to target the

Ku Klux Klan, American Nazi Party, and other white supremacist organizations. This involved extensive infiltration of KKK groups; by 1966 an estimated three hundred Klan members were FBI informers.[6] Another account puts the number of FBI informers at two thousand and reports that they held top-level positions in half of the fourteen Klan organizations.[7]

Some critics of the FBI have argued that COINTELPRO-White Hate was a sham operation that funneled money and information to rightist vigilantes and subjected them to only token harassment.[8] This is inaccurate, as John Drabble and others have shown. Unlike its treatment of the Black Panthers, the FBI did not orchestrate any assassinations of Klansmen or frame any Klansmen on phony murder charges. But the bureau used a variety of other tactics that did significantly damage the Klan. For example, the FBI helped the House Un-American Activities Committee to hold public hearings in 1965–1966 that exposed the Klan to public scrutiny. As a result of these hearings, several top officials of the United Klans of America (UKA, the largest Klan organization) were jailed for contempt of Congress after they refused to provide internal records, and several other leaders resigned or were fired from Klan organizations.[9]

FBI agents targeted Klan groups with many of the dirty tricks that are well known from COINTELPRO operations against the Black Panther Party and other leftist groups:

> FBI mailed thousands of cartoons and hundreds of fake letters depicting embezzlement and personal aggrandizement by Klan leaders, resulting in defections and factionalism as well as conflict between rival Klan organizations. Poison-pen letters snitch-jacketed UKA leaders, i.e. framed them as informers. FBI informants raised controversial issues, aggravated factionalism, and usurped leadership positions. As with the more familiar COINTELPRO operations conducted against black nationalist groups, agents circulated propaganda and informants attacked Klan leaders despite the fact that violent confrontations, including at least one internecine killing, ensued.[10]

The FBI also set up a fake organization, the National Committee for Domestic Tranquility (NCDT), to lure members away from the Klan. The NCDT's newsletter carried the slogan, "Quit the Klan; and back our boys in Vietnam."[11] Bureau agents sent NCDT letters to Klansmen across the country. The letters denounced KKK leaders and heightened dissension and paranoia about informers in the ranks.[12]

COINTELPRO-White Hate contributed to a dramatic decline of the Klan movement in the late 1960s and early 1970s. Total membership in Klan organizations fell from a peak of 14,000–15,000 in 1967 to 4,300 in 1971, and continued falling to 1,500–1,700 in 1974. All of the major Klan organizations declined and several groups split into factions.[13]

Sociologist David Cunningham argues that outside pressure is not the only reason the FBI undertook COINTELPRO-White Hate. Although FBI officials shared the Klan's racist ideology, they saw the Klan as a threat because it carried out organized violence without authorization from the state. They also looked down on most Klansmen as poor, rural, and ignorant (a stereotype shared by many liberals then and now). By contrast, the FBI had no problem with the equally racist but more genteel Citizens Councils.[14] The bureau also did nothing to disrupt either local police brutality or the informal (non-KKK) vigilante networks that enforced white supremacy in many rural areas of the South. As John Drabble comments, the FBI was "focused on preserving domestic security rather than on protecting the civil rights of African Americans...."[15]

Cunningham also draws a useful contrast between COINTELPRO-White Hate and the FBI's simultaneous program against the New Left, whose core ideology it considered far more dangerous than white supremacy:

> Thus, while the [FBI] directorate continually sought to delegitimize and eliminate New Left organizations, a successful counterintelligence program needed not so much to eliminate the Klan as to control the group's actions and minimize its potential for violence. This desire led to two phenomena absent in COINTELPRO-New Left: (1) a campaign to steer members of White Hate groups to selected "acceptable" groups (e.g. groups not actively engaged in violence) and (2) an increased emphasis on infiltrating White Hate groups at a level sufficient to exert some control over the groups' decision-making apparatuses. Both of these attempts to control a target group's activities sometimes involved actually strengthening acceptable White Hate alternatives rather than trying to eliminate these groups altogether.[16]

In the long run, as Drabble points out, the FBI's campaign to exert greater control over the Ku Klux Klan had unintended consequences. Although Klansmen began the decade strongly supportive of the FBI, by the late 1960s the bureau's deliberate efforts to stir up fear of informers eroded most of that goodwill, and the public revelation of COINTELPRO in 1971 killed what was left. Drabble writes:

> By 1971 ... United Klans of America (UKA) Imperial Wizard Robert Shelton had concluded that the FBI was "no longer the respected and honorable arm of justice that it once appeared to be." A year later the UKA's *Fiery Cross* published an editorial written by former American Nazi Party official William Pierce, who declared that the federal government had "been transformed [into] a corrupt, unnatural and degenerate monstrosity," and exhorted Klansmen to launch a bloody revolution against it.[17]

Similarly, the FBI's deliberate efforts to weaken and divide the Klan movement, far from taming it, helped open the door to more militantly oppositional versions of white supremacist politics. Several of the factions that broke away from the UKA began to emphasize paramilitarism, embrace Christian Identity, or interact with Nazis. And with the UKA and other 1960s groups broken and defeated, the field was open for former American Nazi Party member David Duke to set up a new Knights of the Ku Klux Klan that blended elements of Nazi ideology with traditional Klan ritual and symbols.[18]

State-sponsored vigilantism

At the same time, FBI efforts to bring rightist vigilantism under control did not necessarily mean reducing violence. In 1971–1972, the FBI sponsored a group called the Secret Army Organization (SAO), which targeted antiwar leftists with spying, vandalism, mail theft, assassination plots, shootings, and bombings. The SAO was based in San Diego and at its peak had chapters in eleven states. One of the SAO's two main leaders was Howard Godfrey, a former member of the Minutemen who had been an FBI informer for several years. Godfrey later testified in court that the FBI provided or paid for $10,000–$25,000 worth of weapons or explosives for the group. Other court testimony stated that following an SAO shooting that left one person permanently injured, Godfrey's FBI supervisor destroyed evidence and hid the weapon from police for six months.[19] The FBI wasn't the only federal agency involved in this kind of work. Between 1969 and 1972, the U.S. Army's Military Intelligence and the Chicago Police jointly operated a rightist vigilante group called the Legion of Justice, which had several hundred members in and around Chicago, with branches in Indiana, Ohio, and Wisconsin. The Legion burglarized, bugged, vandalized, and assaulted socialist and antiwar groups, often stealing files at the request of the police. The Army supplied the group with tear gas, mace, and electronic bugging equipment, and shared the intelligence proceeds with the Chicago red squad.[20]

One of the most notorious examples of federal complicity in rightist violence against leftists took place in Greensboro, North Carolina, on November 3, 1979, when a group of Klansmen and Nazis opened fire on an anti-Klan rally organized by the Communist Workers Party (CWP), killing five people and injuring ten. The CWP was a Maoist offshoot of the 1960s New Left, which in North Carolina focused largely on organizing textile workers. The attackers were members of the United Racist Front (URF), a local coalition of several Klan and Nazi groups including, among others, the North Carolina Knights of the KKK, the National Socialist Party of America (NSPA). Their caravan that day was led by Ed Dawson, an ex-FBI informer who had founded the North Carolina Knights in 1969 with FBI backing, and who now informed for the Greensboro Police Department. Two days earlier, the police had given Dawson a copy of the anti-Klan march route and permit (which stated that marchers were not allowed to carry weapons). Meanwhile, Bernard Butkovich, an agent of the federal Bureau of Alcohol, Tobacco and Firearms, was working undercover in the NSPA in Winston-Salem. In the days leading up to the November 3 demo, both Dawson and Butkovich urged their respective comrades to confront the CWP, and both attended URF planning sessions for the event. According to court testimony, Butkovich not only urged Nazis to take guns to the confrontation but also encouraged them to illegally convert semi-automatic weapons to fully automatic and offered to obtain explosives for them.[21]

In addition to federal agencies' involvement, many questions surround local police actions before and during the Greensboro massacre.

Although Dawson told police in advance that heavily armed Klansmen would confront the marchers, officers were not told to assemble until 11:30—a full hour after the start time printed on the march permit.[22] The massacre took place at 11:23. "At the time of the killings," writes Joanne Wypijewski, "the police special agent in charge of the Klan informant was at the back of the caravan, having trailed it to the site. He did not intervene, or radio for help, or trip a siren, or pursue the killers as nine of their vehicles got away. Arrests occurred only because two police officers broke ranks and apprehended a van." Although the massacre was captured on video camera and witnessed by many people, two criminal trials before all-white juries resulted in acquittals. Finally in 1985, the killers and the Greensboro Police Department were found liable in a civil trial and ordered to pay $350,000 in damages to the widow of one of those killed.[23]

Cracking down

The Greensboro massacre was a high water mark of federal government collusion with right-wing violence, but by bringing Klansmen and Nazis together it also helped precipitate the rise of a new rightist movement that considered Washington its deadly enemy. One of the participants in the Greensboro massacre, Frazier Glenn Miller, went on to found one the largest and most prominent organizations in the 1980s white supremacist far right: the Carolina (later Confederate) Knights of the Ku Klux Klan, which in 1985 was renamed the White Patriot Party (WPP).[24] Strongly paramilitarist, the WPP stood at the juncture between the new movement's aboveground mass organizing and its vanguardist underground wing, spearheaded by The Order.

The federal apparatus responded aggressively to the new armed revolutionary network. Terrorizing black people and gunning down leftist demonstrators was one thing; robbing banks and armored cars, counterfeiting money, threatening judges, and killing police was something else entirely. In 1984–1985, federal agents killed The Order's leader Robert Jay Mathews in a shootout and rounded up the cell's other members, who received sentences ranging up to 252 years for racketeering, conspiracy, and violating the civil rights of Alan Berg (a Jewish talk show host they had murdered in Denver). Over the following three years, the FBI and other agencies conducted "Operation Clean Sweep," which extended the crackdown to other armed white supremacist groups: Frazier Glenn Miller's White Patriot Party; James Ellison's The Covenant, The Sword, and the Arm of the Lord; William Potter Gale's Committee of the States; Bruder Schweigen Strike Force II (an Aryan Nations offshoot described as a successor to The Order); Arizona Patriots, and others. Defendants received sentences up to thirty-nine years for armed robbery, illegal weapons possession, counterfeiting, conspiring to blow up buildings, and various other crimes.[25] But the biggest federal prosecution effort—the 1988 Fort Smith trial of fourteen white supremacists on seditious conspiracy and other charges—ended in acquittals. Leonard Zeskind argues that the Fort Smith prosecution failed, in part, because the FBI "conceptualized the Aryan underground as a pyramid" and failed to understand its decentralized, weblike structure.[26]

Despite the Fort Smith setback, Operation Clean Sweep helped reverse the neonazi movement's growth, seriously weakening major organizations such as Aryan Nations and the White Patriot Party. At the same time, the 1980s gave the movement a list of martyrs and cemented militant opposition to federal authority as an ideological pole on the far right.

In the early 1990s, deadly and arguably murderous operations by federal officers—at the Weaver home in Ruby Ridge, Idaho, in 1992, and the Branch Davidian compound in Waco, Texas, in 1993—helped spark the explosive growth of the Patriot movement in the mid-1990s. The Patriot movement didn't declare war on the U.S. government, but it did foster an entire subculture that regarded the established federal government apparatus as evil and illegitimate, and built a network of private armed units and "common law courts" claiming to exercise government functions.

At first, federal agencies—wary of another Ruby Ridge or Waco incident—did little to clamp down on the Patriot movement. (Zeskind and others have pointed out that a predominantly black or brown movement spouting anti-government rhetoric and conducting paramilitary training would have been treated very differently.) But in April 1995, neonazi Timothy McVeigh and others blew up the Oklahoma City federal building, killing 168 people, and Patriot militias were widely (but without evidence) blamed for the attack. After that, the FBI pursued a wide-ranging crackdown, which contributed to the Patriot movement's collapse in the late 1990s. Here are a few examples from 1995–1998, drawn from a 2009 Patriot movement timeline compiled by the liberal Southern Poverty Law Center, which works closely with the FBI:

- a tax protester arrested for placing a failed bomb behind the Reno, Nevada, IRS building;

- three members of the Republic of Georgia militia charged with manufacturing shrapnel-packed bombs and training a team to assassinate politicians;

- twelve members of the Arizona Viper Team arrested on federal conspiracy, weapons, and explosives charges;

- seven members of the Mountaineer Militia arrested in a plot to blow up the FBI's national fingerprint records center in West Virginia;

- former Sons of Liberty and other tax protesters set fire to the IRS office in Colorado Springs;

- eight members of a militia group arrested in connection with a plan to invade Fort Hood, Texas, and kill foreign troops mistakenly believed to be housed there;

- three men, including one with ties to the separatist Republic of Texas, charged with conspiracy to use weapons of mass destruction after threatening President Clinton and other federal officials with biological weapons.

The Clinton administration also used the Oklahoma City bombing to help win passage of the 1996 Antiterrorism and Effective Death Penalty Act, which loosened restrictions on the wiretapping and other surveillance of alleged "terrorists," expanded the use of secret evidence to deport non-citizens (which means that the defendants have no opportunity to see the evidence being used against them), and, in the words of legal journalist Lincoln Caplan, "gutted the federal writ of habeas corpus, which a federal court can use to order the release of someone wrongly imprisoned." The law made the death penalty more "effective" by making it much more difficult for death row inmates to appeal their sentences, even though a notoriously high proportion of death sentences have been shown to have serious flaws.[27]

Shifting approaches

As in the past, FBI used infiltration techniques during the 1990s to both monitor and influence far right groups. In 1991, in an undercover operation code-named PATCON, FBI agents in Austin, Texas, created a phony neonazi organization called the Veterans Aryan Movement (VAM), which claimed to be following in The Order's footsteps: robbing banks and armored cars, stockpiling weapons, and building links with like-minded groups around the country. With this cover story, the VAM was well positioned to spy on genuine neonazis and other members of the Patriot movement that was just beginning to coalesce at this time. Officially, PATCON was supposed to investigate specific potential crimes, but in practice it was an open-ended intelligence-gathering operation. PATCON operatives reported lots of talk about violence by Patriot activists, but almost none of this information was used in prosecutions. At one point, PATCON operatives even withheld information from Army investigators about a theft of night vision goggles from Fort Hood, in order to protect their own operation. In July 1993 the FBI ended PATCON, ostensibly because it had failed to uncover actual criminal activity. The operation remained secret until 2007, when investigative reporter J.M. Berger discovered it through a Freedom of Information Act request.[28]

In a separate operation, the FBI recruited Tri-States Militia founder John Parsons as a paid informer in 1995. Based in South Dakota, Parsons ran a Communications Information Center for some nine hundred militia and Patriot groups nationwide, and thus had an unusually strong central role in the decentralized movement. Parsons and his FBI supervisor revealed the arrangement in court testimony during a 1996 trial of other militia activists charged in a bombing plot. Parsons claimed that he relied on the FBI's monthly $1,775 payments to keep the Center going, and his supervisor stated, "The reason [for] trying to keep him in there is I feel he has become a calming voice for these militias across the country." The news stunned members of Tri-States and brought angry denunciations from several militia leaders.[29] As in the 1960s Klan, FBI infiltration fueled paranoia within the movement, but this time it had the effect of reinforcing the movement's core beliefs about the government rather than calling them into question.

With the "War on Terror" that followed the September 11 attacks in 2001, the federal security apparatus shifted its main focus away from domestic threats. The evolution of Islamic rightist paramilitary forces—from CIA clients fighting Communism in Afghanistan to independents waging war against the United States—paralleled the evolution of system-loyal vigilantes into right-wing revolutionaries within the U.S. itself. Similarly, when the U.S. government used the Islamic rightist threat to justify repressive measures such as the Patriot Act, it paralleled earlier use of the danger from U.S. far rightists to justify the Smith Act or the Antiterrorism and Effective Death Penalty Act.

After 2001, federal agencies continued to monitor U.S. far rightists. In 2006, the FBI Counterterrorism Division warned that white supremacists were trying to infiltrate law enforcement agencies, and in 2007, they highlighted the threat from solo white supremacists (prefiguring, for example, Wade Michael Page's 2012 attack on a Sikh temple in Wisconsin, Frazier Glenn Miller's 2014 shooting at a Jewish community center near Kansas City, and Dylann Roof's 2015 mass killing at an African American church in Charleston, South Carolina). However, although U.S. far rightists killed more people than Muslim militants between 2002 and 2015, law enforcement conducted much less surveillance of U.S. far rightists than of Muslim communities. Muslim defendants were more likely to be portrayed as part of a terror network, be charged with more serious crimes, and receive higher sentences than U.S. far rightists. Partly this reflected disparate media treatment. "Mainstream conservative politicians and media personalities protest depictions of right-wing militants as anything more than troubled but patriotic Americans, while Muslim men—particularly young men—are constantly monitored as intrinsic security risks.[30]

Federal agencies have been sensitive to this climate. In 2009, when conservatives denounced the Department of Homeland Security for a report on the resurgence of "Rightwing Extremism," DHS repudiated the report and disbanded the unit that was studying non-Islamic domestic terrorism.[31] Also in 2009, a report about the militia movement from the Missouri Information Analysis Center (one of the DHS-sponsored "fusion centers") met a similar fate.[32]

Fear of conservative criticism probably contributed to federal agencies' seeming hesitation and uncertainty in recent encounters with Patriot movement activists. In the 2014 Bundy Ranch confrontation in Nevada, not only did federal officers back down from enforcing the law when faced with Patriot activists pointing guns at them, but the government waited almost two years before bringing any charges connected to the incident.[33] In the 2016 Malheur wildlife refuge occupation, not only did the FBI leave the occupiers undisturbed for three weeks, but they declined to enforce a movement cordon or shut off water or power to the occupiers throughout that period. When the FBI and Oregon State Police finally did arrest some of the occupation leaders, one of the occupiers, LaVoy Finicum, was shot and killed by state police, becoming a martyr to the cause.[34]

Liberal counterinsurgency

In recent years, some liberal and centrist sections of the political establishment—including the Council on Foreign Relations (CFR) and New America Foundation (NAF, later shortened to New America)—have called for greater emphasis on U.S. far right violence and have criticized security forces' approach for being too reactive and inconsistent. A 2010 op-ed by CFR fellow and counterterrorism analyst Lydia Khalil urged conservatives to stop minimizing "the serious and growing threat of homegrown right-wing extremism" and to identify rightist violence against government institutions as acts of terrorism. A 2011 CFR report by Jonathan Masters on "Militant Extremists in the United States" argued the same points in more detail and advocated a preemptive, intelligence-gathering approach to counter rightist violence. Masters's report outlined the "domestic intelligence infrastructure" available to support such work, including the FBI's Joint Terrorism Task Force, the Department of Homeland Security's Fusion Center program, and the widespread adoption of "intelligence-led policing" by local police departments. While noting civil liberties concerns, the report gave the last word to CFR Adjunct Senior Fellow Richard Falkenrath, who advocated more "permissive" constraints on security forces.

Similarly, in 2011 and 2012, staffers and fellows of the New America Foundation urged in various media that discussions of terrorism be broadened to include homegrown "extremists"—who, they argued, posed a threat as big as or bigger than Islamist groups. Although not as well known as CFR, the New America Foundation, too, has extensive ties with elites in politics, business, media, and academia. The foundation's board of directors has been dominated by Ivy Leaguers and multinationalist business figures such as Google head Eric Schmidt and hedge fund manager Jonathan Soros (son of George Soros). Anne-Marie Slaughter, who became NAF president in 2013, previously spent two years as director of policy planning at the U.S. State Department under Hillary Clinton.[35]

In 2012, NAF published a policy paper by J.M. Berger about PATCON, the FBI undercover operation in the early 1990s that Berger had exposed a few years before. Under PATCON, as mentioned above, the bureau had created a phony organization (the Veterans Aryan Movement) as a way to gather information about the real far right underground. Unlike Berger's other writings about PATCON, his NAF report was framed in terms of "the infiltration dilemma": on one hand, "informants and undercover agents are essential tools for law enforcement officials" investigating "violent extremism"; on the other hand, "aggressive infiltrations can…reinforce extremist narratives" about the government, and "the ripple effects of perceived overreach can also make it more difficult for otherwise friendly community partners to encourage cooperation with law enforcement."[36] Berger argued that the PATCON operation exemplified such overreach. "The reality of the FBI's extensive infiltration of the Patriot movement help[ed] reinforce a paranoid worldview in which the government becomes the perpetrator of crimes like the Oklahoma City bombing, thus exonerating true radical figures and providing a fresh (if usually false) grievance to fuel further radicalization."[37] The report concluded with a set of recommendations for assessing infiltration's "secondary effects" on targeted populations "and how they affect public trust in government and willingness to cooperate with law enforcement."[38] The aim was not to abolish police infiltration of political groups, but to enable security forces to "manage the use of this tool more responsibly."[39]

NAF was concerned with improving infiltration techniques not only against U.S. far rightists but against "potential extremists" more broadly. Coincident with the PATCON report's release in 2012, NAF sponsored a public panel on "Infiltration and Surveillance: Countering Homegrown Terrorism," in which Berger spoke about PATCON and another presenter discussed the New York Police Department's surveillance of Muslim communities. At this event, the moderator asked panelists and audience members to set aside moral and legal issues and focus on the questions, when do infiltration techniques work and how well do they work?

The arguments promoted by the NAF, and to a lesser extent CFR, represented applications of counterinsurgency strategy (COIN) against the far right. Kristian Williams has described COIN as a style of warfare that's characterized by "an emphasis on intelligence, security and peace-keeping operation, population control, propaganda, and efforts to gain the trust of the people."[40] COIN is as much a sophisticated approach to state repression as it is a form of warfare. Williams argues that "the two major developments in American policing since the 1960s—militarization and community policing—are actually two aspects of a domestic counterinsurgency program." In *The New State Repression*, Ken Lawrence highlighted security forces' shift from a reactive approach—targeting groups after they've engaged in some kind of political protest—to a preemptive approach, which assumes that even in periods of calm, opponents of the state are "out there plotting and organizing, so the police must go find them, infiltrate them, and plant provocateurs among them."[41] Lawrence traced this "strategy of permanent repression" to the work of British counterinsurgency expert Frank Kitson in Kenya, Northern Ireland, and elsewhere, which involved, for example, the creation of "pseudo gangs" as a tactic to confuse and weaken genuine opposition forces.

NAF has been a strong proponent of counterinsurgency internationally.[42] An October 2011 article by NAF's Sameer Lalwani criticized the Indian government's heavily militarized approach to combating the leftist Naxalite insurgency as "brutal and incomplete (by western standards)" and urged institutional overhauls to redress the "distribution of power controlled by the state and elite cadres." This approach is in the tradition of the CIA funding European Social Democrats in the 1950s in order to undercut support for Communism. NAF also argued that "the 'global war on terror' is better conceived as a global counterinsurgency campaign, which typically involves a 20% military approach and an 80% 'softer' approach that uses other levers and incentives."[43]

Without using the phrase, Berger's NAF policy paper about PATCON invoked counterinsurgency strategy in several ways. First, it focused on an FBI program which—unlike the bureau's better-known reactive measures—took a preemptive, interventionist approach to the early Patriot movement, and even created a pseudo gang as part of this effort. Second, the report emphasized the need for security forces to tread carefully so as to bolster the state's legitimacy or, in Williams's words, "gain the trust of the people." Third, the report (and associated panel discussion) raised larger questions about how police intelligence work could more effectively stem the rise of "violent extremism" across a range of targeted communities.

It's unclear how much impact NAF's initiative in this area has had, but echoes of counterinsurgency strategy could also be found in the Obama administration's official strategy for "Countering Violent Extremism," which was launched as a program of the Department of Homeland Security in 2011. As summarized in a 2015 fact sheet, the strategy emphasized "the preventative aspects of counterterrorism" and sought to address "the root causes of extremism through community engagement." The White House argued that "CVE efforts are best pursued at the local level, tailored to local dynamics, where local officials continue to build relationships within their communities through established community policing and community outreach mechanisms." The White House noted that "violent extremist threats can come from a range of groups and individuals, including domestic terrorists and homegrown violent extremists in the United States.... " Yet the CVE's main focus was on al-Qaeda and other Islamic rightist groups.[44]

Donald Trump's inauguration as president shifted executive branch priorities further away from tracking domestic far rightists. The new administration considered renaming the Countering Violent Extremism program something like "Countering Radical Islamic Extremism" and proposed a budget that cut CVE funding to zero. These moves, coupled with Trump's tendency to encourage and excuse right-wing violence, have dampened federal security forces' response to right-wing paramilitarism, but it would be a mistake to assume they have ended it.[45]

Conclusion

Federal security forces' role as defenders of elite power and social control has framed their relations with armed right-wing groups. Broadly speaking, security forces may tolerate, work with, or even sponsor violent rightist groups that target the left or oppressed communities, but are much more likely to suppress such groups when they challenge the state. 1980 marks a historical turning point: before then, most right-wing political violence was carried out by groups essentially loyal to the existing system, but this changed as a network of far right groups emerged that was ready and able to take up arms against the "Zionist Occupation Government." At the same time, in both periods federal security forces were also influenced by secondary factors, such as pressure from civil rights groups and liberal politicians (in the 1960s) and from conservative sympathizers with the Patriot movement (in the 2010s). In addition, some federal security initiatives—notably the FBI's COINTELPRO-White Hate operation and the ATF's encouragement of Klan-Nazi collaboration in the Greensboro massacre—unwittingly contributed to the rise of the armed revolutionary right in the first place. Since the 1980s, as far as we know, federal security treatment of the paramilitary far right has largely been reactive and inconsistent, veering between periods of energetic action and passive uncertainty, or between cautious restraint and brutal overreach. It was largely to address this problem that the New America Foundation, representing powerful elite interests, advocated a smarter counterinsurgency-based approach.

New America Foundation's approach to rightist violence made sense from the standpoint of a ruling class trying to maintain social control. If you are serious about combating "terrorism," then you need to deal with the homegrown paramilitary right, which has a persistent base of support and has targeted U.S. government institutions for some thirty years. Since paramilitary rightists may be organizing and planning even when they're not carrying out violent attacks, you want your security forces to get to know rightist networks from the inside instead of just reacting to attacks after they happen. And given that heavy-handed police actions have repeatedly fueled widespread rightist fears about state repression, you need to take these fears into account if you want support for rightist paramilitary violence to shrink instead of grow. The following point by Kristian Williams applies to movements of the right as well as the left: "As a matter of *realpolitik* the authorities have to respond in some manner to popular demands; however, COIN allows them to do so in a way that at least preserves, and in the best case amplifies, their overall control. The purpose of counterinsurgency is to prevent any real shift in power."[46]

10. Leftists, Liberals, and the Specter of Fascism

The rise of a fascist state is one of U.S. leftists' classic fears. Many critics have called Donald Trump a fascist, with his combination of racist and anti-Muslim scapegoating, authoritarian demagoguery, and populist anti-elitism. But the charge has been around for generations, and sections of the left have leveled it against a wide range of opponents—from the George W. Bush administration's apocalyptic militarism and use of torture in the 2000s to FBI/police repression against the Black Panthers in the 1960s, and even Franklin Roosevelt's early New Deal experiments with state-sponsored cartels in the 1930s. Leftists have variously identified the threat of fascism with Joe McCarthy's anticommunist witch-hunts in the 1950s, the Reagan Revolution in the 1980s, and Newt Gingrich's Contract With America in the 1990s, among other developments.

Delineating fascism

Each of these claims that the U.S. government or public officials are driving us toward fascism represents a misuse of the term, one that blurs the line between fascism and the more repressive, racist, and militaristic sides of the United States' liberal-pluralist political system. I addressed this in the 2007 essay, "Is the Bush Administration Fascist?":

It's easy to find commonalities between the U.S. system and fascism, but that is nothing new. The U.S. power structure has always used the state to defend capitalism. It has always been built on a system of racial oppression. It has always promoted militarism and expansionism. It has always used political repression to silence radical dissent. And, at least since Andrew Jackson's followers created the Democratic Party in the 1820s, it has always used mass political organizations to mobilize members of dominant groups around oppressive agendas.

In certain crisis periods, furthermore, the U.S. power structure has expanded and intensified repression dramatically. This happened, for example, in 1917–1920, when radicals, labor organizers, and immigrants were rounded up by the thousands, people were jailed for criticizing the government, anti-Black and anti-Mexican pogroms claimed scores of lives, and the government recruited a wide range of civic organizations to spy on their neighbors. Other repressive high points included World War II (the "anti-fascist" war), when 110,000 people were put in concentration camps because of Japanese ancestry and the FBI compiled dossiers on millions of workers, and the early cold war period, when anti-communist and anti-gay witch hunts created a pervasive climate of fear. Between the late sixties and mid seventies, dozens of Black and American Indian activists were murdered as part of an FBI-spearheaded crackdown against the radical left.

So if the United States is fascist, when did it start? Has the U.S. always been fascist? Has it moved in and out of fascism? If fascism equals capitalist repression plus militaristic nationalism, there's no clear dividing line between then and now.[1]

This fuzziness is one of the reasons I've argued for a sharper, clearer conception of fascism, one that highlights its autonomous, contradictory relationship with capitalist elites; its radical, totalitarian break with liberal-pluralist principles and institutions; and its drive to permanently mobilize large masses of people around an ideology of unity and collective rebirth. Conceptual clarity about fascism isn't just an intellectual exercise; it's strategically important for recognizing qualitatively different opponents so we can respond to them intelligently. Quoting again from "Is the Bush Administration Fascist?":

[M]ilitaristic repression—even full-scale dictatorship—doesn't necessarily equal fascism, and the distinction matters. Some forms of right-wing authoritarianism grow out of established political institutions while others reject those institutions; some are creatures of big business while others are independent of, or even hostile to, big business. Some just suppress liberatory movements while others use twisted versions of radical politics in a bid to "take the game away from the left." These are different kinds of threats. If we want to develop effective strategies for fighting them, we need a political vocabulary that recognizes their differences.[2]

In this chapter I'm going to look at several of the key moments since the 1930s when leftists have declared the U.S. political system was on the brink of—or had already arrived at—fascism. These debates are rarely considered in historical perspective. Impending fascism warnings are urgent and immediate, and they tend to drive out memories of all the similar warnings that came before them. When critics started writing that Donald Trump was leading a drive toward fascism, few of them mentioned that the same charge had been widely leveled against George W. Bush ten years earlier.

Comparing different claims of impending fascism also highlights some of the strategic issues involved. Sometime the f-word is just used for dramatic effect, to highlight the dangers of a new political turn. But sometimes it serves a more specific purpose, such as to rally leftists behind a broad, defensive coalition to protect "democracy" or, conversely, urge more militant or revolutionary action to combat a system whose brutal essence has been exposed.

Communist Party shifts in the 1930s

The U.S. Communist Party's changing responses to President Franklin Roosevelt epitomize the range of purposes that fear of impending fascism has served. In formal terms, the CP's conception of fascism was fixed in 1933, when the Communist International declared: "Fascism is the open, terrorist dictatorship of the most reactionary, most chauvinist and most imperialist elements of finance capital."[3] The Communist

Party has stuck by this definition ever since, but its application of the definition shifted enormously as its overall political line changed and as U.S. politics changed.

President Roosevelt took office in 1933, in the depths of the Great Depression. He called his program of relief and recovery the New Deal; today the New Deal is mostly remembered as a groundbreaking set of welfare state policies such as Social Security, unemployment insurance, and federal recognition for labor unions and collective bargaining. The CP supported all that in the mid- and late 1930s, and Communist labor organizers helped bring the militant Congress of Industrial Organizations (CIO) into close alliance with the Roosevelt administration.

But at first the Communists denounced the New Deal as a move toward fascism. This line was summed up in the 1934 book *Fascism and Social Revolution* by British Marxist R. Palme Dutt. Dutt declared that the Roosevelt administration represented "the transition to Fascist forms, especially in the economic and industrial field,"[4] while the New Deal was "the most comprehensive and ruthless attempt of finance-capital to consolidate its power with the entire strength of the State machine over the whole field of industry"[5] and to intensify workers' exploitation. Dutt warned, "as the advance to war implicit in the whole Roosevelt policy develops, the demand for corresponding political forms of Fascism will inevitably come to the front in the United States."[6]

The CP's initial anti–New Deal stance primarily reflected the left sectarianism of the Communist International's "Third Period" (1928–1934), when Communists rejected any alliance with reformist parties or labor organizations. During this phase, the U.S. Communist Party sharply increased its emphasis on combating white supremacy, arguing that black people in the Deep South constituted a nation with the right of self-determination. But internationally, the Third Period was defined largely by the Communists' emphasis on attacking social democracy as "social fascism"—supposedly as bad as, if not worse than, Hitler's movement. Disastrously, this policy helped keep the German left divided during Hitler's drive for power.

Yet equating the early New Deal with fascism did have some basis in reality. At its start, the Roosevelt administration's political character was not at all clear, and it briefly rallied a broad coalition of liberals and conservatives, including many capitalists who later became staunchly anti-Roosevelt. A cornerstone of the New Deal during FDR's first two years in office was the short-lived National Recovery Administration (NRA), which established "codes of fair competition" to set prices and wages in each major industry. These codes included some protections for workers but mainly reflected big business interests. The NRA embodied the philosophy of *corporatism*—a system of formal, state-sponsored partnerships between official representatives of different social classes and other interest groups. Mussolini's Fascists also championed a version of corporatism, supposedly as a way to eliminate the divisiveness of class conflict and parliamentary debate. In the United States, the NRA represented an extraordinary expansion of the federal government in a time of extraordinary instability, and the men who ran the agency openly admired the Italian Fascist model. But unlike Italian Fascism, the NRA didn't promote a totalitarian ideology or attack representative government, and it was focused on reducing business competition rather than suppressing class conflict.[7] In 1935, the Supreme Court declared the NRA unconstitutional.

Soon after Dutt's book appeared, the Communist International shifted from its sectarian Third Period to the "Popular Front" period of broad antifascist alliances (1934–1939). Meanwhile, facing an increasingly militant working class and growing pressure to address economic inequality (including from Huey Long's populist Share Our Wealth movement), FDR abandoned corporatism for welfare state liberalism and an alliance with organized labor, a move that restabilized the political-economic order. Roosevelt's left turn had backing from a small but influential bloc of businessmen in capital-intensive and internationally oriented industries, who were relatively willing to cut a deal with militant workers and liked Roosevelt's moves toward free trade.[8] A broad majority of capitalists opposed him. So did a large but fragmented far right more or less openly supportive of Nazi Germany, most notably Father Charles Coughlin's organizations, the National Union for Social Justice and the Christian Front. In the mid- and late 1930s, the Communist Party hailed Roosevelt as a defender of "democracy," while attacking all of his opponents as promoters of "fascism."[9] Previously, the CP had lumped together fascists and social democrats; now it lumped together far rightists, laissez-faire conservatives, and Trotskyist revolutionaries under the fascist label.

In a further twist, during the period of the Hitler-Stalin Pact, from 1939 to 1941, the Communist Party abandoned antifascism altogether in favor of a militant opposition to war and Roosevelt, arguing that both sides of the war in Europe were equally at fault.[10] When Germany invaded the Soviet Union in May 1941, the party reverted to Popular Front reformism yet again. In the name of antifascism, the CP helped to break strikes, supported the mass imprisonment of Japanese Americans, and applauded the federal government's imprisonment of Trotskyists under the anti–free speech Smith Act, which made it a crime to advocate the forcible or violent overthrow of the government.[11]

The Communist Party's Popular Front antifascism overlapped with a wide-ranging crusade by liberals in the late 1930s and early 1940s against suspected Axis supporters. As historian Leo Ribuffo has argued, the campaign in this period to root out domestic fascists took the form of a "Brown Scare" that directly anticipated the Red Scare of the early Cold War. Certainly, the far right in this period was a major force and had many ties with mainstream anti–New Dealers. But in exposing it, several liberal investigative journalists distorted facts, used guilt by association, and promoted unsubstantiated conspiracy theories about "the enemy within." Much of this propaganda portrayed all opposition to U.S. entry into World War II as "un-American" and the U.S. far right as a fifth column directed by Hitler's government, rather than a social movement rooted in domestic political traditions. Worse yet, liberal antifascists encouraged the growth of a repressive federal apparatus— encompassing for example the Smith Act, the House Un-American Activities Committee, and the use of the FBI to monitor political dissidents—that was readily turned against leftists and liberals themselves a few years later.[12]

Trotskyists versus the Hudson County Hitler

The Trotskyists who in 1938 founded the Socialist Workers Party (SWP) shared with the Communist Party the assumption that fascism was a tool of big business, but (at least in theory) placed more emphasis on fascism's popular base. As the SWP's Joseph Hansen put it in 1939, fascism "is a wide mass movement of farmers and small business men who face bankruptcy, of youth denied a future under capitalism, of sections of the unemployed," but this movement is "financed and controlled by the very capitalists who above all are anxious to keep the revolutionary violence of the masses from turning against them."[13]

Like the Communist Party, Trotskyists argued that the fascist threat went beyond far rightists such as Father Coughlin to include sections of the established power structure, but they identified the specific threat differently. Frank Hague, who ran Jersey City and the New Jersey Democratic Party from the 1910s until his retirement in 1947, was a prototype of the corrupt political boss. He used local police to suppress dissent, rigged elections, and got rich on bribes and kickbacks. When he started cracking down on labor organizers and leftists in the 1930s, the SWP called him "the Hudson County Hitler" and denounced his operation as "a deliberate mobilization of reaction, backed by big industrial and financial interests, for a serious preliminary test of the workers' capacity to resist fascistic repression." Even Leon Trotsky, commenting from his exile in Mexico, called Hague "an American fascist" and asked, "Why is he aroused? Because the society can no longer be run by democratic means."[14]

The SWP's critique of Frank Hague's local political machine as fascist was more limited than the CP's initial denunciation of the New Deal. But since President Roosevelt depended partly on support from local Democratic Party bosses such as Hague, the SWP's line pointed to interconnections between liberal reformism and capitalist repression. At a time when CIO officials were trying to negotiate a compromise with Hague, the Trotskyists rightly urged the CIO to mobilize a mass counter-demonstration against him, with the "creation of a labor guard to prevent Hague's cops from repeating their brutalities."[15] This kind of militant action would have placed organized labor (another key supporter of Roosevelt) in direct confrontation with the Democratic Party machine, exposing and sharpening tensions within the New Deal coalition.

However, the SWP's portrayal of Hague as fascist indicated that their conception of fascism was not nearly as clear in practice as the profile from Joseph Hansen quoted above. Because Hague didn't lead any sort of popular mass movement and lacked any ideology beyond amassing power and wealth, it's unclear what made him more fascist than other machine politicians who had been suppressing organized labor since the nineteenth century. Far from indicating a breakdown of the existing "democratic" system, as Trotsky suggested, Hague's was one in a long string of repressive enterprises that have been an integral part of the U.S. liberal-pluralist political order.

Confronting McCarthyism

In the 1950s, both the Communist Party and the SWP saw a renewed push toward fascism in the anticommunist witch-hunts spearheaded by Senator Joseph McCarthy. As the Cold War opened in the late 1940s, many liberals joined with conservatives and far rightists in a campaign to drive radical leftists from public life. In 1947, President Harry Truman initiated a loyalty program to root out supposed radicals from the federal civil service, and the purge soon spread across both public and private sectors. Communists and their allies were driven out of positions of influence in the labor movement and civil rights organizations, and dozens of CP members were imprisoned under the Smith Act (as several SWP leaders had been a few years earlier, with CP approval).[16]

Between 1950 and 1954, Senator McCarthy used his congressional soapbox to undertake anticommunist smear campaigns against high-ranking liberals and conservatives in the State Department and other federal agencies—the very officials who were leading the global campaign against the Soviet Union and its allies. It was an attempted purge within the purge, reflecting divisions within the ruling class. McCarthy spoke for ultraconservatives who believed there was a secret alliance between overt radicals and upper class, Ivy League–educated officials. He was supported by midwestern and Sunbelt businessmen against the more powerful Eastern Establishment capitalists who had largely made their peace with the New Deal.[17]

These dynamics were not necessarily clear at the time. The Communist Party warned that "the creeping process of fascization" had intensified and saw McCarthyism as "the most formidable effort to organize a mass fascist movement in the U.S."[18] The SWP saw McCarthy as head of "an incipient fascist movement" with a "political machine [that] is fundamentally independent from the two capitalist party machines" and the beginnings of "a demagogic social program to direct the discontent of farmers, small businessmen, and workers into fascist channels." The Trotskyists argued that capitalism was in its "death agony," social revolution was "imminent," and an organized fascist movement was therefore "an imperative necessity" to the ruling class. They predicted, "If the workers' organizations don't have the answer, the fascists will utilize the rising discontent of the middle class, its disgust with the blundering labor leadership, and its frenzy at being ruined economically, to build a mass fascist movement with armed detachments and hurl them at the unions."[19]

One problem with the SWP's analysis was that McCarthy never actually tried to organize a mass movement or formulate a coherent program other than rooting out supposed traitors. But beyond that, their prediction of a middle class–based fascist backlash against unions was completely out of touch with the realities of U.S. economy and society in the 1950s, as Louis Proyect has pointed out:

> Rather than expressing "rising discontent" or "frenzy," the middle-class was taking advantage of dramatic increases in personal wealth. Rather than plotting attacks on union halls like the Silver Shirts did in 1938, they were moving to suburbia, buying televisions and station wagons, and taking vacations in Miami or Europe. This was not only objectively possible for the average middle-class family, it was also becoming possible for the worker in basic industry. For the very same reason the working-class was not gravitating toward socialism, the middle-class was not gravitating toward fascism. This reason, of course, is that prosperity had become general.[20]

The SWP did note that McCarthy was backed by "a group of fabulously wealthy oil tycoons of Texas" who were "a relatively new sector of Big Business and far from the decisive power in the capitalist class." But the Trotskyists didn't recognize the significance of this connection—that McCarthy served as front man for an *outsider* business faction *against* the Eastern Establishment. Instead, they glossed over the intra-capitalist rivalry and described McCarthy's oil tycoon supporters as "the initial recruits for fascism in America's ruling class" and "a point of contact with other capitalists who can be recruited."[21] Although the SWP declared that a working-class mobilization was needed to stop McCarthy, his crusade was actually halted by a vote of the U.S. Senate, with support from Eastern businessmen.

Black Panther Party's United Front Against Fascism

The charge of government fascism was resurrected in the late 1960s and early 1970s by various sectors of the New Left, notably the Black Panther Party (BPP). Formed in Oakland in 1966, the Panthers soon became a leading force in both the black liberation movement and the Marxist left nationwide. By the end of the decade, they were also a major target of repression by both the FBI and local police. Across the United States, BPP activists were killed, arrested and subjected to lengthy prosecutions on phony charges, and targeted by dirty tricks and smear campaigns designed to isolate and divide them against each other.[22]

Fascism was not initially a major concern for the Black Panther Party. It's not mentioned in their original Ten-Point Program. But as the arrests and police killings of Panthers mounted, the party began increasingly to label the repression they faced as fascist. In July 1969, they convened a national conference to build a "United Front Against Fascism." The BPP conception of fascism borrowed directly from the Communist Party, which funded and participated in the July 1969 conference.[23] In 1970, the BPP newspaper declared:

> As the struggle intensifies, and reaches toward higher levels, the power structure responds with increased levels of repression; insanely murderous violence, and terror, in futile attempts to intimidate or destroy all opposition to its inhuman system. As each day passes, we must cope with … a slow, but sure and purposeful trend toward the establishment of an open fascist dictatorship led by the Nixons, Agnews, Mitchells and Hoovers, and avidly encouraged by the avaricious, power-mad, super-rich hogs of Babylon—Rockefeller, DuPonts, Hunts, Gettys, Mellons, Kennedys, and Company.[24]

Black Panther George Jackson took this point even further, arguing that fascism's "most advanced form" was already in place in the United States. Jackson joined the BPP while serving a "one year to life" prison sentence for robbing a gas station, and became one of the party's leading intellectuals prior to being killed by prison guards in 1971. In his view, U.S. fascism went far beyond repression alone:

> Fascism does indeed exist, with its spies everywhere, its immediate and violent response to all truly revolutionary threats, its multitude of police agencies, police, and its careful attempt to create a police science, its encroachments on the rights of labor to deal with management, its mass expanding consumer economy, and fostering of spectacular sports to ludicrous proportions with the sole intent of diverting attention and energy into harmless channels.[25]

Jackson identified as fascist "the actual totalitarian essence of a consensual political system that forces one forever into the illusion that he is choosing the lesser of two evils, when actually all parties... represent the interest of the same centralized monopoly but with slightly different disguises.... "[26]

In his book *Blood in My Eye*, Jackson argued that the United States' "capitalist orientation and its anti-labor, anti-class nature... almost by themselves identify the U.S. as a fascist-corporative state." He asserted that Franklin Roosevelt had formed "the first fascist regime," which "merge[d] the economic, political and labor elites.... [H]is role was to limit competition, replace it with the dream of cooperation; to put laissez faire to rest, and to initiate the acceptance of government intervention into economic affairs."[27] These comments echoed and expanded upon the Communist Party's Third Period line, while implicitly rejecting the CP's later endorsement of Roosevelt's liberal-reformist turn. Jackson's description of the entire political and cultural apparatus as fascist highlighted the connections between direct physical repression and subtler methods of control, and emphasized the need for comprehensive revolution to effect meaningful change. At the same time, this analysis offered revolutionaries no way to navigate the differences between a liberal-pluralist system, a top-down authoritarian regime, and a dictatorship based on populist mass mobilization.

Leftists versus the George W. Bush administration

Since the 1970s, leftists have sometimes labeled right-wing politicians such as Richard Nixon and Ronald Reagan as fascist, but George W. Bush's presidency gave new life to the charge of a rising fascist state. Bush took office in 2001, after a disputed, close contest that was decided by the Supreme Court and that many opponents considered a stolen election. In the crisis atmosphere following the 9-11 attacks eight months later, Bush spearheaded a number of new repressive measures, such as pushing the USA Patriot Act through Congress and rounding up thousands of South Asian and Middle Eastern men. He promoted a vision of American democracy locked in an apocalyptic, global struggle against evil, and proclaimed a seemingly limitless "War on Terror" against a vaguely defined set of enemies. In the process, Bush's administration invaded and occupied both Afghanistan and Iraq, and oversaw the systematic use of torture against prisoners of war. In both ideological and practical terms, the Bush administration embodied fascism in the eyes of many left and liberal critics.[28]

While the various versions of the "Bush=fascist" claim highlighted important repressive features of the Bush administration, all of them failed to delineate fascism clearly from other forms of right-wing authoritarianism. The most common version used a laundry list approach, in which the Bush administration was measured against a set of vague characteristics to "prove" that it was fascist. For example, many Bush opponents cited a vaguely worded list of "fourteen defining characteristics of fascism" that was adapted from Laurence W. Britt's 2003 article, "Fascism Anyone?," such as militarism, scapegoating of enemies, sexism, obsession with national security, protecting the power of corporations and suppressing the power of labor, disdain for human rights and intellectual freedom, controlled mass media, and fraudulent elections. The themes in Britt's list were either generic to most right-wing governments or defined so broadly as to blur all major differences between the U.S. political system and classical fascism.[29]

The Revolutionary Communist Party, a Maoist group, declared in a 2005 leaflet that Bush and his associates were "Christian Fascists... who aim to make the U.S. a religious dictatorship and to force this upon the world" with backing from "the most powerful capitalists." This exaggerated the power of the Christian right within the Bush coalition and also glossed over important ideological differences between hard-line Christian theocrats and the movement's larger and more opportunistic wing, which sought to amass power within the existing system, not overthrow it.[30]

Michael Novick, editor of the Anti-Racist Action network–affiliated newspaper *Turning the Tide*, has long highlighted fascism's interconnections with colonialism and, in a U.S. context, the centuries-old system of white supremacy. In a 2003 editorial he argued that "fascist methods of rule" had historically been directed against people of color and that being spared these methods was "the fundamental basis of white privilege." Now, however, the Bush administration and its business supporters were "fundamentally transforming the nature of the U.S. state" in ways that extended fascist rule to white working-class people as well.

This implied that white privilege itself was being dismantled. But a lot of Novick's own work has emphasized the continuing reality of racial oppression and white privilege, and Bush administration policies arguably increased racial disparities, not lessened them. In an email discussion about this point Novick wrote that white privilege remained an important reality but was diminishing. While raising important issues, Novick's approach offered no clear way to distinguish fascism from other forms of repression.[31]

Claims that the Bush administration was ushering in fascism were used in different ways. When Bush ran for re-election in 2004, liberal commentator Thom Hartmann urged people to "join together at the ballot box to stop this most recent incarnation of feudal fascism from seizing complete control of our nation." On the other hand, Michael Novick insisted in 2005 that forestalling fascism required "a thorough economic, political and social transformation. ... Passing a law, winning an election, or even impeaching or removing a president won't do it."[32]

Conclusion

Leftist claims of impending fascism in the United States have varied significantly in political content. Some but not all have reflected a larger theory of fascism and its relationship to capitalism and the radical left. Some but not all have served a strategic purpose, either defensive or offensive. But in all of the historical examples I've discussed, claims of impending fascism have brought with them a number of problems. Some of these claims have blurred the line between fascism and liberal reformism. Some have glossed over tensions and conflicts within the ruling class. Many have underestimated the U.S. political system's resilience and elasticity, its ability to shift between openness and repression and to co-opt political challenges. And all of them have either lumped together right-wing insurgency and elite-driven authoritarianism, or ignored right-wing insurgency entirely.

The kernel of truth in these claims is that it's important to address the linkages and points of commonality between fascism and mainstream U.S. politics. Too many discussions obscure the ways in which fascist politics is rooted in U.S. society and dynamically connected with non-fascist actors and institutions. These interconnections are vital for helping us understand right-wing political dynamics. But it's equally important to be able to make distinctions between different kinds of right-wing threats. As the following chapter demonstrates, Donald Trump's rise to power and early presidency exemplify the interplay between far right and system-loyal political currents, and highlight the need for clear analysis and thoughtful use of political terms such as fascism.

11. Trump's Presidency and the Far Right

Donald Trump's presidential campaign and election victory dramatically shifted the terrain on which U.S. far rightists operate. More than any other president in living memory, Trump was aided by far rightists on his path to the White House. And more than any other president in living memory, Trump has given voice to far right political themes, leading people from the left to the conservative right to denounce him as a fascist. Trump's election and many of his early actions as president emboldened organized far rightists and encouraged supremacist violence. But in his first months in office Trump did not break with the established political order or even with the prevailing neoliberal policy framework. Whatever his desires or intentions, it was not clear that he had the power to do either of these things.

The first part of this chapter explores the political character of Donald Trump's presidential campaign and early administration, starting with an assessment of claims that Trump was or is a fascist. (See the Appendix to this book for background on how I approach the concept of fascism.) The second part looks at how various far right currents have responded to Trump and how this has affected their relationship with the established political system. Because I am writing less than a year after Trump took office, this discussion is preliminary and tentative and may well be dated by the time it appears in print. At a minimum, I hope that it will offer a useful baseline of comparison for interpreting later developments.

Trump's campaign: fascist politics?

Trump ran for president in 2015–2016 as a right-wing populist with authoritarian tendencies. He advocated the harshest anti-immigrant measures of any major party presidential candidate in generations, such as barring all Muslim newcomers and rounding up and deporting all eleven million undocumented immigrants. He endorsed the use of torture, encouraged his supporters to use violence against political opponents, bragged about sexually assaulting women, and promoted a cult of personality around himself. He attacked the political establishment and rejected conventional conservatism in ways that recalled earlier right-wing populist presidential candidates—as well as fascist claims to be "neither left nor right." Like George Wallace in 1968, who appealed to working-class whites by defending both racial segregation and expanded welfare state policies, Trump took "liberal" positions on some domestic issues, such as protecting Social Security and calling for universal access to health care. Like Pat Buchanan in the 1990s, Trump rejected Washington's free trade consensus in favor of economic nationalism and protectionism, called for the United States to pull back from its global military role and system of alliances, and denounced globalist financial elites in terms that echoed antisemitic themes. He also broke with the foreign policy establishment in repeatedly praising Russian President Vladimir Putin, calling for closer cooperation between the United States and Russia, and suggesting that he would recognize the Russian annexation of Crimea.[1]

Accusations that Trump was a fascist came not only from leftists and liberals but also from centrists, neoconservatives, and libertarians, and invoked theories of fascism ranging from Leon Trotsky to Ludwig von Mises.[2] Some critics relied on the nebulous statement—incorrectly attributed to Mussolini—that fascism equals a merger of state and corporate power.[3] Others calculated Trump's percentage "score" based on various laundry lists of fascism's supposedly essential characteristics. Umberto Eco's list of fourteen features typical of "ur-fascism" was popular (such as irrationalism, cult of tradition, selective populism, and contempt for the weak), as was Robert Paxton's list of fascism's nine "mobilizing passions" (such as a sense of overwhelming crisis, a feeling of collective victimhood, and a belief in the leader's instincts over reason).[4] Radical journalist Alexander Reid Ross argued that we should look at fascism "as a 'process' rather than an 'outcome'," and that "Trumpism" was "part of a process of 'fascist creep,' meaning a radicalization of conservative ideology that increasingly includes fascist membership while deploying fascist ideology, strategy, and tactics."[5] This approach rightly emphasized that many political initiatives occupy a gray area between fascist and conservative politics and that the political character of such initiatives can change over time. But Ross simply assumed that Trump's campaign—unlike previous right-wing populist candidates such as George Wallace and Pat Buchanan—had an inherent tendency to move toward fascism and would not be co-opted by the established political system.

For many liberals, arguments that Trump was a fascist overlapped with claims that he was acting on behalf of the Russian government. These claims were fueled partly by Trump's public admiration for Putin and calls for a friendlier policy toward Russia, and partly by reports, government leaks, and media speculation about Kremlin interference in the U.S. election and possible links with members of Trump's campaign. Hillary Clinton fueled this theme during the presidential campaign, declaring in an October 2016 speech that "Putin is manipulating Donald... to make Donald the Kremlin's puppet. And it seems to be working."[6] Echoing Cold War–era red-baiting, Franklin Foer in *Slate* argued that "we should think of the Trump campaign as the moral equivalent of Henry Wallace's communist-infiltrated campaign for president in 1948.... A foreign power that wishes ill upon the United States has attached itself to a major presidential campaign."[7] The day before the inauguration, liberal blogger Greg Olear called Trump both "a Fascist" and "a compromised Russian asset."[8] In April 2017, Joe Conason in *AlterNet* wrote that Trump's promotion of "fascist themes" was part of his role as "a political stalking horse for Vladimir Putin," who sought to "disrupt and disorganize the democratic West."[9]

As of this writing, the extent and nature of Russian government involvement in the 2016 U.S. election and its ties to the Trump campaign remain unclear and may well turn out to have been significant. Setting aside claims that Trump is "the Kremlin's puppet," his family has a long history of dealings in the world where Russian business, state security forces, and organized crime are closely intertwined.[10] But as was pointed out by Masha Gessen, a staunch critic of both Putin and Trump, "the protracted national game of connecting the Trump-Putin dots" mingled facts, distortions, unsubstantiated claims, and outright falsehoods, and was driven largely by uncorroborated leaks from U.S.

spy agencies, "setting a dangerous political precedent." It amounted to "promoting a xenophobic conspiracy theory in the cause of removing a xenophobic conspiracy theorist from office."[11] As Doug Henwood commented in December 2016, blaming "shady foreign operators" was all too convenient for Democrats who wanted to avoid confronting their party's own political shortcomings, and for Americans in general who wanted to avoid confronting the U.S. political system's undemocratic nature.[12] The Trump-as-Putin-puppet theme echoed those liberals in the early 1940s who portrayed the movement to keep the United States out of World War II as the result of a Berlin conspiracy, rather than a homegrown social movement. In the end, Putin's greatest leverage over Trump may simply be as a role model of authoritarian nationalist rule.

Clearly, Trump's politics has embodied important elements of fascist politics, and his rise was dynamically interconnected with the growth of the alt-right and other fascist political currents. But several major differences delineate Trump's politics from fascism as I understand the term. First, fascism in power imposes dictatorial control, but in the first months after his inauguration Trump did not even take routine steps to gain control of the executive branch. During his first one hundred days as prime minister, as historian Victoria de Grazia has pointed out, Mussolini started ruling by decree, turned the Fascist Party's paramilitary Blackshirts into a national militia personally loyal to him, and began to massacre leftist workers. During the equivalent period, as political scientist Corey Robin has noted, Donald Trump failed to even nominate people to fill most of the senior positions in the Pentagon or national security agencies, leaving them vacant or, in many cases, still held by Obama appointees.[13]

Second, fascism is not just an "extreme" form of right-wing politics, but a revolutionary one, in that it aims to overthrow the existing political order and create a radically new type of state, culture, and society. Even Italian Fascism, which was far less radical than German Nazism and left major institutions such as the church and the military more or less intact, dramatically transformed the country's cultural, educational, and political landscape to conform to Mussolini's explicitly totalitarian vision, and this transformation got stronger, not weaker, as time went on. By contrast, Trump offered no real vision of cultural or social change and, despite his contempt for democratic principles, did not call the established political system into question.

Third, fascism is populist not just in words but also in actions. Both as a movement and a regime, it seeks to actively and permanently mobilize large masses of people through a network of organizations, public rituals, and—in many versions—paramilitary formations. Although fascists have historically made use of support within existing institutions such as the police, building their own independent bases of support has been crucial to their rise to power, suppression of opponents, and efforts to transform the state and society. By contrast, Trump made skillful use of social media and campaign rallies but did not control or try to build any kind of independent organizational base that would live on past the election.

The political collective Research & Destroy described the gap between Trump and fascism as a kind of Catch-22 dilemma. On the one hand, they argued, in order to "make America great again" in a way that would bring jobs and growth to large numbers of white people (as opposed to just bringing more plunder to the billionaires on his team), Trump would have to bring about "a reorganization of capitalism along new and newly fascistic lines." On the other hand, in order to bring about an actual fascist transformation, Trump "will need loyal people at all levels of the government, as well as extra-governmental forces capable of doing the dirtiest work but also forcing the hand of bureaucrats and judges too loyal to the letter of the law." And to win this kind of loyalty, "he will actually have to put people to work and build infrastructure and increase their living standards."[14]

While not fascist, Trump's rise represented an important challenge to some aspects of neoliberalism—Washington's ruling ideology of deregulation, privatization, relatively open borders, and free trade—and to the related consensus around interventionism in foreign and military policy. In this respect Trump's campaign built on earlier initiatives such as Pat Buchanan's presidential campaigns in the 1990s and, as Benjamin Studebaker argued, was fueled by the Great Recession that began in 2007–2008:

> Economic ideologies change when there is an economic disaster that is seen to discredit the prevailing ideology. The Great Depression discredited the classical economics practiced by right wingers like Calvin Coolidge, allowing for left wing policies that in the 1920s would have sounded insane to ordinary people. The stagflation in the '70s discredited the Keynesian egalitarianism of

FDR and LBJ, allowing Ronald Reagan to implement right wing
policies that would have been totally unthinkable to people living
in the 1960s.

I submit to you that the 2008 economic crisis and the stagnation
that has followed have discredited the neoliberal economic ideology of Reagan and Clinton not just among democrats, but for supporters of both parties, and that new policies and candidates are
possible now that would have been totally unthinkable to people
as recently as 10 years ago.[15]

As Studebaker argued, neoliberalism had dominated both major parties
since the 1980s, but in the 2016 race was challenged from two sides: the
"left egalitarianism" of Bernie Sanders (essentially an updated version
of the New Deal and the Great Society) and the "right nationalism" of
Donald Trump and Ted Cruz. Sanders's unexpectedly strong showing
in the primaries and Trump's surprise victories, first over his Republican
rivals and then over Democrat Hillary Clinton, pointed to broad-based
popular anger at the political establishment and its neoliberal consensus.
Yet as many of his critics pointed out, Trump won the Electoral College
with almost three million fewer popular votes than Clinton.

Trump administration: America first or crony capitalism?

Trump's populist-nationalist campaign positions, coupled with his nas-
tiness toward both liberal and conservative opponents, were applauded
by many far rightists but put him at odds with most Republican officials, many of whom repudiated or barely tolerated Trump during
the campaign. Yet because he lacked an organizational base of his own,
Trump was immediately forced not only to work with establishment
figures in the Republican Party but also to bring them into his own administration. As a result, from the beginning Trump's presidency rested
on an unstable coalition of right-wing factions both opposed to and
aligned with conventional conservatism. The neoliberal consensus was
starting to break down, but populist nationalism was not strong enough
or developed enough to supplant it clearly.

Trump's candidacy also alienated many, if not most, business leaders. The business community has never been able to simply pick the winners of presidential elections, but the 2016 election pointed to a new degree of volatility in capitalists' political role. Historically, campaign finance laws have arguably done little to make the electoral system democratic, but they have helped to mediate conflicting business interests so as to improve the cohesiveness with which the capitalist class influences the political system. But since the U.S. Supreme Court's 2010 *Citizens United* ruling, which removed almost all limits on how much money individuals and corporations can spend on federal elections, it has become much easier for a few extraordinarily wealthy individuals to influence political outcomes far out of proportion to whatever sectoral business interests they may represent. Robert and Rebekah Mercer, who swung their support behind a struggling Trump campaign in the summer of 2016, exemplified this dynamic, as Jane Mayer demonstrated in a lengthy profile of the Mercer father and daughter team.[16] As a computer scientist whose role in an investment management company made him a billionaire, Robert Mercer's support for the Trump campaign probably reflects his own political idiosyncrasies and personal interests rather than any general trend by financial services firms away from the neoliberal consensus.

In the context of Studebaker's analogy between neoliberalism's post-2008 decline and Keynesianism's decline in the 1970s, a useful precedent for understanding Trump's presidency may be that of Richard Nixon. As Thomas Ferguson and Joel Rogers have argued, the Nixon administration was "the product of elaborate compromises among different and commonly competing groups," including both New Deal supporters and opponents. As a result, the Nixon administration sometimes worked to dismantle Lyndon Johnson's Great Society legacy, but also sometimes extended it.[17]

President Trump filled a number of key positions with people who represented the "America First" nationalism he ran on. Of these, the two most significant appointments were Jeff Sessions as attorney general and Steven Bannon as White House chief strategist, both of whom combined thinly veiled white supremacy, an emphasis on excluding immigrants and refugees, economic nationalism, and populist denunciations of corporate crime. After being turned down for a federal judgeship in 1986 for racist comments and actions, Sessions spent twenty years as U.S. senator from Alabama; unlike most Republican officials, he was a longtime opponent of "soulless globalism." Sessions endorsed Trump's presidential bid early, and after the election he helped plan the president's early executive orders and installed close allies in several other important posts.[18]

Bannon was even more of a political outsider than Sessions. Before joining Trump's presidential campaign he spent several years as head of the sensationalist, hard-line conservative *Breitbart News*, and in 2016 he once declared *Breitbart* "the platform of the alt-right." Bannon has long enjoyed the patronage of billionaire Robert Mercer and his daughter Rebekah Mercer. Often misidentified as a leader of the alt-right, Bannon offered Trump his own distinctive version of authoritarian nationalism, combining paleoconservatism's hostility toward globalist elites and non-European immigrants with neoconservatism's grandiose vision of an apocalyptic war between Western civilization and "radical Islam." His image of African and Middle Eastern refugees was shaped by Jean Raspail's *The Camp of the Saints*, one of the most extraordinarily racist novels of the past half-century. As a right-wing populist, Bannon criticized the failure to bring criminal charges against any of the bank executives associated with the 2008 financial collapse. He praised "entrepreneurial" capitalism that is "enlightened" by "Judeo-Christian values," while denouncing "crony capitalism," in which business and the state are too closely connected. Ambiguously, Bannon also denounced the ultralibertarian capitalism of Ayn Rand, while calling for the "deconstruction of the administrative state." He also expressed ambivalence about Russia, criticizing President Vladimir Putin's government as an imperialist, state-capitalist kleptocracy while praising its traditionalism and nationalism.[19]

At the very beginning of Trump's presidency, Sessions and Bannon's politics seemed to be ascendant. Trump's inaugural address struck a starkly nationalist and populist tone. "For too long," he declared, "a small group in our nation's capital has reaped the rewards of government while the people have borne the cost."

> For many decades, we've enriched foreign industry at the expense of American industry; subsidized the armies of other countries while allowing for the very sad depletion of our military; we've defended other nations' borders while refusing to defend our own; and spent trillions of dollars overseas while America's infrastructure has fallen into disrepair and decay.

Trump asserted, "From this moment on, it's going to be America First.... We must protect our borders from the ravages of other countries making our products, stealing our companies and destroying our jobs. Protection will lead to great prosperity and strength." He promised the United States would "follow two simple rules: Buy American and Hire American," and he pledged to "unite the civilized world against Radical Islamic Terrorism, which we will eradicate completely from the face of the Earth."[20]

In this same vein, President Trump quickly signed executive orders to withdraw the United States from the (not yet ratified) Trans-Pacific Partnership Agreement, hire ten thousand more immigration enforcement officers, and dramatically expand the number of undocumented immigrants considered priorities for deportation. He also imposed a hiring freeze on many agencies and halted various environmental and consumer protection regulations. Most controversially, Trump ordered a temporary halt to the refugee program and to all entry by citizens of several majority-Muslim countries. Implementation of this order was rushed, confused, and inconsistent; the order provoked mass protests at airports and was blocked by federal courts on the grounds that it was an attempt to impose an unconstitutional "Muslim ban." A second, slightly more limited executive order was blocked for the same reason.

Many critics regarded President Trump's early actions, especially the Muslim ban orders, as steps in an authoritarian power grab, or even a bid to impose fascism. But others emphasized the administration's disorganization and lack of preparation. For the first executive order on refugees and immigrants, the administration failed to secure the airports, prepare a legal interpretation in advance, or even provide clear implementation instructions to Homeland Security employees. Corey Robin commented, "while some will argue that the spectacle and the chaos are all part of the point, I'm not persuaded. Trump wants displays of power; instead, he got a display of powerlessness." "If Trump is a fascist, he may be the most backassward fascist we've ever seen," Robin argued, "What is the first thing fascists or Nazis do when they come into power, the very first thing? They destroy the left.... Because they know that in order to pursue their maximal agenda, they need to drain the field of all opposition. Trump hasn't done that; in fact, he's done just the opposite."[21]

Coupled with the confusion, disorganization, and protests, America Firsters also faced growing opposition within the administration itself.

From the beginning, the majority of Trump's high-level appointees were not nationalist-populists, but conventional conservatives of various stripes. Some were Christian rightists or Tea Partiers, some were veterans of the Republican political establishment, and some were known mainly for their experience in the military or in business. From early on, America Firsters clashed with neoliberals and establishment figures in the administration and in Congress on issues such as trade policy, which contributed to an unusual degree of chaos and lack of clear direction. The issues on which the different factions agreed, and on which the Trump administration moved forward most effectively, basically represented a hard-line version of neoliberalism's domestic agenda: dismantle environmental regulations and consumer protection rules, open up public lands to corporate exploitation, "reform" the tax system to further redistribute wealth from low- and middle-income people to the rich, make the judicial system more punitive, and speed up militarization of the police. To a large extent, the result seemed to be policies that benefited narrow capitalist interests, such as military contractors, private prison operators, and energy companies, as well as the Trump family's own businesses, more than a coherent unified program.[22]

Because of the administration's internal conflicts and lack of clear direction, many capitalists were uncertain about how to respond. As Robert Cavooris noted, tech companies funded the presidential inauguration yet opposed the executive order restricting Muslim immigrants and refugees, bankers were pleased when Trump picked Steven Mnuchin of Goldman Sachs as treasury secretary yet worried the president's protectionist stance could produce a global trade war, retailers worried about the idea of a 20 percent import tax (which the White House proposed and then dropped), and so on. Even aggressively right-wing billionaires were divided, with Robert Mercer and Peter Thiel (both of whom became rich through innovative use of IT in financial services) supporting Trump, and the Koch brothers (whose oil baron father co-founded the John Birch Society) opposing him.[23] Trump was forced to shut down his major business advisory councils in August 2017 after a raft of business executives resigned in protest of his remarks equating the white supremacists and antifascist protesters who had recently clashed in Charlottesville, Virginia.[24]

Although the America Firsters were more in sync with Trump's campaign rhetoric and long-stated positions, they quickly began to lose skirmishes to the establishment forces. In February 2017, National Security

Advisor Mike Flynn, an America Firster, was forced to resign by the national security establishment on the grounds that he had lied about contacts with Russian officials. Flynn was replaced by H.R. McMaster, who immediately repudiated the Trump administration's anti-Muslim rhetoric.[25] In March, Attorney General Sessions was forced to recuse himself from the investigation of Russian involvement in the presidential election. In April, Bannon was removed from the National Security Council. Two days later, the U.S. launched a missile attack against a Syrian airbase, a move that Bannon opposed and that many far right Trump supporters denounced as a betrayal of the president's America First stance. As a candidate Trump had declared NATO to be obsolete, pledged to withdraw from the North American Free Trade Agreement and abolish the Export-Import Bank, and called for an alliance with Russian President Putin, but as president he quickly abandoned all of these positions.[26] America Firsters' fortunes within the administration rose in early August 2017 when the White House endorsed a bill to cut legal immigration in half, but plummeted later that month when both Bannon and former *Breitbart* staffer Sebastian Gorka were fired.[27]

A world-historical individual?

Far rightists responded to Trump's presidential campaign in various ways. Some found new faith in the possibility for change within the system, while others saw his attacks on the status quo as either quixotic or insincere. Many wavered between these positions. Over the first few months of his administration, as Trump seemed to slide from America First nationalism toward conventional if bellicose conservatism, some far rightists found their skepticism confirmed, some felt betrayed, and some continued to hope that Trump could still advance their politics in some measure.

At the positive response end of the spectrum, the LaRouche network's *Executive Intelligence Review* declared in August 2017 that "this administration has acted with a higher level of wisdom and responsibility than any in living memory," although there was still room for improvement on various issues, such as banking reform. The LaRouchites applauded Trump's economic nationalism, friendliness toward Vladimir

Putin, and interest in infrastructure projects. They also showed an impressive capacity to project their own policy goals onto President Trump, for example speculating (despite overwhelming evidence to the contrary) that he might join with Democrats to establish a single-payer healthcare system. When Trump did something that directly clashed with LaRouchite positions, such as launching the April 2017 missile strike against Syria, they explained this as the result of the British government "manipulating Trump with fake information."[28]

The far right current that had the most important role in Trump's election victory, and that expressed complex reactions to him most fully, was the alt-right. As discussed in chapter 4, alt-rightists' online activism helped discredit Trump's opponents and rally his supporters, and involvement in the Trump campaign dramatically boosted the alt-right's visibility, public legitimacy, and sense of purpose. Most alt-rightists were thrilled by Trump's upset victory over Clinton, but not because they thought that Trump shared their politics or would bring about the changes they wanted. Rather, they believed that a Trump presidency would offer them "breathing room" to promote their ideology and to "move the Overton window" in their favor. In turn, they saw themselves as the Trump coalition's political vanguard, taking hard-line positions that would pull Trump further to the right while enabling him to look moderate by comparison. In Richard Spencer's words, "The Alt Right and Trumpian populism are now aligned much in the way the Left is aligned with Democratic politicians like Obama or Hillary.... We—*and only we*—can say the things Trump can't say ... can criticize him in the right way ... and can envision a new world that he can't quite grasp."[29] The Traditionalist Youth Network was more specific: "We cannot and will not back down on the Jewish Question or our explicit racial identity. We won't. Don't worry. But we will join those who aren't as radical as we are in pulling politics in our direction."[30]

Joining the Trump coalition gave alt-rightists unprecedented access to mainstream conservatives via the media and networks such as the College Republicans, but it did not mean pledging loyalty to the political system. Jef Costello of *Counter-Currents* was "agog about Donald Trump" and "for the first time in years feeling hopeful," yet cautioned, "In spite of my support for Trump I do yearn for the destruction of this awful country, which should never have been in the first place." Put another way, "the Donald is a World-Historical Individual. But this is NOT because he is going to 'save America.' It is because he is acting as an agent of destruction … helping to bring about the end of globalism and multiculturalism."[31]

Pro-Trump alt-rightists generally took a wait-and-see approach during the first few months after the election, applauding Trump's anti-immigrant executive orders and appointments such as Bannon and Sessions and Flynn, but increasingly unhappy as mainstream Republicans garnered more and more of the other posts and seemed more and more to be in charge. For many alt-rightists, who not only opposed military interventionism but had increasingly aligned themselves with the governments of Bashir al-Assad and his supporter Vladimir Putin, the U.S. missile strike against Syria was the last straw. At *American Renaissance,* John Derbyshire wrote, "There was always the possibility that Trump would cuck on us. Still, I don't think any of us thought the cucking would come so swiftly."[32] At *The Daily Stormer,* neonazi Andrew Anglin called the event "soul-crushing" and urged his fellow alt-rightists to "take care of each other in this very difficult time."[33] The fact that many conventional politicians and mainstream media organs praised the missile strike underscored alt-rightists' sense of betrayal. In response to claims that Trump had at last accepted the roles of commander-in-chief and leader of the Free World, Brad Griffin blogged in *Occidental Dissent*:

> The Alt-Right doesn't believe in the concept of the "Free World." We didn't vote for another "Leader of the Free World." Instead, we voted *against* being the world's policeman. We voted *against* the West's human rights dogma. We voted *against* the burden of the US Empire. More than anything else, we voted *against* the endless foreign wars in the Middle East that have been raging since our childhood because we wanted nothing to do with that quagmire.[34]

Alt-rightists blamed the administration's change of direction on political and corporate insiders, the intelligence community, and Trump's Jewish advisors (above all his son-in-law Jared Kushner), and speculated about whether Trump had acted out of weakness or was being blackmailed. They debated how best to revise their strategy. Some, such as "Pseudo-Laurentius" at *The Right Stuff,* argued for continuing to play a vanguard role, just more aggressively: "unless Trump crosses the very specific line of enacting anti-White agenda items, we should remain demanding but supportive, not become hostile opposition," because "to fully switch from support to opposition would shut us completely out. We need a Trump administration that becomes increasingly nationalist, not less."[35] But other alt-rightists found this approach no longer tenable. "Meinrad Gaertner" at *Occidental Dissent* envisioned a United States quickly descending into economic collapse and civil war and declared, "No elected official can salvage this nation. There is no reforming the system—it is beyond repair. We can only rebuild from the ashes."[36]

Unlike neonazis who were part of the alt-right, those neonazis who remained separate from it tended to be more skeptical of Donald Trump from the beginning. On the *Iron March* discussion forum ("the Online HQ for the IronMarch Global Fascist Fraternity"), a July 2016 discussion thread about the election tended toward the view that the whole thing was a farce. One participant commented, "I think Trump is like Reagan of his time, in a sense that he is there to pacify the population amidst growing popularity of right-wing ideas. There is a chance he legitimately is right-wing (not in N[ational] S[ocialist] sense, but more in paleoconservative kind of way), but even that won't fix the problem. In any case, whoever wins I hope it will result in a massive civil war in US and a global recession."[37]

In December 2016, American Nazi Party leader Rocky Suhayda offered cautious praise for the president-elect:

> Mr Trump had the savvy AND the courage to break the "PC curtain" of SILENCE that virtually ALL systemite politicians toe the line to.... The Donald had from the FIRST the understanding of the ANGER and FRUSTRATION of those TENS of MILLIONS of White American workers, MEN and/or WOMEN, BLUE or White collar, that the usual political whores dare not appeal to—and he took a logical gamble and pulled it off.[38]

But Suhayda also commented that Trump's picks for his administration had been "nothing more or less than a role [sic] call of the USUAL political vermin that we're used to seeing." By January 2017, Suhayda's assessment was harsher:

> [T]he Blacks THOUGHT that Obama was going to be their Savior in the White House. LMAO! Just "WHAT" did the Mighty Mulatto DO for THEM? NOTHING. *Does* ANYONE reading these words honestly think that the MULTI-BILLIONAIRE

Mega 1%er is going out on a limb for YOU Whitey? Yet, as the ALTERNATIVE is rolling up your sleeves and DOING what needs to be done by every White man AND woman—the appeal of the "Hero on the White Horse" doing it FOR you, still stands as the #1 choice of White America.

The ONLY thing that the election of Trump SHOWS, is that there IS viable, mass support for many of our key issues—IF we swear to take advantage of utilizing them![39]

On the *Iron March*–affiliated website *Noose*, "Max Macro" blogged in February 2016 that "Donald Trump functions as a jewish measuring stick for emerging racial consciousness—the objective is for him to act as a relief valve and to keep all related discourse within a *semitically*-correct, patriotard frame, preventing it from reaching a point of explicit racial consciousness and organization." He also commented that white nationalists who supported Trump were "hilariously oblivious to the fact that *Donnie* would have absolutely no problem Ruby Ridging these people's families on behalf of his Jewish friends," referring to the 1992 incident in which federal agents attempting to arrest Aryan Nations sympathizer Randy Weaver shot and killed his wife and teenage son.[40] After Trump's victory, Macro wrote a follow-up post in a similar vein: "The second Trump actually steps into office, he becomes our enemy to be held accountable for the promises he'll no doubt fail to deliver on. And no, Steve Bannon of Kikebart is not gonna do our job for us either, conflating his semitically correct civic nationalism with our cause just confuses people into thinking we've scored more than we actually have."[41]

The anti-globalist he claims to be?

Patriot groups were not prominently involved in Trump's presidential campaign, but like alt-rightists they predominantly supported him. Patriot activists applauded Trump's denunciations of the political establishment and globalist elites; his attacks on Muslims, immigrants, and Black Lives Matter; and his hostility toward environmental regulation.

And while alt-rightists hoped to pull Trump's administration from civic nationalism to white nationalism, most Patriot groups shared Trump's disavowal of explicit racial politics.

Yet like alt-rightists, Patriots' enthusiasm about Trump was tinged with caution. After the election, the Oath Keepers' "Shorty Dawkins" asked, "Is [Trump] the anti-globalist he claims to be? ... I sincerely hope so, but the proof is in the pudding."[42] Soon after Trump's inauguration, Dawkins added, "Hillary, and the leftist/Globalist cabal, lost the election. People everywhere are waking up to what Globalism is all about, and they are rejecting it. That is the message of the election. Trump may be the answer. If not, the people will find someone else."[43] Georgia Security Forces leader Chris Hill warned, "We have to be just as vigilant in January as we are today. Revolution is still on the table."[44]

Over the early months of Trump's administration, Patriot activists applauded many of his actions, from his executive orders barring people from several majority-Muslim countries to his call to slash federal land acquisition for national parks.[45] Yet this support was not unanimous. When the White House announced a budget proposal that called for eliminating nineteen federal agencies, one commenter at *ThreePercenter. org* called it "a great starting point" since the agencies targeted were "just more ways to funnel money to Leftist causes." But another activist, expressing the movement's long-term worries about federal repression, asked why the Bureau of Alcohol, Tobacco, Firearms and Explosives and other "jack boot agencies" were not on the list.[46] On a different discussion thread, a Three Percenter wrote, "We got the president that we needed into the White House," but complained that Trump had made no moves to kick out the "100,000 United Nations foreign troops" who were supposedly garrisoned on military bases across the United States. Another commenter agreed that these UN troops were "WAY WORSE than any immigrant threat," and added, "If trump is so pro constitution, why was one of his first acts of office not to roll back the patriot act and the NDAA [National Defense Authorization Act]?"[47]

Despite these concerns about Trump, Patriot groups were much more worried about the liberal and leftist opposition he faced. In the days before the election, Oath Keepers warned that Black Lives Matter and other groups might try to disrupt the voting with violence. Afterwards, as Trump opponents took to the streets in a series of protests across the country, Patriot activists reacted angrily, sometimes in language tinged with racism or antisemitism. Patriot groups claimed that anti-Trump demonstrators were "brain-washed" by the mass media, or "ventrilo-quist dummies" mouthing slogans written by globalist elites. Some claimed that Barack Obama was behind the protests, others that they were bankrolled and organized by liberal Jewish financier George Soros.[48] Oath Keepers openly launched an operation to infiltrate and spy on anti-Trump protest groups and then reported on their findings about the ideologies, tactics, and demographics of the different anti-Trump currents: "liberal socialists" were "primarily coming out of our higher education system"; "communists" represented "a much broader spectrum of society" and had "no ethical boundaries"; and "anarchists" were "by far the most dangerous," "organized like militias," and had "zero tolerance for weakness."[49] Oath Keepers declared that it was shar-ing spy reports with law enforcement and hoped they would be used to prosecute protesters for their "treasonous attacks on our nation and our constitution."[50] Patriot activists rationalized this repressive, system-loyal activity by treating it as resistance to abusive power—supposedly they were defending a populist upsurge against an elite-sponsored cam-paign to suppress it. Over the following months, Patriot activists in sev-eral states provided security or worked for pro-Trump elected officials or local politicians.[51]

Like alt-rightists, many Patriot activists were shocked and angered by President Trump's April 2017 missile strike against Syria. Comments on the website *A Well Regulated Militia* ... spoke for many: "On the campaign trail, Trump was criticizing past administrations for med-dling in the Middle East with useless wars. ... But it looks like he's go-ing down that same road again." "I didn't join the Marine Corps to fight for al Qaeda in a Syrian civil war." "Can someone please show me where this country has the right to bomb another country when no American was killed."[52] The Oath Keepers' NavyJack commented, "as a candidate, Donald Trump was severely critical of U.S. foreign inter-ventionism. ... It's difficult for me to accept that President Trump could reverse course on Syria so quickly. ... Is President Trump so impetuous as to risk war with Russia over what could just be a Syrian bomb strik-ing a chemical munition in a known al-Nusra Front munition ware-house?" Or, as the article's headline asked, "Has President Trump Been Blackmailed or Deceived by the NEOCONs?"[53] But unlike many alt-rightists, Patriot groups tended to get over their anger about the Syria strike and return to more favorable coverage of Trump.[54]

An instrument of God?

Many Christian right voters supported Donald Trump in November 2016, thanks to their hatred of Hillary Clinton, Trump's hurried shift to Christian right positions on questions such as abortion rights, and his choice of Mike Pence for vice president. As president, Trump also chose evangelical Christians for a majority of cabinet posts.[55] Hard dominionists, however, were sharply split over Trump. The issue highlighted and further crystallized the political divide between the New Apostolic Reformation movement, which seemed to step back from its theocratic goals to a more clearly system-loyal stance, and many Christian Reconstructionists, who continued to reject the established political order.

In June 2016, about four months before his death, New Apostolic Reformation founder C. Peter Wagner published an article endorsing Donald Trump for president. This was the first time that Wagner had issued a presidential endorsement. He argued that "much of America's malady has been caused over the years by the establishment politics of both parties in Washington, D.C." and that Trump, as "someone whose life has been business before politics, who finances his own campaign, and who is beholden to no one in Washington" offered the best prospects of turning the country around. Acknowledging that Trump wasn't much of a Christian, Wagner argued that "God is not limited to using Christians to accomplish His purposes" and compared Trump to Cyrus, "the idolatrous king of Persia, whom God used to help get His people back to Jerusalem."

In the same article, Wagner also argued that Trump's rise was in keeping with the NAR goal to transform the "Seven Mountains" or seven areas of cultural influence. Previously, Wagner had called for achieving Christian dominion over society by having "kingdom-minded people" (those oriented toward God's kingdom) influencing each of the seven mountains, but now he declared that this was only important in the Religion Mountain.[56] For the other cultural areas, it was simply important to have "successful people" in charge, and Trump was a successful businessman. "I want to vote for a commander-in-chief, not a bishop-in-chief."[57] The conservative Lutheran website *Pirate Christian* commented that Wagner was abandoning dominionism in favor of the philosophy that "anyone with a big ego and bank account is on the Lord's side."[58]

Several other NAR leaders also praised Trump, generally in terms that were vague about substantive policies. In August 2016, motivational speaker and NAR apostle Lance Wallnau portrayed Trump as a "wrecking ball" to political correctness who would help Christians wrest control of cultural institutions from Satan.[59] After the election, Johnny Enlow, author of *The Seven Mountain Prophecy*, wrote that Trump would reform governmental systems such as prisons and criminal justice, boost the national and global economies, and expose "corrupting influences in media" to bring about far-reaching reform.[60] Cindy Jacobs, co-founder of Generals International, prophesied that Trump would "restore America's relationship with Israel" and that the United States would "receive blessing from the hand of the Lord" as a result.[61] As protests mounted against President Trump, MorningStar Ministries head Rick Joyner commented that Trump's opponents were manifesting Satan's rage at being displaced from power.[62] Lou Engle, co-founder of the prayer meeting organization TheCall, called for three days of fasting and prayer to save Trump and his associates from a curse by witches.[63]

Discussion of Trump among Christian Reconstructionists was dramatically different. Facing the choice between Trump and Clinton, Reconstructionists debated whether a Christian should ever vote for the lesser of two evils. *Eagle Rising* editor Gary DeMar said yes, noting that "no one is without evil." DeMar urged support for Trump, arguing tepidly that establishment politicians "would serve as a check on any outrageous policies he might propose."[64] But others argued that lesser-evil voting was never justified. Joel McDurmon, DeMar's successor as president of American Vision, wrote that "The question is akin to asking whether we must support Caligula or Nero Caesar" and declared that "the only way to make American great again lies in Restoring America not in a presidential election, but *one county at a time.*"[65] John M. Otis of *Theonomy Resources* commented that Trump "does not present a credible profession of faith and [his] character is contemptible on multiple levels."[66]

Reversing claims by NAR leaders and many other Christian rightists that Trump was an instrument of God, Kevin Swanson of Christian Home Educators of Colorado declared that if Trump were elected president it would reflect God's plan—not to make America great, but to destroy it. "He sets up over empires the basest of men and prepares the empires for the dismantlement, as He did to Babylon, as He did to Assyria, as He did to Persia, as He did to Greece, as He did to

Rome.... You're talking about the absolute lowest, least qualified, basest of men [who] are put in position in order that these kingdoms, these empires may come down."[67]

McDurmon denounced Trump's approach to health care policy as "socialist."[68] Yet he also warned that with President Trump's "attempt to get tough on crime and terrorism" he feared "a tremendous ramp-up in the police state, and since it will no longer be Obama behind it, Republicans will be far less likely to resist...."[69] Expanding on this point elsewhere, McDurmon argued that Trump was "at least very close to a fascist, if not one," but "by the technical definitions of fascism, America has always been to some degree *fascist*."

> Virtually every American president and much of our government since the Constitution actually fit these descriptors. We have always been a nation at war; and always gloried in it. Our national anthem is literally about warfare. We have always had national corporatism since *at least* George Washington's first state of the union address. This *certainly* includes every American president since the great *American fascist*, Theodore Roosevelt, who set the mold for it. But there were many lesser fascist lights before him, too.[70]

It was left to Gary North, Christian Reconstructionism's surviving patriarch, to repudiate Trump most clearly in far right terms. Four days after the November 2016 election, North declared, "Trump's Revolution is Over." North predicted, "The revolution is going to die a stillbirth. Trump is going to cooperate with [House Speaker Paul] Ryan. He is going to cooperate with [Senate Majority Leader Mitch] McConnell. He is going to cooperate with the Council on Foreign Relations. It has already begun." Deflecting conspiracist interpretations of this development, North argued that the revolution had not been betrayed, but rather, "there was never any institutional arrangement by which the revolution could be implemented." Moreover, "Trump is the most naïve elected senior politician in the history of Western civilization. He has no skills whatsoever for the position which he has now been elected [to]. He is what is sometimes called a babe in the woods. More to the point, he is a sitting duck."[71]

Conclusion

Donald Trump has presented far rightists with a political dilemma that will be familiar to many people on the radical left: To what extent and under what circumstances should you support a system-loyal politician who shares many of your politics? How do you balance the importance of holding fast to political principles against the value of expanded visibility, legitimacy, and influence? While some far rightists found these questions easy to answer, others—in the alt-right particularly—were conflicted and struggled to plot a new course.

President Trump, while building on the work of his predecessors, has intensified the U.S. government's white supremacist and authoritarian tendencies beyond what any conventional conservative would have done. But Trump's ability to effect change has been limited by his lack of organizational and political skills coupled with conventional conservatism's entrenched power. The early result, as I described it in August 2017, has been "a harsher, more repressive, more chaotic version of neoliberalism with some America First elements."[72] Trump has made U.S. foreign policy more belligerent and unpredictable without offering any radical change of direction, accelerated deregulation and privatization to help capitalists accumulate wealth even faster, bolstered the repressive apparatus to hold off growing social conflict, and mixed in a few high-profile measures to make life harder for Muslims, immigrants, and Black Lives Matter activists.

The Trump administration may well continue on this same course. But surprises could happen, too: another war or major attack by the Islamic State or al-Qaeda could reinvigorate Trump's America First politics; or, a major scandal could make Trump such a liability to political elites and his own party that he could be forced out of office.

Whatever his shortcomings as a political strategist or organizer, and whatever direction his presidency takes, Trump's rise to power indicates that the political system—a system designed to translate the interests of the capitalist elite into terms that a majority of the electorate would embrace—is in crisis. Neoliberalism, both as a set of policies to keep the economy stable and profitable for big business and as a system of social control, is breaking down, and so far there is no agreement among the ruling class about a backup plan. Trump has shown that a combination of right-wing populism, economic nationalism, and thinly veiled racist scapegoating can attract mass support. Whether it can attract substantial elite support remains to be seen. In this period of uncertainty, far right-ists will have more openings to promote their supremacist visions and either draw more people into oppositional politics or at least widen the space for intensified scapegoating and oppression within the existing system.

Conclusion: Disloyalty in Motion

I have argued that the U.S. far right is best defined not by one specific ideology, but rather by its withdrawal of loyalty to the state. Far rightists reject the established political system because they believe it gets in the way of the social order they want, an order based on or committed to human inequality. Far right anti-egalitarianism can be framed in terms of race, as in the case of neonazis and other white nationalists, but it can also be framed in terms of religion (Christian theocrats), individual property rights (Patriot activists), gender (male tribalists), or a generic elitism (LaRouchites). This expands the scope of which political forces are included under the far right label, and it encourages us to address ideological dimensions and interconnections that standard accounts of the far right tend to minimize or miss completely.

For example, critics of the Patriot movement routinely point out its ideological debt to Posse Comitatus and other white nationalists, but they often ignore its debt to Christian Reconstructionists, who had been advocating "local militias" for years before Larry Pratt brought their ideas to the 1992 Estes Park meeting that helped launch the Patriot movement. Similarly, when alt-rightists first gained prominence in 2015–2016, many critics insisted they were really just neonazis or white supremacists in new clothes, until some of us pointed out the alt-right's profound debt to other rightist currents, such as the intense misogyny propagated by the manosphere.

The issue of loyalty to the existing state is a key question that divides right-wingers who share other political views, in the same way that it divides the left between reformists and revolutionaries. Most Christian rightists function as a power bloc within the Republican Party and push for specific measures such as banning abortion and same-sex marriage, but Reconstructionists aren't interested in piecemeal change, because they want a radically different kind of state, where Christian men hold near-absolute authority via the institutions of church and family. Similarly, the difference between alt-right and alt-lite isn't just that alt-rightists are openly racist while alt-lite activists try to pretend they aren't; more importantly, it's that alt-lite activists want white people and white culture to be openly dominant in the United States once again, while alt-rightists want to split off from the United States or destroy it altogether.

As we've seen, there are borderline cases. The New Apostolic Reformation movement's call for right-thinking Christians to seize control of all "seven mountains" of society is fundamentally at odds with the existing political system, but in practical terms the movement has functioned more like a power bloc than a force for revolution, and in endorsing Trump for president, NAR founder C. Peter Wagner seemed to abandon a big part of his movement's demand for theocracy. The Patriot movement promotes an ideology that disavows the legitimacy of the U.S. government in the name of loyalty to the Constitution, yet since Trump's election leading sections of the movement have shifted much of their focus to helping the state repress leftists, whom they claim are secretly acting on behalf of sinister elites. But borderline cases such as these don't erase the distinction between revolutionary right and system-loyal right, any more than the existence of twilight erases the distinction between night and day.

Given the long history of rightist support for the established order, are far rightists sincere when they talk about abandoning or overthrowing the United States? Of course, some may be bluffing or spouting rhetoric they would abandon if the stakes got too high, in the same way that leftists sometimes call for revolution and then retreat into reformism under pressure. But there are sections of the right that have consistently disavowed loyalty to the political system for years or even decades. And there are rightists who have stuck to this position despite losing their jobs, their liberty, and in some cases risking their very lives.

Disloyalty to the state enables the far right to tap into people's rebellious energy, their sense of disempowerment and anger at those in power. It enables the far right to repurpose elements of leftist politics in distorted form, or even seek alliances with leftists around shared points of opposition. Disloyalty to the state also enables the far right to push the envelope, to stake out positions beyond where others are willing to go, which expands the political space in which system-loyal rightists can operate. This fosters the kind of dynamic tension we have seen in the alt-right's relationship with Donald Trump, allowing the far right to exert an influence well beyond its small numbers.

The far right is often portrayed as backward looking, regimented, and lacking new ideas. Yet the movement has repeatedly defied this stereotype and has shown itself to be ideologically diverse, multifaceted, continually remaking itself in response to external and internal factors. Each of the three big far right upsurges of the past several decades—the neonazi movement in the 1980s, the Patriot movement in the 1990s, and the alt-right in the 2010s—resulted from a new confluence of several different rightist currents. This capacity to change and bounce back from political setbacks in a new and unexpected form is—as much as anything else—what makes the far right dangerous.

The U.S. far right's history over the past four decades has highlighted several issues that are likely to remain pivotal:

- Far rightists' anti-imperialism, while rooted in anti-egalitarian and exclusionary principles, places them genuinely at odds with both U.S. military interventionism and multinational capitalist power. We are likely to see continuing debates among far rightists about whether to ally with countervailing powers (at this time, Russia first and foremost) and whether to seek common ground with left-wing anti-imperialists.

- Most of the far right has moved away from classical fascism's faith in large-scale dictatorship toward various forms of smaller-scale authoritarianism. This speaks not only to widespread suspicion of big government but also to the shift from an era of colonial empires, rising nationalism, and massive factories, to an era of regional separatism, privatization, and flexible supply chains.

- Far rightists have promoted many forms of explicit, aggressive, and often genocidal supremacism—positions that have simultaneously bolstered systems of oppression and expressed a militant defiance of establishment multiculturalism. Yet they have also qualified their supremacist politics in a number of ways—such as neonazis celebrating Aryan women warriors in quasi-feminist terms or Patriot activists offsetting their harsh Islamophobia with color-blind ideology— sometimes in a calculated effort to deflect criticism, but often as an expression of genuinely contradictory politics. The tension between these two impulses is likely to persist, because the far right doesn't simply react against social changes but also co-opts them for its own purposes.

- Far rightists have used a wide variety of strategies. Neonazis have tried everything from electoralism to street fighting and underground paramilitarism; Patriot groups built dual power institutions in defiance of the existing state; Christian Reconstructionists spread their message through homeschooling networks and exhorting families to wage demographic warfare; and alt-rightists used online activism in a "metapolitical" bid to shift the parameters of acceptable discourse. We should expect this experimentation and diversity of approaches to continue and new strategies and tactics to emerge. For example, we may see far rightists expand their use of cyberattacks against leftist, establishment, and governmental targets.

Recent events have demonstrated the far right's changeability. In the spring and summer of 2017, alt-rightists were on the upswing. They were frustrated by the Trump administration's moves toward conventional conservatism, but they weren't particularly surprised, and they weren't standing still. Branching out from internet activism, alt-rightists were building actual organizations, turning out for public rallies, and strengthening ties with other rightists. A series of demonstrations under the banner of "free speech" (protecting political space against supposed suppression by antifascists) or "against Sharia" (vilifying Muslims) brought together alt-rightists, neonazis, pro-Trump Republicans, and Patriot movement activists in a new alliance that writer Spencer Sunshine dubbed "independent Trumpism."[1] For Patriot groups, in particular, to show up at the same rallies with white nationalists was a new and ominous development. Worse yet, both alt-rightists and alt-lite militant conservatives were developing a street-fighting presence—squaring off in physical clashes with antifascists, organizing and training for combat, and in some cases working closely with neonazi skinheads.[2]

But independent Trumpism had a lot of fault lines as well, including conflicts over personality, tactics, and ideology. Both Patriot groups and alt-lite activists disavowed white nationalism, and Patriot activists tried to present themselves as neutral defenders of free speech and quasi law enforcements officers, rather than demonstrators. There were tensions and even some physical altercations between the different forces.[3] While shared hostility to antifascists provided a degree of unity, disagreements over long-term direction—notably the question of loyalty to the United States versus building a white homeland—would have to be faced sooner or later.

A "Unite the Right" rally in Charlottesville, Virginia, in August 2017 marked a turning point. The event was the largest white nationalist demonstration in decades, drawing some one thousand participants from various alt-right, neonazi, neo-Confederate, and Ku Klux Klan groups, as well as some Patriot movement organizations. The far rightists clashed violently with their opponents, and one of them rammed his car into a group of counterprotesters, killing antifascist Heather Heyer and injuring nineteen others.[4]

In the aftermath of Charlottesville, some alt-rightists were thrown on the defensive, but others called for increased militancy or even "leaderless resistance" against the state.[5] Meanwhile, public opinion turned sharply against the far right. A small rightist rally in Boston a week later drew forty thousand counterprotesters. National rallies planned by Jack Posobiec, a leading alt-lite figure, and ACT for America, a leading anti-Muslim organization, were cancelled, and several internet companies shut down many alt-right and neonazi accounts, for example closing down both the *Daily Stormer* and *Stormfront*. When Donald Trump vaguely condemned "hatred, bigotry and violence on many sides" at Charlottesville he was widely criticized, including by Republicans, for drawing a false equivalence between fascists and antifascists.[6]

Then, in another rapid shift, a wide swath of media organs and political figures, from conservatives to social democrats, embraced the spirit of Trump's words and mounted a propaganda campaign against antifascists, exaggerating and distorting their violence and calling them a "gang" and "the moral equivalent of neo-Nazis." The Department of Homeland Security was reported to have labeled antifa activities "domestic terrorist violence." The Anti-Defamation League urged the FBI to infiltrate and spy on antifascists (though it later retracted the recommendation).[7]

These developments highlight several points: that the far right is constantly in motion, and its political fortunes and activities may look very different from one moment to the next; that the far right encompasses multiple currents, which sometimes but not always share common positions; and that centrist pro-establishment forces are threatened by autonomous, militant antifascism at least as much as they are by fascists killing people in the streets.

The centrist backlash against antifa is also a reminder that the far right's contradictory relationship with the established order cuts both ways: in some ways the far right threatens those invested in the status quo, and in other ways it doesn't. The far right wants the political freedom to pursue its supremacist visions, but those visions grow out of the oppressive, exploitative reality that exists now. The conflict between the far right and the existing system of power is real, but a politics of liberation calls on us to defeat both.

Appendix:
Two Ways of Looking at Fascism*

Introduction

Fascism is an important political category, but a confusing one. People use the word fascism in many different ways, and often without a clear sense of what it means.

Political events since the September 11, 2001, attacks have raised the issue of fascism in new ways. People on both the right and the left have described Islamic rightist forces such as al Qaeda and the Taliban as fascist—but for very different reasons. Neoconservatives and Bush administration officials have denounced "Islamofascists" to help justify the so-called war on terrorism and the military occupations of Iraq and Afghanistan. By contrast, some leftists describe some of these same groups as fascist—not to rationalize U.S. expansion, but to highlight the fact that there are major political forces today that are deadly enemies of both the left and U.S. imperialism.

At the same time, a number of liberals and leftists have warned that the United States itself is headed in a fascist direction. As I've argued elsewhere, the Bush administration's authoritarian and militaristic policies are a serious threat, but they're a world apart from fascism's volatile mix of oppression and anti-elitism, order and insurgency. Fascism doesn't just terrorize and repress; it uses twisted versions of radical

* This essay was first published in the journal *Socialism and Democracy* issue 47 (vol. 22, no. 2; July 2008) and is reprinted here courtesy of Taylor & Francis.

politics in a bid to "take the game away from the left," as neonazi leader Tom Metzger urged his followers in the 1980s. We need different strategies to fight these different forms of right-wing authoritarianism, and we need a political vocabulary that lets us tell them apart.[1]

Claims of impending fascism tend to reflect two underlying problems—first, the idea that fascism is essentially a tool or strategy of big business to defend capitalist rule; second, vagueness about what delineates fascism from other forms of capitalist repression. We can see both of these problems in pronouncements from several different U.S. leftist organizations (such as the Communist Party, Socialist Workers Party, Revolutionary Communist Party, and Socialist Labor Party), in leftist and left-liberal media organs such as *CounterPunch* and *Common Dreams*, and in numerous websites and online discussions among U.S. activists.[2]

A recent sophisticated example of both problems comes from Marxist academicians Gregory Meyerson and Michael Joseph Roberto. In an October 2006 *Monthly Review* article, "It Could Happen Here," they argue that "fascism is a plausible response by the U.S. bourgeoisie to the general crisis of Pax Americana" and, although the outcome of the crisis remains unclear, "evidence is mounting for what we are calling a fascist trajectory." Meyerson and Roberto see fascism as an intrinsic structural tendency of capitalism in crisis, a form of rule that is promoted strictly from the top down. ("Only the ruling class can institute fascist processes.") Although they acknowledge the existence of fascist movements, "the Marxist view," they claim, "does not focus primarily on fascist mass movements because they are not primary engines of fascism."[3]

Even if we accept this concept of fascism (and of Marxism), Meyerson and Roberto never explain concretely what they mean by fascist rule. They emphasize that fascism needs to be understood in functional terms, as a form of capitalist rule in crisis, and they criticize descriptive definitions of fascism on the grounds that these obscure its changing historical character. A U.S. fascist trajectory "will look quite different from past fascist trajectories," and will "unfold in a bipartisan context, liberals and conservatives acting in concert—the whole ruling class." But since Meyerson and Roberto don't tell us what fascism will look like, how will we know it's happening? The substance of their argument seems to be that the growing crisis may persuade most representatives of capital that they need to establish a much more repressive and authoritarian state. This is a serious and wholly justified concern, but it's a simple point that doesn't require elaborate arguments about functionalism and structural tendencies. And we gain nothing, but lose much, by calling the result fascism.

The concept of fascism is indeed highly relevant for analyzing current political threats, but not in the way that Meyerson and Roberto maintain. Fascism can help us understand a range of political phenomena that the U.S. ruling class didn't initiate and does not control. These phenomena are part of a crisis that goes far beyond the decline of U.S. global hegemony and the American welfare state, to include the following:

- across eastern Europe and northern Asia, the collapse of the Soviet bloc, followed in many countries by a drastic decline of living standards and the rise of large-scale criminality and a host of right-wing nationalist movements;

- in many parts of Asia, Africa, and Latin America, the co-optation or defeat of revolutionary leftist insurgencies and governments and the growth of diverse populist or religious-based oppositional forces;

- in much of the world, the acceleration of capitalist globalization dynamics such as capital flight, international mass migration, commodification of women's labor, the growth of international mass culture, and the erosion of traditional local institutions—and the upsurge of ambivalent or hostile responses to all of these from various points on the political spectrum.

In this volatile mix, fascism is an important reference point—not just as a developed political force but also as a tendency or potential within broader movements. It is both distinct from and at odds with top-down capitalist authoritarianism. In addition, while fascism takes shape in a capitalist context, it isn't a functional consequence of capitalist development, analogous (as Meyerson and Roberto suggest) to imperialism. Rather, it is a political current, which—like socialism, liberalism, or conservatism—embodies its own set of ideas, policies, organizational forms, and bases of support. Like all major political currents, fascism exists in multiple variations and evolves dynamically to address new historical conditions. This means that no definition of fascism is the one true, final answer. But defining—or at least describing—fascism can help us to grasp fascism's key features, delineate its relationship with other forces, and explore how it develops and how it can be fought.

Unlike many discussions among left activists in the United States today, this essay offers a concept of fascism that speaks to its double-edged reality—bolstering oppression and tyranny but also tapping into real popular grievances and overturning old conventions and forms of rule. To do this, I bring together two distinct but complementary approaches. First, I draw on a current within Marxist thought that emphasizes fascism's contradictory relationship with the capitalist class. As a movement or a regime, fascism attacks the left and defends class exploitation but also pursues an agenda that clashes with capitalist interests in important ways. Since the 1920s, several independent Marxists have analyzed fascism along these lines; I will look specifically at the work of August Thalheimer, Tim Mason, Mihaly Vajda, Don Hamerquist, and J. Sakai.

These writers are strong in analyzing fascism's class politics—its relationship with capital and other class forces, its roots in capitalist crisis, and its impact on the socioeconomic order. They are weaker in discussing fascist ideology, which is important for positioning fascism within the political right and for understanding why people—sometimes millions of people—are attracted to fascist movements. To address these issues, I draw on the work of Roger Griffin, a non-leftist scholar who has done pathbreaking work on fascist ideology over the past two decades. Griffin treats fascism as a form of revolutionary nationalism that attacks both the left and liberal capitalist values, an approach that resonates strongly with some of the most promising leftist discussions of fascism. Griffin's focus on ideology neglects fascism's structural dimensions but offers a helpful complement to a class-centered analysis.

The body of this essay is divided into three parts. First, I discuss the work of several independent Marxists who have grappled with fascism's relationship with capitalism, from Thalheimer's "Bonapartism" theory to Hamerquist and Sakai's treatments of fascism as a right-wing revolutionary movement. Next I explore Griffin's ideology-centered approach, particularly his argument that fascism represents a blend of populist ultranationalism and a myth of collective rebirth. Lastly, I offer a new draft definition of fascism that incorporates aspects of both approaches, and discuss how this stereoscopic vision can help us understand fascist movements and tendencies today.

From Bonapartism to right-wing revolution

Many Marxists have treated fascism as a tool of big business to defend capitalism in times of crisis. There have been many different versions of this approach. During the Communist movement's so-called Third Period, roughly 1928–1935, leaders of the Communist International (Comintern) argued that fascism wasn't really a distinct political movement, but rather a counterrevolutionary trend within all bourgeois parties. This meant that the rising Nazi movement in Germany posed no specific danger. In fact, it was more important for Communists to fight against the Social Democratic Party ("social fascists") to win workers to revolutionary politics. This conception blocked German Communists from seeking an alliance with Social Democrats against their common Nazi enemy—the one thing that could have saved Germany from Nazi rule at that point.

After Hitler's rise to power, the Comintern shifted course. In December 1933, the Comintern executive committee declared that "Fascism is the open terrorist dictatorship of the most reactionary, most chauvinistic and most imperialist elements of finance capital."[4] By identifying fascism with a specific wing of the capitalist class, this approach soon contributed to a new Popular Front strategy of broad antifascist alliances with Social Democrats and liberal capitalists. In practice, this meant abandoning revolutionary politics for liberal reformism. Over the following decades, the Comintern's 1933 definition was embraced by radicals of various persuasions and became the most well-known and influential leftist definition of fascism.

Leon Trotsky, in opposition to the Comintern, emphasized that fascism developed as an autonomous mass movement, based primarily in the petty bourgeoisie, whose plebian and violent character frightened big capitalists. Nevertheless, he argued, fascism's main purpose was to smash the workers' organizations in the service of capitalism. Once in power, fascism lost its mass support and became "a most ruthless dictatorship of monopolist capital."[5] Some other leftists have echoed Trotsky's distinction between fascism as a movement and fascism as a regime. For example, Canadian Marxist David Lethbridge endorses the Comintern definition but acknowledges that fascists initially criticize big business and sometimes disrupt political stability in ways that the ruling class does not want. But, he argues, fascism falls into line and gives up its radicalism "as soon as it becomes financed by substantial circles within the ruling class."[6]

All of these approaches oversimplify fascism's complex relationship with capitalism. Certainly, both Italian and German fascists received crucial support in winning state power from sections of the business community, the military, and the state apparatus. Once established, the fascist regimes aided capitalism and boosted profits by suppressing the left, smashing the labor movement, and—at first—stabilizing the economy and society. Both Mussolini's and Hitler's governments initially included some traditional conservatives as junior members, and old elites kept control of some sectors, such as the army. The "radical" wings of the fascist movement that wanted to challenge old elites more directly were either frustrated, as in Italy, or suppressed, as in Germany.

But as the fascist regimes consolidated themselves, the capitalist class increasingly lost political control: it lost the power to determine the main direction of state policy. Fascism installed a new political elite that advanced its own ideological agenda. While capitalists remained an important constituent in the overall system of rule, they were progressively reduced to a reactive role at the level of national policy, adapting themselves to the fascists' agenda, not the reverse.

An important statement of this view came from British Marxist historian Timothy Mason, who was a specialist on the working class under Nazism. In his 1966 essay, "The Primacy of Politics," Mason argued that "both the domestic and the foreign policy of the National Socialist government became, from 1936 onwards, increasingly independent of the economic ruling classes, and even in some essential respects ran contrary to their interests."[7]

In Mason's view, the representatives of capital handed state power to Hitler in the mistaken belief that they would be able to retake it once the Nazis had crushed the left and restabilized civil society. During the first few years of Nazi rule, business elites played little role in shaping foreign or military policy but continued to control economic policy through Hjalmar Schacht, minister of economics and Reichsbank president. But starting in 1936, the Nazis intensified rearmament and demanded economic self-sufficiency for Germany. Leaders of heavy industry, who had previously dominated the business community and had been among Nazism's staunchest allies, opposed this shift toward economic isolation because they relied on international trade. The IG Farben chemical trust gained influence in their place by promising to provide synthetic replacements for strategic imports (notably petroleum and rubber), thereby furthering the Nazis' self-sufficiency goal. The shift not only "broke the economic and political supremacy of heavy industry," it also "meant an end to the formation of any general and unified political will or representation of interests on the part of German capital... all that was left were the special interests of individual firms, at most of certain branches of the economy."[8] Each big firm cultivated its own ties with state agencies in order to win contracts, but big business lost its collective voice as a player in shaping overall policy.

Mason acknowledged that capitalists took advantage of the rearmament drive and the German military victories to expand, increase profits, and smash foreign competitors. But the overall direction of Nazi war policy was based on political aims, not economic ones. The war helped alleviate certain economic shortages, but those shortages were the direct result of the forced rearmament drive itself.

In this context, Mason emphasized, the Nazi state pursued ideologically driven goals—the genocide and mass enslavement of Jews and other peoples—that were "in flat contradiction to the interests of the war economy":

> Among the first Polish Jews who were gassed in the extermination camps were thousands of skilled metal workers from Polish armament factories.... The army emphasized the irrational nature of this action in view of the great shortage of skilled labour, but was unable to save the Jewish armament workers for industry.... The same internal power relationship lay behind the use of scarce railway installations for the deportation of persecuted Jews towards the end of the war, instead of for the provisioning of the forces on the Eastern Front.[9]

Similarly, the Nazi leadership decided to import millions of enslaved eastern European workers for the war economy—rather than draft German women for industrial work—even though the official in charge of labor deployments warned that slave labor was unproductive, unreliable, and a "racial danger" to the German people.

Mason's essay has held up well, with some qualifications. Ian Kershaw, after weighing two decades of later scholarship on the topic, endorsed the main line of Mason's argument but cautioned that Mason separated politics and economics too sharply and exaggerated industrialists' loss of political influence under Nazi rule. Jane Caplan suggested that the concept "autonomy" was preferable to "primacy" of politics, so as not to imply a hierarchy of politics over economics.[10]

Mason claimed that the Nazi state's relationship with capitalists was "unique." But the dynamic under Italian Fascism was in fact strikingly similar. Non-leftist historian Franklin Hugh Adler, in one of the few detailed English-language studies of Italian Fascism's relationship with big business, describes how Mussolini's regime helped industrialists to intensify workplace exploitation and control—both by destroying working-class organizations and by overruling the Fascist movement's own syndicalist wing. At the same time, the Fascist state pursued a long series of policies that industrialists did not initiate and did not want, from overvaluing the lira's exchange rate to imposing a corporatist bureaucracy on the economy, from encouraging Italians to move to the countryside and have lots of babies to allying with Hitler against Britain and France. Adler summarizes this dynamic as follows:

> Although absolute managerial authority was preserved at the factory level, and Confindustria [the confederation of Italian industrialists] came to assume significant authority in administering economic policy, it is nevertheless the case that the *context* of economic policy became increasingly political and irrational from a strictly economic point of view.... At the level of public policy, both foreign and domestic, Confindustria exercised little or no initiative. Here the association, at best, could negotiate subsequent trade-offs to the relative advantage of industry *once fundamental decisions had already been made*; it reacted rather than acted. [italics in original][11]

Adler's discussion suggests that capitalists held onto more political power under Italian Fascism than they did under German Nazism. But in both cases they increasingly lost control of core government policy.

Although Mason did not offer any theoretical framework to explain the "primacy of politics" under Nazism, his analysis meshes closely with the Bonapartism theory of fascism first proposed by August Thalheimer in the late 1920s and early 1930s. Thalheimer was a leading theoretician of the German Communist Party (KPD), who was expelled in 1928 for opposing the Third Period line and helped form the Communist Party–Opposition (KPO). Thalheimer rejected the Comintern's campaign against "social fascism" and called instead for broad-based working-class defense against the Nazis through extraparliamentary action.

Thalheimer argued that Marx's analysis of the Louis Bonaparte dictatorship in mid nineteenth-century France offered the best starting point for understanding fascism. The fascist dictatorship, like that of Louis Bonaparte, represented "the autonomisation of the executive power," in which the capitalist class gave up control of the state in order to protect its socioeconomic status. Thalheimer quoted a passage from Marx's *The Eighteenth Brumaire of Louis Bonaparte* that described this move:

> the bourgeoisie confesses that its own interests dictate that it should be delivered from the danger of its *own rule*; ... that in order to preserve its social power intact, its political power must be broken; that the individual bourgeois can continue to exploit the other classes and to enjoy undisturbed property, family, religion and order, only on condition that their class be condemned along with the other classes to like political nullity; ... and the sword that is to safeguard it must at the same time be hung over its own head as a sword of Damocles.[12]

Like Bonapartism, Thalheimer argued, fascism came to power after "an unsuccessful proletarian onslaught ended with the demoralization of the working class, while the bourgeoisie, exhausted, distraught and dispirited, cast around for a saviour to protect its social power."[13] This interpretation had far more accuracy than the Comintern's Third Period line that fascism was capitalism's last-ditch defense against the *rising* threat of proletarian revolution. And while the Comintern claimed that fascist rule was a natural outgrowth of bourgeois parliamentarianism, Thalheimer argued that it marked a "sudden leap." Parliamentary governments helped lay the groundwork for fascism with their own anti-labor repression, but fascism itself "only begins at the point when and where the bayonet becomes independent and turns its point against bourgeois parliamentarians as well."[14]

Thalheimer saw the fascist party, like Louis Bonaparte's Society of December 10th, as consisting of "socially uprooted elements from every class, from the aristocracy, the bourgeoisie, the urban petty bourgeoisie, the peasantry, the workers," while the fascist militia paralleled the Bonapartist army, "and like it provides a source of livelihood for the socially uprooted." Fascist ideology echoed Bonapartism in its nationalism, rhetorical denunciations of economic and political elites, and glorification of the heroic leader. But while Bonaparte's organization mirrored French working-class secret societies, the fascist party mirrored the Soviet Communist Party. As a mass formation, the fascist party was in some ways stronger than Bonaparte's organization, but this also intensified its internal contradictions "between the social interests of this mass following and the interests of the dominant classes which it has to serve."[15]

Thalheimer regarded fascism as inherently unstable, a regime pulled simultaneously in opposite directions. "Fascism, like Bonapartism, seeks to be the benefactor of all classes; hence it continually plays one class off against another, and engages in contradictory maneuvers internally." He predicted that the conflicting policy demands of fascism's various constituencies, "combined with the nationalist imperialist ideology, push the dictator to external violations of the peace, and finally to war" — a process that would bring about fascism's ruin.[16]

Thalheimer's discussion amounts to just a skeletal analysis of fascism. He offered only brief, general comments on fascism's ideology, organization, and social base; the dynamics of capitalist-fascist relations; and the historical context that promoted fascism's rise. Some have criticized him for applying the concept of Bonapartism mechanically. But given that Thalheimer wrote early — only a few years after Mussolini consolidated his dictatorship and before the Nazi seizure of power — his outline matches the fascist regimes' later trajectories strikingly well.

Thalheimer's work has influenced a number of later scholars. Jane Caplan, for example, echoed and reformulated his point about fascism's inherent instability:

> Fascism is the most extreme form yet observed of the exceptional capitalist state, and the essential contradiction of exceptional states is that they represent a type of coercive structure in which the control of the extraction of surplus value is displaced from the labor process to the political process, in a vast enhancement of the state's role. The fascist regime is the extreme form of the autonomization of politics under capitalism. It is the product of an immense dislocation of the capitalist mode of production and … is unlikely to persist in the long term, for it manifestly bristles with contradictions. …

Under National Socialism, for example, one term of the fundamental contradiction in the role of the state is expressed in the tendency toward the ultimate autonomization of the political police, with its disruptive implications for the process of production.[17]

Hungarian Marxist philosopher Mihaly Vajda incorporated a Bonapartist approach into a general theory of fascism in his book *Fascism as a Mass Movement*, which was written in 1969–1970 and first published in 1976. Vajda was a member of the "Budapest School" of intellectuals around George Lukacs, whose members became increasingly critical of orthodox Soviet-style Marxism, particularly after the Warsaw Pact's military suppression of the Czechoslovak Spring in 1968. In 1973, Vajda and several other members of the Budapest School were fired from their academic posts and expelled from the Hungarian Workers Party (Communist Party) for their political views.

Vajda drew on both Thalheimer and Mason in arguing that fascism is "a capitalist form of rule" in which "the bourgeoisie does not itself exercise political power, and…lacks a voice in the decisions of those who are ruling politically."[18] As a general rule, Vajda asserted that "fascism in no way restricted the bourgeoisie's economic power within the factory. It did not thwart their economic interests and even helped them obtain increased satisfaction." On the other hand, fascism "creates extraordinary political conditions and replaces normal bourgeois everyday life with a situation of constant tension, and the bourgeoisie finds this at least 'uncomfortable.'" Beyond that, fascism "openly contradicts the interests of the ruling class in some cases," specifically in the conduct of World War II. Vajda's account of the dynamics of German Nazi rearmament and war closely followed Mason's. On Italy, Vajda wrote, "if Mussolini had not bound his fate to Hitler's absolutely, none of his political objectives would have endangered the bourgeoisie's particular interests in any way whatsoever." But Mussolini's alliance with Hitler, like the Nazi war drive itself, reflected fascism's inherent tendency toward aggressive expansionism.[19]

Vajda went beyond a Bonapartist argument to address several other aspects of fascism, such as its social psychology and the contrasting historical functions it served in Italy and Germany. As his book's title suggests, Vajda emphasized that a fascist regime comes to power as a mass movement, which gives it both organized popular support and a recruiting pool for the new political elite. The fascist movement centers on combat organizations such as the stormtroopers, whose paramilitary activism is the driving force in fascism's bid for state power. Although helpful for understanding the Italian and German examples, this focus on paramilitary formations arguably does not apply to all fascist movements.

Vajda also argued that fascism has a distinctive ideology: a form of aggressive, totalistic nationalism. Within the nation-state, this doctrine subordinates "every kind of particularity to the 'total,' 'natural-organic' whole, 'the nation'"; externally, it promotes national uplift "even at the expense of the very existence of other nations." Fascist ideology negates bourgeois democracy and liberalism (which involve the promotion of particular group interests over the national totality) and rejects the principle of human equality in favor of national chauvinism or racism. But fascist ideology does not challenge the principle of private property; therefore its vision of national unity "is not a negation of the basis and framework of the existing class society" and "represents an illusory transcendence of particularity."[20]

Vajda argued that "the 'uplifting' of the 'nation'…is the only constant element in [fascism's] very varied programmes, which in other respects are always subject to radical change." This nationalism and racism "enabled fascism to avoid conflict between, on the one hand, the particular interests of the masses who joined it and were represented by it, and on the other hand, the basic principles of the existing social system."[21]

Vajda's discussion sheds a useful light on fascist ideology and prefigures several points in Roger Griffin's more developed treatment. Vajda's formulation is not precise enough to distinguish fascist ideology from other forms of right-wing nationalism and overlooks the fact that some fascist movements, such as Romania's Iron Guard, were not expansionist. In addition, as I will argue later, some fascist ideologies don't center on nationalism at all.

Thalheimer, Mason, and Vajda wrote about the fascism of the 1920s–1940s. The 2002 book *Confronting Fascism: Discussion Documents for a Militant Movement* [reprinted in 2017] is concerned with fascism today as much as "classical" fascism—its points of reference are not just Hitler and Mussolini but also the World Church of the Creator and Alexander Dugin, Israeli West Bank settlers and the Taliban. As outlined in the Introduction by Xtn (then of Chicago Anti-Racist Action), the book grew out of discussions among antifascist and revolutionary leftists (both anarchist and Marxist) about the relationship between fighting fascism and fighting the capitalist state. It was published in the wake of the September 11th attacks, which sparked a new wave of state repression and racist attacks, while highlighting the fact that some of the U.S. power structure's most militant opponents were on the far right.[22]

Confronting Fascism centers on an essay by Don Hamerquist, formerly of the Sojourner Truth Organization, and an extended reply by J. Sakai, a Maoist best known for his book *Settlers: The Mythology of the White Proletariat.* Hamerquist and Sakai are both independent Marxists who have worked with anarchist antifascists and been influenced by anti-authoritarian critiques of dogmatic Marxism. Like Thalheimer, Mason, and Vajda, they emphasize that fascism is an independent political force, not a capitalist puppet or policy. But Hamerquist and Sakai go much further than this, presenting fascism as a right-wing revolutionary force. In Sakai's words, "Fascism is a revolutionary movement of the right *against* both the bourgeoisie and the left, of middle class and declassed men, that arises in zones of protracted crisis." It is not revolutionary in the socialist or anarchist sense: "Fascism is revolutionary in a simpler use of the word. It intends to seize State power for itself... in order to violently reorder society in a new class rule."[23]

Hamerquist and Sakai argue that most leftists seriously underestimate fascism's potential to attract mass support within the United States and worldwide. Capitalism's developing contradictions, they argue, create growing opportunities for a resurgence of fascist movements. Far from being a frozen relic of the past, fascism is a dynamic political force that includes a range of factions and tendencies and is evolving in response to changing conditions. Fascist groups feed on popular hostility to big business and the capitalist state, and some of them present an oppositional militance that looks more serious and committed than that of most leftist groups today. (Hamerquist particularly cites "third position" fascists, who claim to reject both the left and the right, but the argument is not limited to these groups.) The main danger of fascism today, Hamerquist argues, is not that it will seize power, but that it "might gain a mass following among potentially insurgent workers and declassed strata through an historic default of the left," causing "massive damage to the potential for a liberatory anti-capitalist insurgency."[24]

A related danger that Hamerquist raises is a convergence between fascists and sections of the radical left. He points to leftward overtures from sections of the far right, and tendencies within much of the left that mesh dangerously with fascism, such as male supremacy, glorification of violence, leader cultism, hostility to open debate and discussion, and elitism. Hamerquist notes that German Communists in the early 1930s sometimes made tactical alliances with the Nazis against the Social Democrats because they considered Social Democrats the bigger threat.

Hamerquist warns that U.S. fascist groups are actively organizing around a number of issues that leftists often consider to be "ours"—such as labor struggles; environmentalism; and opposition to police repression, U.S. imperialism, and corporate globalization. This kind of fascist popular appeal is nothing new. As Sakai points out, both Mussolini and Hitler galvanized people largely by attacking established elites and promoting an anti-bourgeois militance that seemed much more exciting and dynamic than conventional left politics. "Many youth in 1930s Germany viewed the Nazis as liberatory. As opposed to the German social-democrats, for example, who preached the dutiful authority of parents over children, the Hitler Youth gave rebellious children the power to keep their own hours, have an active sex and political life, smoke, drink and have groups of their own."[25]

In different ways, both Hamerquist and Sakai argue that fascism's radical approach shapes its relationship with capitalism. Of the two writers, Sakai's position is closer to a Bonapartist model. He describes fascism as "*anti-bourgeois* but not anti-capitalist." Under fascist regimes, "capitalism is restabilized but the bourgeoisie pays the price of temporarily no longer ruling the capitalist State." But for Sakai this conflict is much starker than it is for Bonapartism theorists. Today's fascism "is opposed to the big imperialist bourgeoisie..., to the transnational corporations and banks, and their world-spanning 'multicultural' bourgeois culture. Fascism really wants to bring down the World Bank, WTO and NATO, and even America the Superpower. As in destroy."[26]

Sakai argues that fascism radically reshapes the capitalist social order to create an economy of "heightened parasitism": "a lumpen-capitalist economy more focused on criminality, war, looting and enslavement." He describes how Hitler's regime elevated millions of German workers into a new parasitic class of soldiers, policemen, and bureaucrats and replaced them with a new proletariat of foreign and slave laborers, retirees, and women. This process "created an Aryan society that had never existed before," giving Nazi racial categories a concrete, social reality that was qualitatively new (but which paralleled the color-line divisions of U.S. society).[27]

Sakai's discussion belies claims that Hitler's regime had little or no impact on the socioeconomic order. We should remember, however, that this discussion does *not* apply to Italian Fascism, which lacked Nazism's overarching racialist imperative and never consolidated the same degree of control over the state. Its effect on the socioeconomic order was far more limited.

Hamerquist takes fascist anti-capitalism more seriously than Sakai does. He notes that current-day fascist movements encompass various positions on how to relate to the capitalist class, from opportunists who want to cut a deal, to pro-capitalist revolutionaries who want to pressure big business into accepting fascist rule, to some third positionists who want to overthrow the economic ruling class entirely. It is unclear how serious a challenge to capitalist economic power any fascists would mount in practice. Where it has been tested, fascist anti-capitalism has meant opposition to "bourgeois values," specific policies, or a "parasitic" wing of capital (such as Jewish bankers)—not the capitalist system. On the other hand, as Hamerquist warns, it would be dangerous for leftists to dismiss the prospect of a militantly anti-capitalist fascism simply because it doesn't fit our preconceptions.

Hamerquist's concept of fascist anti-capitalism rests partly on his analysis (following German left communist Alfred Sohn-Rethel) that German Nazism foreshadowed "a new 'transcapitalist' exploitative social order." In particular, Hamerquist argues, German fascism's genocidal labor policy broke with capitalist principles. Not just labor power, but workers themselves were "consumed in the process of production just like raw materials and fixed capital," thus obliterating "the distinctively capitalist difference between labor and other factors of production." True, "normal" capitalist development involves genocide "against pre-capitalist populations and against the social formations that obstruct the creation of a modern working class." But by contrast, "the German policy was the genocidal obliteration of already developed sections of the European working classes"—i.e., the importation of colonial-style mass killing into Europe's industrial heartland.[28]

This doesn't necessarily mean that Nazism was in the process of overthrowing the capitalist system. The labor policies Hamerquist describes did not call into question the economic power of big business, and arguably could not be sustained for more than a brief period. But the very fact that they were not sustainable may be part of the point. As Hamerquist reminds us, Marx warned that the contradictions of capitalism might end, not in socialist revolution, but in "barbarism," "the common ruin of the contending classes." Fascist revolution could be one version of this scenario.[29]

Here we should remember Thalheimer's and Caplan's point that the fascist state's contradictory relationship with the business class—defending its economic power but pursuing policies that eventually conflict with capitalist economic rationality—is inherently unstable. In theory, this conflict could be resolved in various ways: (1) the collapse or overthrow of the fascist regime (as happened in Italy and Germany), (2) the conversion of fascist rule into a more conventional pro-capitalist regime, or (3) some kind of fascist overthrow of capitalist economic power. The last of these alternatives is the hardest to imagine, but cannot simply be dismissed as impossible or nonsensical. It would not abolish economic exploitation but would reshape it in fundamental ways, as Hamerquist suggests in his discussion of Nazi labor policy.

Sakai and Hamerquist also differ on the question of fascism's class base. Like many others before him, Sakai links fascism to middle-class and declassed strata threatened or uprooted by rapid social and economic change—historical losers who hate the big capitalists and want to get back the privilege they used to have. Sakai sees this dynamic in the Germans who rallied to Hitler during the Depression, the Timothy McVeigh figures who turn to neonazism as the old U.S. system of white privilege crumbles, and the Muslim world's shopkeepers and unemployed college graduates hit by globalization, who are at the core of the pan-Islamic right. "To the increasing mass of rootless men fallen or ripped out of productive classes—whether it be the peasantry or the salariat—[fascism] offers not mere working class jobs but the vision of payback. Of a land for real men, where they and not the bourgeois will be the one's [sic] giving orders at gunpoint and living off of others."[30]

This discussion is helpful but oversimplified. The dynamics Sakai describes represent part of fascism's appeal, and there is evidence that the middle classes and sections of the unemployed disproportionately supported fascism in the interwar period. But it would be a serious distortion to pigeonhole fascism as a movement of historical losers. Pre–World War II fascism didn't just attract declining and uprooted middle classes such as small merchants, but also groups at the core of the new corporate economy, such as white-collar workers and professionals.

The fascist vision criticizes modern decadence but also embraces many aspects of modernity. For example, as David Roberts argues, Italian Fascism appealed to petty bourgeois activists as a vehicle for national integration, political reform, and large-scale industrial development.[31]

Furthermore, as Geoff Eley has pointed out about German Nazism, the movement's dependence on a particular social class is less striking than its ability "to broaden its social base in several different directions"—to construct "a broadly based coalition of the subordinate classes" "without precedent in the German political system." In contrast to the Social Democrats and Communists, who remained focused on the industrial working class, the Nazis (and to a lesser extent Italian Fascists) unified "an otherwise disjointed ensemble of discontents within a totalizing populist framework."[32]

Hamerquist does not directly expand on his warning that militant fascism could build a mass base among insurgent workers (a possibility that Sakai questions). Although definitions of "working class" are subject to debate, several fascist movements in the 1930s seem to have attracted substantial numbers of workers, such as the Arrow Cross in Hungary and Father Coughlin's Social Justice movement in the United States. In 1930–1933, workers made up about 30 percent of German Nazi Party members and a majority within the SA (Stormtroopers), the Nazis' paramilitary wing.[33]

While they disagree about fascism's class base, Hamerquist and Sakai agree that we need to rethink old leftist assumptions about fascism's racial politics. As Hamerquist puts it, "there is no reason to view fascism as necessarily white just because there are white supremacist fascists. To the contrary there is every reason to believe that fascist potentials exist throughout the global capitalist system. African, Asian, and Latin American fascist organizations can develop that are independent of, and to some extent competitive with Euro-American 'white' fascism."[34] Coupled with this, some white fascists support Third World anti-imperialism or even disavow racial supremacy, and some have started to build links with right-wing organizations of color, such as the Nation of Islam.

Sakai notes that the mass displacement of Black workers over the past generation, coupled with the defeat of 1960s left Black nationalism, has fueled an unprecedented growth of authoritarian rightist organizations in the Black community. Sakai also argues that fascism's key growth area now is in the Third World, where "pan-Islamic fascism" and related movements have largely replaced the left as the major anti-imperialist opposition force.

Unfortunately, Sakai and Hamerquist have little to say about what fascism means for women, as Xtn notes in the Introduction to *Confronting Fascism*. Sakai asserts that fascism is basically a male movement both in composition and outlook. In reality, as Xtn points out, fascist movements intensify patriarchy but often rely on mass support from both women and men. As I have argued elsewhere, all fascist movements are male supremacist, but they have embodied a range of doctrines on women and gender issues, both traditionalist and anti-traditionalist, and even including twisted versions of feminism. Fascism has sometimes recruited large numbers of women as active participants, largely by offering them specific benefits and opportunities—in education, youth groups, athletics, volunteer work, and certain paid jobs—even as it sharpened and centralized male dominance.[35]

Hamerquist and Sakai offer a fuller, livelier picture of fascism than the earlier writers we have considered. Their discussion of current-day movements highlights the immediacy of the issue, and their emphasis on fascist radicalism helps to explain fascism's appeal much more than Bonapartism theory does. At the same time, they are not always clear about which movements they consider fascist (and why) or about fascism's relationship to other right-wing forces. Their discussions of fascist ideology are fragmentary and sometimes vague. For a fuller and more systematic look at these areas, I turn now to someone outside the Marxist tradition.

The myth of national rebirth

British historian Roger Griffin has been a leading figure in the academic field of fascist studies since publishing *The Nature of Fascism* in 1991. In this and later works, Griffin draws on a wide body of historical material to develop an innovative theory of fascism. He is a self-described liberal whose premises, focus, and method contrast sharply with the Marxist writers I discussed above. This makes the complementarity of their analyses all the more striking.

Griffin's approach builds on the work of historian George Mosse, who he credits with "establishing several points which herald a new phase in fascist studies":

> First, though Nazism is to be conceived as unquestionably a manifestation of generic fascism, it is no longer to be seen as paradigmatic or its quintessential manifestation. Second, at bottom fascism is neither a regime, nor a movement, but first and foremost an ideology, a critique of the present state of society and a vision of what is to replace it. Third, when this vision is dissected it reveals fascism to be a revolutionary form of nationalism.... Fourth, its ideology expresses itself primarily not through theory and doctrines, but through a bizarre synthesis of ideas whose precise content will vary significantly from nation to nation but whose appeal will always be essentially mythic rather than rational. Equally importantly, it is an ideology which expresses itself through a liturgical, ritualized form of mass political spectacle.[36]

Like Mosse (but unlike many leftists), Griffin takes seriously fascists' own statements of belief. He argues that an analysis of fascist ideology—like socialist, liberal, or conservative ideology—should be based on how its proponents themselves articulate a social critique and vision, an approach he calls "methodological empathy."[37] Although some critics wrongly interpret this as lack of critical distance or even political sympathy for fascism, methodological empathy is in fact crucial for understanding what draws people to support fascist movements.

Another basic premise of Griffin's work is that "generic" fascism (as opposed to the specific Fascism headed by Mussolini) represents an "ideal type," a term coined by Max Weber. This means it is a theoretical construct that can only approximate historical phenomena. Definitions of fascism, Griffin argues, are not objectively "true" in the descriptive sense—rather, they are more or less useful as conceptual frameworks for interpreting and classifying events and mapping relationships. For some reason, historian Robert Paxton claims that this approach "condemn[s] us to a static view, and to a perspective that encourages looking at fascism in isolation." As I will show, Griffin's own work belies both of these criticisms.[38]

Griffin's definition of fascism can be boiled down to three words: "palingenetic populist ultra-nationalism."[39] Each of these terms needs explanation:

Palingenetic—from the Greek *palin* (again or anew) + *genesis* (creation or birth)—refers to a myth or vision of collective rebirth after a period of crisis or decline.

Populist, in Griffin's usage, means a form of politics that draws its claims of legitimacy from "the people" (as opposed, for example, to a monarchical dynasty or divine appointment) and uses mass mobilization to win power and transform society.

Ultra-nationalism treats the nation as a higher, organic unity to which all other loyalties must be subordinated. Ultra-nationalism rejects "anything compatible with liberal institutions or with the tradition of Enlightenment humanism which underpins them."[40]

As a form of populist ultra-nationalism, fascism fundamentally rejects the liberal principles of pluralism and individual rights, as well as the socialist principles of class-based solidarity and internationalism, all of which threaten the nation's organic unity. At the same time, fascism rejects traditional bases for authority, such as the monarchy or nobility, in favor of charismatic politics and a new, self-appointed political elite that claims to embody the people's will. Fascism seeks to build a mass movement of everyone considered part of the national community, actively engaged but controlled from above, to seize political power and remake the social order. This movement is driven by a vision "of the national community rising phoenix-like after a period of encroaching decadence which all but destroyed it."[41] Such rebirth involves systematic, top-down transformation of all social spheres by an authoritarian state, and suppression or purging of all forces, ideologies, and social groups the fascists define as alien.

By demanding a sweeping cultural and political transformation and break with the established order, the vision of renewal sets fascism apart from conservative forms of ultra-nationalism as a revolutionary ideology. The fascist revolution, Griffin argues, is above all a cultural one. "The dominant world-view...was for the fascist mindset the primary reality, the principal locus of the nation's rebirth, and the foremost object of its regeneration and metamorphosis. Indeed, the Marxist stress on socio-economics as the motor of historical change was for fascists a symptom of its essential materialism, its 'atheism,' and hence of its decadence." "In the new order 'culture' would cease to be an individualized, privatized, marginalized sphere of modern life. ... Instead it would once more be what Lewis Mumford calls the 'megamachine,' the matrix for all the mythopoiea, rituals, institutions, values, and artistic creativity of an entire society. ... "[42]

Despite this emphasis on the subjective, Griffin argues, fascism also pursues major objective structural changes. "While neither the Fascist nor Nazi state wanted to abolish capitalist economics and private property, they had no scruples about involving themselves with the economy on a scale unprecedented in any liberal state except in wartime," including vast public works programs, a drive for economic self-sufficiency (autarky), and, in the Nazi case, creating a vast empire and enslaving millions of workers. "Both regimes also indulged in a massive programme of social engineering which involved creating mass organizations for every social grouping, retooling the educational system, symbolically appropriating all aspects of leisure, sport, culture, and technology. ... "[43]

In emphasizing fascism's revolutionary side, Griffin obscures the extent to which fascism has acted as a bulwark of capitalism and established social hierarchy. He notes in passing that "fascism in practice colluded with traditional ruling elites in order to gain and retain power and left capitalist structures substantially intact." But for him the crucial point is that "at the level of ideological intent both Fascism and Nazism aimed to coordinate all the energies of the nation, including conservative and capitalist ones, in a radically new type of society ... and went some way towards doing this."[44] Griffin offers no indication that the tension between these two statements needs to be addressed at a basic theoretical level—for him, ideology is simply more important.

Nevertheless, Griffin's focus on fascism's myth of collective rebirth represents a conceptual breakthrough, which has widely influenced the field of fascism studies. The palingenetic element gives Griffin's model of fascism more precision than some earlier ones (such as Mihaly Vajda's), which identify fascist ideology simply with ultra- or "organic" nationalism. The focus on palingenetic myth also clarifies fascism's apparent contradiction between forward- and backward-looking tendencies. As Griffin notes, although some forms of fascism invoke the glories of an earlier age, they do so as inspiration for creating a "new order," not restoring an old one. Fascism "thus represents an alternative modernism rather than a rejection of it."[45]

The concept of palingenetic myth sheds light not only on fascism, but also a number of related political currents. For example, the Ku

Klux Klan was formed in the late 1860s around a vision of restoring the white supremacist South after its near destruction in the Civil War and Reconstruction. Since the 1860s, white supremacists have repeatedly invoked this vision of rebirth to help them interpret and address other crises in the U.S. racial order. That helps to explain why the Klan, unlike many other racist institutions, has been revived again and again—and how the Klan helped to prepare the ground for fascist ideas imported from Europe.

Griffin's definition of fascism has other advantages. It is flexible enough to encompass many different versions of fascist politics. As Griffin notes, fascism may or may not involve paramilitary organization, a cult of the supreme leader, corporatist economic policies, or a drive for imperialist expansion. (Some fascist movements, such as Oswald Mosley's British Union of Fascists, have preached neutralism or even a community of regenerated nations.) And while all forms of fascism are racist, Griffin argues, in the sense that they promote ethnic chauvinism and mono-cultural societies, this racial ideology may or may not be defined in biological terms and can range from relatively mild ethnocentrism all the way to systematic programs for genocide.

Unlike many definitions of fascism, Griffin's model is also specific enough to map fine-grained distinctions and relationships between fascism and other branches of the right. Griffin delineates fascism from formations that share a related ideology but make no effort to build a mass base or to overthrow a liberal political system. He recognizes that there can be borderline cases. Griffin argues, notably, that Italy's National Alliance, successor to the neo-fascist Italian Social Movement, represents a contradictory but genuine hybrid between fascist ideology and an acceptance of the liberal democratic rules of the game. Griffin's name for this hybrid, "democratic fascism," is unfortunate, but the basic point holds true that some formations straddle the line between revolutionary and reformist branches of the right.[46]

Griffin's definition of fascism also excludes most of the dictatorships that have often been labeled fascist. He has suggested the term *para-fascist* to describe many of these.[47] A para-fascist regime is imposed from above (often by the military) and represents traditional elites trying to preserve the old order, but surrounds its conservative core with fascist trappings. These trappings may include an official state party, paramilitary organizations, a leader cult, mass political ritual, corporatism, and the rhetoric of ultra-nationalist regeneration. Para-fascist regimes may be just as ruthless as genuine fascist ones in their use of state terrorism. Unlike true fascism, para-fascism does not represent a genuine populist mobilization and does not substantively challenge established institutions. During the 1920s and 1930s, Griffin argues, para-fascist regimes arose in several European countries, such as Spain, Portugal, Hungary, Romania, and Austria, joined by the Vichy government after France surrendered to Germany in 1940. Para-fascist regimes regarded genuine fascist movements as a threat and used various strategies to contain, co-opt, or crush them. In Spain during the Civil War, for example, General Franco "imposed a shot-gun marriage between Falangists and the traditional (that is non-fascist) radical right" as part of his strategy to establish a para-fascist dictatorship.[48]

Contrary to claims that an "ideal type" definition freezes our image of fascism in the past, Griffin is also alert to ways that fascism has changed. He writes in some detail about *neo-fascism*, by which he means post-1945 forms of fascism that have substantially modified or replaced inter-war versions of fascist ideology.[49] Many fascists have concealed their politics behind a democratic facade through the use of coded rhetoric, helping to blur the line between hard-line conservatism and the far right. Some have advanced new philosophical systems for rationalizing fascist politics, such as the Nouvelle Droit (New Right) of Alain de Benoist's GRECE think-tank in France or the Traditionalism of Julius Evola in Italy. Third Position groups have embraced the "leftist" anti-capitalist current on the margins of traditional fascism, rather than the mainstream of Hitler or Mussolini.

Among a range of neo-fascist innovations, Griffin highlights one trend in particular: a shift toward increased internationalism. From the 1960s on, international networking increased substantially, through both informal contacts and organizations such as CEDADE (Spanish Circle of Friends of Europe), the NSDAP/AO (National Socialist German Workers Party/Overseas Organization), and WUNS (World Union of National Socialists). Such networking has fostered the sense of belonging to an international movement, and a belief that fascist principles can regenerate many nations, not just one's own.

Despite the many advantages of Griffin's approach, several assumptions sharply limit its usefulness for understanding current politics. This is evident, for example, when Griffin addresses the social and political factors that promote fascism's rise. He argues that the growth of a strong fascist movement is only possible under a special combination of circumstances: a liberal democracy (where there is political space for fascist organizing) experiencing a major crisis (which gives visions of radical rebirth broad appeal) and without strong non-fascist right-wing forces (which block fascism's ability to build mass support). For a fascist seizure of political power, the window of opportunity is even narrower: the liberal democracy must be "mature enough institutionally to preclude the threat of a direct military or monarchical coup, yet too immature to be able to rely on a substantial consensus in the general population" around liberal values. Griffin argues that fascist movements have reached such an opportunity in only four countries: Italy (1918–22), Germany (1918–23, 1929–33), Finland (1929–32), and South Africa (1939–43).[50]

Unlike his definition of fascism, this part of Griffin's discussion is too static, trapped in a description of classical fascism's rise between the world wars. As the history of the left shows, oppositional forces can organize on a mass scale (and even take power) under many different political systems, not just liberal democracies. Even weaker is Griffin's claim that fascists will never again be able to break out of their marginal status to bid for state power, because "the structural factors that turned Fascism and Nazism into successful revolutions have simply disappeared."[51] As support for this, Griffin argues that since 1945 liberal nation-states have raised living standards, strengthened popular commitment to democratic principles, and improved the handling of structural crises. The naiveté and shortsightedness of these assertions is jarring, given Griffin's level of insight on other points. Here Griffin seems particularly limited by his liberalism and lack of radical analysis.

Another weak spot in Griffin's discussion concerns fascism's relationship with religion. He argues that fascism is a secular ideology that is fundamentally incompatible with "genuine" religion. To Griffin, fascism's "earthly aspirations" contrast with religion's focus on an infinite, metaphysical reality above all human activity, and fascism's brutality and ethnocentrism are irreconcilable with "authentic" religion's recognition of the interconnectedness and beauty of all life. It's true, Griffin admits, that many ostensibly religious people have embraced fascism, but this represents a "confusion" of their faith. Yes, many fascist ideologies have incorporated religious themes, but in doing so fascism has "corrupted," "desecrated," even "mongrelized" religion.[52]

Given the history of religion worldwide, it's hard to understand how Griffin could argue that violent or oppressive versions of religious belief are simply not authentic. Who is he to say that his concept of religion is the only true one? In doing so, Griffin is throwing his own commitment to methodological empathy out the window. If analysis of fascist ideology is supposed to "penetrate fascist self-understanding...in order to grasp how people saw the movement,"[53] then we need to try to understand what religion has meant to fascists—not dismiss their beliefs as phony or corrupt because they don't match an external yardstick. Griffin is clear about this when it comes to fascist conceptions of revolution, but for him religion is a blind spot.

More defensible, but still flawed, is Griffin's insistence that there is a basic conceptual difference between fascism and religious "fundamentalism." Although both promote a vision of collective rebirth out of a corrupt and disintegrated modern society, he argues, fascism calls for the rebirth of a particular nation and claims "the people"—defined by a specific cultural or genetic heritage—as its source of authority. By contrast, "fundamentalists conceive 'the people' as a community of believers created by a divine force for a metaphysical mission" and define God—not the nation or race—as the ultimate reality and source of legitimacy. Furthermore, fundamentalism "attempts to reestablish what it conceives to be traditional or orthodox religious values based on divine revelation," which means that its response to the modern world is "not revolutionary but reactionary and conservative."[54]

Griffin concedes that, in practice, "hybrids" between fascism and fundamentalism can occur, and even that "the boundaries between the religious right and neo-fascism have become increasingly fuzzy over the last two decades."[55] His discussion of this point is somewhat confused, because he uses the term fundamentalism in different ways, not all of which match his description of fundamentalism quoted above. In general, the examples he gives of fascist-fundamentalist hybrids (Kahanism in Israel, the Bharatiya Janata Party in India, Christian Identity in the United States) are movements that are not particularly concerned with religious orthodoxy but rather use religion as a marker for national or ethnic identity and persecution. As Nikki Keddie has argued, such movements are better described as *religious nationalist*, and the term *fundamentalist* is better reserved for movements (such as the Christian Right) that try to impose a specific set of religious beliefs or practices on society.[56] Fundamentalist movements in Keddie's narrower sense have relatively little overlap with fascism as Griffin defines it.

Contrary to Griffin, there are good reasons to extend the concept of fascism to include some religious fundamentalist movements (in the narrower sense). This means rethinking the idea that fascism is always a form of nationalism. In the era of globalization, fascism is less closely tied to nationhood than it was seventy-five years ago. Griffin himself notes a trend toward internationalism among neo-fascists, and some neo-fascists have also worked to break up nation-states into smaller, ethnically pure units (such as the neonazi call for an independent white homeland in the Pacific Northwest). A British Third Positionist magazine declares, "Highly centralized states are likely to lead to extreme conflict in these times. The practical alternative of decentralized states based on homogeneous groupings co-operating through Confederacies and allowing bi-lateral agreements between Regions is the only long-term answer."[57] (Such decentralist visions remain totalitarian in that they seek to impose rigid ideological conformity on all spheres of society, but would enforce this through local, regional, or nongovernmental institutions, not nation-states.)

In the context of these shifts away from traditional fascist nationalism, the difference between rebirth of a nation and rebirth of a community of believers remains important, but it isn't more important than the difference between Mussolini's cultural chauvinism and Hitler's biological racism.

Coupled with this, I disagree with Griffin's claim that the drive to impose religious orthodoxy is never revolutionary. The most radical branches of both the Christian Right and the Islamic Right demand a "return" to supposedly ancient scriptural laws. But adapted to modern conditions and combined with modern technology and organizational strategies, this means a coordinated, elite-controlled project to reshape all social spheres, which closely resembles the fascist cultural revolution Griffin describes. It also means that some religious fundamentalists pursue ideological goals that may clash with capitalist policies (such as promoting consumerism or exploiting women's labor power) in ways that parallel secular fascism's contradictory relationship with business elites.

Combining two approaches

In their analyses of fascism, Griffin and the independent Marxists I discussed above share several important points. In broad terms, both regard fascism as an autonomous political force, a distinct form of right-wing politics that opposes the left but also challenges the established order, including conventional capitalist politics and culture. Two of the Marxists (Hamerquist and Sakai) join with Griffin in labeling fascism as revolutionary. Within both approaches there is also a recognition that fascism is not a static entity, but one that evolves to address new historical conditions and opportunities. Along with these points of commonality, each side also brings something to the table that the other lacks. Griffin brings an incisive and detailed portrait of fascist ideology, while the Marxists bring a careful assessment of fascism's contradictory relationship with capitalism.

All of this offers a lot of room for useful interchange, but little work has been done in this area. Griffin himself often treats Marxist discussions of fascism as an intellectual dead end, trapped by a supposed dismissal of fascism's revolutionary claims and what he calls "the axiomatic assumption that fascism is primarily to be understood in relation to the crisis of the capitalist state."[58] However, Griffin does recognize significant variation among Marxist analyses and in one 2001 essay hails "the prospects for synergy between Marxist and liberal" approaches to fascist aesthetics.[59]

On the other side, few Marxists have even addressed Griffin's work. Trotskyist Dave Renton offers a mean-spirited polemic that falsifies many of Griffin's views. Renton claims, for example, that Griffin wants to "rescue fascist Italy from stigma" and that he believes "fascism cannot be blamed for the Holocaust." In contrast, Mark Neocleous makes a serious effort to synthesize class analysis with an exploration of fascist ideology that is partly influenced by Griffin. But Neocleous underplays fascism's insurgent dimension—precisely the area that should be central to such an interchange—and instead portrays fascism one-sidedly as "a counter-revolutionary phenomenon in defense of capitalism"[60]

As a step toward bringing the two approaches together, I offer the following draft definition: *Fascism is a revolutionary form of right-wing populism, inspired by a totalitarian vision of collective rebirth, that challenges capitalist political and cultural power while promoting economic and social hierarchy.*[61]

In this definition, *revolutionary* means an effort to bring about a fundamental, structural transformation of the political, cultural, economic, or social order. Fascism seeks, first of all, to overthrow established political elites and abolish established forms of political rule, whether liberal-pluralist or authoritarian. Second, fascists also attack "bourgeois" cultural patterns such as individualism and consumerism, and aim to systematically reshape all cultural spheres—encompassing education, family life, religion, the media, arts, sports and leisure, as well as the culture of business and the workplace—to reflect one unified ideology. Third, some (not all) forms of fascism promote a socioeconomic revolution that transforms but does not abolish class society—as when German Nazism restructured the industrial heart of Europe with a system of exploitation based largely on plunder, slave labor, and genocidally working people to death.

By *right-wing* I mean a political orientation that reinforces or intensifies social oppression as part of a backlash against movements for greater equality, freedom, or inclusiveness. *Populism* means a form of politics that uses mass mobilization to rally "the people" around some form of anti-elitism. (This definition, borrowed from Margaret Canovan, differs slightly from Griffin's use of the term populism.) Combining these two concepts, *right-wing populism* mobilizes a mass movement around a twisted anti-elitism (often based on conspiracy theories) at the same time that it intensifies oppression. In place of leftist conceptions of class struggle, fascists often draw a phony distinction between "producers" (including "productive" capitalists, workers, and middle classes) and "parasites" (defined variously as financiers, bureaucrats, foreign corporations, Jews, immigrants, welfare mothers, etc.) Right-wing populism appeals largely to middle groups in the social hierarchy, who have historically formed an important part of fascism's mass base.[62]

The phrase *totalitarian vision of collective rebirth* draws on Griffin's work but broadens his category of ultra-nationalism to encompass certain religious-based and other non-nationalist movements. The fascist vision is *totalitarian* in that it (a) celebrates one group—national, ethnic, religious, or racial—as an organic community to which all other loyalties must be subordinated; (b) uses mass organizations and rituals to create a sense of participation and direct identification with that community; (c) advocates coordinated top-down control over all institutions; and (d) rejects in principle the concepts of individual rights, pluralism, equality, and democratic decision-making. The *collective rebirth* aspect of the vision declares that the community must be rescued from a profound inner crisis, largely by purging "alien" ideologies and groups of people that are considered threats to the community's unity and vitality. This vision often draws on romanticized images of the past but points toward a radically new cultural and political order.

Fascist regimes *challenge capitalist political and cultural power* by taking dominance of the state away from the representatives of big business and subordinating capitalist interests to their own ideological agenda. At the same time, fascism *promotes economic and social hierarchy*, either within or (potentially) outside a capitalist framework. Historically, fascists have colluded with capitalists and bolstered the economic power of big business. Although fascists have often targeted specific capitalist features and even specific sectors of the business class, no fascist movement has substantively attacked core capitalist structures such as private property and the market economy. A fascist revolution of the future might radically reshape economic exploitation but would not abolish it.

By combining insights from the two approaches I have explored, the proposed definition—with its twin focus on ideology and class rule—offers a fuller, more rounded model of fascism. In the process, it gives us a more powerful tool to map divisions, relationships, and changes in right-wing politics, and to understand how these dynamics relate to changes in capitalism.

The past thirty years have seen an upsurge of right-wing movements in many parts of the world. Many of these movements promote some form of authoritarian populism—either nationalist or religious in focus—that incorporates themes of anti-elitism and collective regeneration out of crisis. In this context, some commentators treat explicit racism or antisemitism as the decisive markers of fascism, but racism and antisemitism can be found among non-fascists as well, and not all fascists today fit the classic profile for ethnic bigotry. A more critical dividing line is between "reformists" who are content to work within existing channels and "revolutionaries" (including but not limited to fascists) who advocate a radical break with the established order. This division often cuts across movements rather than between them. As of this writing in 2008,* the United States has seen two major examples of

---

* For a more up to date and in-depth survey of these movements, see chapters 2 and 3.

this in recent years: the Patriot movement and the Christian right.[63]

The Patriot movement, which included armed "citizens militias" and peaked in the mid/late 1990s, represented the United States' first large-scale coalition of committed nazis and non-fascist activists since World War II. The Patriot movement promoted the apocalyptic specter of an elite conspiracy to destroy U.S. sovereignty and impose a tyrannical collectivist system run by the United Nations. The movement's program centered on forming armed "militias" to defend against the expected crackdown, but more extreme proposals circulated widely, such as bogus "constitutional" theories that would relegalize slavery, abolish women's right to vote, and give people of color an inferior citizenship status. A loose-knit and unstable network mainly based among rural, working-class whites, the Patriot movement attracted millions of supporters at its height. It fed not only on fears of government repression but also reactions to economic hardship connected with globalization (such as the farm crisis of the 1980s), the erosion of traditional white male privilege, the decline of U.S. global dominance, and disillusionment with mainstream political options. (Many of the same impulses fueled grassroots support for Pat Buchanan's 1992 and 1996 Republican presidential campaigns. Buchanan blended attacks on immigrants, homosexuals, and feminists with a critique of corporate globalization and an anti-interventionist foreign policy, but did not challenge the established political framework.)

The Christian Right has promoted a program of cultural traditionalism in response to perceived social breakdown and a supposed elite secular humanist conspiracy to destroy American freedom. The movement's agenda centers on reasserting traditional gender roles and heterosexual male dominance, but also includes strong subthemes of cultural racism. The Christian right is based mainly among middle-class Sunbelt suburbanites and has fostered a dense network of local, regional, and national organizations that actively engage millions of people. The movement includes a small fascist wing, spearheaded by advocates of Christian Reconstructionism. Reconstructionists, who have played a key role in the most terroristic branch of the anti-abortion rights movement, reject pluralist institutions in favor of a full-scale theocracy based on their interpretation of biblical law. However, the bulk of the Christian Right has (so far) advocated more limited forms of Christian control and has worked to gain power within the existing political system, not overthrow it.

In many other parts of the world, too, fascism operates as a tendency or a distinct faction within a larger movement. In western and central Europe, many right-wing nationalist movements encompass small hardcore neofascist groups alongside mass parties such as the National Front (France), the Freedom Party of Austria (FPO), and the National Alliance (Italy).[64] All three of these parties were built largely by (ex?)-fascists and promote political themes (especially anti-immigrant racism) that are widely identified as the opening wedge for a fascist agenda. Note that both the FPO and the National Alliance have participated in coalition governments at the national level. This may be part of a long-term strategy to "fascisticize" the political climate and institutions from within, but it also suggests the possibility that fascists—like socialists—can be co-opted into a liberal capitalist political system.

The Islamic right encompasses a great diversity of organizations, political philosophies, strategies, and constituencies across the Muslim world.[65] Although some branches (notably Saudi Arabia's religious power structure) are conservative or reactionary, others represent a kind of right-wing populism that aims not to reject modernity but reshape it. These branches use modern forms of political mobilization to rally Muslims against western imperialism, Zionism, global capitalist culture, and/or local elites. They envision a collective religious and national (or international) rebirth through re-Islamizing society or throwing off foreign domination.

Within this framework, Afghanistan's Taliban and Lebanon's Hezbollah represent opposite poles. The Taliban have promoted a totalitarian form of Islamic rule that combines virulent misogyny, Pashtun ethnic chauvinism, and warlord capitalism—politics that fully deserve the fascist label. Hezbollah, in contrast, offsets its call for a theocracy modeled on Iran with an everyday practice that respects religious, ethnic, and political diversity, does not impose special strictures on women, and focuses its populist critique mainly on the realities of Israeli aggression and the hardships faced by Lebanon's Shiite majority.[66] (Iran's Islamic Republic falls somewhere between these two poles. Although authoritarian, it preserves too much openness and pluralism to be labeled fascist, which highlights the fact that right-wing revolutionary anti-imperialism does not necessarily equal fascism.)

India's massive Hindu nationalist movement advocates Hindu unity and supremacy as the key to revitalizing India as a nation. The movement promotes hatred of—and mass violence against—Muslims and claims that India's political leaders have long pursued anti-Hindu policies and favoritism toward Muslims and other minorities. Hindu nationalism, or "Hindutva," has disproportionately appealed to upper-caste, middle-class Hindus from northern and west-central India. The movement centers on the Rashtriya Swayamsevak Sangh (Association of National Volunteers, or RSS), an all-male cadre organization that promotes a paramilitary ethos and a radical vision to reshape Indian culture along authoritarian corporatist lines. The RSS's political spinoff, the Bharatiya Janata Party (Indian People's Party, or BJP), has often favored a more pragmatic electoral strategy that blends a toned-down version of Hindu chauvinism with populist economic appeals. (The BJP headed India's coalition government from 1998 to 2004 and now leads the parliamentary opposition.)* There are also tensions within the movement between advocates of free trade and economic nationalists who warn of the dangers posed by foreign investment. In contrast to many fascists and other right-wing nationalists, Hindutva forces have sought close strategic ties with both the United States and Israel, especially since George W. Bush proclaimed the War on Terror.[67]

This array of movements looks different from classical fascism, in large part, because the capitalist world has changed. Classical fascism took shape in an era of European industrialization and nation-building, competing colonial empires, and an international Communist movement inspired by the recent Bolshevik Revolution. Now both old-style colonialism and state socialism have almost vanished, while corporate globalization is shifting industries across the world and reshaping nation-states. Far-right movements are responding to these changes in various ways. They promote nostalgia for old empires but also right-wing anti-imperialism, old-style nationalisms but also internationalist and decentralized versions of authoritarian politics. They feed off of a backlash against the left but also grow where the left's weakness has

---

* Since this essay way originally published in 2008, the BJP spent ten years out of office; however, in 2014, longtime Gujarat Chief Minister Narendra Modi—a man who had been personally implicated in the anti-Muslim pogroms of 2002 in which over two thousand people were killed—led the party to a landslide victory in the country's general election. Since that election, Modi has headed the BJP-led coalition government as prime minister, and as of July 2017 the same coalition governs eighteen of India's twenty-nine states.

opened space for other kinds of insurgent movements. And they promote different versions of anti-elitism, often targeting U.S. or multinational capital but sometimes focusing more on local elites.

Many commentators have argued that fascist movements today represent a right-wing backlash against capitalist globalization. Martin A. Lee argues, for example, that in Europe "the waning power of the nation-state has triggered a harsh ultra-nationalist reaction." Here far rightists have exploited a range of popular issues associated with international economic restructuring—not only scapegoating immigrants but also criticising the European Union, the introduction of a single European currency, and the rise of a globalized culture. "Global commerce acts as the great homogenizer, blurring indigenous differences and smothering contrasting ethnic traits. Consequently, many Europeans are fearful of losing not only their jobs, but their cultural and national identities."[68]

In Europe and elsewhere, far-right politics is indeed largely a response to capitalist globalization, but this response is more complex than a simple backlash. For example, the Patriot/militia movement in the United States denounced "global elites," the "new world order," the United Nations, international bankers, etc. But their attack on government regulation, as People Against Racist Terror has pointed out, dovetailed with "the actual globalist strategy of the International Monetary Fund and World Bank to end all environmental and labor codes that restrict untrammeled exploitation."[69] In India, Hindu nationalists have denounced multinational capital and globalized culture, but the movement's dominant approach has been to seek a stronger role for India within the context of global capitalism. The BJP-led coalition government of 1998–2004 promoted privatization, deregulation, foreign investment, consumer credit growth, and expansion of the information technology sector. These policies are tailored to India's rising upper and middle classes, eager to participate more effectively in the global economy—not historical "losers" trying to gain back their old status by attacking the forces of change.[70]

The gender politics of the Christian and Islamic right, too, are sometimes seen as a reaction against capitalist globalization—a drive to force women out of the wage labor force and back into full domestic submission, depriving multinational capital of a crucial source of labor. There is truth to this, but here again the dynamic is more complex than a simple backlash. To begin with, many Christian rightists and Islamic rightists consider it acceptable for women to work outside the home, as long as they do it in a way that is "modest" and doesn't challenge male authority. And even the religious traditionalist claim that women's place is in the home can make it easier for employers to exploit women economically. As Maria Mies argues in *Patriarchy and Accumulation on a World Scale*, defining homemaking as women's natural role trivializes women's paid work as a source of "supplementary" income (which justifies paying women much less than men) and isolates women workers from each other and from male workers (which hinders collective labor activism).[71] This means that there is potential for both conflict and accommodation on gender politics between religious rightists and global (or local) capital.

This essay is intended to challenge the prevailing view among U.S. leftist organizations that fascism equals a tool of capitalist repression— because that view not only distorts history but also hides major political threats in today's world. Fascism is better understood as an autonomous right-wing force that has a contradictory relationship with capital and that draws mass support largely by advocating a revolution against established values and institutions. Several Marxists discussed above have helped to develop this counter-model of fascism, but their work is limited by an unsystematic analysis of fascist ideology. By contrast, Roger Griffin's analysis of fascism centers on a careful treatment of ideology, although his conception neglects class dynamics and does not adequately address fascism's scope and prospects today. Combining the two approaches gives us a stronger model of fascism than either approach can offer on its own.

This essay does not offer a comprehensive theory of fascism. Many important aspects of fascism merit a fuller treatment than I have been able to give them here, and the writers I have discussed are only a sampling of those (both Marxist and non-Marxist) who have written insightfully about fascism. I hope that this discussion will encourage further efforts at synthesis.

The concept of fascism as a right-wing revolutionary force has spawned the idea that we are facing a "three-way fight" between fascism, conventional global capitalism, and (at least potentially) leftist revolution. This approach is an improvement over widespread dualistic models that try to divide all political players between the "forces of oppression" and the "forces of liberation." As some radical antifascists have pointed out for years, "my enemy's enemy" is not necessarily my friend. At the same time, like any theoretical model, the three-way fight itself only approximates reality. There are more than three sides in the struggle, and to understand the different forces and their interrelationships, we have a lot of work to do.

Thanks to Dan Berger, Chip Berlet, Roger Griffin, Don Hamerquist, Karl Kersplebedeb, Jonathan Scott, Victor Wallis, and Xtn for critical comments and suggestions.

Endnotes

NOTES TO THE INTRODUCTION

1. Matthew N. Lyons, "Calling them alt-right helps us fight them," *Three Way Fight* (blog), November 22, 2017; Matthew N. Lyons, "Alt-right: more misogynistic than many neonazis," *Three Way Fight*, December 3, 2017.

2. Chip Berlet and Matthew N. Lyons, *Right-Wing Populism in America: Too Close for Comfort* (New York: Guilford Press, 2000), 2–3.

3. Matthew N. Lyons, "Is the Bush Administration Fascist?" *New Politics* 11, no. 2 (Winter 2007).

4. Don Hamerquist et al., *Confronting Fascism: Discussion Documents for a Militant Movement* (Montreal: Kersplebedeb Publishing, 2017); Roger Griffin, *The Nature of Fascism* (London: Pinter Publishers, 1991; New York: Routledge, 1996).

5. "About Us," *Three Way Fight* (blog), June 12, 2005.

6. Matthew N. Lyons, *Arier, Patriarchen, Übermenschen: die extreme Rechte in den USA* [Aryans, Patriarchs, Supermen: The far right in the USA], trans. Gabriel Kuhn (Münster, Germany: Unrast Verlag, 2015).

7. Berlet and Lyons, *Right-Wing Populism in America*, chapters 3 and 7.

8. Ibid., chapters 9 and 10.

9. Kevin Coogan, *Dreamer of the Day: Francis Parker Yockey and the Postwar Fascist International* (Brooklyn, Autonomedia, 1999), 255, 418–420, 457–461; Michael J. McVicar, *Christian Reconstruction: R.J. Rushdoony and American Religious Conservatism* (Chapel Hill: University of North Carolina Press, 2015), chapter 3.

10. Thomas Ferguson, *Golden Rule: The Investment Theory of Party Competition and the Logic of Money-Driven Political Systems* (Chicago: University of Chicago Press, 1995); Thomas Ferguson and Joel Rogers, *Right Turn: The Decline of the Democrats and the Future of American Politics* (New York: Hill and Wang; Farrar, Straus and Giroux, 1986).

11. Berlet and Lyons, *Right-Wing Populism in America*, chapter 10.

12. Ferguson and Rogers, *Right Turn*, chapter 3.

13. Berlet and Lyons, *Right-Wing Populism in America*, chapters 10 and 11.

14. Mike Davis, *Prisoners of the American Dream: Politics and Economy in the History of the US Working* Class (London: Verso, 1986), chapters 5 and 6; Amy Elizabeth Ansell, *New Right, New Racism: Race and Reaction in the United States and Britain* (Washington Square, NY: New York University Press, 1997).

15. George Monbiot, "Neoliberalism—the ideology at the root of all our problems," *The Guardian*, April 15, 2016.

16. Arun Gupta, "How the Democrats Became the Party of Neoliberalism," *teleSUR* (website), October 31, 2014; Thomas Ferguson, Paul Jorgensen, and Jie Chen, "Party Competition and Industrial Structure in the 2012 Elections," *International Journal of Political Economy* 42, no. 2 (Summer 2013): 3–41; Jeremy Scahill and Anthony Arnove, "Rebranding war and occupation," *Socialist Worker*, no. 699 (June 17, 2009).

17. Michael Omi and Howard Winant, "How Colorblindness Co-Evolved With Free-Market Thinking," *The Public Eye*, Fall 2014 [Political Research Associates]; Richard P. Appelbaum, "Multiculturalism and Flexibility: Some New Directions in Global Capitalism," in *Mapping Multiculturalism*, ed., Avery F. Gordon and Christopher Newfield (Minneapolis: University of Minnesota Press, 1986), 297–316; Catherine Rottenberg, "The Rise of Neoliberal Feminism," *Cultural Studies* (2013); Nancy Fraser, "How feminism became capitalism's handmaiden—and how to reclaim it," *Guardian*, October 14, 2013; Sarah Jaffe, "Neoliberal Feminists Don't Want Women to Organize," *The Public Eye*, Fall 2014; Karma Chavez, Ryan Conrad, and Yasmin Nair, "Occupying Gay Rights: Against Equality and the Neoliberal Project of 'Equality,'" *AREA Chicago* (website), nd [c. 2012]; Mehlab

Jameel, "Rainbows and Weddings: The Neoliberal and Imperialist Politics of LGBT Rights," *Solidarity* (website), July 6, 2015.

18. On right-wing politics' complex relationship with global capitalism in the current period, see "Morbid Symptoms: The Rise of Trump," *Unity and Struggle* (website), November 15, 2016; "Morbid Symptoms: The Downward Spiral," *Unity and Struggle*, December 19, 2016; Bromma, "Notes on Trump," *Kersplebedeb* (website), December 2016, revised January 2017.

19. See Butch Lee and Red Rover, *Night Vision: Illuminating War & Class on the Neo-Colonial Terrain* (New York: Vagabond Press, 1993); Bromma, "Exodus and Reconstruction: Working-Class Women at the Heart of Globalization," *Kersplebedeb* (website), September 11, 2012.

NOTES TO CHAPTER 1. NEONAZIS

1. "Watch IREHR President Leonard Zeskind Discuss White Nationalism" (video), *Institute for Research and Education for Human Rights* (website), April 28, 2015. For a contrasting interpretation, see Chip Berlet, "What is White Nationalism?" *Research for Progress* (website), July 28, 2016.

2. Ken Lawrence, "Klansmen, Nazis, Skinheads: Vigilante Repression," *CovertAction Quarterly*, no. 31 (1989): 29–33; James Ridgeway, *Blood in the Face: The Ku Klux Klan, Aryan Nations, Nazi Skinheads, and the Rise of a New White Culture* (New York: Thunder's Mouth Press, 1990), 27–33, 37–44; Moshe Postone, "Anti-Semitism and National Socialism," in *Germans and Jews since the Holocaust*, ed., Anson Rabinbach and Jack Zipes (New York: Holmes and Meier, 1986).

3. Chip Berlet and Matthew N. Lyons, *Right-Wing Populism in America: Too Close for Comfort* (New York: Guilford Press, 2000), 172–173; Leonard Zeskind, *Blood and Politics: The History of the White Nationalist Movement from the Margins to the Mainstream* (New York: Farrar Straus Giroux, 2009), 71; William L. Pierce [Andrew Macdonald, pseud.], *The Turner Diaries* (Arlington, VA: National Vanguard Books, 1978).

4. Matthew N. Lyons, "Notes on Women and Right-Wing Movements—Part One," *Three Way Fight* (blog), September 27, 2005; Martin Durham, *White Rage: The extreme right and American politics* (New York: Routledge, 2007), chapter 6.

5. Berlet and Lyons, *Right-Wing Populism in America*, 54–62.

6. Alexander Saxton, *The Indispensable Enemy: Labor and the Anti-Chinese Movement in California* (Berkeley: University of California Press, 1971); Berlet and Lyons, *Right-Wing Populism in America*, 62–68.

7. Berlet and Lyons, *Right-Wing Populism in America*, 95–103; Kathleen M. Blee, *Women of the Klan: Racism and Gender in the 1920s* (Berkeley: University of California Press, 1991).

8. Karen Brodkin, *How Jews Became White Folks and What That Says About Race in America* (New Brunswick, NJ: Rutgers University Press, 1998).

9. Marc Parry, "How U.S. Law Inspired the Nazis" (interview with James Q. Whitman), *Chronicle of Higher Education*, March 19, 2017; Berlet and Lyons, *Right-Wing Populism in America*, chapter 6.

10. Berlet and Lyons, *Right-Wing Populism in America*, 131–149.

11. Gregory Hood, "Rockwell as Conservative," *Counter-Currents Publishing* (website), March 2013.

12. Ibid.; Kevin Coogan, *Dreamer of the Day: Francis Parker Yockey and the Postwar Fascist International* (Brooklyn: Autonomedia, 1999), 457–461; Stephen E. Atkins, *Encyclopedia Of Right-Wing Extremism In Modern American History* (Santa Barbara, CA: ABC-CLIO, 2011), 89–90.

13. Ridgeway, *Blood in the Face*, 60–63; Sara Diamond, *Roads to Dominion: Right-Wing Movements and Political Power in the United States* (New York: Guilford Press, 1995), 58, 88.

14. Eric K. Ward, "Skin in the Game: How Antisemitism Animates White Nationalism," *Political Research Associates* (website), June 29, 2017.

15. Zeskind, *Blood and Politics*, 367–380, 420–423, 466–469. "Federation for American Immigration Reform," *Southern Poverty Law Center* (website), nd.

16. Zeskind, *Blood and Politics*, 17–26; Durham, *White Rage*, 27–30; Pierce, *The Turner Diaries*; "James Mason Interview with Race and Reason," interview by Tom Metzger, *Race and Reason*, 1993; reposted to *YouTube* by Atomwaffen Division, March 26, 2017.

17. Zeskind, *Blood and Politics*, 34–35, 37–41, 40–45, 87–93; Durham, *White Rage*, 39–42; Ridgeway, *Blood in the Face*, 85–88.

18. Frank P. Mintz, *The Liberty Lobby and the American Right: Race, Conspiracy, and Culture* (Westport, CT: Greenwood Press, 1985); Zeskind, *Blood and Politics*, 32.

19. Ridgeway, *Blood in the Face*, 109–129; Thomas Murphy, with Steve Vetzner, "The Posse Comitatus in Wisconsin," *Public Eye* 3, nos. 1 and 2 (1981): 17–24 [Political Research Associates].

20. Michael Barkun, "Essay: The Christian Identity Movement," *Southern Poverty Law Center* (website), nd; Durham, *White Rage*, 66–72.

21. "Agent Tells of '79 Threats by Klan and Nazis," *New York Times*, May 12, 1985; JoAnn Wypijewski, "Whitewash," *Mother Jones*, November 2005.

22. Ken Lawrence, "The Ku Klux Klan and Fascism" [speech to the National Anti-Klan Network conference, Atlanta, June 19, 1982], *Urgent Tasks*, no. 14 (Fall/Winter 1982).

23. Pierce, *The Turner Diaries*, 63.

24. Ibid., 51.

25. Ibid., 101.

26. Ibid., 206–207.

27. "Dominica Coup Plot Described to Court," *New York Times*, June 18, 1981; Matthew Lauder, "Operation Red Dog: Canadian neo-nazis were central to the planned invasion of Dominica in 1981," *Canadian Content* (website), [2011]; republished on *Operation Red Dog—Bayou of Pigs* (website), April 9, 2017.

28. Anti-Defamation League, *Tattered Robes: The State of the Ku Klux Klan in the United States* (New York: Anti-Defamation League, 2016).

29. Sara Diamond, *Roads to Dominion: Right-Wing Movements and Political Power in the United States* (New York: Guilford Press, 1995), 262–265, 270–273; Durham, *White Rage*, 44–45, 121–122.

30. Zeskind, *Blood and Politics*, 205–218, 341–346, 448–449; Durham, *White Rage*, 30–31.

31. Durham, *White Rage*, 28.

32. Zeskind, *Blood and Politics*, 91–93.

33. Ibid., 97–99.

34. Durham, *White Rage*, 101–102; Zeskind, *Blood and Politics*, 96–99; Ridgeway, *Blood in the Face*, 89–100.

35. *Terror from the Right: Plots, Conspiracies and Racist Rampages Since Oklahoma City* (Montgomery, AL: Southern Poverty Law Center, 2012); Zeskind, *Blood and Politics*, 406, 413–416.

36. See Durham, *White Rage*, chapter 5.

37. Louis Beam, "Leaderless Resistance," *Inter-Klan Newsletter*, 1983; republished in *The Seditionist*, no. 12 (February 1992); Durham, *White Rage*, 103–110; Zeskind, *Blood and Politics*, 91–93.

38. The Order, "Declaration of War," unpublished typescript, November 25, 1984.

39. Zeskind, *Blood and Politics*, 64–65; Durham, *White Rage*, 44.

40. Zeskind, *Blood and Politics*, 103–104.

41. Devin Burghart and Leonard Zeskind, "The Northwest Imperative Redux," *Institute for Research & Education on Human Rights* (website), 2012; Dan Stern, "The Fascist White Aryan Nation: The Historic Compromise of the Fascist Ideal," unpublished typescript, 1988.

42. *What Is the National Alliance?* (Hillsboro, WV: National Vanguard Books, 1993), 4; "What We Stand For," *American Nazi Party* (website), 2012; "25 Points of American National Socialism," *National Socialist Movement* (website), nd.

43. "Neofascism, European Style," *Intelligence Report*, no. 97 (Winter 2000) [Southern Poverty Law Center]; Ridgeway, *Blood in the Face*, 169–76; Spencer Sunshine, "Nazi Skinhead Economics," *Souciant* (website), August 7, 2014.

44. "The New Resistance Manifesto," *Open Revolt!*, January 10, 2012; "Neo-Nazi Leader James Porrazzo Mixes Racism with Leftist Ideology," *Intelligence Report*, no. 148 (Winter 2012) [Southern Poverty Law Center].

45. Anton Shekhovtsov, "Aleksandr Dugin's Neo-Eurasianism: The New Right *à la Russe*," *Religion Compass* 3, no. 4 (2009): 697–716; Marlène Laruelle, *Aleksandr Dugin: A Russian Version of the European Radical Right?* Kennan Institute Occasional Paper #294 (Washington, DC: Woodrow Wilson International Center for Scholars, 2006); "The New Resistance Manifesto," *Open Revolt!* (website), 2012.

46. Russ Bellant, *Old Nazis, the New Right, and the Republican Party: Domestic fascist networks and their effect on U.S. cold war politics*, third edition (Cambridge, MA: South End Press, 1999). This occasional unity can be traced unbroken back to the Second World War; see Christopher Simpson, *Blowback: America's Recruitment of Nazis and Its Effects on the Cold War* (New York: Collier Books, 1989).

47. Matthew N. Lyons, "Fragmented Nationalism: Right-Wing Responses to September 11 in Historical Context," *Pennsylvania Magazine of History and Biography* 127, no. 4 (December 2003): 398–401.

48. Zeskind, *Blood and Politics*, 347–354, 506–510, 530.

49. Durham, *White Rage*, 34–35.

50. "Extremist Files: Groups," *Southern Poverty Law Center* (website), c. 2016.

51. Ibid.

52. "William Pierce," *Anti-Defamation League* (website), c. 2002; "Extremist Files: Groups."

53. Martin Durham, "White Hands across the Atlantic: the Extreme Right in Europe and the United States, 1958– ," in *New Perspectives on the Transnational Right*, ed., Martin Durham and Margaret Power (New York: Palgrave Macmillan, 2010), 149–169.

54. David Holthouse, "Leaders of Racist Prison Gang Aryan Brotherhood Face Federal Indictment," *Intelligence Report*, no. 119 (Fall 2005) [Southern Poverty Law Center]; Leonard Zeskind, "Aryan Brotherhood a Danger, But Not Part of White Nationalist Movement," *Institute for Research & Education on Human Rights* (website), October 21, 2014.

55. "Extremists," *Southern Poverty Law Center* (website), c. 2016.

56. Henry Schuster, "An Unholy Alliance: Aryan Nation Leader Reaches Out to al Qaeda," *CNN* (website), March 29, 2005.

57. Heidi Beirich, "White Supremacists Find Common Cause with Pam Geller's Anti-Islam Campaign," *Hatewatch* (blog), August 25, 2010 [Southern Poverty Law Center].

58. Don Terry, "Chattanooga Braces for Neo-Nazi Rally Against Immigration," *Hatewatch* (blog), April 8, 2014 [Southern Poverty Law Center].

59. Durham, *White Rage*, 133–134; Chip Berlet, *Right Woos Left: Populist Party, LaRouchite, and Other Neo-fascist Overtures To Progressives, And Why They Must Be Rejected* (Cambridge, MA: Political Research Associates, 1994; revised 1999); Spencer Sunshine, "The Right Hand of Occupy Wall Street: From Libertarians to Nazis, the Fact and Fiction of Right-Wing Involvement," *The Public Eye*, Winter 2014: 9–14 [Political Research Associates]; Nick Mamatas, "Fascists for Che: White supremacists infiltrate the anti-globalization movement," *In These Times*, September 13, 2002; Anti-Fascist Forum, ed., *My Enemy's Enemy: Essays on Globalization, Fascism and the Struggle Against Capitalism* (Montreal: Kersplebedeb Publishing, 2002).

60. Antifascist Front, "NeoFascist: Heathen Harvest, Neofolk, and Fascist Subculture Entryism," *Anti-Fascist News* (website), February 13, 2016; Hatewatch Staff, "NYC Oi! Fest Returns to New York City With New Kind of Hate," *Hatewatch* (blog), May 27, 2016 [Southern Poverty Law Center].

NOTES TO CHAPTER 2. THEOCRATS

1. Frank Newport, "In U.S., 42% Believe Creationist View of Human Origins," *Gallup* (website), June 2, 2014; Art Swift, "In US, Belief in Creationist View of Humans at New Low," *Gallup*, May 22, 2017.

2. "Resolution On Racial Reconciliation On The 150th Anniversary Of The Southern Baptist Convention," *Southern Baptist Convention* (website), 1995; Tanya Erzen, "Immigration Policy and the Christian Right," *Talk to Action* (website), May 4, 2006; Tarso Luís Ramos and Pam Chamberlain, "Nativist Bedfellows: The Christian Right Embraces Anti-Immigrant Politics," *The Public Eye Magazine* 23, no. 2 (Summer 2008) [Political Research Associates]; Jean Hardisty,

"Kitchen Table Backlash: The Antifeminist Women's Movement," in *Unraveling the Right: The New Conservatism in American Thought and Politics*, ed., Amy E. Ansell (Boulder, CO: Westview Press, 1998), 121–123; Ann Withorn, "Fulfilling Fears and Fantasies: The Role of Welfare in Right-Wing Social Thought and Strategy," in *Unraveling the Right*, 126–147.

3. Lisa McGirr, *Suburban Warriors: The Origins of the New American Right* (Princeton, NJ: Princeton University Press, 2001), 242; Brian Auten, "The 'Sunbelt Argument' and the Rise of Christian Reconstructionism," *Political Theology Today*, August 27, 2014; Sara Diamond, *Spiritual Warfare: The Politics of the Christian Right* (Boston: South End Press, 1989), 2, 113.

4. "U.S. Religious Landscape Survey: Affiliations," Religion and Public Life Project, *PewResearch* (website), 2007; Larry Eskridge, "How Many Evangelicals Are There?" *Institute for the Study of American Evangelicals* (website), 2012; Bradley Wright, "How Many Americans are Evangelical Christians? Born-Again Christians?" *Black, White and Gray* (blog) [*Patheos* (website)], March 28, 2013; Steven Waldman, "The Religious Left is As Big As The Religious Right," *Huffington Post*, November 1, 2008, updated May 25, 2011; "The Twelve Tribes of American Politics in the 2008 Election," *BeliefNet* (website), [2008].

5. Michael W. Cuneo, *The Smoke of Satan: Conservative and Traditionalist Dissent in Contemporary American Catholicism*, (Baltimore: Johns Hopkins University Press, 1999).

6. Frederick Clarkson, "The Rise of Dominionism: Remaking America as a Christian Nation," *The Public Eye* 19, no. 3 (Winter 2005) [Political Research Associates]; Paul Rosenberg, "Exposing religious fundamentalism in the US," *Al Jazeera*, September 6, 2011.

7. Sara Diamond, *Roads to Dominion: Right-Wing Movements and Political Power in the United States* (New York: Guilford Press, 1995), chapter 7.

8. Diamond, *Spiritual Warfare*; Diamond, *Roads to Dominion*, chapter 10.

9. Chip Berlet and Matthew N. Lyons, *Right-Wing Populism in America: Too Close for Comfort* (New York: Guilford Press, 2000), 229–237.

10. Diamond, *Roads to Dominion*, 237–241; Matthew N. Lyons, "Fragmented Nationalism: Right-Wing Responses to September 11 in Historical Context," *Pennsylvania Magazine of History and Biography* 127, no. 4 (December 2003): 406–412; Rachel Tabachnick, "The New Christian Zionism and the Jews: A Love/Hate Relationship," *The Public Eye* (Winter 2009/Spring 2010) [Political Research Associates].

11. Frederick Clarkson, "Christian Reconstructionism: Theocratic Dominionism Gains Influence," *The Public Eye* 8, nos. 1 and 2 (March and June 1994) [Political Research Associates]; Diamond, *Spiritual Warfare*, 136–138.

12. Clarkson, "Christian Reconstructionism."

13. Michael J. McVicar, "The Libertarian Theocrats: The Long, Strange History of R.J. Rushdoony and Christian Reconstructionism," *The Public Eye*, vol. 22, no. 3 (Fall 2007) [Political Research Associates]; Philip Bump, "Ron Paul's Home Schooling Curriculum Will Turn Your Kid into a Little Ron Paul," *The Atlantic*, April 9, 2013.

14. Diamond, *Spiritual Warfare*, 136–139; Diamond, *Roads to Dominion*, 247–249; John Sugg, "A Nation Under God," *Mother Jones*, December 2005; Rachel Tabachnick, "The Rise of Charismatic Dominionism," *Talk To Action* (website), January 3, 2011.

15. James Risen and Judy L. Thomas, *Wrath of Angels: The American Abortion War* (New York: Basic Books, 1998).

16. National Abortion Federation, "Anti-Abortion Extremists: Army of God," *National Abortion Federation* (website), nd; Risen and Thomas, *Wrath of Angels*, 75–76, 87, 275, 349–370; Frederick Clarkson, "Anti-Gay Ideas of the Army of God Going Mainstream?" *Talk to Action* (website), May 25, 2011; Dan Holman, "Vengeance vs. Defensive Action," *Army of God* (website), [2009?]; "The Army of God Manual," third edition, *Army of God* (website), nd.

17. Risen and Thomas, *Wrath of Angels*, 299, 347; Mark Juergensmeyer, "The Return of Christian Terrorism," *Religion Dispatches*, April 9, 2010.

18. "League of the South Works to Take Over Churches," *Intelligence Report*, no. 101 (Spring 2001) [Southern Poverty Law Center]; Edward H. Sebesta and Euan Hague, "The US Civil War as a Theological War: Confederate Christian Nationalism and the League of the South," *Canadian Review of American Studies* 32, no. 3 (2002); Rachel

Tabachnick with Frank Cocozzelli, "Nullification, Neo-Confederates, and the Revenge of the Old Right," *Political Research Associates*, November 22, 2013; Rachel Tabachnick, "Rushdoony and Theocratic Libertarians on Slavery," *Talk to Action*, July 13, 2010; Frederick Clarkson, "If Democracy is a Crime Under Religious Right's Biblical Law, What is the Punishment?" *Political Research Associates* (website), August 21, 2014.

19. Lyons, "Fragmented Nationalism," 410–412; Mark R. Rushdoony, "What My Armenian Father Taught Me about Islam," *Chalcedon Report*, January 2002: 6–8.

20. Sugg, "A Nation Under God"; Frederick Clarkson, "Charles Koch, Gary North, Libertarianism & Holocaust Denial," *Talk to Action* (website), October 6, 2013.

21. "Klan Shows its True Colors," *Choice-Net Report* (website), August 27, 1994; Frederick Clarkson, "Anti-Abortion Bombings Related," *Intelligence Report*, no. 91 (Summer 1998) [Southern Poverty Law Center]; James Ridgeway, "A Brief History of the Radical Right," *Mother Jones*, June 2, 2009.

22. Clarkson, "Christian Reconstructionism"; William Edgar, "The Passing of R.J. Rushdoony," *First Things*, August/September 2001.

23. Kathryn Joyce, *Quiverfull: Inside the Christian Patriarchy Movement* (Boston: Beacon Press, 2009), 3.

24. Joyce, *Quiverfull*.

25. Gary North, "The Intellectual Schizophrenia of the New Christian Right," *Christianity and Civilization* 1 (1982): 25.

26. Frederick Clarkson, "Rumblings of Theocratic Violence," *Political Research Associates* (website), June 11, 2014; David Lane, "Wage War to Restore a Christian Nation," *World Net Daily* (website), June 2013 [full text preserved at *Friendly Signal* (website), July 3, 2013].

27. C.J. McCloskey, "Hope for the Pro-Life Movement," *Truth and Charity Forum* (website), January 13, 2013; Frank Cocozzelli, "Opus Dei Priest's Secessionist Roadmap to Theocracy," *Talk to Action* (website), April 1, 2014.

28. Rachel Tabachnick, "Spiritual Warriors with an Anti-Gay Mission: The New Apostolic Reformation," *Political Research Associates*, March 22, 2013; Holly Pivec, "The New Apostolic Reformation:

Influence and Teachings," *Apologetics Index* (website), 2013; Trevor O'Reggio, "The Rise of the New Apostolic Reformation," *Perspective Digest* (website), nd; C. Peter Wagner, "The New Apostolic Reformation," *Renewal Journal* (website), April 12, 2012.

29. Julie Ingersoll, "Dominion Theology, Christian Reconstructionism, and the New Apostolic Reformation," *Religion Dispatches* (website), August 30, 2011.

30. Tabachnick, "Spiritual Warriors with an Anti-Gay Mission"; Pivec, "New Apostolic Reformation."

31. Tabachnick, "Spiritual Warriors with an Anti-Gay Mission."

32. Pivec, "New Apostolic Reformation."

33. Ibid.

34. Tabachnick, "The New Christian Zionism and the Jews."

35. Paul Rosenberg, "Exposing religious fundamentalism in the US," *Al Jazeera*, September 6, 2011.

NOTES TO CHAPTER 3. THE PATRIOT MOVEMENT

1. Spencer Sunshine et al., *Up in Arms: A Guide to Oregon's Patriot Movement* (Scappoose, OR: Rural Organizing Project; Somerville, MA: Political Research Associates, 2016), 11, 19.

2. *The Second Wave: Return of the Militias* (Montgomery, AL: Southern Poverty Law Center, 2009), 5, 8; Alexander Zaitchick, "'Patriot' Paranoia: A Look at the Top Ten Conspiracy Theories," *Intelligence Report*, no. 139 (Fall 2010) [Southern Poverty Law Center].

3. Chip Berlet and Matthew N. Lyons, *Right-Wing Populism in America: Too Close for Comfort* (New York: Guilford Press, 2000), 295–297; Robert H. Churchill, *To Shake Their Guns in the Tyrant's Face: Libertarian Political Violence and the Origins of the Militia Movement* (Ann Arbor: University of Michigan Press, 2009), 204–206.

4. Leonard Zeskind, *Blood and Politics: The History of the White Nationalist Movement from the Margins to the Mainstream* (New York: Farrar Straus Giroux, 2009), 359–360.

5. Mark Rupert, "Articulating Neoliberalism and Far-Right Conspiracism: The Case of the American 'Gun Rights' Culture," paper presented at the annual meeting of the International Studies Association, New Orleans, LA, February 2015; Churchill, *To Shake Their Guns in the Tyrant's Face*, 213–215.

6. James Scaminaci III, *The Christian Right's Fourth Generation Warfare in America*, Book 2, chapter 15: "The Christian Right and the Formation of the Patriot Militia," *Academia.edu* (website), nd, 15–16.

7. Ibid., 23.

8. Ryan Lenz and Mark Potok, "War in the West: The Bundy Ranch Standoff and the American Radical Right," *Southern Poverty Law Center* (website), July 9, 2014, 19–20; William Kevin Burke, "The Wise Use Movement: Right-Wing Anti-Environmentalism," in *Eyes Right! Challenging the Right Wing Backlash*, ed., Chip Berlet (Boston: South End Press, 1995), 135–145.

9. James A. Aho, *The Politics of Righteousness: Idaho Christian Patriotism* (Seattle: University of Washington Press, 1990), 17–21.

10. Justin King, "Larry Pratt," *Southern Poverty Law Center* (website), nd.

11. Tom Burghardt, "A Small Circle of Friends: Larry Pratt, the Council for Inter-American Security and International Fascist Networks," *Antifa Info-Bulletin* 1, no. 5 (March 7, 1996).

12. Berlet and Lyons, *Right-Wing Populism in America*, 287–288.

13. Ibid., 258–260.

14. Bob Moser, "Constitution Party Hopes to Take Politics to the Extreme in 2004," *Intelligence Report*, no. 111 (Fall 2003) [Southern Poverty Law Center].

15. Patrick J. Buchanan, "Why I Am Running for President," *Human Events*, December 28, 1991, 11.

16. Berlet and Lyons, *Right-Wing Populism in America*, 290–292.

17. Churchill, *To Shake Their Guns in the Tyrant's Face*, 188–189; Timothy J. Dunn, *The Militarization of the U.S.-Mexico Border, 1978–1992: Low-Intensity Conflict Doctrine Comes Home* (Austin: Center for Mexican American Studies, University of Texas at Austin, 1996).

18. Juan González et al., "MOVE Bombing at 30: 'Barbaric' 1985 Philadelphia Police Attack Killed 11 & Burned a Neighborhood,"

Democracy Now!, May 13, 2015; Zaid Jilani, "30 Years Ago Today, Philadelphia Police Dropped a Bomb on a Black Liberation Group," *Alternet*, May 13, 2015.

19. Zeskind, *Blood and Politics*, 310–19

20. Scaminaci, *The Christian Right's Fourth Generation Warfare*, Book 2, chapter 11: "First Contacts: Christian Reconstructionism and Christian Identity," *Academia.edu* (website), no date.

21. Churchill, *To Shake Their Guns in the Tyrant's Face*, 224.

22. Ibid., 201.

23. Ibid., 243.

24. Ibid., 203–206.

25. "Patriot Movement Timeline," *Intelligence Report*, no. 128 (Summer 2010) [Southern Poverty Law Center]; *The Second Wave: Return of the Militias.*

26. Heidi Beirich, "Midwifing the Militias," *Intelligence Report*, no. 137 (Spring 2010) [Southern Poverty Law Center]; *Articles of Freedom: The Works of the Continental Congress* (Queensbury, NY: We the People Foundation for Constitutional Education, 2009) [available on *National Liberty Alliance* website].

27. "Meet the 'Patriots,'" *Intelligence Report*, no. 138 (Summer 2010) [Southern Poverty Law Center]; Justine Sharrock, "Oath Keepers and the Age of Treason," *Mother Jones*, March/April 2010; Spencer Sunshine, "Profiles on the Right: Three Percenters," *Political Research Associates*, January 5, 2016; Sunshine et al., *Up in Arms*, 5, 22.

28. Devin Burghart and Leonard Zeskind, "Tea Party Nationalism: A Critical Examination of the Tea Party Movement and the Size, Scope, and Focus of Its National Factions," *Institute for Research & Education on Human Rights* (website), October 2010, 63; Sunshine et al., *Up in Arms*, 7; David Holthouse, "Nativists to Patriots," in *The Second Wave: Return of the Militias*, 11–12; David Holthouse, "New Nativist-'Patriot' Coalition Formed," *Hatewatch* (blog), April 16, 2009 [Southern Poverty Law Center].

29. Sunshine et al., *Up in Arms*, 7, 27.

30. Ibid., 28, 34.

31. J.J. Johnson, "A Heartfelt Invitation to Black Americans," *The Buffalo Soldiers* (website), nd; "False Patriots," *Intelligence Report*,

Notes from pages 50 to 52

Summer 2001 [Southern Poverty Law Center]; Sunshine et al., *Up in Arms*, 33.

32. Matthew N. Lyons, "Oath Keepers, Ferguson, and the Patriot movement's conflicted race politics," *Three Way Fight*, August 28, 2015.

33. "Oath Keepers Joins Coalition Supporting Hundreds of Protests Against Illegal Immigration on July 18–19. Members Encouraged to Participate," *Oath Keepers* (website), July 17, 2014; Jon Levine, "Two Images Show the Double Standard for Black and White Protesters in Ferguson," *Mic* (website), August 11, 2015.

34. Miranda Blue, "'Sodomites, Go To Hell!': Right-Wing July 4th Event Warns Hurricanes Create 'Sodomite Heaven,'" *Right Wing Watch* (website), July 8, 2015.

35. Lyons, "Oath Keepers, Ferguson, and the Patriot movement's conflicted race politics"; NYOathKeeper, "An Oath Keeper Speaks Out: All Lives Matter—Including the Lives of Police Officers," *OK New York* (website), December 22, 2014.

36. Missouri Oath Keepers, "Open Letter of Warning to Governor Nixon From Missouri Oath Keepers," *Oath Keepers* (website), August 22, 2014; "Oath Keepers Open Letter to the People of Ferguson, Missouri," *Oath Keepers* (website), November 24, 2014.

37. Jay Syrmopoulos, "Oath Keepers to Arm 50 Black Protesters in Ferguson with AR-15's for an Epic Rights Flexing March," *Free Thought Project* (website), August 15, 2015; Justin King, "Exclusive: Oath Keepers leave organization in protest after leadership reportedly fails to support armed Ferguson march," *The Fifth Column* (website), August 26, 2015; see also Alan Feuer, "The Oath Keeper Who Wants to Arm Black Lives Matter," *Rolling Stone*, January 3, 2016.

38. Adam Winkler, "The Secret History of Guns," *The Atlantic*, September 2011.

39. "Sovereign Citizens Movement," *Southern Poverty Law Center* (website), nd; J.J. MacNab, "'Sovereign' Citizen Kane," *Intelligence Report*, no. 139 (Fall 2010) [Southern Poverty Law Center].

40. Kevin Carey, "Too Weird for The Wire," *Washington Monthly*, May/June/July 2008; Leah Nelson, "'Sovereigns' in Black," *Intelligence Report*, no. 143 (Fall 2011), [Southern Poverty Law Center].

41. Sunshine et al., *Up in Arms*, 7.

42. Ibid., 38.

43. Ibid., 9, 43, 44.

44. Ibid., 8, 38–40.

45. Lenz and Potok, "War in the West," 6.

46. Ibid.; Paul Rosenberg, "'A much larger and more dangerous movement': Right-wing militias thrive post-Bundy—and the media won't talk about it," *Salon*, July 22, 2014.

47. "Anatomy of a Standoff: The Occupiers of the Malheur National Wildlife Refuge Headquarters," *Anti-Defamation League*, 2016; Carli Brosseau, "Oregon occupation planned for months by Bundy and Montana militia leader," *The Oregonian*, January 11, 2016; Spencer Sunshine, "What the Oregon Standoff Is Really About," *Yes! Magazine*, January 15, 2016.

48. Conor Friedersdorf, "Oregon and the Injustice of Mandatory Minimums," *The Atlantic*, January 5, 2016.

49. Ammon Bundy et al., "Militia Members Outline Their Plan" [video by Sarah Dee Spurlock], *The Oregonian*, January 2, 2016.

50. Zach Schwartz-Weinstein, "Bundy's Oregon Occupation Is Capitalist at Its Core," *Truthout*, January 8, 2016.

51. Rupert, "Articulating Neoliberalism and Far-Right Conspiracism."

NOTES TO CHAPTER 4. THE ALT-RIGHT

1. Chip Berlet and Matthew N. Lyons, *Right-Wing Populism in America: Too Close for Comfort* (New York: Guilford Press, 2000), 243–244, 283–284.

2. Rachel Tabachnick and Frank L. Cocozzelli, "Nullification, Neo-Confederates, and the Revenge of the Old Right," *Political Research Associates* (website), November 22, 2013.

3. Matthew N. Lyons, "Fragmented Nationalism: Right-Wing Responses to September 11 in Historical Context," *Pennsylvania Magazine of History and Biography* 127, no. 4 (December 2003): 398–404.

4. Roger Griffin, "Plus ça change! The Fascist Pedigree of the Nouvelle Droite," chapter written for *The Development of the Radical Right in France 1890–1995*, ed., Edward Arnold (London: Routledge: 2000) [available on *ResearchGate* (website)]; Anton Shekhovtsov, "Aleksandr Dugin's Neo-Eurasianism: The New Right a la Russe," *Religion Compass* 3, no. 4 (2009): 697–716.

5. See Alain de Benoist and Charles Champetier, "The French New Right in the Year 2000," *Telos*, no. 115 (Spring 1999): 117–144.

6. In the 1990s, the ex-leftist journal *Telos* was instrumental in translating European New Right texts into English and engaging with ENR ideas. See for example the *Telos* Winter 1993–Fall 1994 (nos. 98–99), special double issue on "The French New Right: New Right—New Left—New Paradigm?"

7. See, for example, Richard Spencer, "The Conservative Write," *Taki's Magazine*, August 6, 2008; Kevin DeAnna, "The Alternative Right," *Taki's Magazine*, July 26, 2009; and Jack Hunter, "Whither the Alternative Right?" *Taki's Magazine*, November 3, 2009.

8. Matthew N. Lyons, "AlternativeRight.com: Paleoconservatism for the 21st Century," *Three Way Fight* (blog), September 19, 2010.

9. Greg Johnson, "Theory & Practice," *Counter-Currents Publishing* (website), September 2010.

10. James Kirchick, "American Racist Richard Spencer Gets to Play the Martyr in Hungary," *The Daily Beast*, October 7, 2014.

11. Antifascist Front, "Alternative Internet Racism: Alt Right and the New Fascist Branding," *Anti-Fascist News* (website), December 18, 2015.

12. Lawrence Murray, "Fashism," *The Right Stuff* (website), October 24, 2015.

13. "The Rich Kids of Fascism: Why the Alt-Right Didn't Start with Trump, and Won't End With Him Either," *It's Going Down* (website), December 16 2016; republished in *Ctrl-Alt-Delete: An Antifascist Report on the Alternative Right* (Montreal: Kersplebedeb Publishing, 2017); see also Leonard Zeskind, "Standing at the Crossroads: An Analysis of Events in Charlottesville, Virginia," *Institute for Research & Education on Human Rights* (website), August 16, 2017; Antwan Herron, "How White Millennials Became Neo-Nazis," *Wear Your Voice* (website), April 19, 2017.

14. Richard Hoste, "Why an Alternative Right is Necessary," *AlternativeRight.com*, February 24, 2010, reposted in *Radix Journal*.

15. Johnson, "Theory & Practice."

16. Lawrence Murray, "The Fight for the Alt-Right: The Rising Tide of Ideological Autism Against Big-Tent Supremacy," *The Right Stuff* (website), March 6, 2016.

17. Alfred W. Clark, "What is the #Altright?" *Radix Journal* (website), January 20, 2016.

18. Dylan Matthews, "Why the alt-right loves single payer health care," *Vox* (website), April 4, 2017; Ahab, "Environmentalism and the Alt Right," *AltRight.com* (website), June 6, 2017.

19. Richard B. Spencer, "Identitarianism—A Conversation Starter," *Radix Journal* (website), June 15, 2015.

20. Darth Stirner, "Fascist Libertarianism: For a Better World," *The Right Stuff* (website), January 23, 2013.

21. Antifascist Front, "#Cuckservative: How the 'Alt Right' Took Off Their Masks and Revealed Their White Hoods," *Anti-Fascist News* (website), August 16, 2015.

22. Ibid.

23. "Joshua Blakeney Interviews Greg Johnson, Part 2," *Counter-Currents Publishing* (website), December 2014; "Richard Bertrand Spencer," *Southern Poverty Law Center* (website), nd; Antifascist Front, "Meet the Exterminationist Wing of the Alt Right Who is Open About Wanting to Kills Jews and Non-Whites," *Anti-Fascist News* (website), April 3, 2017.

24. Ben Lorber, "Understanding Alt-Right Antisemitism," *Doikayt* (website), March 24, 2017.

25. Andrew Anglin, "Intensified Jewing: Vox Covers the Alt-Right," *Daily Stormer*, April 18, 2016.

26. Auschwitz Soccer Ref, "Zero Tolerance: Why Aren't White Nationalists and Jewish Nationalists Fellow Travelers?" *The Right Stuff*, April 11, 2016.

27. Jared Taylor, "Jews and American Renaissance," *American Renaissance*, April 14, 2006.

28. Chuck Tanner, "Richard Spencer: Alt-Right, White Nationalist, Anti-Semite," *Institute for Research & Education on Human Rights* (website), January 5, 2017.

29. Eugene Girin, "Is the Alt Right Anti-Semitic?" *AlternativeRight.com*, July 29, 2010, reposted in *Radix Journal*.

30. M.K. Lane, "Will Jews Change Sides?" *Counter-Currents Publishing*, February 17, 2016.

31. Jeff Sharlet, "Are You Man Enough for the Men's Rights Movement?" *GQ*, February 3, 2014.

32. Paul Elam, "Jury duty at a rape trial? Acquit!" *A Voice for Men*, July 20, 2010.

33. Paul Elam, "October is the fifth annual Bash a Violent Bitch Month," *A Voice for Men*, September 30, 2015.

34. Roosh V [Daryush Valizadeh], "Women Must Have Their Behavior And Decisions Controlled By Men," *Roosh V* (website), September 21, 2015.

35. Quoted in David Futrelle, "Why Elliot Rodger's misogyny matters," *We Hunted the Mammoth* (blog), May 25, 2014.

36. Roosh V [Daryush Valizadeh], "No One Would Have Died If PUAHate Killer Elliot Rodger Learned Game," *Return of Kings* (website), May 25, 2014.

37. Stephen Totilo, "Another Woman in Gaming Flees Home Following Death Threats," *Kotaku* (website), October 11, 2014.

38. Amanda Hess, "Why Women Aren't Welcome on the Internet," *Pacific Standard*, January 6, 2014.

39. Roosh V [Daryush Valizadeh], "The Damaging Effects Of Jewish Intellectualism And Activism On Western Culture," *Return of Kings* (website), May 4, 2015.

40. Dota, "Manosphere Rising," *Alternative Right* (alternative-right.blogspot.com), May 14, 2015.

41. Matt Parrott, "An Endorsement of Roosh's 'Neomasculinity' Manifesto," *Traditionalist Worker Party*, May 27, 2015, updated January 19, 2016.

42. David Futrelle, "Hitler-loving dudes named Andrew agree: Roosh V is a-OK! (Even though he's not white.)" *We Hunted the Mammoth* (blog), August 15, 2015.

43. David Futrelle, "Roosh V shocked to discover that white supremacist movement is full of white supremacists," *We Hunted the Mammoth* (blog), February 24, 2016.

44. Greg Johnson, "Roosh Really is a Rape Advocate (& a Rapist, if He's Telling the Truth)," *Counter-Currents Publishing* (website), February 10, 2016.

45. Roosh V [Daryush Valizadeh], "The Alt Right Is Worse Than Feminism in Attempting to Control Male Sexual Behavior," *Return of Kings* (website), February 22, 2016; quoted in Futrelle, "Roosh V shocked to discover."

46. Jack Donovan, *The Way of Men* (Milwaukie, OR: Dissonant Hum, 2012), 138–139.

47. Jack Donovan, "A Time for Wolves," *Jack Donovan* (website), June 14, 2014.

48. "The Wolves of Vinland: a Fascist Countercultural 'Tribe' in the Pacific Northwest," *Rose City Antifa* (website), November 7, 2016.

49. Jack Donovan, *A Sky Without Eagles: Selected Essays and Speeches 2010–2014* (Milwaukie, OR: Dissonant Hum, 2014), 166.

50. Jack Donovan, "Why I Am Not A White Nationalist," *Jack Donovan* (website), May 31, 2017, update added August 19, 2017.

51. Jack Donovan, "Anarcho-Fascism," *Jack Donovan* (website), March 3, 2013.

52. Jack Donovan, *A Sky Without Eagles*, 14

53. F.T. Marinetti, "The Futurist Manifesto" (1909), in James Joll, *Three Intellectuals in Politics* (New York: Pantheon Books, 1960), 182.

54. Donovan, "Anarcho-Fascism."

55. Antifascist Front, "Queer Fascism: Why White Nationalists Are Trying to Drop Homophobia," *Anti-Fascist News* (website), November 6, 2015.

56. Spencer Sunshine, "Rebranding Fascism: National-Anarchists," *The Public Eye Magazine* 23, no. 4 (2008) [Political Research Associates]; Graham D. Macklin, "Co-opting the Counter Culture: Troy Southgate and the National Revolutionary Faction," *Patterns of Prejudice* 39, no. 3 (2005).

57. Greg Johnson, "Bay Area National Anarchists: An Interview with Andrew Yeoman, Part 1," *The Occidental Quarterly* (website), August 21, 2009; "THIRD WAY: Introducing the National-Anarchist Movement," *National-Anarchist Movement* (website), October 3, 2010.

58. Troy Southgate, "N-AM Manifesto," *National-Anarchist Movement* (website), 2010).

59. "National-Anarchist Movement (n-am) faq," *National-Anarchist Movement* (website), November 21, 2012.

60. Matthew N. Lyons, "Rising Above the Herd: Keith Preston's Authoritarian Anti-Statism," *New Politics* (website), April 29, 2011.

61. American Revolutionary Vanguard, "Statement of Purpose," *Attack the System* (website), 2016.

62. Keith Preston, "The National-Anarchist Litmus Test," *Attack the System* (website), April 24, 2009; Keith Preston, "The Thoughts That Guide Me," *Attack the System* (website), 2005; Lyons, "Rising Above the Herd."

63. Keith Preston, "Mass Immigration and Totalitarian Humanism," speech at 2011 National Policy Institute Conference, Washington, DC, *YouTube*, June 23, 2013; Preston, "Thoughts That Guide Me."

64. Keith Preston, Introduction to "The Alt-Right: History, Ideology, and the Future of a Fascist Movement," *Attack the System*, November 15, 2017.

65. Keith Preston, "What, Exactly, is the 'Alternative Right?'" [introductory comments], *Attack the System* (website), December 23, 2015.

66. Francisco Albanese, "Rethinking White Tribalism: Anarchy in the Southern Cone," *Counter-Currents Publishing* (website), June 5, 2014.

67. Keith Preston, "Anarchist Economics Compared and Contrasted: Anarcho-Capitalism vs Anarcho-Syndicalism/Communism," *Attack the System* (website), March 21, 2015; McVicar, "Libertarian Theocrats."

68. Keith Preston, "Anarcho-Pluralism and Pan-Secessionism: What They Are and What They Are Not," *Attack the System* (website), August 8, 2010.

69. Keith Preston, "Third North American Secessionists Convention—A Review," *Attack the System* (website), November 19, 2008.

70. Park MacDougald, "The Darkness Before the Right," *The Awl* (website), September 28, 2015.

71. Peter Thiel, "The Education of a Libertarian," *Cato Unbound* (website), April 13, 2009.

72. Klint Finley, "Geeks for Monarchy: The Rise of the Neoreactionaries," *TechCrunch* (website), November 22, 2013.

73. Scharlach, "Neoreaction = Monarchy?" *Habitable Worlds* (blog), November 23, 2013.

74. Nick Land, "The Dark Enlightenment: Part 1," *The Dark Enlightenment* (website), 2013.

75. Finley, "Geeks for Monarchy."

76. Hubert Collins and Hadley Bishop, "Two Prominent Identitarians Give Us Their Thoughts On Neoreaction" [interview with Michael McGregor and Gregory Hood], *Social Matter* (website), October 15, 2014.

77. Dylan Matthews, "The alt-right is more than warmed-over white supremacy. It's that, but way way weirder," *Vox* (website), April 18, 2016.

78. Mencius Moldbug [Curtis Yarvin], "Why I am not an anti-Semite," *Unqualified Reservations* (website), June 23, 2007.

79. Collins and Bishop, "Two Prominent Identitarians."

80. Keith Preston, "The Growth of the Alternative Right," *Attack the System* (website), January 4, 2016.

81. "Point of Contention: A Fractured White Supremacist Take on Immigration," *Anti-Defamation League* (website), May 5, 2015.

82. Lawrence Murray, "White Nationalism FAQ," *The Right Stuff* (website), April 14, 2016.

83. Jack Donovan, "Becoming the New Barbarians," *Radix Journal*, December 23, 2013.

84. Jack Donovan, "The Bright Side of Illegal Immigration," *Jack Donovan* (website), November 13, 2012.

85. Richard Spencer, "The Majority Strategy: The Essential Argument—Why the GOP Must Win White America," *V Dare* (website), September 8, 2011.

86. Richard Spencer, "Facing the Future as a Minority," *The National Policy Institute* (website), April 30, 2013.

87. Ted Sallis, "Democratic Multiculturalism: Strategy & Tactics," *Counter-Currents Publishing*, November 19, 2014.

88. Matthew Heimbach, "The Trump Train and the Southern Strategy: The Only Hope for the GOP," *Traditionalist Worker Party* (website), October 19, 2015.

89. Professor Evola-Hitler, "Trump's Our Guy for the 2016 Election. We Have No Choice," *The Right Stuff* (website), April 29, 2016.

90. Auschwitz Soccer Ref, "Trump's Not Our Guy. It's Time to Stop Pretending Otherwise," *The Right Stuff* (website), April 25, 2016.

91. Jack Donovan, "No One Will Ever Make America Great Again," *Jack Donovan* (website), July 7, 2016.

92. Keith Preston, "The Alternative Right—An Autopsy," *Attack the System* (website), May 21, 2016.

93. Joseph Bernstein, "Behind The Racist Hashtag That Is Blowing Up Twitter," *BuzzFeed*, July 27, 2015.

94. Ibid.

95. Antifascist Front, "#Cuckservative."

96. Robert Evans, "5 Things You Learn Being Attacked By The Alt-Right," *Cracked* (website), September 20, 2016.

97. David French, "The Price I've Paid for Opposing Donald Trump," *National Review*, October 21, 2016.

98. Don Caldwell, "#DraftOurDaughters," *Know Your Meme* (website), 2016.

99. Eric Striker, "#DraftOurDaughters: Feminist Hillary Supporters Vow To Fight War With Russia For Us," *The Daily Stormer*, October 28, 2016; Vox Day [Theodore Beale], "Draft our Daughters," *Vox Popoli* (blog), October 28, 2016.

100. Abby Ohlheiser, "What was fake on the Internet this election: #DraftOurDaughters, Trump's tax returns," *The Washington Post*, October 31, 2016.

101. Ian Tuttle, "The Racist Moral Rot at the Heart of the Alt-Right," *National Review*, April 5, 2016.

102. Stephen Piggott, "Is Breitbart.com Becoming the Media Arm of the 'Alt-Right'?" *Hatewatch*, April 28, 2016 [Southern Poverty Law Center].

103. Allum Bokhari and Milo Yiannopoulos, "An Establishment Conservative's Guide to the Alt-Right," *Breitbart*, March 29, 2016.

104. Antifascist Front, "Going Full Fash: Breitbart Mainstreams the 'Alt Right,'" *Anti-Fascist News* (website), April 5, 2016.

105. Antifascist Front, "Meet the Alt Lite, the People Mainstreaming the Alt Right's White Nationalism," *Anti-Fascist News* (website), November 3, 2016.

106. Sarah Posner, "How Donald Trump's New Campaign Chief Created an Online Haven for White Nationalists," *Mother Jones*, August 22, 2016; Michelle Goldberg, "*Breitbart* Calls Trump Foe 'Renegade Jew.' This Is How Anti-Semitism Goes Mainstream," *Slate*, May 16, 2016.

107. Richard B. Spencer, "Make Trump Trump Again," *Radix Journal*, August 17, 2016.

108. Hunter Wallace [Brad Griffin], "Alt-Right vs. Alt-Lite," *Occidental Dissent*, November 23, 2016. On Yiannopoulos's downfall, see Hunter Wallace [Brad Griffin], "MILO Press Conference," *AltRight.com* (website), February 21, 2017, and especially the comments section.

NOTES TO CHAPTER 5. THE LAROUCHE NETWORK

1. Dennis King, *Lyndon LaRouche and the New American Fascism* (New York: Doubleday, 1989); Helen Gilbert, *Lyndon LaRouche: Fascism Restyled for the New Millennium*, Red Banner Reader No. 8 (Seattle: Red Letter Press, 2003).

2. King, *Lyndon LaRouche*, chapters 2–4.

3. Ibid., chapters 11–14 and pages 139–144.

4. Ibid., chapters 18–20, 22–24, 31–38.

5. Ibid., 314–322, 377.

6. Joseph Brewda, "Anglo-American war has made Iraq into a vast death camp," *Executive Intelligence Review* 18, no. 17 (May 3, 1991); Umberto Pascali, "Kosovo Liberation Army: a pawn in the British game," *Executive Intelligence Review* 26, no. 40 (October 8, 1999); Spencer Sunshine, "The Right Hand of Occupy Wall Street: From Libertarians to Nazis, the Fact and Fiction of Right-Wing Involvement," *The Public Eye*, Winter 2014: 9–14.

7. Matthew N. Lyons, "The LaRouche Network's Russia Connection," *Three Way Fight* (blog), July 3, 2015; Anton Shekhovtsov, "Sergey Glazyev and the American fascist cult," *Anton Shekhovtsov's blog*, June 7, 2015.

8. Hartmut Cramer, "FDR's 'New Deal': An Example of American System Economics," *Executive Intelligence Review* 27, no. 24 (June 16, 2000); Lyndon LaRouche, "The Wicked Witches of Obama," *LaRouche Political Action Committee* (website), March 8, 2014.

9. Lyndon LaRouche, *LaRouche's Emergency Reconstruction Policy: Recreate Our Economy!* (pamphlet) (Leesburg, VA: Lyndon LaRouche PAC, 2005), 5–7; L. Wolfe and Nancy Spannaus, "LaRouche's Solution: Maintain a Strong Social Security With A Strong Physical Economy," in *Stop George Schultz's Drive Toward Fascism!* (Leesburg, VA: Lyndon LaRouche PAC, 2005), 30–32.

10. "U.S. Labor Party Convention: Rule The World With Reason," *Executive Intelligence Review* 5, no. 26 (July 11, 1978); Hector A. Rivas, Jr., "George Soros: Hit-man for The British Oligarchy," in *Your Enemy, George Soros* (pamphlet) (Leesburg, VA: LaRouche Political Action Committee, 2008), 2–6; Richard Freeman, "Cato Institute: Wall Street's Predators in Charge of Taking Social Security," in *Stop George Schultz's Drive Toward Fascism!* (Leesburg, VA: Lyndon LaRouche PAC, 2005), 33–37; LaRouche, *LaRouche's Emergency Reconstruction Policy*; Joseph Brewda, "Israel's apartheid system shows Zionism is racism," *Executive Intelligence Review* 18, no. 32 (August 23, 1991); Anton Chaitkin, "The Christian Coalition: The Nature of the Beast," *Executive Intelligence Review* 32, no. 16 (April 22, 2005): 68–79; William Jones, "The Ugly History of The Cheney Warmongers," *Executive Intelligence Review* 31, no. 14 (April 9, 2004): 64–68; Editors of *Executive Intelligence Review*, *Dope, Inc.: Boston Bankers and Soviet Commissars* (New York: New Benjamin Franklin House, 1986); Lyndon H. LaRouche, Jr., *The Case of Walter Lippmann: A*

Presidential Strategy (New York: Campaigner Publications, 1977); Kathleen Klenetsky, "The child molesters in the classroom," *Executive Intelligence Review* 20, no. 28 (July 23, 1993); Michelle Lerner, "How the Counterculture Ushered in Fascism," *Executive Intelligence Review* 31, no. 14 (April 9, 2004): 18–27.

11. King, *Lyndon LaRouche*, 38–46; Gilbert, *Lyndon LaRouche*, 23–26.

12. Michael Lewis, "The Speculator," *New Republic*, January 10, 1994; Adam Holland, "LaRouche promoting anti-Obama Soros conspiracy theory," *Adam Holland* (blog), May 31, 2008.

13. King, *Lyndon LaRouche*, 136–137, 370; Dennis King, "Birds of a feather? President Trump and Lyndon LaRouche," *Socialist Currents* (website), November 4, 2016.

14. Chip Berlet and Matthew N. Lyons, *Right-Wing Populism in America: Too Close for Comfort* (New York: Guilford Press, 2000), 105–107, 146; LaRouche, *Case of Walter Lippmann*, 67, 142, 144; Lyndon H. LaRouche, Jr., *Creating a Republican Labor Party* (pamphlet) (New York: Citizens for LaRouche, 1979), 1.

15. Quoted in King, *Lyndon LaRouche*, 290.

16. Quote is from King, *Lyndon LaRouche*, 290; see also *Ibid.*, 34–36, 197–207, 289–290; Gilbert, *Lyndon LaRouche*, 26–30; LaRouche, *Case of Walter Lippmann*, 30; Thomas Murphy, with Steve Vetzner, "The Posse Comitatus in Wisconsin," *Public Eye* 3, nos. 1 and 2 (1981).

17. "LaRouche-Bevel campaign brings a message of hope: An interview with Rev. James Bevel," *Executive Intelligence Review* 19, no. 39 (October 2, 1992); Amelia Boynton Robinson, "Amelia Boynton Robinson to Detroit LPAC: Wake Up America! Go With LaRouche!" *New Federalist*, April 4, 2005: 4; Louis Farrakhan, "Farrakhan sends message to Schiller Institute conference," *Executive Intelligence Review* 22, no. 10 (March 3, 1995); Dennis Speed, "The African-American Spiritual and the Resurrection of Classical Art," *New Federalist*, October 9, 1995.

18. King, "Birds of a feather?"

19. Gilbert, *Lyndon LaRouche*, 18–23; Lyn Marcus [Lyndon H. LaRouche, Jr.], "The Sexual Impotence of the Puerto Rican Socialist Party," *The Campaigner* 7, no. 1 (November 1973); LaRouche, *Case of Walter Lippmann*, 48, 110.

20. LaRouche, "Wicked Witches of Obama"; Lyndon H. LaRouche, Jr., "Rumsfeld as 'Strangelove II," in *Children of Satan: The 'Ignoble Liars' Behind Bush's No-Exit War* (pamphlet) (Leesburg, VA: LaRouche in 2004, 2004), 8.

21. Lyndon H. LaRouche, Jr., *A Draft Constitution For The Commonwealth of Canada* (Montreal: Committee for the Republic of Canada, 1981; republished 1984), 21–22; Lyndon LaRouche, *Creating a Republican Labor Party*, 9.

22. LaRouche, *Draft Constitution*, 3, 21, 22, 24; LaRouche, *Case of Walter Lippmann*, 127, 129.

23. Lyndon H. LaRouche, Jr., "Lyndon LaRouche on the Alex Jones Show, March 22, 2012" (video), *LaRouche Political Action Committee* (website), 2012; Lyndon H. LaRouche, Jr., "Lyndon LaRouche on Alex Jones Show" (video), *LaRouche Political Action Committee* (website), October 17, 2013; Chip Berlet, *Right Woos Left: Populist Party, LaRouchite, and Other Neo-fascist Overtures To Progressives, And Why They Must Be Rejected* (Cambridge, MA: Political Research Associates, 1994; revised 1999); Chip Berlet, "Webster G. Tarpley's Toxic Waste is Polluting the Antiwar Movement," *Chip Berlet* (blog), September 17, 2007; Chip Berlet, "Crackpots, the Left, and Jewish Banker Cabals," *Research for Progress* (website), April 28, 2016.

NOTES TO CHAPTER 6.
GENDER AND SEXUAL IDENTITY

1. Bromma, "Exodus and Reconstruction: Working-Class Women at the Heart of Globalization," *Kersplebedeb* (website), September 11, 2012.

2. Jack Donovan, *No Man's Land: Masculinity Maligned, Reimagined, Jack Donovan* (website), 2011; Jack Donovan, *The Way of Men* (Milwaukie, OR: Dissonant Hum, 2012), 138.

3. Mab Segrest and Leonard Zeskind, *Quarantines and Death: The Far Right's Homophobic Agenda* (pamphlet) (Atlanta: Center for Democratic Renewal, 1989), 11.

4. Dennis King, *Lyndon LaRouche and the New American Fascism* (New York: Doubleday, 1989), 25–28, 140–144.

5. Betty A. DeBerg, *Ungodly Women: Gender and the First Wave of American Fundamentalism* (Minneapolis: Fortress Press, 1990); Kathleen M. Blee, *Women of the Klan: Racism and Gender in the 1920s* (Berkeley: University of California Press, 1991).

6. Richard Drinnon, *Facing West: The Metaphysics of Indian-Hating and Empire-Building* (New York: Schocken Books, 1990), 232.

7. Theodore Roosevelt, *An Autobiography* (New York: Macmillan, 1913), chapter 5 [available on *Bartleby.com*]; Linda Gordon, *Woman's Body, Woman's Right: Birth Control in America* (New York: Penguin Books, 1976), 136.

8. Arnaldo Testi, "The Gender of Reform Politics: Theodore Roosevelt and the Culture of Masculinity," *The Journal of American History* 81, no. 4 (March 1995): 1522.

9. Lutz Kaelber, "Eugenics: Compulsory Sterilization in 50 American States," honors course research project, University of Vermont (website), 2009, updated 2011 and 2012.

10. Kathryn Krase, "History of Forced Sterilization and Current U.S. Abuses," *Our Bodies Ourselves* (website), October 1, 2014; Jane Lawrence, "The Indian Health Service and the Sterilization of Native American Women," *American Indian Quarterly* 24, no. 3 (Summer 2000).

11. Chip Berlet and Matthew N. Lyons, *Right-Wing Populism in America: Too Close for Comfort* (New York: Guilford Press, 2000), 94, 365n32.

12. Glen Jeansonne, *Women of the Far Right: the Mothers' Movement and World War II* (Chicago: University of Chicago Press, 1996), 71, 114.

13. Jeansonne, *Women of the Far Right*, 64.

14. Ibid., 90–91.

15. John D'Emilio, *Sexual Politics, Sexual Communities: The Making of a Homosexual Minority in the United States, 1940–1970* (Chicago: University of Chicago Press, 1983), 49.

16. Andrea Dworkin, *Right-Wing Women* (New York: Coward-McCann, 1983), 21.

17. Sara Diamond, *Spiritual Warfare: The Politics of the Christian Right* (Boston: South End Press, 1989), 104–106.

18. Susan Faludi, *Backlash: The Undeclared War Against American Women* (New York: Anchor Books, Doubleday, 1991), 250–252.

19. Tim LaHaye and Beverly LaHaye, *The Act of Marriage: The Beauty of Sexual Love* (Grand Rapids, MI: Zondervan Publishing House, 1976).

20. "About Us," *Concerned Women for America* (website), nd; Penny Young Nance, "There is no war on women," *Politico*, October 4, 2013.

21. Crystal Goodremote, "Award Winning Display of Ignorance," *Concerned Women for America* (website), February 23, 2015.

22. CWALAC Staff, "Make Love Not War (on Women)," *Concerned Women for America* (website), October 7, 2013.

23. CWALAC Staff, "Why Homosexual 'Marriage' is Wrong," *Concerned Women for America* (website), September 16, 2003.

24. CWALAC Staff, "Christ Restoring a Male/Female Identity in a Sexually Confused World," *Concerned Women for America* (website), May 13, 2016.

25. Joel McDurmon, "12 Reasons homosexual marriage will wreck the nation," *American Vision* (website), May 8, 2015.

26. Brian Tashman, "GOP Confab Ends With Call to Execute Gays Who Don't Repent, Send Queen Elsa Back to Hell," *Right Wing Watch*, November 10, 2015.

27. Michael J. McVicar, *Christian Reconstruction: R.J. Rushdoony and American Religious Conservatism* (Chapel Hill: University of North Carolina Press, 2015), 130–131; Julie J. Ingersoll, *Building God's Kingdom: Inside the World of Christian Reconstruction* (New York: Oxford University Press, 2015), 215–216; Tashman, "GOP Confab Ends With Call"; Warren Throckmorton, "What Would Dominionists Do With Gays?" *Patheos*, August 29, 2011.

28. Quoted in Throckmorton, "What Would Dominionists Do With Gays?"

29. Ibid.

30. "Profile on the Right: Lou Engle," *Political Research Associates* (website), nd.

31. Quoted in Ingersoll, *Building God's Kingdom*, 165.

32. Joyce, *Quiverfull*, ix.

33. Ibid., 27, 101.

34. Joyce, *Quiverfull*, 3–10; Ingersoll, *Building God's Kingdom*, 114, 140–166; Julie Anne Smith, "Christian Patriarchy is Alive and Well: NCFIC Director Scott Brown Moves into Position to Fill the Void Left by Doug Phillips/Vision Forum," *Spiritual Sounding Board* (website), January 31, 2014.

35. Joyce, *Quiverfull*, x, 13–16.

36. Ibid., 206.

37. Ibid., 17, 50, 93–94, 98–99, 102.

38. Ibid., 81, 96–97, 135, 208.

39. Ingersoll, *Building God's Kingdom*, 161–162.

40. Joyce, *Quiverfull*, 184, 189–192.

41. Rick Joyner, "The High Calling of Womanhood," *MorningStar Ministries* (website), 2003; Rachel Tabachnick, "Resource Directory for the New Apostolic Reformation," *Talk To Action* (website), January 20, 2010.

42. Joyner, "High Calling of Womanhood."

43. Cindy Jacobs, "Empowering Women: Breaking Strongholds That Strangle Destiny," *Generals International* (website), May 2, 2016.

44. Diane Lake, "A Great Company of Women," *Generals International* (website), May 9, 2016.

45. Lonnie Crowe, "Redeeming Eve," *Generals International* (website), May 23, 2016.

46. Tisha Sledd, "Return to Eden: Equality for Women in God's Kingdom," *Generals International* (website), May 16, 2016.

47. Tisha Sledd, "How Patriarchy Is Killing the American Church," *Tisha Sledd Ministries* (website), April 4, 2016.

48. Tisha Sledd, "My Journey Out of Bondage to Male Headship," *Tisha Sledd Ministries* (website), April 6, 2016.

49. Barbara Perry, "'White Genocide': White Supremacists and the Politics of Reproduction," in *Home-Grown Hate: Gender and Organized Racism*, ed., Abby L. Ferber (New York: Routledge, 2004), 85–86.

50. Quoted in Segrest and Zeskind, *Quarantines and Death*, 25.

51. Segrest and Zeskind, *Quarantines and Death*, 7; Leonard Zeskind, *Blood and Politics: The History of the White Nationalist Movement from the Margins to the Mainstream* (New York: Farrar Straus Giroux, 2009), 132, 460–462.

52. Quoted in Segrest and Zeskind, *Quarantines and Death*, 13.

53. "What We Stand For," *American Nazi Party* (website), 2012.

54. "25 Points of American National Socialism," *National Socialist Movement* (website), nd.

55. Martin Durham, *White Rage: The extreme right and American politics* (New York: Routledge, 2007), 88–89.

56. Quoted in Kathleen M. Blee, "Women and Organized Racism," in *Home-Grown Hate*, 66.

57. Alex Linder, "Alex Linder on Women vs. Men," *Vanguard News Network* (website), September 21, 2009.

58. Alex Linder, "The Female Vote: a Terrible Idea Since 1920," *Vanguard News Network*, February 9, 2016.

59. Molly Gill, *The Radical Feminist*, vol. 5, no. 2 (Spring 1991).

60. Molly Gill, *The Rational Feminist*, vol. 8, no. 9 (Fall 1994), 6.

61. Durham, *White Rage*, 95.

62. "Women," *White Aryan Resistance* (http://resist.com), [2000 or earlier].

63. "Mission Statement," *Women for Aryan Unity* (website), nd; "Women of History," *Women's Frontier: The Creativity Movement Sisterhood, The Creativity Movement* (website), nd.

64. Blee, "Women and Organized Racism," 49.

65. Ibid., 68, 69.

66. Ibid., 73.

67. Jason Vest, "The Spooky World of Linda Thompson," *Washington Post*, May 11, 1995; see also Elinor Burkett, *The Right Women: A Journey Through the Heart of Conservative America* (New York: Scribner, 1998), 89–92.

68. Spencer Sunshine et al., *Up in Arms: A Guide to Oregon's Patriot Movement* (Scappoose, OR: Rural Organizing Project; Somerville, MA: Political Research Associates, 2016), 34–38.

69. Amanda Peacher, "Meet the Women of the Occupied Refuge," *Oregon Public Broadcasting* (website), January 22, 2016.

70. Patriot Patricia, "The Patriot Movement Needs Real Women," *Love, Guns & Freedom* (website), July 6, 2014.

71. Burkett, *Right Women*, 113, 118.

72. Ibid., 181.

73. "The Homosexual agenda!" discussion thread on *ThreePercenter.org* website, 2011.

74. Jason Van Tatenhove, "Oath Keepers Offers Kim Davis Protection From Further Imprisonment by Judge," *Oath Keepers* (website), September 9, 2015.

75. Shorty Dawkins, "Boycott Target Petition!," *Oath Keepers* (website), April 25, 2016.

76. Miranda Blue, "'Sodomites, Go To Hell!': Right-Wing July 4th Event Warns Hurricanes Create 'Sodomite Heaven,'" *Right Wing Watch* (website), July 8, 2015.

77. Northman, "Women Should Hate Freedom," *The Right Stuff* (website), December 2, 2013; Danielle Paquette, "The alt-right isn't only about white supremacy. It's about white male supremacy," *Chicago Tribune*, November 25, 2016; Gregory Hood, "A Cat Lady Culture," *Radix Journal*, June 2, 2015.

78. Greg Johnson, "Abortion & White Nationalism," *Counter-Currents Publishing* (website), April 2016; see also Aylmer Fisher, "The Pro-Life Temptation," *Radix Journal*, April 8, 2016; Brad Griffin [Hunter Wallace], "The Pro-Choice Temptation," *Occidental Dissent* (blog), April 12, 2016; T.M. Goddard, "Unintended Consequences," *Radix Journal*, April 13, 2016.

79. Roosh V [Daryush Valizadeh],"What is Neomasculinity?" *Roosh V* (website), May 6, 2015; "Travel Books," *Roosh V Store* (website), nd.

80. Roosh V [Daryush Valizadeh], "Why Homosexual Marriage Matters For Straight Men," *Return of Kings* (website), October 12, 2015.

81. Matt Forney, "Are Transsexuals Who Sleep With Straight Men Guilty of Rape?" *Return of Kings* (website), December 8, 2014.

82. Paul Elam, "Andy Bob exposes feminist hatred of gay men in new book," *A Voice for Men* (website), January 7, 2016.

83. Jack Donovan, *A Sky Without Eagles: Selected Essays and Speeches 2010–2014* (Milwaukie, OR: Dissonant Hum, 2014), 160, 158.

84. Jef Costello, "Jack Donovan's *A Sky Without Eagles*" [review], *Counter-Currents Publishing* (website), July 2014.

85. Chip Smith, "The First Rule of Androphilia: An Interview with Jack Malebranche," *The Hoover Hog* (website), January 2009.

86. Donovan, *Way of Men*, 60–62.

87. Jack Donovan, comment on "Jack Donovan" discussion thread, *Roosh V Forum* (website), November 16, 2012.

88. Donovan, *The Way of Men*, 137, 148, 150.

89. Greg Johnson, "The Woman Question in White Nationalism." *Counter-Currents Publishing*, May 25, 2011.

90. Andrew Yeoman, "We Will Lose," *AlternativeRight.com*, June 9, 2010, reposted in *Radix Journal*.

91. Johnson, "Woman Question in White Nationalism."

92. Matt Parrott, "Where the White Women At?" *Traditionalist Worker Party* (website), April 13, 2015.

93. "White Supremacists Feud Over the Racist Gender Gap," *Anti-Defamation League* (blog), April 26, 2016; Paquette, "Alt-right isn't only about white supremacy."

94. E.W., "Women and the Alt-Right," *The Economist*, February 1, 2017; Flavia Dzodan, "Alt-Feminism and the white nationalist women who love it," *This Political Woman* (website), March 7, 2017.

95. Matt Parrott, "Jews Destroy Women: A Response to 'Women Destroy Nations," *Traditionalist Worker Party* (website), February 18, 2016.

96. Matthew Heimbach, "The Homosexual Lobby," *Traditionalist Worker Party* (website), June 19, 2013.

97. Eric Striker, "The Majority of Homosexuals Are Spreading HIV On Purpose, and It's being Covered Up," *Traditionalist Worker Party* (website), September 8, 2015.

98. Matthew Heimbach, "African Traditionalists Against the Globalist Homosexual Agenda," *Traditionalist Worker Party* (website), July 29, 2015.

99. Greg Johnson, "Homosexuality & White Nationalism," *Counter-Currents Publishing*, October 4, 2010 [originally published on *Vanguard News Network*, June 28, 2002, under the pseudonym F.C.I. Clarke].

100. Quoted in Ann Sterzinger, "Fashy Homos & Green Nazis in Space" [review of *Green Nazis in Space! New Essays on Literature, Art, and Culture* by James J. O'Meara], *Counter-Currents Publishing*, May 20, 2016.

101. Andy Nowicki, "The Homo and the Negro: An Interview with James O'Meara," *Alternative Right* (alternative-right.blogspot.com), April 6, 2014 [originally published December 10, 2012].

102. Butch Leghorn, "Wedging Gays and Muslims," *The Right Stuff* (website), June 14, 2016.

103. Lucas Nolan, "Milo in Orlando: Gays, Like Jews, Should Say 'Never Again!'" *Breitbart*, June 15, 2016.

NOTES TO CHAPTER 7. ANTI-IMPERIALISM

1. Franz Schurmann, *The Logic of World Power: An Inquiry into the Origins, Currents, and Contradictions of World Politics* (New York: Pantheon, 1974), 56–57; see also Bruce Cumings, *The Origins of the Korean War*, vol. 2, *The Roaring of the Cataract, 1947–1950* (Princeton, NJ: Princeton University Press, 1990), 80–102.

2. Patrick J. Buchanan, "Why I Am Running for President," *Human Events*, December 28, 1991, 11.

3. On the paleoconservatives, see Sara Diamond, *Roads to Dominion: Right-Wing Movements and Political Power in the United States* (New York: Guilford Press, 1995), 275, 281–288.

4. David D. Roberts, *The Syndicalist Tradition and Italian Fascism* (Chapel Hill: University of North Carolina Press, 1979), 118.

5. Roberts, *The Syndicalist Tradition and Italian Fascism*, 120–121.

6. See Kevin Coogan, *Dreamer of the Day: Francis Parker Yockey and the Postwar Fascist International* (Brooklyn, Autonomedia, 1999), 191, 276, 285.

7. Ibid., 385; Leila Nathoo, "Subhas Chandra Bose: Secret files on India's lost freedom fighter made public," *Independent*, February 7, 2016.

8. Coogan, *Dreamer of the Day*, 382–383; see also Martin A. Lee, *The Beast Reawakens* (Boston: Little, Brown and Company, 1997), especially chapter 4.

9. On Yockey, see Coogan, *Dreamer of the Day;* Loren Goldner, "An American National Bolshevik: Review of Kevin Coogan, *Dreamer of the Day,*" *Race Traitor*, no. 15 (2001) [available on *Break Their Haughty Power* (website)].

10. Quoted in Coogan, *Dreamer of the Day*, 460.

11. Moyote Project [Franco Berteni, Denis Giordano and Caterina Sartori], "Casa Pound and the new radical right in Italy," *libcom.org* (website), June 8, 2011.

12. Moyote Project, "Casa Pound."

13. Graham D. Macklin, "Co-opting the Counter Culture: Troy Southgate and the National Revolutionary Faction," *Patterns of Prejudice* 39, no. 3 (2005).

14. Robert de Herte, quoted in Alberto Spektorowski, "The French New Right: Differentialism and the Idea of Ethnophilian Exclusionism," *Polity* 33, no. 2 (Winter 2000): 297.

15. Alain de Benoist and Charles Champetier, "The French New Right in the Year 2000," *Telos*, no. 115 (Spring 1999): 117–144.

16. Some of the points in this section appeared in Matthew Lyons and Efe Can Gürcan, "Exchange on Eurasianism," *Socialism and Democracy* 28, no. 1 (March 2014): 165–168. On Dugin, see also Andreas Umland, "'Neo-Eurasianism,' the Issue of Russian Fascism, and Post-Soviet Political Discourse," *OpEdNews*, June 11, 2008; Anton Shekhovtsov, "Aleksandr Dugin's Neo-Eurasianism: The New Right à la Russe," *Religion Compass* 3/4 (2009): 697–716; Marlène Laruelle, "Aleksandr Dugin: A Russian Version of the European Radical Right?" Kennan Institute Occasional Paper #294 (Washington, DC: Woodrow Wilson International Center for Scholars, 2006).

17. Aleksandr Dugin, "Fascism—borderless and red," [1997], trans. Andreas Umland, *Russian-Studies listserv archives*, 2009.

18. Aleksandr Dugin, *Misterii Evrazii* [*The Mysteries of Eurasia*], quoted in Laruelle, "Aleksandr Dugin," 14; Aleksandr Dugin, "To Understand is To Defeat," *Den* (newspaper), 1992; republished on *Arctogaia* (website).

19. Laruelle, "Aleksandr Dugin," 13.

20. "'United by Hatred': Manuel Ochsenreiter interviews Alexander Dugin on the Ukraine Crisis," *Counter-Currents Publishing* (website), January 30, 2014.

21. "Alexander Dugin on 'White Nationalism' and other Potential Allies in the Global Revolution," *Open Revolt* (website), May 19, 2013.

22. "'United by Hatred.'"

23. Sara Diamond, *Roads to Dominion: Right-Wing Movements and Political Power in the United States* (New York: Guilford Press, 1995), 228–229; Matthew N. Lyons, "Business Conflict and Right-Wing Movements," in *Unraveling the Right: The New Conservatism in American Thought and Politics*, ed., Amy E. Ansell (Boulder, CO: Westview Press, 1998), 96–97.

24. Gary North, "The American Empire vs. Your Retirement Prospects," *Gary North's Specific Answers* (website), May 5, 2014.

25. John Crawford, "Russia, the Ukraine and the Extension of Peace in History," *American Vision* (website), April 8, 2014.

26. Tom Rose, "Contra Imperium: The Christian Case Against American Imperialism and the Security/Police State," *Chalcedon Foundation* (website), November 1, 2006.

27. Rob Slane, "Another day, another phoney war," *American Vision* (website), August 29, 2013.

28. Alexander Zaitchik, "Patriot Paranoia: A Look at the Top Ten Conspiracy Theories," *Intelligence Report*, August 1, 2010 (Fall 2010 issue) [Southern Poverty Law Center].

29. Lyndon H. LaRouche, Jr., *The Power of Reason: 1988* (Washington: DC: Executive Intelligence Review, 1987), 191; see also Lyndon H. LaRouche, Jr., "Globalization, The New Imperialism," *Executive Intelligence Review*, October 28, 2005.

30. See Chip Berlet, *Right Woos Left: Populist Party, LaRouchite, and Other Neo-fascist Overtures To Progressives, and Why They Must Be Rejected* (Cambridge, MA: Political Research Associates, 1994; revised 1999).

31. Matthew N. Lyons, "The LaRouche Network's Russia Connection," *Three Way Fight* (blog), July 3, 2015.

32. Natalia Vitrenko, "United States and EU, with Ukrainian Terrorists, Establish Nazi Regime," *Executive Intelligence Review*, February 28, 2014; "Nuland-Nazi Regime Takes Power in Ukraine," *LaRouchePAC* (website), March 1, 2014; Nancy Spannaus, "Anglo-Saudis Go In for the Kill Against Syria," *Executive Intelligence Review*, March 29, 2013; Ulf Sandmark, "Eyewitness Report: Will the West Take the Damascus Road?" *Executive Intelligence Review*, November 28, 2014.

33. Nick Mamatas, "Fascists for Che: White supremacists infiltrate the anti-globalization movement," *In These Times*, September 13, 2002.

34. Tom Metzger, quoted in George Michael, *Confronting Right Wing Extremism and Terrorism in the USA* (New York: Routledge, 2003), 67.

35. PolishPatriot82, "Third Positionism—Selling it to Leftists, Liberals and Moderates," *Stormfront* (website), February 2011.

36. James Porrazzo, "Is Rodrigo Duterte a Monster?" *Open Revolt!* (website), February 20, 2017.

37. "Joshua Blakeney Interviews Greg Johnson," Part 1, *Counter-Currents Publishing*, November 28, 2014.

38. "Joshua Blakeney Interviews Greg Johnson," Part 4, *Counter-Currents Publishing*, December 3, 2014.

39. "Joshua Blakeney Interviews Greg Johnson," Part 2, *Counter-Currents Publishing*, December 1, 2014.

40. "Joshua Blakeney Interviews Greg Johnson," Part 3, *Counter-Currents Publishing*, December 2, 2014.

41. Eugene Montsalvat, "The Necessity of Anti-Colonialism," *Counter-Currents Publishing*, February 2015.

42. Matt Parrott, "Against Eurasianist Anti-Nationalism," *Traditionalist Worker Party* (website), November 30, 2016.

43. Casey Michel, "Beyond Trump and Putin: The American Alt-Right's Love of the Kremlin's Policies," *The Diplomat*, October 13, 2016; Neil MacFarquhar, "Right-Wing Groups Find a Haven, for a Day, in Russia," *New York Times*, March 22, 2015; Alina Polyakova, "The Kremlin's support for right-wing parties is no game. It's trying to subvert the European idea," *Foreign Policy*, February 23, 2016.

44. Greg Johnson, "Dugin on Heidegger," *Counter-Currents Publishing*, November 2014; Greg Johnson, "The Ukraine Crisis," *Counter-Currents Publishing*, March 2014; Colin Liddell, "The Failure of Putin," *Alternative Right* (alternative-right.blogspot.com), December 18, 2014; Duns Scotus, "The Boundless Insanity of Neo-Russian Imperialism," *Alternative Right* (alternative-right.blogspot.com), March 22, 2015.

45. See Matthew N. Lyons, "Far rightists divided over Hugo Chávez," *Three Way Fight* (blog), March 24, 2013.

46. Gregory Hood, "Two Cheers for Chávez," *Counter-Currents Publishing*, March 2013; Kerry Bolton, "Viva Chávez!," *Counter-Currents Publishing*, March 2013.

47. Colin Liddell, "The Grand Invisible Alliance," *Alternative Right* (alternative-right.blogspot.com), March 6, 2013.

48. Matt Parrott, "Syrian Conflict: Identity and Sovereignty Are Winning," *Traditionalist Worker Party* (website), September 28, 2015; see also Matthew N. Lyons, "U.S. fascists debate the conflict in Ukraine," *Three Way Fight* (blog), March 12, 2014.

49. Gregory Hood, "Standing With Syria," *Counter-Currents Publishing*, September 2013.

50. See Workers World Party, "Stop U.S. war against Syria!" *Workers World* (website), April 6, 2017; Caleb T. Maupin, "Syria, Linda Sarsour & The New Left & New Right," *Mint Press News* (website), May 2, 2017. For an example of a leftist analysis that is critical of both the Syrian government and the opposition, see for example Enrab Feroz, "Syria, The Left, and The World," interview by Yassin al-Haj Saleh, *Yassin al-Haj Saleh* (website), April 6, 2017.

NOTES TO CHAPTER 8. DECENTRALISM

1. People Against Racist Terror, "PART's Perspective on the Militias," *Turning the Tide*, 8, no. 2 (Summer 1995).

2. Matthew N. Lyons, "Rising Above the Herd: Keith Preston's Authoritarian Anti-Statism," *New Politics* (website), April 29, 2011.

3. Gabriel Kolko, *Main Currents in Modern American History* (New York: Harper & Row, 1976), 2.

4. Ibid., 4.

5. Mike Davis, *Prisoners of the American Dream: Politics and Economy in the History of the US Working* Class (London: Verso, 1986), 163.

6. Robert Justin Goldstein, *Political Repression in Modern America: From 1870 to the Present* (Boston: G.K. Hall & Co., 1978), 12.

7. Ibid., 10–11.

8. Alexander Saxton, *The Indispensable Enemy: Labor and the Anti-Chinese Movement in California* (Berkeley: University of California Press, 1971), 81; Wyn Craig Wade, *The Fiery Cross: The Ku Klux Klan in America* (New York: Simon & Schuster, 1987), 107.

9. Michael J. McVicar, "The Libertarian Theocrats: The Long, Strange History of R.J. Rushdoony and Christian Reconstructionism," *The Public Eye*, vol. 22, no. 3 (Fall 2007) [Political Research Associates]; Brian Doherty, *Radicals for Capitalism: A Freewheeling History of the Modern American Libertarian Movement* (New York: Public Affairs, 2007), 93, 271–275.

10. Sara Diamond, *Roads to Dominion: Right-Wing Movements and Political Power in the United States* (New York: Guilford Press, 1995), 123–127; Doherty, *Radicals for Capitalism*, 335–346.

11. Brian Doherty, "The Roots of Modern Libertarian Ideas," *Cato Institute* (website), March–April 2007.

12. Murray N. Rothbard, *Egalitarianism as a Revolt Against Nature and Other Essays*, second edition (Auburn, AL: The Ludwig von Mises Institute, 2000), 160.

13. Peter Vallentyne, "Left-Libertarianism as a Promising Form of Liberal Egalitarianism," *Philosophic Exchange* 39, no. 1 (2009), article 1.

14. Rothbard, *Egalitarianism*, 20, 8; Llewellyn H. Rockwell, Jr., "The Menace of Egalitarianism," *Mises Institute* (website), October 8, 2015.

15. Antifascistfront, "Capitalists Against Cops: Cop Block, Christopher Cantwell, and the Libertarian Paradox," *Anti-Fascist News*, December 15, 2015.

16. Gregory Hood, "Review: 'Right Wing Critics Of Conservatism' by George Hawley," *Radix Journal*, May 4, 2016.

17. Greg Johnson, "The Refutation of Libertarianism," *Counter-Currents Publishing*, October 2015.

18. Justin Raimondo, "Nationalists Without a Nation," *Taki's Magazine*, May 28, 2009.

19. Vox Day [Theodore Beale], "Greg Johnson Interviews Vox Day," *Counter-Currents Publishing*, November 2015.

20. Klint Finley, "Geeks for Monarchy: The Rise of the Neoreactionaries," *TechCrunch* (website), November 22, 2013.

21. McVicar, "Libertarian Theocrats"; Michael J. McVicar, *Christian Reconstruction: R.J. Rushdoony and American Religious Conservatism* (Chapel Hill: University of North Carolina Press, 2015), 227–228.

22. McVicar, *Christian Reconstruction*, 132–134, 126, 182.

23. Ibid., 130–131.

24. Ibid., 125.

25. Dan Levitas, "Tracing the Opposition to Taxes in America," *Intelligence Report*, November 29, 2001 [Southern Poverty Law Center].

26. Scott W. Reed, "The County Supremacy Movement: The Mendacious Myth Marketing," *Idaho Law Review*, vol. 30 (1994): 525–554.

27. See Mark Pitcavage, "Common Law and the Uncommon Courts: An Overview of the Common Law Court Movement," *Militia Watchdog* (website), July 25, 1997 [Anti-Defamation League].

28. Ibid.

29. Leonard Zeskind, *Blood and Politics: The History of the White Nationalist Movement from the Margins to the Mainstream* (New York: Farrar Straus Giroux, 2009), 103–104.

30. Louis Beam, "Leaderless Resistance," *Inter-Klan Newsletter*, 1983; republished in *The Seditionist*, no. 12 (February 1992).

31. William S. Lind et al., "The Changing Face of War: Into the Fourth Generation," *Marine Corps Gazette*, October 1989.

32. James Scaminaci III [interviewed by Chauncey Devega], "How '4th Generation Warfare' helps to explain the rise of Donald Trump," *Salon*, July 5, 2017.

33. Lucian Tudor, "Organic Democracy," *New European Conservative* (website), October 17, 2014 [excerpt from "The Philosophy of Identity"].

34. Alain de Benoist, "Ten Theses on Democracy," *New European Conservative*, June 28, 2013 (London: Arktos Media, 2011), 100–103 [excerpt from *The Problem of Democracy*].

35. Tudor, "Organic Democracy."

36. De Benoist, "Ten Theses on Democracy."

37. Alain de Benoist and Charles Champetier, "The French New Right in the Year 2000," *Telos*, no. 115 (Spring 1999): 117–144.

38. George Whale, "Review of Faye's 'Archeofuturism,'" *New European Conservative*, May 6, 2012; Michael Walker, "*Archeofuturism* by Guillaume Faye," *Amerika* (website), December 30, 2010.

39. Quoted in Walker, "*Archeofuturism* by Guillaume Faye."

40. Troy Southgate, "N-AM Manifesto," *National-Anarchist Movement* (website), 2010.

41. Lyons, "Rising Above the Herd."

NOTES TO CHAPTER 9. FEDERAL SECURITY FORCES AND THE PARAMILITARY RIGHT

1. See Frank J. Donner, *The Age of Surveillance: The Aims and Methods of America's Political Intelligence System* (New York: Alfred A. Knopf, 1980).

2. Michael Cohen, "'The Ku Klux Government': Vigilantism, Lynching, and the Repression of the IWW," *Journal for the Study of Radicalism* 1, no. 1 (2006): 32.

3. Chip Berlet and Matthew N. Lyons, *Right-Wing Populism in America: Too Close for Comfort* (New York: Guilford Press, 2000), 153–154.

4. Don Hamerquist, "Thinking and Acting in Real Time and a Real World," *Three Way Fight*, January 27, 2009.

5. Michael T. Kaufman, "Gary T. Rowe Jr., 64, Who Informed on Klan In Civil Rights Killing, Is Dead," *New York Times*, October 4, 1998.

6. John Drabble, "The FBI, COINTELPRO-WHITE HATE, and the Decline of Ku Klux Klan Organizations in Alabama, 1964–1971," *Alabama Review* 61 (January 2008), 28.

7. William Karl Ziegenhorn, *"No Rest for the Wicked": The FBI Investigations of White Supremacist Groups, 1983–1988* (Master's thesis, San Jose State University, 1995), 16 [available on *SJSU ScholarWorks*].

8. Brian Glick, *War at Home: Covert Action Against U.S. Activists and What We Can Do About It* (Boston: South End Press, 1989), 12–13.

9. John Drabble, "From White Supremacy to White Power: The FBI, COINTELPRO-WHITE HATE, and the Nazification of the Ku Klux Klan in the 1970s," *American Studies* 48, no. 3 (Fall 2007): 53.

10. Ibid., 55.

11. William W. Keller, *The Liberals and J. Edgar Hoover: Rise and Fall of a Domestic Intelligence State* (Princeton, NJ: Princeton University Press, 1989), 83.

12. Drabble, "The FBI," 32–37.

13. Drabble, "From White Supremacy to White Power," 55–56.

14. David Cunningham, *There's Something Happening Here: The New Left, the Klan, and FBI Counterintelligence* (Berkeley: University of California Press, 2004), 122–125.

15. Drabble, "The FBI," 12.

16. Cunningham, *There's Something Happening Here*, 128.

17. Drabble, "From White Supremacy to White Power," 49.

18. Ibid., 57, 61.

19. Ward Churchill and Jim Vander Wall, *Agents of Repression: The FBI's Secret War Against the Black Panther Party and the American Indian Movement* (Boston: South End Press, 1988), 182; Everett R. Holles, "A.C.L.U. Says F.B.I. Funded 'Army' to Terrorize Antiwar Protesters," *New York Times*, June 27, 1975; Noam Chomsky, "Domestic Terrorism: Notes on the State System of Oppression," *New Political Science* 21, no. 3 (September 1999): 303–324.

20. Frank Donner, *Protectors of Privilege: Red Squads and Police Repression in Urban America* (Berkeley: University of California Press, 1990), 146–150.

21. Michael Newton, *The FBI and the KKK: A Critical History* (Jefferson, NC: McFarland & Company, Inc., 2005), 170.

22. Ibid.

23. JoAnn Wypijewski, "Whitewash," *Mother Jones*, November 2005.

24. Martin Durham, *White Rage: The extreme right and American politics* (New York: Routledge, 2007), 44.

25. Ziegenhorn, *"No Rest for the Wicked,"* 65–76; Zeskind, *Blood and Politics*, 146.

26. Leonard Zeskind, *Blood and Politics: The History of the White Nationalist Movement from the Margins to the Mainstream* (New York: Farrar Straus Giroux, 2009), 146.

27. Lincoln Caplan, "The Destruction of Defendants' Rights," *The New Yorker*, June 21, 2015; Elaine Cassel, "Anti-Terrorism," *CounterPunch*, October 19, 2002.

28. J.M. Berger, "PATCON Revealed: An Exclusive Look Inside The FBI's Secret War With The Militia Movement," *IntelWire* (website), October 8, 2007.

29. "The Neo-Militia News Archive: January–June 1996: Militia Leader Revealed to have FBI Connections," *The Militia Watchdog*, June 19, 1996 [archived at *Anti-Defamation League* website]; Bill Swindell, "Militia Coordinator On Federal Payroll," *Tulsa World*, April 7, 1996.

30. Naomi Braine, "Terror Network or Lone Wolf?" *Public Eye* (website), Spring 2015, [Political Research Associates].

31. Department of Homeland Security, Office of Intelligence Analysis, *Rightwing Extremism: Current Economic and Political Climate Fueling Resurgence in Radicalization and Recruitment*, April 7, 2009 [available on *Federation of American Scientists, Intelligence Resource Program* (website)]; Amy Goodman, "Former DHS Analyst Daryl Johnson on How He Was Silenced for Warning of Far-Right Militants in U.S." [interview with Daryl Johnson], *Democracy Now!* (website), August 9, 2012.

32. Chuck Baldwin, "Missouri Scraps MIAC Report," *RenewAmerica* (website), March 27, 2009.

33. Ryan Lenz and Mark Potok, "War in the West: The Bundy Ranch Standoff and the American Radical Right," *Southern Poverty Law Center* (website); Maxine Bernstein, "Cliven Bundy, 4 others face federal indictments in Nevada," *The Oregonian*, February 17, 2016.

34. Spencer Sunshine, "Interview with Spencer Sunshine on the Oregon Militia Occupation," *It's Going Down* (website), January 11,

2016; Les Zaitz, "LaVoy Finicum shot 3 times as he reached for gun, investigators say," *The Oregonian*, March 8, 2016.

35. Peter Bergen and Andrew Lebovich, "Study Reveals the Many Faces of Terrorism," *New America Foundation* (website), September 20, 2011; Peter Bergen and Jennifer Rowland, "Right-wing extremist terrorism as deadly a threat as al Qaeda?" *CNN* (website), August 8, 2012; New America Foundation, "Our people," *New America Foundation* (website), nd.

36. J.M. Berger, "PATCON: The FBI's Secret War Against the 'Patriot' Movement, and How Infiltration Tactics Relate to Radicalizing Influences" (policy paper), *New America Foundation* (website), May 21, 2012, 2; see also J.M. Berger, "Patriot Games: How the FBI spent a decade hunting white supremacists and missed Timothy McVeigh," *Foreign Policy*, April 18, 2012.

37. Berger, "PATCON: The FBI's Secret War," 22.

38. Ibid., 23.

39. Ibid., 22.

40. Kristian Williams, "The other side of the COIN: counterinsurgency and community policing," *Interface* 3, no. 1 (May 2011): 84.

41. Ken Lawrence, *The New State Repression*, second edition (Chicago: International Network Against New State Repression, 1985); reprint, with an introduction by Kristian Williams (Portland, OR: Tarantula, 2006), 6 [page citation is to the reprint edition].

42. Douglas Ollivant, "Countering the New Orthodoxy" (policy paper), *New America Foundation* (website), June 28, 2011; Parag Khanna and Ayesha Khanna, "How Pakistan Can Fix Itself," *New America Foundation* (website), May 2009.

43. "Counterterrorism and Counterinsurgency Initiative" (information sheet), *New America Foundation* (website), [c. 2008].

44. The White House, Office of the Press Secretary, "Fact Sheet: The White House Summit on Countering Violent Extremism" (press release), February 18, 2015, available at *ObamaWhiteHouse.archives.gov*.

45. Casey Quinlan, "Homeland Security effort to track white supremacists remain intact, for now," *ThinkProgress* (website), June 1, 2017; Michael Kalin, "Trump's Emerging Policy on Countering Violent Extremism," *Political Violence at a Glance* (website), June 20, 2017.

46. Williams, "The other side of the COIN," 85.

NOTES TO CHAPTER 10.
LEFTISTS, LIBERALS, AND THE SPECTER OF FASCISM

1. Matthew N. Lyons, "Is the Bush Administration Fascist?" *New Politics* 11, no. 2 (Winter 2007): 22.

2. Ibid., 21.

3. R. Palme Dutt, *Fascism and Social Revolution*, revised edition (New York: International Publishers, 1934), 110.

4. Ibid., 271.

5. Ibid., 267.

6. Ibid., 271.

7. James Q. Whitman, "Of Corporatism, Fascism, and the First New Deal," *American Journal of Comparative Law 39* (1991), 766–770, available in *Yale Law School Legal Scholarship Repository*.

8. Thomas Ferguson, *Golden Rule: The Investment Theory of Party Competition and the Logic of Money-Driven Political Systems* (Chicago: University of Chicago Press, 1995), chapters 2 and 4.

9. A.B. Magil and Henry Stevens, *The Peril of Fascism: The Crisis of American Democracy* (New York: International Publishers, 1938), 101, 271.

10. Mark Naison, *Communists in Harlem during the Depression* (New York: Grove Press, 1984), 290.

11. Michael Goldfield, "Recent Historiography of the Communist Party," *Year Left* 1 (1985), 338; J. Sakai, *Settlers: The Mythology of the White Proletariat from Mayflower to Modern*, fourth edition (Montreal: Kersplebedeb and Oakland: PM Press, 2014), 294–296; Steve Clark, "How CP USA backed Smith Act convictions of SWP, Teamster leaders," *The Militant* 69, no. 20 (May 23, 2005).

12. Leo P. Ribuffo, *The Old Christian Right: The Protestant Far Right from the Great Depression to the Cold War* (Philadelphia: Temple University Press, 1983), chapter 5.

13. Joseph Hansen, *Father Coughlin: Fascist Demagogue* (pamphlet) (New York: Pioneer Publishers, 1939), 9, posted on *Marxist update* (blog), October 3, 2012.

14. James P. Cannon and Joseph Hansen, *What Is American Fascism? Writings on Father Coughlin, Mayor Frank Hague, and Senator Joseph*

McCarthy (pamphlet) (New York: Socialist Workers Party, 1976), 15, 18, 21.

15. Ibid., 15.

16. David Caute, *The Great Fear: The Anti-Communist Purge Under Truman and Eisenhower* (New York: Simon and Schuster, 1978), 187–199.

17. Bruce Cumings, *The Origins of the Korean War*, vol. 2, *The Roaring of the Cataract, 1947–1950* (Princeton, NJ: Princeton University Press, 1990), 91–92, 106–117.

18. George Blake, "New Features in the Struggle Against Fascism," *Political Affairs* 30 (10, 1951), 41, 42.

19. Cannon and Hansen, *What Is American Fascism?*, 22, 23, 29, 23.

20. Louis Proyect, "Is Donald Trump a fascist?" *Louis Proyect: The Unrepentant Marxist* (blog), December 8, 2015.

21. Cannon and Hansen, *What Is American Fascism?*, 37.

22. Ward Churchill and Jim Vander Wall, *Agents of Repression: The FBI's Secret War Against the Black Panther Party and the American Indian Movement* (Boston: South End Press, 1988); Frank Donner, *Protectors of Privilege: Red Squads and Police Repression in Urban America* (Berkeley: University of California Press, 1990).

23. Alice Echols, *Daring to Be Bad: Radical Feminism in America, 1967–1975* (Minneapolis: University of Minnesota Press, 1989), 127–128.

24. Chris Booker, "Lumpenization: A Critical Error of the Black Panther Party," in *The Black Panther Party [Reconsidered]*, ed. Charles E. Jones (Baltimore: Black Classic Press, 1998), 348 [available on *libcom.org* (website)].

25. George Jackson, "A Tribute to Three Slain Brothers," *The Black Panther*, January 16, 1970 [available on *It's About Time — Black Panther Party Legacy & Alumni* (website)].

26. Ibid.

27. George Jackson, *Blood In My Eye* (New York: Random House, 1972), 140.

28. Lyons, "Is the Bush Administration Fascist?"

29. Laurence W. Britt, "Fascism Anyone?" *Free Inquiry Magazine* 23, no. 2 (March 31, 2003).

30. Revolutionary Communist Party, "The Battle for the Future Will Be Fought From Here Forward!" *Revolutionary Worker*, no. 1262 (December 19, 2004) [available on *RevCom.us* (website)]; see also Larry Everest, "The Rise of the Christian Fascists: The Specter of a U.S. Theocracy and Why the People Must Stop It," *Revolutionary Worker,* no. 1263 (December 26, 2004) [available on *RevCom.us* (website)].

31. Michael Novick, "Fascism and What Is Coming," *Turning the Tide* 16, no 2. (Summer 2003); republished in *Dissident Voice* (website), June 10, 2003.

32. Thom Hartmann, "Dismantling Democracy: What's behind the magic trick of war?" *Common Dreams* (website), September 22, 2002; Michael Novick, "The Five Faces of Fascism," *Turning the Tide* 18, no. 5 (November–December 2005); republished in *4strugglemag* (website), February 11, 2006.

NOTES TO CHAPTER 11.
TRUMP'S PRESIDENCY AND THE FAR RIGHT

1. Matthew N. Lyons, "Trump: 'anti-political' or right wing?" *Three Way Fight* (blog), March 13, 2016; Niraj Chokshi, "Trump Accuses Clinton of Guiding Global Elite Against U.S. Working Class," *New York Times*, October 13, 2016; Elise Viebeck, Jerry Markon, and Karen DeYoung, "Trump, Putin agree in phone call to improve unsatisfactory relations between their countries, Kremlin says," *Washington Post*, November 14, 2016.

2. Matthew N. Lyons, "Oath Keepers, Ferguson, and the Patriot movement's conflicted race politics," *Three Way Fight*, August 28, 2015.

3. Chip Berlet, "'Trumping' Democracy: Right-Wing Populism, Fascism, And The Case For Action," *Political Research Associates* (website), December 12, 2015.

4. Umberto Eco, "Ur-Fascism," *New York Review of Books*, June 22, 1995; Robert Paxton, *The Anatomy of Fascism* (New York: Robert A. Knopf, 2004).

5. Alexander Reid Ross, "Trumpism, Pt. 3: Propaganda of the Deal," *It's Going Down* (website), December 11, 2015.

6 Alex Mohajer, "Hillary Clinton's Stunning Campaign Statement About Trump's Ties To Russia," *Huffington Post*, March 23, 2017.

7. Franklin Foer, "Putin's Puppet," *Slate*, July 4, 2017.

8. Greg Olear, "Trump is a Fascist, This is a Coup, I'm Not Normalizing it on Facebook," *The Weeklings* (website), January 19, 2017.

9. Joe Conason, "With Le Pen, Trump (and Putin) Are Still Pushing Fascist 'Nationalism,'" *AlterNet*, April 23, 2017.

10. Charles P. Pierce, "What Do the Russians 'Have' on the Trump Family? Fear," *Esquire*, July 10, 2017; Craig Unger, "Trump's Russian Laundromat," *New Republic*, July 13, 2017.

11. Masha Gessen, "Russia: The Conspiracy Trap," *New York Review of Books*, March 6, 2017.

12. Doug Henwood, "Putin didn't win this election for Trump. Hillary Clinton did," *The Guardian*, December 13, 2017.

13. Antonia De Grazia, "Many call Trump a fascist. 100 days in, is he just a reactionary Republican?" *The Guardian*, April 30, 2017; Corey Robin, "Think Trump is an authoritarian? Look at his actions, not his words," *The Guardian*, May 2, 2017.

14. Research & Destroy, "The Landing: Fascists Without Fascism," *research & destroy* (website), February 20, 2017.

15. Benjamin Studebaker, "Why Bernie Sanders is More Electable Than People Think," *Huffington Post*, February 12, 2016.

16. Jane Mayer, "The Reclusive Hedge-Fund Tycoon Behind the Trump Presidency," *The New Yorker*, March 27, 2017.

17. Thomas Ferguson and Joel Rogers, *Right Turn: The Decline of the Democrats and the Future of American Politics* (New York: Hill and Wang/Farrar, Straus and Giroux, 1986), 68–69.

18. Sharon LaFraniere and Matt Apuzzo, "Jeff Sessions, a Lifelong Outsider, Finds the Inside Track," *New York Times*, January 8, 2017; Philip Rucker and Robert Costa, "Trump's hard-line actions have an intellectual godfather: Jeff Sessions," *Washington Post*, January 30, 2017.

19. Paul Blumenthal and J.M. Rieger, "This Stunningly Racist French Novel Is How Steve Bannon Explains The World," *Huffington Post*, March 4, 2017; J. Lester Feder, "This Is How Steve Bannon Sees The Entire World" [transcript of Bannon's remarks via Skype to the Third

International Conference on Human Dignity, Vatican City, Summer 2014], *BuzzFeed News*, November 15, 2016; Max Fisher, "Stephen K. Bannon's CPAC Comments, Annotated and Explained," *New York Times*, February 24, 2017; see also Joshua Green, "Inside the Secret, Strange Origins of Steve Bannon's Nationalist Fantasia," *Vanity Fair* (website), July 17, 2017.

20. Donald J. Trump, "Transcript of President Trump's inauguration speech," *USA Today*, January 20, 2017.

21. Corey Robin, "If Trump is a fascist, he may be the most backassward fascist we've ever seen," *Corey Robin* (website), January 29, 2017.

22. David A. Graham, "Trump Has Quietly Accomplished More Than It Appears," *The Atlantic*, August 2, 2017; Danielle Ivory and Robert Faturechi, "The Deep Industry Ties of Trump's Deregulation Teams," *New York Times*, July 11, 2017; "Trump to undo Obama-era limits on military-style gear for US police," *Guardian*, August 28, 2017.

23. Robert Cavooris, "One Step Back, Two Steps Forward: Trump and the Revolutionary Scenario," *Viewpoint*, February 21, 2017.

24. Damian Paletta and Jena McGregor, "Trump's business advisory councils disband as CEOs abandon president over Charlottesville views," *Washington Post*, August 16, 2017.

25. Mark Landler and Eric Schmitt, "H.R. McMaster Breaks With Administration on Views of Islam, *New York Times*, February 24, 2017.

26. Doyle McManus, "Trump's populist revolution is already over—for now," *Los Angeles Times*, April 16, 2017.

27. Peter Baker, "Trump Supports Plan to Cut Legal Immigration by Half," *New York Times*, August 2, 2017; "Gorka, a Trump adviser and Bannon ally, is out: White House," *Reuters*, August 25, 2017.

28. Stanley Ezrol, "Tillerson Charts a Course Toward a New Era of International Collaboration for Peaceful Growth," *Executive Intelligence Review* (website), August 11, 2017; "Will Democrats and Trump Join Forces for Real Healthcare?" *Executive Intelligence Review*, March 27, 2017; "Press Release: Hersh: Trump's Decision To Launch Cruise Missiles Against Syria Ran Counter to Intelligence That There Was No Chemical Attack," *Executive Intelligence Review*, June 26, 2017.

29. Richard B. Spencer, "We the Vanguard Now," *Radix Journal*, November 9, 2016.

30. Matt Parrott, "Trump Apocalypse Now," *Traditionalist Worker Party* (website), November 10, 2016.

31. Jef Costello, "I Keep Forgetting That I'm Not an American," *Counter-Currents Publishing* (website), March 15, 2017.

32. John Derbyshire, "Collapse Of Trumpism—On War AND Immigration?" *V Dare*, April 7, 2017.

33. Andrew Anglin, "An Extremely Unfortunate Turn of Events," *Daily Stormer*, April 7, 2017.

34. Hunter Wallace [Brad Griffin], "Donald Trump is Now the Leader of the Free World," *Occidental Dissent* (blog), April 8, 2017.

35. Pseudo-Laurentius, "Deploying Tactical Blackpills: The Alt Right Versus Trump," *The Right Stuff* (website), April 14, 2017.

36. Meinrad Gaertner, "A Reflection and Foreshadowing," *Occidental Dissent* (blog), April 17, 2017.

37. IronSaxon et al., U.S. election discussion thread, *Iron March Forums*, July 22, 2016.

38. Rocky Suhayda, "ANP Report for December 09, 2016," *American Nazi Party* (website), December 9, 2016.

39. Rocky Suhayda, "ANP Report for January 14, 2017," *American Nazi Party* (website), January 14, 2017.

40. Max Micro, "TrumpCucks," *Noose* (website), February 16, 2016.

41. Max Micro, "Trump Victory," *Noose* (website), December 6, 2016.

42. Mark Pitcavage, "The Militia's Election: Extremists React to Trump Victory with Celebration—and Anger," *Anti-Defamation League* (website), November 10, 2016.

43. Shorty Dawkins, "The Hypocrisy of the Left," *Oath Keepers* (website), January 31, 2017.

44. Sara Rathod, "Militia Groups Are Basking in Trump's Victory," *Mother Jones*, November 10, 2016.

45. Michael Cutler, "Trump's Immigration Executive Orders and the Constitution," *Oath Keepers* (website), February 20, 2017; Ben Kew, "Trump Budget Proposes to End Obama's Federal Land Grab," *Oath Keepers* (website), March 16, 2017.

46. Pastor Mike et al., "The 19 Federal Agencies Trump Wants to Eliminate" (discussion thread), *Three Percenter* (website), March 17–18, 2017.

47. Bangfly59 et al., "Could Someone Explain This To Me?" (discussion thread), *Three Percenter* (website), March 5–7, 2017.

48. Pitcavage, "Militia's Election"; NavyJack, "NavyJack—Operation HYPO After Action Report: Infiltrating Violent Protest Organization," *Oath Keepers* (website), January 29, 2017; Robert R. Owens, "Trump Protestors Professional Patsies," *Oath Keepers* (website), March 11, 2017.

49. NavyJack, "NavyJack—Operation HYPO: Infiltrating Violent Protests Against the President Elect," *Oath Keepers* (website), November 11, 2016; NavyJack, "NavyJack—Operation HYPO After Action Report."

50. NavyJack, "NavyJack—Operation HYPO: Infiltrating Violent Protests."

51. Alex Yablon, "Gun-Toting Militias Are Now Part of Local Politics Thanks to Trump," *Vice* (website), August 7, 2017.

52. air force, "'Regime Change' in Syria" (discussion thread), *A Well Regulated Militia...* (website), April 6, 2017.

53. NavyJack, "Has President Trump Been Blackmailed or Deceived by the NEOCONs?" *Oath Keepers* (website), April 6, 2017.

54. Jeffrey Folks, "To Sink Trump Is to Sink Ordinary Americans," *Oath Keepers* (website), July 24, 2017; Awr Hawkins, "Freedom Winning as Pres. Trump Trades Gun Control for Crime Control," *Oath Keepers*, August 3, 2017.

55. Bob Eschliman, "Sonny Perdue Becomes the 9th Evangelical to Join the Trump Cabinet," *Charisma News* (website), January 19, 2017.

56. C. Peter Wagner, "The New Apostolic Reformation Is Not a Cult," *Charisma News*, August 24, 2011.

57. C. Peter Wagner, "I like Donald Trump," *Charisma News*, June 10, 2016.

58. Steven Kozar, "C. Peter Wagner Alters the '7 Mountain Mandate'—An Act of Desperation," *Pirate Christian* (website), June 14, 2016.

59. Miranda Blue, "Lance Wallnau: Trump Can Help Stop Satan From Taking Control Of The Seven Mountains," *Right Wing Watch*, August 18, 2016.

60. Johnny Enlow, "Johnny Enlow: 'Trump Quake! What's Next?'" *Elijah List* (website), December 6, 2016.

61. Cindy Jacobs, "2017: Year of the Breakthrough," *Charisma Magazine*, January 5, 2017.

62. Mernant Mehta, "Televangelist Rick Joyner: People Who Oppose Donald Trump Are Under the Influence of Satan," *Patheos*, February 3, 2017.

63. Peter Montgomery, "Lou Engle Calls For National Fast To Save Donald Trump From Witchcraft Curse," *Right Wing Watch*, March 6, 2017. On NAR support for Trump, see also Sunnivie Brydum, "A President 'Anointed By God': POTUS Shield And Religious Right's Affair With Trump," *Religion Dispatches* (website), August 4, 2017; Peter Montgomery, "POTUS Shield: Trump's Dominionist Prayer Warriors and the 'Prophetic Order of the United States,'" *Right Wing Watch* (website), August 2017.

64. Gary DeMar, "To Trump Skeptics: 7 Reasons Trump is the Only Viable Option," *Eagle Rising* (website), July 2016.

65. Joel McDurmon, "Power and Authority: putting Hillary v. Trump in perspective," *American Vision* (website), August 9, 2016.

66. John M. Otis, "Should A Christian Vote For Trump to Avoid a Hillary Clinton Presidency?" *Theonomy Resources* (website), November 5, 2016.

67. Kyle Mantyla, "Kevin Swanson: President Trump Is God's Plan For Bringing About The Destruction Of America," *Right Wing Watch*, May 6, 2016.

68. Joel McDurmon, "Trump's attack on the Freedom Caucus speaks volumes," *American Vision* (website), March 27, 2017.

69. Joel McDurmon, "Comments on the 2016 Trumpocalypse," *American Vision* (website), November 11, 2016.

70. Joel McDurmon, "Is Trump *really* a fascist?" *American Vision* (website), March 13, 2017.

71. Gary North, "Trump's Revolution Is Over," *Gary North's Specific Answers* (website), November 12, 2016.

72. Matthew N. Lyons, "An Alt Right Update," *Political Research Associates* (website), August 7, 2017.

NOTES TO THE CONCLUSION:
DISLOYALTY IN MOTION

1. Spencer Sunshine, "The Growing Alliance Between Neo-Nazis, Right Wing Paramilitaries and Trumpist Republicans," *ColorLines*, June 9, 2017; see also "Based Reserve Army: How the Right is Changing Its Strategy," *It's Going Down*, April 25, 2017; Spencer Sunshine, "Islamophobia is the Glue that Unites Diverse Factions of the Far Right," *Truthout*, July 14, 2017; David Neiwert, "Far Right Descends on Berkeley for 'Free Speech' and Planned Violence," *Hatewatch*, April 17, 2017 [Southern Poverty Law Center]; "Oath Keepers Call to Action: Stand and Defend Free Speech at Berkeley Patriots Rally, April 15, 2017," *Oath Keepers (website)*, April 1 2017.

2. Antifascist Front, "The Alt Right Has Taken the Public Step Towards Violence," *Anti-Fascist News*, April 28, 2017; Emma Grey Ellis, "Don't Look Now, But Extremists' Meme Armies are Turning Into Militias," *Wired*, April 20, 2017; "Gavin McInnes' 'Alt-Right' Fan Club Drifts Toward Neo-Nazi Violence," *IdaVox*, May 18, 2017; Northern California Anti-Racist Action, "How 'Based Stickman' & Proud Boys are Working with Neo-Nazis in So-Cal," *It's Going Down*, July 8, 2017.

3. Taly Krupkin, "The Jewish Provocateur Caught in the Turf War as the 'Alt-right' Battles the 'Alt-light,'" *Ha'aretz*, June 22, 2017; "'Alt-Right' declares flame war on Oath Keepers," *Southern Poverty Law Center* (website), June 15, 2017; "Armed Militias Face Off With The 'Antifa' In The New Landscape Of Political Protest" [interview with Mark Pitcavage], *Fresh Air*, *National Public Radio* (website), August 23, 2017.

4. Spencer Sunshine, "I Almost Died in Charlottesville," *Colorlines*, August 15, 2017; Jason Wilson, "Charlottesville reveals an emboldened far right that can no longer be ignored," *Guardian*, August 14, 2017.

5. Vincent Law, "Leaderless Resistance," *AltRight.com* (website), August 31, 2017.

6. Spencer Sunshine, "Has the 'Alt-Right' Met Its Gettysburg?" *Truthout*, August 26, 2017; Samuel Osborne, "Neo-Nazi Website Stormfront Forced Offline 'By Its Own Host," *Independent*, August 28, 2017; Keith Collins, "A running list of websites and apps that have banned, blocked, deleted, and otherwise dropped white supremacists," *Quartz* (website), August 16, 2017; Joanna Walters and

Jason Wilson, "Charlottesville: Trump under fire for failure to condemn far right," *Guardian*, August 14, 2017.

7. Shane Bauer, "What the Media Got Wrong About Last Weekend's Protests in Berkeley," *Mother Jones,* August 29, 2017; Chris Hedges, "How 'Antifa' Mirrors the 'Alt-Right,'" *TruthDig* (website), August 27, 2017; "Berkeley Mayor: We Should Classify Antifa 'As A Gang,'" *CBS SF Bay Area* (website), August 28, 2017; Mark A. Thiessen, "Yes, antifa is the moral equivalent of neo-Nazis," *Washington Post*, August 30, 2017; Nancy Pelosi, "Pelosi Statement Condemning Antifa Violence in Berkeley" (press release), *Nancy Pelosi: Democratic Leader* (website), August 29, 2017; "'Antifa' groups only help the hateful forces they claim to oppose" (editorial), *Washington Post*, August 29, 2017; Josh Nathan-Kazis, "ADL Tells Cops To Infiltrate Antifa—And Film Protests," *Forward*, August 30, 2017.

NOTES TO APPENDIX:
TWO WAYS OF LOOKING AT FASCISM

1. Matthew N. Lyons, "Is the Bush Administration Fascist?" *New Politics* 11, no. 2 (Winter 2007).

2. See for example, Gus Hall, "The hidden GOP agenda: Right-wing control of Republican Party stands as a wake-up call to the nation," *People's Weekly World*, August 24, 1996; Jack Barnes, "Fascism: not a form of capitalism but a way to maintain capitalist rule," *The Militant*, September 4, 2006; Revolutionary Communist Party, USA, "The Battle For the Future Will Be Fought From Here Forward!" (leaflet), [c. December 2004]; Eric Hass, *The Reactionary Right: Incipient Fascism* (New York Labor News: 1963; online edited edition 2007) [available on *Socialist Labor Party of America* (website)]; Anis Shivani, "Is America Becoming Fascist?" *CounterPunch*, October 26, 2002; Alan Nasser, "The Threat of U.S. Fascism: An Historical Precedent," *Common Dreams*, August 2, 2007; and the numerous progressive websites that invoke Laurence Britt's "Fourteen Identifying Characteristics of Fascism" or Bertram Gross's *Friendly Fascism: The New Face of Power in America* (Cambridge, MA: South End Press, 1980).

3. Gregory Meyerson and Michael Joseph Roberto, "It Could Happen Here," *Monthly Review* (website), October 21, 2006.

4. Extract from 13th Enlarged Executive of the Communist International (ECCI) Plenum (held in December 1933) on "Fascism, the War Danger, and the Tasks of the Communist Parties"; republished in *International Fascism: Theories, Causes and the New Consensus*, ed., Roger Griffin (New York: Oxford University Press, 1998), 59.

5. Leon Trotsky, "What is National Socialism?" 1933, published 1943; republished in *The Age of Permanent Revolution: A Trotsky Anthology*, ed., Isaac Deutscher (New York: Dell Publishing Co., 1964), 181.

6. David Lethbridge, "The Marxist-Leninist Theory of Fascism," The Bethune Institute for Anti-Fascist Studies, 1999.

7. T.W. Mason, "The Primacy of Politics — Politics and Economics in National Socialist Germany," in *The Nature of Fascism: Proceedings of a conference held by the Reading University Graduate School of Contemporary European Studies* (London: Weidenfeld and Nicolson, 1968), 165–195.

8. Ibid., 179.

9. Ibid., 191–192.

10. Ian Kershaw, *The Nazi Dictatorship: Problems and Perspectives of Interpretation*, second edition (London: Edward Arnold, 1989), 44–60; Jane Caplan, "Theories of Fascism: Nicos Poulantzas As Historian," 1977; republished in *Radical Perspectives on the Rise of Fascism in Germany, 1919–1945*, ed., Michael N. Dobkowski and Isidor Walliman (New York: Monthly Review Press, 1989), 149n29.

11. Franklin Hugh Adler, *Italian Industrialists from Liberalism to Fascism: The political development of the industrial bourgeoisie, 1906–1934* (Cambridge, UK: Cambridge University Press, 1995), 347.

12. August Thalheimer, "On Fascism," 1928; republished in *Marxists in the Face of Fascism: Writings by Marxists on Fascism from the Interwar Period*, ed., David Beetham (Totowa, NJ: Barnes & Noble, 1984), 188.

13. Ibid., 191.

14. Thalheimer, "So-called Social-fascism," 1929; republished in *Marxists in the Face of Fascism*, ed., Beetham, 196.

15. Thalheimer, "On Fascism," 191, 194.

16. Ibid., 190, 192–93.

17. Caplan, "Theories of Fascism," 143–44.

18. Mihaly Vajda, *Fascism as a Mass Movement* (New York: St. Martin's Press, 1976), 13, 93.

19. Ibid., 93, 75, 8, 105.

20. Ibid., 17, 24, 19–20.

21. Ibid., 24–25.

22. Xtn, "Introduction," in Don Hamerquist et al., *Confronting Fascism: Discussion Documents for a Militant Movement* (Montreal: Kersplebedeb Publishing, 2017), 9–25.

23. J. Sakai, "The Shock of Recognition," in *Confronting Fascism*, 115, 124.

24. Don Hamerquist, "Fascism & Anti-Fascism," in *Confronting Fascism*, 29.

25. Hamerquist, "Fascism & Anti-Fascism," 53; Sakai, "Shock of Recognition," 135–136.

26. Sakai, "Shock of Recognition," 122, 115, 122.

27. Ibid., 119, 157.

28. Hamerquist, "Fascism & Anti-Fascism," 42–43.

29. Ibid., 39.

30. Sakai, "Shock of Recognition," 123.

31. David D. Roberts, *The Syndicalist Tradition and Italian Fascism* (Chapel Hill: University of North Carolina Press, 1979); Geoff Eley, "What Produces Fascism: Preindustrial Traditions or a Crisis of the Capitalist State?" 1983; republished in *Radical Perspectives on the Rise of Fascism in Germany*, ed., Dobkowski and Walliman, 78–79.

32. Eley, "What Produces Fascism," 85.

33. Ibid., 83; Conan Fischer, *Stormtroopers: A Social, Economic and Ideological Analysis, 1929–1935* (Boston: George Allen & Unwin, 1983).

34. Hamerquist, "Fascism & Anti-Fascism," 60.

35. Xtn, "Introduction," 22–24; Matthew N. Lyons, "Notes on Women and Right-Wing Movements" [two-part essay], *Three Way Fight* (blog), September–October 2005.

36. Roger Griffin, "Section II: The Search for the Fascist Minimum: Presentation," in *International Fascism*, 52–53.

37. Roger Griffin, "Notes towards the definition of fascist culture: the prospects for synergy between Marxist and liberal heuristics," *Renaissance and Modern Studies* 42 (Autumn 2001).

38. Roger Griffin, *The Nature of Fascism* (London: Pinter Publishers, 1991; New York: Routledge, 1996), 11; Robert Paxton, *The Anatomy of Fascism* (New York: Robert A. Knopf, 2004), 21.

39. Griffin, *Nature of Fascism*, 32–39.

40. Ibid., 37.

41. Ibid., 38.

42. Griffin, "Notes towards the definition of fascist culture," 12, 13.

43. Roger Griffin, "Revolution from the Right: Fascism," in *Revolutions and Revolutionary Tradition in the West 1560–1989*, ed., David Parker (New York: Routledge, 1999).

44. Griffin, *Nature of Fascism*, 48.

45. Ibid., 47.

46. Roger Griffin, "The 'Post-Fascism' of the Alleanza nazionale: A case-study in Ideological Morphology," *Journal of Political Ideologies* 1, no. 2 (1996): 123–146.

47. Griffin, *Nature of Fascism*, 121.

48. Ibid., 123.

49. Ibid., 166–174; Roger Griffin, "Europe for the Europeans: Fascist Myths of The European New Order 1922–1992," Humanities Research Centre Occasional Paper, no. 1, 1994.

50. Griffin, *Nature of Fascism*, 208–211.

51. Ibid., 220.

52. See Roger Griffin's essays entitled "Fascism" written for *Encyclopedia of Fundamentalism*, ed., Brenda Brasher (Great Barrington, MA: Berkshire Reference Works, 2001); *The Encyclopedia of Religion and Nature*, ed., Bron Taylor and Jeffrey Kaplan (London: Continuum International Publishers, 2003); and *The Encyclopedia of Religion and Politics* (draft), February 11, 2000.

53. George Mosse, quoted in Griffin, "Notes towards the definition of fascist culture."

54. Griffin, "Fascism," *Encyclopedia of Fundamentalism*.

55. Ibid.

56. Nikki Keddie, "The New Religious Politics and Women Worldwide: A Comparative Study," *Journal of Women's History* 10, no. 4 (Winter 1999): 11–34.

57. "Nation State—Out of Date?" *Third Way*, no. 8 (July 25, 1991): 3.

58. Griffin, "Introduction," in *International Fascism*, 4.

59. Griffin, "Notes towards the definition of fascist culture."

60. Dave Renton, *Fascism: Theory and Practice* (London: Pluto Press, 1999), 24; Mark Neocleous, *Fascism*, Concepts in Social Thought Series (Minneapolis: University of Minnesota Press, 1997), 38.

61. In a previous draft of this essay, I offered a version of this definition that had a different final clause, stating that fascism *"challenges capitalist control of the state while defending class exploitation."* Thanks to Don Hamerquist for pointing out that this violated methodological empathy, since many neofascists either ignore or disavow class exploitation, although they glorify hierarchy, authority, and discipline.

62. Chip Berlet and Matthew N. Lyons, *Right-Wing Populism in America: Too Close for Comfort* (New York: Guilford Press, 2000); Margaret Canovan, *Populism* (New York: Harcourt Brace Jovanovich, 1981).

63. The following sketches of the Patriot movement and the Christian right are based on Berlet and Lyons, *Right-Wing Populism in America*, chapters 11, 12, and 14.

64. See Martin A. Lee, *The Beast Reawakens* (Boston: Little Brown and Company, 1997); Jérôme Jamin, "The Extreme Right in Europe: Fascist or Mainstream?" *The Public Eye* 19, no. 1 (Spring 2005) [Political Research Associates]; Luciano Cheles, Ronnie Ferguson, and Michalina Vaughan, eds., *Neo-Fascism in Europe* (New York: Longman Publishing, 1991).

65. See Joel Beinin and Joe Stork, ed., *Political Islam: Essays from Middle East Report* (Berkeley: University of California Press, 1997); Said Amir Arjomand, "Iran's Islamic Revolution in Comparative Perspective," *World Politics* 38, no. 3 (April 1986): 383–414; Abdel Azim Ramadan, "Fundamentalist Influence in Egypt: The Strategies of the Muslim Brotherhood and the Takfir Groups," in *Fundamentalisms and the State: Remaking Polities, Economies, and Militance*, ed., Martin E. Marty and R. Scott Appleby, The Fundamentalism Project, Volume 3 (Chicago: University of Chicago Press, 1993), 152–183;

Ahmed Rashid, *Taliban: Militant Islam, Oil and Fundamentalism in Central Asia* (New Haven, CT: Yale University Press, 2001); Amal Saad-Ghorayeb, *Hizbu'llah: Politics and Religion* (London: Pluto Press, 2002); Nikki R. Keddie and Farah Monian, "Militancy and Religion in Contemporary Iran," in *Fundamentalisms and the State*, ed., Marty and Appleby, 511–538.

66. See Matthew N. Lyons, "Defending my enemy's enemy," *Three Way Fight* (blog), August 3, 2006; Matthew N. Lyons, "Further thoughts on Hezbollah," *Three Way Fight*, August 26, 2006.

67. See Arun R. Swamy, "Hindu Nationalism—What's Religion Got to Do With It?" Occasional Papers Series, Asian-Pacific Center for Security Studies, 2003; Christophe Jaffrelot, *The Hindu Nationalist Movement and Indian Politics, 1925 to the 1990s* (New Delhi: Penguin Books India, 1999); Thomas Blom Hansen, *The Saffron Wave: Democracy and Hindu Nationalism in Modern India* (New Delhi: Oxford University Press, 1999); Vijay Prashad, *Namaste Sharon: Hindutva and Sharonism Under US Hegemony*, Signpost Series (New Delhi: LeftWord Books, 2003).

68. Martin A. Lee, "The Fascist Response to Globalization," *Los Angeles Times*, November 28, 1999. For a parallel argument, see Roberto Lovato, "Far From Fringe: Minutemen Mobilizes Whites Left Behind by Globalization," *The Public Eye* 19, no. 3 (Winter 2005) [*Political Research Associates*].

69. People Against Racist Terror, "PART's Perspective on the Militias," *Turning the Tide* 8, no. 2 (Summer 1995).

70. Radhika Desai, "Forward March of Hindutva Halted?" *New Left Review* 30 (November–December 2004): 61. On Hindu national-ist ambivalence about globalization, see Jaffrelot, *Hindu Nationalist Movement*, 432, 492–493; Hansen, *Saffron Wave*, 171–172.

71. Maria Mies, *Patriarchy and Accumulation on a World Scale: Women in the International Division of Labour* (London: Zed, 1986), 118. Regina Cochrane has criticized Mies for "populist and maternal feminist tendencies" that are anti-modernist, essentialize motherhood, and romanticize poverty. However, I believe that Mies's point about homemaking that I cite here remains valid and reflects a useful critique of capitalist globalization's gender dynamics. (See Cochrane, "They Aren't Really Poor": Ecofeminism, Global Justice, and "Culturally-Perceived Poverty," *Center for Global Justice* (website), 2006.

Selected Bibliography

The following is a selected list of secondary sources, cited in this book, that discuss modern U.S. far right currents; their origins; or their interactions with the state, system-loyal political forces, or the left. I have also included a few articles analyzing the politics of Donald Trump's presidential campaign or administration. For space reasons, I have excluded works by far rightists themselves and works that focus on political currents in other time periods or other parts of the world. For a more complete list of useful readings, please consult the endnotes.

In researching this book I relied heavily on internet sources. I have omitted URLs from the citations because they are both cumbersome and unreliable. The web is constantly in flux, and an article's URL may change without warning when its website is reorganized or it is reposted on a new domain, or it may disappear altogether. Compounding this issue, political pressure has recently forced a number of far right websites to close down, switch service providers, or move behind a paywall. To locate online works cited here, I recommend that readers use browser searches and the Internet Archive's Wayback Machine. If you are really stuck, please contact me.

Anti-Fascist Forum, ed. *My Enemy's Enemy: Essays on Globalization, Fascism and the Struggle Against Capitalism*. Montreal: Kersplebedeb Publishing, 2002.

Antifascist Front. "#Cuckservative: How the 'Alt Right' Took Off Their Masks and Revealed Their White Hoods." *Anti-Fascist News* (website), August 16, 2015.

———"Going Full Fash: Breitbart Mainstreams the 'Alt Right.'" *Anti-Fascist News* (website), April 5, 2016.

———"Queer Fascism: Why White Nationalists Are Trying to Drop Homophobia." *Anti-Fascist News* (website), November 6, 2015.

Berger, J.M. "PATCON Revealed: An Exclusive Look Inside The FBI's Secret War With The Militia Movement." *IntelWire* (website), October 8, 2007.

———"PATCON: The FBI's Secret War Against the 'Patriot' Movement, and How Infiltration Tactics Relate to Radicalizing Influences" (policy paper). *New America Foundation* (website), May 21, 2012.

Berlet, Chip. *Right Woos Left: Populist Party, LaRouchite, and Other Neo-fascist Overtures To Progressives, and Why They Must Be Rejected.* Cambridge, MA: Political Research Associates, 1994; corrected 1999.

Berlet, Chip, and Matthew N. Lyons. *Right-Wing Populism in America: Too Close for Comfort.* New York: Guilford Press, 2000.

Bromma. "Exodus and Reconstruction: Working-Class Women at the Heart of Globalization." *Kersplebedeb* (website), September 11, 2012.

Burghardt, Tom. "A Small Circle of Friends: Larry Pratt, the Council for Inter-American Security and International Fascist Networks." *Antifa Info-Bulletin* 1, no. 5 (March 7, 1996).

Burkett, Elinor. *The Right Women: A Journey Through the Heart of Conservative America.* New York: Scribner, 1998.

Cavooris, Robert. "One Step Back, Two Steps Forward: Trump and the Revolutionary Scenario." *Viewpoint* (website), February 21, 2017.

Churchill, Robert H. *To Shake Their Guns in the Tyrant's Face: Libertarian Political Violence and the Origins of the Militia Movement.* Ann Arbor: University of Michigan Press, 2009.

Clarkson, Frederick. "Christian Reconstructionism: Theocratic Dominionism Gains Influence." *The Public Eye* 8, nos. 1 and 2 (March and June 1994) [Political Research Associates].

Coogan, Kevin. *Dreamer of the Day: Francis Parker Yockey and the Postwar Fascist International*. Brooklyn, Autonomedia, 1999.

Cunningham, David. *There's Something Happening Here: The New Left, the Klan, and FBI Counterintelligence*. Berkeley: University of California Press, 2004.

Diamond, Sara. *Roads to Dominion: Right-Wing Movements and Political Power in the United States*. New York: Guilford Press, 1995.

——*Spiritual Warfare: The Politics of the Christian Right*. Boston: South End Press, 1989.

Drabble, John. "From White Supremacy to White Power: The FBI, COINTELPRO-WHITE HATE, and the Nazification of the Ku Klux Klan in the 1970s." *American Studies* 48, no. 3 (Fall 2007).

Durham, Martin. *White Rage: The extreme right and American politics*. New York: Routledge, 2007.

Ferber, Abby L., ed. *Home-Grown Hate: Gender and Organized Racism*. New York: Routledge, 2004.

Gilbert, Helen. *Lyndon LaRouche: Fascism Restyled for the New Millennium*. Red Banner Reader No. 8. Seattle: Red Letter Press, 2003.

Griffin, Roger. *The Nature of Fascism*. London: Pinter Publishers, 1991; New York: Routledge, 1996.

Hamerquist, Don, et al. *Confronting Fascism: Discussion Documents for a Militant Movement*. Montreal: Kersplebedeb Publishing, 2017.

Ingersoll, Julie J. *Building God's Kingdom: Inside the World of Christian Reconstruction*. New York: Oxford University Press, 2015.

———"Dominion Theology, Christian Reconstructionism, and the New Apostolic Reformation." *Religion Dispatches* (website), August 30, 2011.

Joyce, Kathryn. *Quiverfull: Inside the Christian Patriarchy Movement.* Boston: Beacon Press, 2009.

King, Dennis. *Lyndon LaRouche and the New American Fascism.* New York: Doubleday, 1989.

Lawrence, Ken. "The Ku Klux Klan and Fascism" [speech to the National Anti-Klan Network conference, Atlanta, June 19, 1982]. *Urgent Tasks*, no. 14 (Fall/Winter 1982).

Lenz, Ryan, and Mark Potok. "War in the West: The Bundy Ranch Standoff and the American Radical Right." *Southern Poverty Law Center* (website), July 9, 2014.

Lorber, Ben. "Understanding Alt-Right Antisemitism." *Doikayt* (website), March 24, 2017.

Lyons, Matthew N. "Is the Bush Administration Fascist?" *New Politics* 11, no. 2 (Winter 2007).

———"The LaRouche Network's Russia Connection." *Three Way Fight* (blog), July 3, 2015.

———"Rising Above the Herd: Keith Preston's Authoritarian Anti-Statism." *New Politics* (website), April 29, 2011.

McVicar, Michael J. *Christian Reconstruction: R.J. Rushdoony and American Religious Conservatism.* Chapel Hill: University of North Carolina Press, 2015.

———"The Libertarian Theocrats: The Long, Strange History of R.J. Rushdoony and Christian Reconstructionism." *The Public Eye*, vol. 22, no. 3 (Fall 2007) [Political Research Associates].

Mintz, Frank P. *The Liberty Lobby and the American Right: Race, Conspiracy, and Culture.* Westport, CT: Greenwood Press, 1985.

"Morbid Symptoms: The Rise of Trump." *Unity and Struggle* (website), November 15, 2016.

"Morbid Symptoms: The Downward Spiral." *Unity and Struggle* (website), December 19, 2016.

O'Reggio, Trevor. "The Rise of the New Apostolic Reformation." *Perspective Digest* (website), nd.

People Against Racist Terror. "PART's Perspective on the Militias." *Turning the Tide*, 8, no. 2 (Summer 1995).

Pivec, Holly. "The New Apostolic Reformation: Influence and Teachings." *Apologetics Index* (website), 2013.

Research & Destroy. "The Landing: Fascists Without Fascism." *research & destroy* (website), February 20, 2017.

"The Rich Kids of Fascism: Why the Alt-Right Didn't Start with Trump, and Won't End With Him Either." *It's Going Down* (website), December 16 2016; republished in *Ctrl-Alt-Delete: An Antifascist Report on the Alternative Right*. Montreal: Kersplebedeb Publishing, 2017.

Ridgeway, James. *Blood in the Face: The Ku Klux Klan, Aryan Nations, Nazi Skinheads, and the Rise of a New White Culture*. New York: Thunder's Mouth Press, 1990.

Risen, James, and Judy L. Thomas. *Wrath of Angels: The American Abortion War*. New York: BasicBooks, 1998.

Rupert, Mark. "Articulating Neoliberalism and Far-Right Conspiracism: The Case of the American 'Gun Rights' Culture." Paper presented at the annual meeting of the International Studies Association, New Orleans, LA, February 2015.

Scaminaci, James, III. *The Christian Right's Fourth Generation Warfare in America*. Available on *Academia.edu* (website), nd.

Second Wave, The: Return of the Militias. Montgomery, AL: Southern Poverty Law Center, 2009.

Segrest, Mab, and Leonard Zeskind. *Quarantines and Death: The Far Right's Homophobic Agenda*. Pamphlet. Atlanta: Center for Democratic Renewal, 1989.

Sunshine, Spencer. "Rebranding Fascism: National-Anarchists." *The Public Eye*, Winter 2008: 1, 12-19 [Political Research Associates].

——"The Right Hand of Occupy Wall Street: From Libertarians to Nazis, the Fact and Fiction of Right-Wing Involvement." *The Public Eye*, Winter 2014: 9–14 [Political Research Associates].

Sunshine, Spencer, et al. *Up in Arms: A Guide to Oregon's Patriot Movement*. Scappoose, OR: Rural Organizing Project; Somerville, MA: Political Research Associates, 2016.

Tabachnick, Rachel. "The Rise of Charismatic Dominionism." *Talk To Action* (website), January 3, 2011.

——"Spiritual Warriors with an Anti-Gay Mission: The New Apostolic Reformation." *Political Research Associates*, March 22, 2013;

Ward, Eric K. "Skin in the Game: How Antisemitism Animates White Nationalism." *Political Research Associates* (website), June 29, 2017.

Wypijewski, JoAnn. "Whitewash." *Mother Jones*, November 2005.

Zeskind, Leonard. *Blood and Politics: The History of the White Nationalist Movement from the Margins to the Mainstream*. New York: Farrar Straus Giroux, 2009.

Ziegenhorn, William Karl. *"No Rest for the Wicked": The FBI Investigations of White Supremacist Groups, 1983–1988*. Master's thesis, San Jose State University, 1995 [available on *SJSU ScholarWorks*].

Index

abortion politics: alt-right and, 116; Army of God, 18, 33, 34, 35, 40, 155; Christian right and, 28, 30, 33–34, 256; eugenics and, 7–8, 94, 97–98, 116; insurgent politics, 33–34; Ku Klux Klan and, 35; militias and, 34, 45; neonazism and, 6, 35, 108–109; Quiverfull movement, 36; spiritual warfare and, 36; violence and, 18, 33–34, 35, 40, 155; white nationalists and, 35. *See also* reproductive rights

Adler, Franklin Hugh, 234

Aho, James A., 44

al-Assad, Bashar, 134

Albanese, Francisco, 73–74

al-Husseini, Haj Amin, 127

AlternativeRight.com (website), 59–60, 61, 70, 72, 150

alt-right: overview, i–ii, 56, 82; use of term, 59; abortion politics, 116; alliance building, 74; alt-lite and, 80–82, 122; androphilia and, 71–72, 118–119; anti-egalitarianism and, 25, 62, 64; anti-feminism, 68–69, 116, 119–120; anti-immigrant politics, 62–63;

anti-imperialism and, 139–142; anti-Islamic politics, 81, 121–122; antisemitic politics, 56, 62–63, 65–66, 81–82; authoritarianism, 56, 73; demographic shift within, 61, 64–65; electoral activism and, 115–116; environmentalism and, 63; European New Right and, 57–58, 139–142, 140; fascist politics and, 60–61; feminist politics, 66–70, 116, 119–120; gender politics, i–ii, 66–70, 70–72, 79–80, 115–122; growth of, 59–61; identitarianism, 63; ideological roots of, 56–58; inside/outside political strategy debates, 76–79; intellectualism of, 61, 63, 64–65; interventionism and, 207; Jewish people within, 65–66, 81–82; leaderless resistance and, 223; leftist politics and, 63, 139; libertarianism, 63–64; loyalty to the state and, 22, 220; mainstream media coverage of, i–ii, 81–82; male tribalism, 70–72, 117–119; manosphere and, 66–69, 116–119; multiculturalism and, xiv, 62,

activism, 15, 21; international ties, 23; Knights of the Ku Klux Klan, 10, 15, 169; National Association for the Advancement of White People and, 10, 15, 22

Dutt, R. Palme, 184, 185

Dworkin, Andrea, 99

Eco, Umberto, 196

economic nationalism, 73, 196, 201, 205

8chan (website), 60, 68

The Eighteenth Brumaire of Louis Bonaparte (Marx), 235

Elam, Paul, 67, 117

electoral activism: alt-right and, 115–116; Christian right and, 30, 212–214, 220; far right movements and, 199–200; neonazism and, 15, 21; paleoconservatives and, 21; Trump campaign and, 199–200, 206

Eley, Geoff, 243

Engdahl, William, 89

Engle, Lou, 101, 213

Enlow, Johnny, 101, 213

environmentalism, xii, 43–44, 63, 150

Eurasianism, 20, 131–132, 136, 141

Euromaidan movement, 136

European New Right (ENR), xiv, 57–58, 60, 129–130, 130–132, 140, 156–158. *See also* de Benoist, Alain; Dugin, Aleksandr

Evola, Julius, 58, 59, 73, 129, 249

evolutionary psychology, 65, 70, 118

Falkenrath, Richard, 176

Falwell, Jerry, 30, 40

Farrakhan, Louis, 23, 87, 129

far right movements: overview, x–xv; use of term, ii–v, x; anti-egalitarianism and, ii, iii, x, 123, 142, 219, 221; authoritarianism and, ii, 144, 183, 221, 255, 257–258; disloyalty to the state and, 219–224; gender politics and, 94–96; legitimacy of U.S. government and, ii–iii, x–xv; multiculturalism and, 221–222; racial politics, ii, iv–v; sexual identity politics, 95–96; system-loyal politics and, ii–iii, v–vi, ix–x, xiv, 3, 101, 133–134, 175, 194

fascism: use of term, ix–x, 181–183, 227–230, 231, 253–255; anarcho-fascism, 71; anti-egalitarianism and, 238; anti-imperialism and, 125–127; antisemitic politics, 8; authoritarianism and, vii–viii, 192, 193–194, 228–230, 239; black nationalism and, 243–244; Black Panther Party and, 51–52, 167, 181, 189–191; Bonapartism, 234–238; George W. Bush and, vii–viii; capitalism and, 232–234, 239–244, 255, 258–259, 260; Christian right and, 256; classical fascism *vs.* contemporary fascism, 258–261; class politics and, 242–244, 255; Communist Party and, 183–186; European movements, 257; gender politics, 244, 259–260; globalization and, 259; internationalism and, 249–250, 256–258; Islamic right and,

ABOUT PM PRESS

PM Press was founded at the end of 2007 by a small collection of folks with decades of publishing, media, and organizing experience. PM Press co-conspirators have published and distributed hundreds of books, pamphlets, CDs, and DVDs. Members of PM have founded enduring book fairs, spearheaded victorious tenant organizing campaigns, and worked closely with bookstores, academic conferences, and even rock bands to deliver political and challenging ideas to all walks of life. We're old enough to know what we're doing and young enough to know what's at stake.

We seek to create radical and stimulating fiction and non-fiction books, pamphlets, T-shirts, visual and audio materials to entertain, educate, and inspire you. We aim to distribute these through every available channel with every available technology—whether that means you are seeing anarchist classics at our bookfair stalls, reading our latest vegan cookbook at the café, downloading geeky fiction e-books, or digging new music and timely videos from our website.

PM Press is always on the lookout for talented and skilled volunteers, artists, activists, and writers to work with. If you have a great idea for a project or can contribute in some way, please get in touch.

PM Press
PO Box 23912
Oakland, CA 94623
www.pmpress.org

FRIENDS OF PM PRESS

These are indisputably momentous times—the financial system is melting down globally and the Empire is stumbling. Now more than ever there is a vital need for radical ideas.

In the years since its founding—and on a mere shoestring— PM Press has risen to the formidable challenge of publishing and distributing knowledge and entertainment for the struggles ahead. With over 300 releases to date, we have published an impressive and stimulating array of literature, art, music, politics, and culture. Using every available medium, we've succeeded in connecting those hungry for ideas and information to those putting them into practice.

Friends of PM allows you to directly help impact, amplify, and revitalize the discourse and actions of radical writers, filmmakers, and artists. It provides us with a stable foundation from which we can build upon our early successes and provides a much-needed subsidy for the materials that can't necessarily pay their own way. You can help make that happen—and receive every new title automatically delivered to your door once a month—by joining as a Friend of PM Press. And, we'll throw in a free T-shirt when you sign up.

Here are your options:

- **$30 a month** Get all books and pamphlets plus 50% discount on all webstore purchases

- **$40 a month** Get all PM Press releases (including CDs and DVDs) plus 50% discount on all webstore purchases

- **$100 a month** Superstar—Everything plus PM merchandise, free downloads, and 50% discount on all webstore purchases

For those who can't afford $30 or more a month, we have **Sustainer Rates** at $15, $10 and $5. Sustainers get a free PM Press T-shirt and a 50% discount on all purchases from our website.

Your Visa or Mastercard will be billed once a month, until you tell us to stop. Or until our efforts succeed in bringing the revolution around. Or the financial meltdown of Capital makes plastic redundant. Whichever comes first.

Catastrophism: The Apocalyptic Politics of Collapse and Rebirth

Sasha Lilley, David McNally, Eddie Yuen, and James Davis with a foreword by Doug Henwood

ISBN: 978-1-60486-589-9
$16.00   192 pages

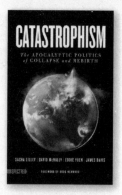

We live in catastrophic times. The world is reeling from the deepest economic crisis since the Great Depression, with the threat of further meltdowns ever-looming. Global warming and myriad dire ecological disasters worsen—with little if any action to halt them—their effects rippling across the planet in the shape of almost biblical floods, fires, droughts, and hurricanes. Governments warn that no alternative exists than to take the bitter medicine they prescribe—or risk devastating financial or social collapse. The right, whether religious or secular, views the present as catastrophic and wants to turn the clock back. The left fears for the worst, but hopes some good will emerge from the rubble. Visions of the apocalypse and predictions of impending doom abound. Across the political spectrum, a culture of fear reigns.

Catastrophism explores the politics of apocalypse—on the left and right, in the environmental movement, and from capital and the state—and examines why the lens of catastrophe can distort our understanding of the dynamics at the heart of these numerous disasters—and fatally impede our ability to transform the world. Lilley, McNally, Yuen, and Davis probe the reasons why catastrophic thinking is so prevalent, and challenge the belief that it is only out of the ashes that a better society may be born. The authors argue that those who care about social justice and the environment should eschew the Pandora's box of fear—even as it relates to indisputably apocalyptic climate change. Far from calling people to arms, they suggest, catastrophic fear often results in passivity and paralysis—and, at worst, reactionary politics.

"This groundbreaking book examines a deep current—on both the left and right—of apocalyptical thought and action. The authors explore the origins, uses, and consequences of the idea that collapse might usher in a better world. Catastrophism is a crucial guide to understanding our tumultuous times, while steering us away from the pitfalls of the past."
—Barbara Epstein, author of *Political Protest and Cultural Revolution: Nonviolent Direct Action in the 1970s and 1980s*